Renaissance & Reformation Almanac

Renaissance & Reformation Almanac

Volume 2

PEGGY SAARI &
AARON SAARI, EDITORS
Julie Carnagie, Project Editor

Detroit • New York • San Diego • San Francisco • Cleveland • New Haven, Conn. • Waterville, Maine • London • Munich

THOMSON
GALE

Renaissance and Reformation: Almanac

Peggy Saari and Aaron Saari

Project Editor
Julie L. Carnagie

Permissions
Kimberly Davis

Imaging and Multimedia
Robert Duncan, Kelly A. Quin

Product Design
Pamela A. Galbreath

Composition
Evi Seoud

Manufacturing
Rita Wimberly

LIBRARY OF CONGRESS CATALOGING-IN-PUBLICATION DATA

Saari, Peggy.
  Renaissance and Reformation. Almanac / Peggy Saari and Aaron Saari ; Julie L. Carnagie, editor.
    p. cm.
Includes bibliographical references and index.
    ISBN 0-7876-5467-1 (set hardcover : alk. paper)
    1. Renaissance–Juvenile literature. 2. Reformation–Juvenile literature. I. Saari, Aaron Maurice. II. Carnagie, Julie. III. Title.
    CB359 .S23 2002
    940.2'1–dc21
                                                                            2002006152

Vol. 1. 0-7876-5468-X; Vol. 2. 0-7876-5469-8; Set 0-7876-5467-1

Printed in the United States of America
10 9 8 7 6 5 4 3 2

Contents

Volume 1

Volume 2

Reader's Guide

Renaissance and Reformation: Almanac provides a wide range of historical information on the period in European history between the mid-1300s and the early 1600s. The two-volume set explores both the Italian and Northern Renaissance as well as the Protestant and Catholic Reformations. Arranged in fourteen subject chapters, *Renaissance and Reformation: Almanac* includes topics such as the rise of European monarchies, Martin Luther and his role in the Protestant Reformation, Italian and Northern Renaissance culture, science during the Renaissance, education and training, women in Renaissance society, and daily life.

Additional Features

Renaissance and Reformation: Almanac includes numerous sidebars, some focusing on people associated with the Renaissance and Reformation era, others taking a closer look at pivotal events. More than one hundred black-and-white illustrations enliven the text, while cross-references are made to people or events discussed in other chapters. Both volumes contain a timeline, a glossary, research and activity ideas, a bibliography, and a cumulative index providing access to the subjects discussed in *Renaissance and Reformation: Almanac.*

Comments and suggestions

We welcome your comments on this work as well as your suggestions for topics to be featured in future editions of *Renaissance and Reformation: Almanac.* Please write: Editors, *Renaissance and Reformation: Almanac,* U•X•L, 27500 Drake Rd., Farmington Hills, MI 48331-3535; call toll-free: 1-800-877-4253; fax: 248-699-8097; or send e-mail via www.gale.com.

Introduction

Renaissance and Reformation: Almanac presents an overview of the most significant revolution in Western history. Beginning with the Italian Renaissance in the mid-1300s and lasting until the end of the Protestant and Catholic Reformations in the early 1600s, this revolution essentially turned the European world upside down. By the close of the seventeenth century, unprecedented changes had taken place in politics, religion, science, economics, education, the arts, and society throughout Europe. Scholars and teachers are still intrigued by this historical period, but the twenty-first century student might wonder, "Why should I want to read about the Renaissance and Reformation? How could anything that happened hundreds of years ago possibly be relevant to my life?" The answer to the first question is that it was a fascinating time, filled with dramatic events, interesting people, and great achievements. The answer to the second question is that we can understand more about the world today by studying this era, which historians consider the beginning of the modern age.

The Renaissance produced many innovations that are now ordinary facts of modern life. Among them was the printing press, which facilitated mass communication and became the first step in advanced information technology. Of even greater importance was the scientific revolution led by astronomers who used the newly perfected telescope to make observations of celestial bodies. Their discoveries paved the way for present-day knowledge about the universe. Renaissance scientists pioneered modern medicine, introducing chemical-based drugs and acquiring new knowledge about human anatomy. Navigators and explorers led the way for European settlement of the Americas, expanding the borders of the Western world to the other side of the globe. The Renaissance brought the rise of the middle class and the emergence of feminist thinking, which became hallmarks of Western society. Economic innovations included capitalism and global banking, which are now the basis of the world economy. The Protestant Reformation led to the founding of the Protestant faiths that still exist today, and the Catholic Reformation established Catholic Church policies that remained in place for more than four hundred years. Finally, the human-centered view of the world promoted by Italian humanists established individualism and secularism as dominant themes in modern Western culture.

The Renaissance and Reformation also set in motion political and social tensions that had a profound impact during the modern era. European settlement of the Americas ultimately resulted in the destruction of native cultures. The first worldwide war took place in Europe in the seventeenth century, setting the stage for conflicts that involved all the major world powers in the twentieth century. Anti-Semitism steadily increased, as did the expansion of the African slave trade: two developments that had tragic consequences in the nineteenth and twentieth centuries. And throughout the three hundred years of the Renaissance and Reformation period, Europeans in the West and Muslims in the East became increasingly bitter enemies. The result was a widening gap between East and West that has continued into the present day.

Renaissance and Reformation: Almanac traces all of these developments, and more, with the goal of establishing a direct link between our twenty-first century world and the not-so-distant past.

Timeline of Events

c. 300 Jews arrive in Spain.

395 The Roman Empire is split into the West Roman Empire and the East Roman (Byzantine) Empire.

711 Moors invade Spain.

late 700s–c. 1000 Feudalism is established in Europe.

800 Emperor Charlemagne claims to revive ancient Roman Empire.

1076 Pope Gregory VII excommunicates Holy Roman Emperor Henry IV.

1096 Christians launch the Crusades against the Muslims.

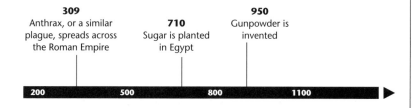

309
Anthrax, or a similar plague, spreads across the Roman Empire

710
Sugar is planted in Egypt

950
Gunpowder is invented

200   500   800   1100

1233	Pope Gregory IX establishes the medieval Inquisition.
1291	The Crusades end when the Muslims defeat the Christians.
1300	Pope Boniface issues *Unam Sanctam,* declaring all people to be subjects of the pope.
1305	The Papacy is moved to Avignon, France, beginning the Babylonian Captivity.
1327	Italian poet Petrarch begins writing *Canzoniere,* a series of love lyrics in which he departs from the medieval convention of seeing a woman as a spiritual symbol and depicts Laura as a real person.
1337	France and England begin the Hundred Years' War over control of the French throne.
1347–50	The Black Death, or bubonic plague, sweeps Europe.
1376	The Babylonian Captivity ends with the return of the papacy to Rome.
1378	The Great Schism in the Roman Catholic Church begins with the election of Pope Urban VI.
1396	Greek scholar Manuel Chrysoloras comes to Florence, Italy, to teach Greek.
1402	Mongol warrior Timur Lenk (Tamerlane) conquers the Ottoman Empire.
1414	The Council of Constance is convened to discuss problems within the Roman Catholic Church.
1415	Czechoslovakian priest Jan Hus is executed by the Council of Constance because of his criticism of the Catholic Church.
c. 1417	Italian architect Filippo Brunelleschi invents linear perspective, a system derived from mathematics in

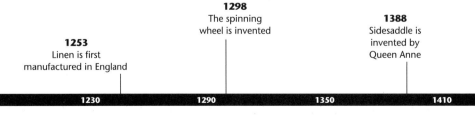

1253
Linen is first manufactured in England

1298
The spinning wheel is invented

1388
Sidesaddle is invented by Queen Anne

1230 1290 1350 1410

which all elements of a composition are measured and arranged from a single point of view, or perspective.

1418 The Council of Constance ends the Great Schism.

1420 Florentine artist Massaccio is the first to use linear perspective in painting.

1420 Filippo Brunelleschi begins work on the dome of the Florence Cathedral.

1421 Sultan Mehmed II restores the Ottoman Empire.

1423 Italian educator Vittorino da Feltre establishes a humanist school.

1440 Italian scholar Lorenzo Valla questions the legitimacy of the pope.

1450 Francesco I Sforza starts an eighty-year dynasty in Milan.

1451 Italian scholar Isotta Nogarola writes "On the Equal and Unequal Sin of Eve and Adam," which is considered the first piece of feminist writing.

1453 Constantinople falls to the Ottoman Turks.

1454 German printer Johannes Gutenberg perfects movable type.

1455 The houses of York and Lancaster begin the War of the Roses in England.

1458 Margaret of Navarre's *Heptaméron* is published and becomes an important work of the Renaissance period.

1461 Wanting to be separate from the continents of Asia and Africa, and thus the Muslims, Pope Pius II introduces the idea of Europe as separate continent.

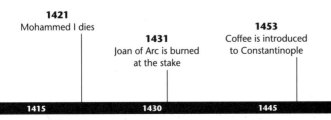

1421
Mohammed I dies

1431
Joan of Arc is burned
at the stake

1453
Coffee is introduced
to Constantinople

1415   1430   1445   1460

1469 Italian merchant Lorenzo de' Medici takes control of Florence and becomes famous for his contributions to countless artists.

1474 Catholic monarchs Ferdinand II and Isabella I begin the Spanish Inquisition to enforce Christianity as the sole religion of Spain.

1485 The War of Roses ends and the Tudor dynasty begins in England

1490s German artist Albrecht Dürer raises woodcut to the level of high art.

1492 Ferdinand II and Isabella I issue the Edict of Expulsion, ordering all Jews to leave Spain.

1492 Italian navigator Christopher Columbus makes his first voyage to the New World.

1494 Pope Alexander VI issues the Treaty of Tordesillas that gives Portugal authority over Brazil.

1494 Italian preacher Girolamo Savonarola influences a new pro-French government in Florence.

1494 King Charles VIII of France invades Italy, initiating the Italian Wars with Spain.

1495 Italian painter Leonardo da Vinci begins *The Last Supper,* in which he experimented with oil-based paint, which is more easily blended.

1495 Alexander VI organizes the Holy League, an alliance between the Papal States, the Holy Roman Empire, Spain, Venice, and Milan against France.

1497 Italian navigator John Cabot begins his search for the Northwest Passage, a water route to the Indies.

1457
Donatello moves
to Florence

1467
Turkish forces
enter
Herzegovina

1475
World's first coffee
house opens

| 1455 | 1465 | 1475 | 1485 |

1498 Girolamo Savonarola is executed for heresy, or the violation of church laws.

1498 Italian sculptor Michelangelo starts the *Pietà,* his first important commission.

1498 Albrecht Dürer introduces humanism, a human-centered intellectual movement based on the revival of classical culture, into northern European art.

c. 1500 The *Querelle des femmes* movement begins. It refers to the literary debate over the nature and status of women.

c. 1500 Germany replaces Italy as the center of European banking.

1503 Leonardo begins work on the *Mona Lisa,* one of the most famous portraits in the Western world.

1511 Italian artist Raphael paints *School of Athens,* considered to be one of his greatest achievements.

1512 Michelangelo completes the decoration of the Sistine Chapel ceiling at the Vatican in Rome.

1513 Italian diplomat Niccolò Machiavelli writes *The Prince,* in which he proclaimed his controversial political philosophy.

1516 Dutch humanist Desiderius Erasmus publishes *Praise of Folly,* a satire of the Roman Catholic Church and its clergy. That same year Erasmus published his translation of the New Testament of the Bible, the first published Greek text.

1516 English humanist Thomas More publishes his greatest work *Utopia.* Modeled on Plato's *Republic, Utopia* describes an imaginary land that is free of grand displays of wealth, greed, and violence.

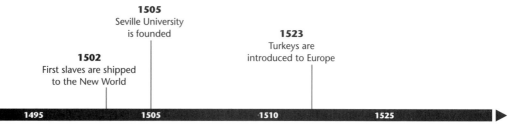

1505
Seville University
is founded

1523
Turkeys are
introduced to Europe

1502
First slaves are shipped
to the New World

1495   1505   1510   1525

1517 German priest Martin Luther posts his *Ninety-Five Theses,* initiating the Protestant Reformation.

1519 King Charles I of Spain is elected Holy Roman Emperor Charles V, leading to the spread of the Spanish empire east from Spain to include the kingdoms of Germany, Hungary, Bohemia, Naples, and Sicily. The empire also extends south and west to include possessions in North Africa and the Americas.

1520 King Francis I of France and King Henry VIII of England meet at the Field of the Cloth of Gold in order to form an alliance against Holy Roman Emperor Charles V.

1520s Swiss-born physician Theophrastus Paracelsus pioneers the use of chemicals to treat disease.

1520 Paris *collèges* adopt classical Latin and Greek studies.

1521 At the Diet of Worms, Charles V declares Martin Luther an "outlaw of the church."

1521 The Ottoman Empire begins to reach it height when the sultan Süleyman I defeats Hungary in the Battle of Mohács.

1523 Swiss priest Huldrych Zwingli issues "Sixty-Seven Articles," or proposed reforms, which become the basis for the Reformation in Switzerland.

1524–26 The German Peasants' Revolt challenges the rule of Catholic noblemen.

1525 French king Francis I is captured by the Spanish at the Battle of Pavia.

1526 The Diet of Speyer permits German princes to determine which religion is practiced in their regions.

1527 Armies of Holy Roman Emperor Charles V sack Rome.

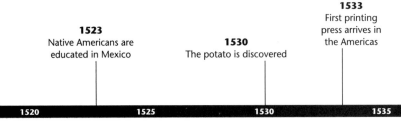

1523
Native Americans are educated in Mexico

1530
The potato is discovered

1533
First printing press arrives in the Americas

1520   1525   1530   1535

1527 King Gustav I Vasa begins establishing Lutheranism in Sweden.

1528 French diplomat Baldassare Castiglione publishes *Book of the Courtier.* The book is an immediate success, and quickly becomes a guide to etiquette for both the bourgeoisie and the aristocracy in Europe.

1534 King Henry VIII is declared supreme head of the Church of England, completing the break between England and the Roman Catholic Church.

1534 French author François Rabelais begins publishing his most popular work, *Gargantua and Pantagruel.*

1535 Thomas More is beheaded by Henry VIII after refusing to acknowledge the Act of Supremacy that made Henry supreme head of the Church of England.

1536 French-born Protestant reformer John Calvin writes the first edition of *Institutes of the Christian Religion,* which outlines his beliefs and gains him attention as an important religious leader.

1536 Ottoman sultan Süleyman I forms an alliance with France.

1540 Spanish priest Ignatius of Loyola founds the Society of Jesus (Jesuits). His Jesuit order eventually becomes the single most powerful weapon of the Catholic Reformation.

1543 *On the Revolution of Celestial Spheres* by Polish astronomer Nicolaus Copernicus is published. The book gives important information about the orbits of the planets and begins a revolution in human thought by serving as the cornerstone of modern astronomy.

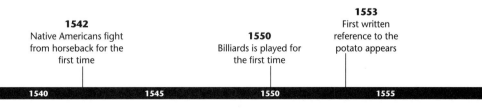

1542
Native Americans fight from horseback for the first time

1550
Billiards is played for the first time

1553
First written reference to the potato appears

1540 1545 1550 1555

1543 Belgian anatomist Andreas Vesalius publishes *On the Fabric of the Human Body,* one of the most important contributions to human anatomy.

1545 Pope Paul III convenes the Council of Trent, a meeting to discuss reforming the Roman Catholic Church from within.

1547 Michelangelo directs construction of the new Saint Peter's Basilica in Rome.

1547 Charles V defeats German Protestant princes at the Battle of Mühlberg. Charles hopes his victory will stop the spread of Protestantism throughout the Holy Roman Empire.

1548 Ignatius of Loyola publishes *Spiritual Exercises.* This short but influential book outlines a thirty-day regimen, or systematic plan, of prayer and acts of self-denial and punishment, with the understanding that devotion to God must be central.

1550s Italian architect Andrea Palladio popularizes the villa.

1550s Italian composer Giovanni Pierluigi da Palestrina creates the oratorio, a lengthy religious choral work that features recitatives, arias, and choruses without action or scenery.

1553 Queen Mary I restores Catholicism in England and begins persecuting Protestants after ascending to the English throne.

1555 John Calvin organizes an evangelical government in Geneva, Switzerland.

1555 French astrologer Nostradamus begins publishing *Centuries,* his best-selling book of predictions.

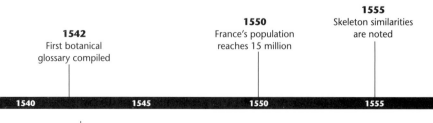

1542
First botanical
glossary compiled

1550
France's population
reaches 15 million

1555
Skeleton similarities
are noted

1540   1545   1550   1555

1555   Italian artist Sofonisba Anguissola paints *The Chess Game.* This painting is meant to demonstrate female excellence at an intellectual game.

1556   Charles V abdicates the throne after building one of the largest empires in history.

1558   Elizabeth I begins her forty-five-year reign as queen of England and Ireland.

1559   The Italian Wars end with the Treaty of Cateau-Cambrésis.

1560   Catherine de Médicis is named regent of France after the death of her husband King Henry II.

1560s   King Philip II of Spain begins building the Escorial, an enormous complex of buildings north of Madrid.

1562   The French Wars of Religion begin.

1562   Teresa de Ávila founds the Reformed Discalced Carmelite Order.

1563   The Council of Trent adjourns and issues *Canons and Decrees of the Council of Trent,* a statement that upholds Catholic doctrine, or religious rules, but shows more tolerance of opposition.

1563   German artist Pieter Bruegel paints *Tower of Babel,* one of his most famous works.

1566   Revolt against Spanish rule begins in the Netherlands.

1567   Philip II introduces the Spanish Inquisition in the Netherlands.

1570   Flemish mapmaker Abraham Ortel publishes the first world atlas.

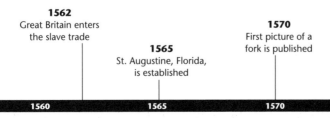

1562
Great Britain enters
the slave trade

1565
St. Augustine, Florida,
is established

1570
First picture of a
fork is published

1560   1565   1570   1575

1571   The European Christian alliance defeats the Ottoman fleet at the Battle of Lepanto, ending Ottoman control of the Mediterranean Sea.

1572   Catholics kill Huguenots in the Saint Bartholomew's Day Massacre in Paris.

1572   Danish astronomer Tycho Brahe introduces the term "nova" for an exploding star.

1580   French author Michel de Montaigne publishes *Essays*. The work created a new literary genre (form), the essay, in which he used self-portrayal as a mirror of humanity in general.

1580–1640 Witchcraft trials reach peak in Europe.

1582   Pope Gregory XIII issues the Gregorian calendar.

1587   Elizabeth I orders the execution of Mary, Queen of Scots after a conspiracy to assassinate Elizabeth is discovered.

1588   Spanish Armada is defeated by the English fleet, marking the high point of Elizabeth's reign.

1592   English playwright William Shakespeare begins his career in London.

1595   The Edict of Nantes grants religious and civil liberties to Huguenots.

1605   Spanish author Miguel de Cervantes publishes the first part of *Don Quixote,* one of the great masterpieces of world literature.

1606   Foremost English playwright Ben Jonson's dramatic genius is fully revealed for the first time in *Volpone, or the Fox,* a satiric comedy that contains the playwright's harshest and most unrelenting criticism of human vice.

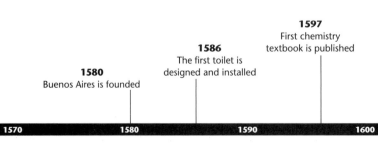

1597
First chemistry
textbook is published

1586
The first toilet is
designed and installed

1580
Buenos Aires is founded

1570   1580   1590   1600

1607	Italian composer Claudio Monteverdi publishes his first opera, *La favola d'Orfeo.*
1609	English scientist Thomas Harriot makes the first recorded use of the telescope.
1609	German astronomer Johannes Kepler publishes his first two laws of planetary motion.
1609	Philip II begins expelling Moriscos (Jews) from Spain.
1610	Italian astronomer Galileo publishes *The Starry Messenger.*
1611	*The Life of Teresa of Jesus* is published.
1611	King James I of England approves a new English translation of the Bible.
1614	Scottish mathematician John Napier discovers logarithms.
1616	Galileo is ordered to cease promoting new science.
1616	Italian painter Artemisia Gentileschi becomes the first woman to be admitted to the Florentine Academy of Art.
1618	Johannes Kepler publishes his third law of planetary motion.
1618	Thirty Years' War begins; it becomes the first armed conflict involving all major world powers.
1620	English philosopher Francis Bacon publishes *New Method.*
1621	English mathematician William Oughtred makes the first slide rule.
1624	Peter Paul Rubens paints his famous *Self-portrait.*

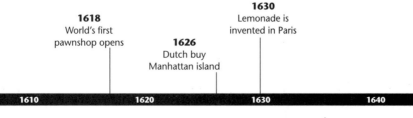

1618
World's first
pawnshop opens

1626
Dutch buy
Manhattan island

1630
Lemonade is
invented in Paris

1610   1620   1630   1640

1628   English anatomist William Harvey announces the discovery of the circulatory system.

1630s   French noblewoman Madame de Rambouillet presides over one of the first salons.

1642   English Civil War begins.

1648   Thirty Years' War ends with the Peace of Westphalia.

1648   English Civil War ends.

1651   Leonardo's *Treatise on Painting* is published.

1666   Margaret Cavendish publishes *The Description of a New World Called the Blazing World*, considered to be one of the first works of science fiction.

1636
Harvard College
is founded

1644
Ming dynasty ends

1657
London's first
chocolate shop opens

1625   1640   1655   1670

Words to Know

A

Abbey: A church connected with a monastery.

Abbot: A head of a monastery.

Abbess: A head of a convent.

Abdicate: To step down from the throne.

Absolution: Forgiveness of sins pronounced by a priest.

Absolutism: The concentration of all power in the hands of one ruler.

Adultery: Having sexual relations with someone who is not the person's husband or wife.

Agriculture: The growing of crops for food and other products.

Alchemy: The medieval science devoted to changing common metals into gold and silver.

Algebra: A form of arithmetic in which letters represent numbers.

Allegory: A story featuring characters with symbolic significance.

Altarpiece: A work of art that decorates an altar of a church.

Anatomy: The study of the structure of the body.

Annulment: An order that declares a marriage invalid.

Anti-Semitism: Prejudice against Jews.

Apprentice: One who learns a craft, trade, or profession from a master.

Aristocracy: The upper social class.

Armor: A protective suit made of iron worn by a soldier in battle.

Artillery: Various types of weapons.

Astrolabe: A device used to observe and calculate the distance of celestial bodies.

Astrology: The study of the heavens to predict future events.

Astronomy: The study of celestial bodies, such as planets, stars, the Sun, and the Moon.

Atheist: One who does not believe in God.

Augsburg Confession: An official statement of Lutheran churches prepared in 1530.

Auto da fé: Act of faith; public expression of commitment to Christianity required of supposed heretics during the Inquisition.

Autopsy: The dissection and examination of a corpse to determine the cause of death.

Axiom: A statement accepted as being true.

B

Babylonian Captivity: The name given to the period from 1307 to 1376 when the Roman Catholic pope lived in Avignon, France.

Baptism: A Christian ceremony in which a person is blessed with water and admitted to the Christian faith.

Barbarism: A lack of refinement or culture.

Baroque: The term used to describe the music, art, literature, and philosophy of the seventeenth century; exuberant, sensuous, expressive, and dynamic style.

Battle of Lepanto (1571): A sea battle in which the European Christian naval alliance defeated the fleet of the Ottoman Empire.

Battle of Mohács (1526): A conflict in which the Ottoman Empire conquered much of Hungary.

Battle of Mühlberg (1547): A conflict in which Holy Roman Emperor Charles V defeated the Schmalkaldic League.

Battle of Pavia: A conflict during the Italian Wars, in which Spain defeated France; resulted in the Treaty of Madrid (1526), requiring France to give up claims to Italy, Burgundy, Flanders, and Artois.

Battle of Preveza (1538): A sea battle in which the Ottoman navy defeated the Genoan fleet and gained control of the eastern Mediterranean Sea.

Bewitch: To cast a spell over someone or something.

Bible: The Christian holy book.

Biology: The study of living organisms and their processes.

Bishop: The head of a church district.

Black Death: A severe epidemic of the bubonic plague that started in Europe and Asia in the fourteenth century.

Blasphemy: An expression of contempt toward God.

Bleeding: The procedure of draining blood from the body to cure disease.

Bourgeoisie: The middle class.

Brethren of the Common Life: The Protestant organization that founded humanist schools.

Bull: An order issued by a pope.

C

Cadaver: A dead body used for study purposes.

Canon: Church law or degree; clergyman at a cathedral.

Canonized: Named as a saint, or a person declared holy by the Roman Catholic Church.

Canton: A province or state.

Cardinal: A Roman Catholic Church official ranking directly below the pope.

Carnival: A celebration of a holy day.

Cartography: The study of maps and map-making.

Cartoon: A preparatory design or drawing for a fresco.

Castle: The residence of a lord and his knights, family, servants, and other attendants; eventually the center for a village and local government.

Catechism: A book of religious instructions in the form of questions and answers.

Cathedral: A large Christian house of worship.

Catholic Reformation: The reform movement within the Roman Catholic Church of the sixteenth and seventeenth centuries; also called the Counter Reformation.

Cavalry: Soldiers who ride horses in battle.

Censored: Suppressed or prohibited, as by the church.

Chamber music: Music composed for performance in a private room or small auditorium, usually with one performer for each part.

Chancellor: A chief secretary or administrator.

Chivalric code: A complex system of honor observed by knights during the Middle Ages.

Christ: The name for Jesus of Nazareth, founder of Christianity.

Christendom: The kingdom of Christ; name given to Europe by the Christian church.

Christianity: The religion founded by Jesus of Nazareth, who was also called the Christ.

City-state: A geographic region under the governmental control of a central city.

Classical period: The ancient Greek and Roman world, especially its literature, art, architecture, and philosophy.

Clergy: Church officials, including bishops, priests, and monks.

Cloister: Walkways with an arched open side supported by columns; also a term for an enclosed monastery or convent.

Coat of arms: An emblem signifying noble rank.

Commedia dell' arte: A type of comedy performed by professional acting companies that improvise plots depending on the materials at hand and the talents of the actors.

Commune: A district governed by a group of leaders called a corporation.

Communion: A Christian religious ceremony in which bread and wine represent the body and blood of Jesus of Nazareth (Christ).

Concordat of Bologna (1516): The agreement in which the Catholic Church in France came under direct control of the king.

Confession: An admission of sins to a priest; statement of belief forming the basis of a religious faith or denomination.

Confirmation: The act of conferring the gift of the Holy Spirit.

Confraternity: A society devoted to a charitable or religious cause.

Conscription: The requirement of all men above a certain age to serve in the military.

Constitution: A document that specifies the laws of a state and the rights of its citizens.

Consubstantiation: The concept that bread and wine in the Christian communion service are only symbolic of the body and blood of Christ, not transformed into the actual body and blood.

Convent: A house for women who are dedicated to religious life; also called a nunnery.

Conversion: The act of leaving one religion to accept another.

Converso: The Spanish word for a Jew who converted to Christianity.

Coup d'etat: A violent overthrow of a government.

Courtier: A member of a court; a gentleman.

Courtly love: Part of the chivalric code according to which a knight undertakes a quest (religious journey) or a tournament (game of combat) dedicated to a special lady.

Creed: A statement of religious beliefs.

Crucifix: A carved image of Christ crucified on a cross.

Crusades (1096–1291): A series of wars waged by Christians against Muslims in an effort to recapture the city of Jerusalem in the Holy Land; also wars against other non-Christians and Christians who challenged the church.

Curate: A clergyman in charge of a parish.

D

Democracy: A government based on the will of the majority of people.

Dialectic: Conversation based on discussion and reasoning.

Dialogue: A written work in which two or more speakers discuss a topic.

Diet: A meeting of representatives from states and districts in the Holy Roman Empire.

Diet of Augsburg (1530): A meeting in which Protestants and Catholics tried unsuccessfully to reach a compromise.

Diet of Nuremberg (1532): A meeting in which Protestant princes forced Emperor Charles V to continue toleration of Lutheranism indefinitely.

Diet of Speyer (1526): A meeting in which it was decided that each prince was responsible for settling religious issues in his own territory "until a general council of the whole Church could be summoned."

Diet at Speyer (1529): A meeting in which the 1526 Diet of Speyer decision was revoked; some Lutheran reformers protested, thus gaining the name "Protestants."

Diet of Worms (1521): A meeting in which Martin Luther refused to recant his beliefs and was declared an outlaw of the church by Emperor Charles V.

Diocese: A territorial district of a bishop.

Diplomat: A political negotiator or representative of a government.

Disciple: One who spreads the doctrines of a religious leader; one of the twelve followers of Jesus of Nazareth (Christ).

Disputation: A formal debate.

Divine right: The concept that a ruler is chosen directly by God.

Doctrine: Official church teachings.

Doge: The duke of Venice, Italy.

Dowry: Money, goods, or the estate that a woman brings to her husband in marriage.

Ducat: A gold coin used in various European countries.

Duel: A form of combat with weapons, usually pistols, between two persons in the presence of witnesses.

Dynasty: Rulers from the same family who hold political power for many generations.

E

East Roman Empire: In the Middle Ages, the countries of eastern Europe; based in Byzantium (now Istanbul, Turkey) and formed after the split of the Roman Empire in A.D. 395; also known as the Byzantine Empire.

East-West Schism (1052): The splitting of the Christian church into the Eastern Orthodox Church at Constantinople and the Roman Catholic Church in Rome.

Easter: The commemoration of Christ's resurrection, or rising from the dead.

Eclipse: The total or partial obscuring of one celestial body by another, as in the eclipse of the Sun by the Moon.

Edict of Worms: The statement issued by Emperor Charles V at the Diet of Worms in 1521; it condemned Lutheranism in all parts of the Holy Roman Empire.

The Elect: A few people chosen by God to receive salvation and to lead others who are not chosen for salvation.

Elector: A German prince entitled to vote for the Holy Roman Emperor.

Elegy: A poem expressing sorrow.

Epic: A literary work, usually a poem, in which the main character undertakes a long journey.

Epidemic: A widespread outbreak of disease.

Etiquette: Rules for proper manners.

Evangelism: A personal commitment to the teachings of Jesus of Nazareth (Christ).

Excommunicate: The act of being expelled from membership in a church.

Exile: Forcibly sending a person away from his or her native country or state.

F

Fable: A story with animal characters that teaches a moral lesson.

Facade: The outer front wall of a building.

Factions: Opposing sides in a conflict.

Faith: The acceptance of truth without question; also a profession of religious belief.

Farce: Literary or theatrical work based on exaggerated humor.

Fasting: Abstaining from food.

Feudalism: The social and political system of the Middle Ages, under which rulers granted land to lords in exchange for loyalty.

Fief: Territory granted to a nobleman by a king or emperor under feudalism.

First Helvetic Confession (1536): A statement of Protestant reform goals.

Florin: A coin made in Florence, Italy; later used by various European countries.

Free will: Exercise of individual choice independent of the will of God.

French Wars of Religion (1562–98): Series of conflicts between Catholics and Huguenots (Protestants) in France.

Fresco: A wall painting made by applying paint over a thin layer of damp lime plaster.

Friar: A man who belongs to a religious order that takes a vow of poverty.

G

Galaxy: A very large group of stars.

Galley: A ship propelled by oars.

Genre: A form of literature.

Geography: The study of the physical and cultural features of the Earth's surface.

Geometry: The branch of mathematics that deals with points, lines, angles, surfaces, and solids.

German Peasants' War (1524–26): Rebellion staged by peasants against Catholic princes in Germany.

Gospel: The word of God delivered by Jesus of Nazareth (Christ).

Grammar school: An elementary school; in the Renaissance, called Latin grammar school because students were required to learn Latin as the basis of the humanist curriculum.

Great Schism (1378–1418): The name given to a period of time when there were two Roman Catholic popes, one in Rome and one in Avignon, France.

Guild: An association of craftsmen, merchants, and professionals that trained apprentices and set standards of production or business operation.

H

Habit: The garment worn by a nun.

Hanseatic League: A trading network formed in the Middle Ages among cities around the Baltic Sea and the North Sea.

Heliocentric: Sun-centered.

Heresy: Violation of church laws.

Heretic: One who violates or opposes the teachings of the church.

Hermit: A member of a religious order who retires from society and lives in solitude.

Holy Roman Empire: A revival of the ancient Roman Empire; established by Otto the Great in A.D. 962.

Holy Spirit: The third person of the Christian Trinity (God the Father, the Son, and the Holy Spirit).

House: A family of rulers.

Huguenots: French Protestants.

Humanism: A human-centered literary and intellectual movement based on the revival of classical culture that started the Renaissance.

Humanistic studies: Five academic subjects consisting of grammar (rules for the use of a language), rhetoric (art of effective speaking and writing), moral philosophy (study of human conduct and values), poetry, and history.

Hundred Years' War (1337–1453): A series of intermittent conflicts between England and France over the French throne.

I

Idolatry: The worship of images, or false gods.

Incarnate: The spirit in bodily form.

Index of Prohibited Books: A list of books banned by the Roman Catholic Church.

Indulgence: The Roman Catholic Church practice of granting a partial pardon of sins in exchange for money.

Infantry: Soldiers trained to fight in the front line of battle.

Inquisition: An official court established by the Roman Catholic Church in 1233 for the purpose of hunting down and punishing heretics; during the Renaissance, it continued under the Spanish Inquisition (1492) and Roman Inquisition (1542).

Investiture struggle: An eleventh-century conflict between popes and rulers over the right to appoint bishops.

Islam: A religion founded by the prophet Muhammad.

Italian Wars (1494–1559): A conflict between France and Spain over control of Italy.

J

Janissaries: An elite army of the Ottoman Empire, composed of war captives and Christian youths forced into service.

Journeyman: The stage of apprenticeship during which one travels from job to job working in the shop of a master craftsman.

Joust: Combat on horseback between two knights with lances.

K

Kabbalah: Also cabala; system of Jewish religious and mystical thought.

Knight: A professional warrior who rode on horseback in combat; also known as a vassal, or one who pledged his loyalty to a lord and a king.

L

Laity: Unordained church members.

Lance: A long polelike weapon with a sharpened steel point.

Lent: The forty week days prior to Easter, the celebration of Christ's rising from the dead; a time devoted to prayer, penance, and reflection.

Limbo: A place where the unbaptized remain after death.

Linear perspective: A system derived from mathematics in which all elements of a composition are measured and arranged according to a single point (perspective).

Liturgy: Rites and texts used in a worship service.

Logarithms: A system of numbers with points that move on two lines of numbers, one point on increasing arithmetic value and the other moves on decreasing geometric values.

Loggia: An open, roofed porchlike structure with arches that overlooks a courtyard.

Logic: A system of thought based on reason.

Lord: One who was granted a large estate by a king in exchange for loyalty.

M

Madrigal: A song based on a poem or sacred text.

Magic: The use of spells or charms believed to have supernatural powers over natural forces; black magic is the use of evil spirits for destructive purposes; white magic is beneficial use of magic.

Magistrate: A government official similar to a judge; a mayor.

Marburg Colloquy (1529): Gathering of Protestant theologians who met to create a common creed (statement of beliefs) as a united front against Catholics.

Martyr: A person who voluntarily suffers death for a religious cause.

Masque: Court entertainment featuring masked actors, elaborate costumes, music, and dance.

Mass: The Roman Catholic worship service in which communion is taken.

Medical practitioner: An unlicensed healer who treats illness and disease.

Medieval: A term for the Middle Ages.

Mercenary: A hired soldier.

Mercury: A silver-colored, poisonous metallic element.

Metallurgy: The study and use of metals.

Metaphysics: The study of the nature of reality and existence.

Meteorology: The science that deals with the study of weather patterns.

Middle Ages: A period in European history that began after the downfall of the West Roman Empire in the fourth and fifth centuries and continued into the fifteenth century; once called the Dark Ages.

Midwife: One who assists in childbirth.

Mistress: A woman who has a continuing sexual relationship with a married man and is not his wife.

Monarchs: Kings and queens who have sole ruling power.

Monastery: A house for monks, members of a religious order.

Monk: A man who is a member of a religious order and lives in a monastery.

Monopoly: Exclusive control or possession of a trade or business.

Moors: Muslim Arab and Berber conquerors of Spain.

Morisco: The Spanish word for a Muslim who converted to Christianity.

Mortal sin: An act of wrongdoing that causes spiritual death.

Mosque: A Muslim house of worship.

Muslim: A follower of the Islamic religion.

Mysticism: Religion based on intense spiritual experiences.

N

Natural history: An ancient and medieval term for the study of nature.

New Testament: The second part of the Bible, the Christian holy book.

New World: The European term for the Americas.

Nobility: Members of the upper social class.

Novella: A form of short fictitious story originating in Italy.

Nun: A woman who is a member of a religious order and lives in a convent.

O

Occult: An aspect of religion that relies on magic and mythology.

Old Testament: The first part of the Bible, the Christian holy book.

Opera: A musical work that combines choruses in complex harmony, solo ensembles, arias, dances, and independent instrumental pieces.

Oratorio: A lengthy religious choral work that features singing that resembles speaking in the form of arias and choruses without action or scenery.

Oratory: Public speaking.

Orbit: The path of a heavenly body such as a planet.

P

Pagan: A person who has no religious beliefs or worships more than one god.

Papacy: The office of the pope.

Papal: Relating to a pope or the Roman Catholic Church.

Papal State: The territory owned by the Roman Catholic Church and governed by the pope.

Parish: A local church community.

Parliament: The main governing body of Britain.

Patron: A financial supporter.

Peace of Westphalia (1648): An agreement that ended the Thirty Years' War; by it, Catholic and Protestant states were given equal status within the Holy Roman Empire.

Penance: An act performed to seek forgiveness of sins.

Persecution: Harassment for religious beliefs.

Philosophy: The search for a general understanding of values and reality through speculative thinking.

Physics: The science that deals with energy and matter and their interactions.

Piety: Dutifulness in religion.

Pilgrimage: A religious journey.

Plague: A widespread communicable disease.

Planetary motion: The movement of planets around the Sun.

Pope: The supreme head of the Roman Catholic Church.

Predestination: The belief that the fate of all humans is determined by a divine force.

Prince: A political and military leader; Renaissance ruler.

Prior: The head of a monastery.

Protestantism: Christian religion established by reformers who separated from the Roman Catholic Church.

Protestant Reformation: The reform movement that established a Christian religion separate from the Roman Catholic Church.

Purgatory: A place between heaven and hell.

Q

Quadrant: A device in the shape of a quarter circle that measures angles up to 90 degrees and is used for determining altitudes.

Quest: A religious journey.

R

Regent: One who rules in place of a minor or an absent monarch.

Relief: A carving or sculpture with detail raised above the surface.

Renaissance: The transition period in European history from medieval to modern times, marked by a revival of classical culture, which brought innovations in the arts and literature and initiated modern science.

Rhetoric: Art of effective speaking and writing.

Roman Catholic Church: Christian religion based in Rome, Italy, and headed by a pope.

S

Sack of Rome (1527): Destruction of parts of Rome by armies of Emperor Charles V.

Sacraments: Rites of the Catholic Church: communion, baptism, confirmation, penance, anointing of the sick, marriage, and holy offices.

Sacrilege: The violation of anything considered sacred to God.

Saint: A person who is declared holy by the Catholic Church.

Salic law: A law stating that a male could be the only legitimate heir to the throne.

Salon: A gathering of nobles for discussion of literature and ideas.

Salvation: The forgiveness of sins.

Satire: Criticism through the use of humor.

Schmalkaldic League: A military alliance of German Protestant princes formed in 1531.

Scholasticism: Medieval scholarly method that combined Christian teachings with Greek philosophy.

Scriptures: The text of the Bible, the Christian holy book.

Sect: A small religious group.

Secular: Nonreligious; worldly.

Seignor: An owner of a large estate; also called a lord.

Seignorialism: European social system inherited from the Roman practice of forcing poor people to be dependent on a large landowner called a seignor or lord.

Serf: A peasant who was loyal to a lord and worked on land under the system of feudalism.

Sextant: An instrument used for measuring angular distances.

Simony: The selling of offices in the Roman Catholic Church.

Smallpox: A contagious disease caused by a virus that produces severe skin sores.

Soul: Eternal spirit.

Spanish Armada: The fleet of heavily armored ships built by Spain to defeat England.

Sultan: Arabian king.

Swiss Brethren: A Protestant group who believe in adult baptism; also called Anabaptists.

Swiss Confederation: An alliance of cantons (states) in Switzerland.

Synagogue: Jewish house of worship.

T

Tapestry: A large embroidered wall hanging.

Telescope: A tube-shaped instrument with a lens or mirror used for viewing distant objects.

Theologian: A scholar who studies and teaches religion.

Thirty Years' War (1618–48): A social, religious, and political conflict involving all major world powers; known as the first "world war."

Tithe: Contribution of one-tenth of a church member's income to the church.

Topography: The study of natural and man-made features of a place.

Tournament: A game in which knights engaged in combat with lances on horseback.

Tragedy: A drama that portrays the rise and fall of an honorable man.

Transubstantiation: The belief that bread and wine actually become the body and blood of Christ.

Treatise: A written study of a topic or issue.

Treaty of Cateau-Cambrésis (1559): The peace agreement between France and Spain that ended the Italian Wars, giving Spain control of Italy.

Trigonometry: The branch of mathematics dealing with the study of triangles.

Triptych: A three-panel artwork.

Troubadours: French and Italian poet-musicians.

U

Universe: The totality of the world, including the Earth and the heavens.

V

Vassal: A knight; nobleman soldier who pledged loyalty to a lord.

Vatican: The palace of the pope.

Vestimentary laws: Laws relating to the clothes, or vestments, worn by clergymen.

Villa: A country house; a popular architectural style during the Renaissance.

Vulgate: The official Latin version of the Bible.

W

War of the Roses (1455–85): Conflict between the houses of York and Lancaster in England that resulted in the founding of the House of Tudor.

West Roman Empire: Countries of western Europe; based in Rome, Italy, and formed after the split of the Roman Empire in A.D. 395.

Witchcraft: The practice of communicating with supernatural spirits to bring about certain events or results.

Y

Year of Jubilee: A special spiritual celebration held every twenty-five years by the Catholic Church.

Research and Activity Ideas

The following list of research and activity ideas is intended to offer suggestions for complementing English, social studies, and history curricula; to trigger additional ideas for enhancing learning; and to suggest cross-disciplinary projects for library and classroom use.

Activity 1: Living history: Life in the Renaissance

Assignment: Your social studies class has been selected to create a "living history" presentation on life in the Renaissance. The presentation will be featured in a school program that will be attended by fellow students, parents, and members of the community. You will determine the format of your presentation, but you are expected to make it informative, involve all members of the class, and engage the imagination of the audience.

Preparation: The first task is to hold a class discussion and plan your presentation. One possibility is to assign specific roles, such as kings, queens, dukes, duchesses, courtiers, peasants, slaves, merchants, clergymen, scholars, scientists, patrons, *salonnières,* artists, writers, playwrights, and musicians. Once you have assigned roles, gather information about the lives of the people you will portray. Focus on food, clothing, housing, community and family life, work, recreation, religion, education, and other relevant topics. Each class member might do individual research for his or her role, or teams of students could conduct general research on two or three topics. Using *Renaissance and Reformation: Almanac* as a starting point, find information at the library and on Internet Web sites. Search for sources such as historians' accounts and documents from the period. Try to find little-known or especially interesting facts.

Presentation: After you have gathered information, prepare a fifty-minute group presentation. Use various strategies to dramatize your roles: wear Renaissance-style clothing, give speeches, act out skits, read excerpts from documents of the period, play recordings of Renaissance music, and exhibit color photocopies of artworks. Explore other possibilities to draw upon the knowledge and talents of each class member.

Activity 2: Renaissance science fair

Assignment: Your class has completed a unit on the history of science and is now planning a science fair that will highlight the Renaissance period. You have invited another class in your school to attend the fair. The assignment is to plan and stage the fair, which will feature five- to ten-minute individual presentations and ten- to fifteen-minute group presentations on aspects of Renaissance science.

Preparation: In planning the fair, it is necessary to do some preliminary research. The teacher has distributed a list of general topics such as astronomy, mathematics, geography, navigation, medicine, technology, and scientific instruments. Hold a class meeting in which you assign teams of three or four students to research a topic. Using *Renaissance and Reformation: Almanac*

Chapter 10 as a starting point, find additional information at the library and on Internet Web sites. After the teams have completed their research, hold another class meeting to make assignments for individual and group presentations. Individual presentations might focus on a particular scientist, invention, or scientific experiment; group presentations might cover the methods and discoveries in a specific field. The goal should be to give a comprehensive overview of science in the Renaissance period.

Presentation: After you have made assignments, prepare your presentations. Concentrate on engaging the audience's interest with such techniques as demonstrating an experiment and distributing photocopies of scientists' portraits, diagrams of theories, and illustrations of instruments. Think of other techniques that draw upon the knowledge and talents of individual and group presenters.

Activity 3: Renaissance and Reformation literature

Assignment: Your English class is completing a unit on Renaissance and Reformation literature. The teacher has distributed a list of topics for independent projects that will enable class members to learn more about a particular writer. Your project will involve preparing a paper that (1) presents biographical information about the writer, (2) explains the writer's significance to the Renaissance or Reformation, and (3) interprets a brief excerpt from an example of the writer's work. You will present your paper as an oral report to the class.

Preparation: The first step is to choose a subject for your paper. Then you will need to conduct research on (1) the writer's life, (2) his or her significance to the Renaissance or Reformation, and (3) locate one of the writer's works. Using *Renaissance and Reformation: Almanac* as a starting point, find additional material in the library and on Internet Web sites. After deciding on an example of the writer's work, choose a one-page excerpt (250–300 words). Once you have completed your research, write a paper at least five pages in length (excluding the excerpt of the writer's work).

Presentation: Your teacher has requested that, after you have completed your paper, you make a photocopy of it for each person in the class. You will then present a five-minute oral report, summarizing the results of your research. At the end of the report you might also lead a brief discussion of the writer and his or her work.

Italian Renaissance Culture

"Humanism" is the modern term for the intellectual movement that initiated the Italian Renaissance, which later spread to northern Europe. The humanist movement originated in Florence in the mid-1300s and began to affect other countries shortly before 1500. Humanist scholars believed that a body of learning called *studia humanitatis* (humanistic studies), which was based on the literary masterpieces of ancient Greece and Rome, could bring about a cultural rebirth, or renaissance. Humanistic studies consisted of five academic subjects: grammar (rules for the use of a language), rhetoric (the art of effective speaking and writing), moral philosophy (study of human conduct and values), poetry, and history. The texts included not only classical literature but also the Bible and the works of early Christian thinkers. Many texts had been known throughout the Middle Ages, or medieval period, while others had been recently rediscovered. Humanists believed the study of ancient works would help end the "barbarism," or lack of refinement and culture, of the Middle Ages.

Although humanism began with an emphasis on classical Latin literature, the movement reached its height when scholars mastered Greek language and literature. This part of the ancient heritage had been little known to medieval scholars. Humanists were always eager to discover and share ancient texts, and in the 1450s the new art of printing greatly aided this goal. They also embraced reform of the church through a return to ancient biblical and early Christian works. They were able to adapt their ideas to the different political and cultural situations in the various Italian city-states. The movement spread rapidly from Florence to the elite social classes in Venice, Padua, Verona, Bologna, Milan, and Genoa, then extended south to Rome and Naples. By the turn of the sixteenth century the center of humanism had shifted from Florence to Venice, where the humanist scholar Aldus Manutius (1449–1515) opened a printing press in 1493.

The political autonomy, or self-rule, of Italian city-states ended with the French invasion of Italy in 1494. The French presence escalated into the Italian Wars (1494–1559), a long conflict between France and Spain over control of Italy (see "Italian Wars dominate Renaissance" in Chapter 2). The final blow to Italian independence was dealt when Rome was sacked, or attacked, by the army of Holy Roman Emperor Charles V in 1527. The political and cultural environment that had produced humanism was now past in Italy. Humanism did not end, however, as scholars in northern Europe continued to develop a new method of historical study. By this time the movement had transformed every aspect of intellectual and cultural life—literature, painting, sculpture, music, and theater—not only in Italy but also throughout Europe.

Humanist literature

Many scholars, writers, intellectuals, and patrons contributed to the development of humanism in Italy. Several figures stand out as being the most influential writers. Among them is the scholar Petrarch, who founded humanism. The statesman Coluccio Salutati established Florence, Italy, as the center of humanist activity. Scholar Lorenzo Valla, historian Leonardo Bruni, and philosopher Giovanni Pico della Mirandola expanded the concept of humanism into the culture of their own day. Political theorist Niccolò Machiavelli and social commentator Baldassare both wrote books that spread humanist ideas throughout Europe and eventually became classics of Western literature.

Petrarch studies classics The Italian poet Petrarch (Francesco Petrarca; pronounced PEE-trark; 1304–1374) is considered the founder of humanism. He has been called the first modern man because he rejected the medieval tradition of focusing on religion and spiritual matters. Instead, he analyzed his own thoughts and emotions. Conscious of the fleeting nature of human existence, he felt it was his mission to save works by classical authors for future generations. He also perfected the sonnet form of poetry and is considered by many to be the first modern poet. Petrarch's personal letters mark a distinct break with medieval traditions and a return to the classical and early Christian practice of private letter writing. He provided the great stimulus to the cultural movement that culminated in the Renaissance.

Writes *Canzoniere* Petrarch was born in Arezzo, Italy. When he was eight his family moved to Carpentras, France, near Avignon, which was then the seat of the papacy, the office of the pope. Beginning in 1316, Petrarch pursued legal studies at the University of Montpellier, but already he preferred reading classical poetry to studying law. After his father died in 1326 Petrarch abandoned law and participated in the fashionable social life of Avignon. The following year, in the church of Saint Clare, Petrarch saw and fell in love with a young woman whom he called Laura. She did not return his love. The true identity of Laura is not known, but there is no doubt regarding her existence or the intensity of the poet's passion. He began writing the *Canzoniere* (Song book), a series of love lyrics inspired by Laura. In these poems he departed from the medieval convention of seeing a woman as a spiritual symbol and depicted Laura as a real person.

In 1330 Petrarch entered the service of Cardinal Giovanni Colonna. Over the next few years Petrarch traveled widely and continued writing poetry. In early 1337 he visited Rome for the first time. The ancient ruins of the city deepened his admiration for the classical age. Later that year he returned to France and went to live at Vaucluse, where he led a solitary life and composed his major Latin works. In 1341 Petrarch was crowned poet laureate in Rome. By this time he was the best-known private citizen in Europe. During the same year Petrarch wrote a letter to Colonna recalling the ancient sites they had seen together in Rome. In this letter Petrarch also made his now-famous assertion that the reign of the Roman emperor Constantine (died A.D. 337; ruled 306–37), rather than the birth of Christ, was the great dividing point in history. Petrarch gave the name "dark age" to the period that followed the end of Constantine's reign in the fourth century and continued until Petrarch's own time. Petrarch is thus an important source for our concept of three major periods in Western (non-Asian) history: ancient, medieval, and modern.

In 1345, while studying at the cathedral library in Verona, Petrarch discovered letters of the ancient Roman statesman Marcus Tullius Cicero (106–43 B.C.). Petrarch personally transcribed these letters, which inspired him to plan a formal collection of his own correspondence. By 1348 Petrarch was in Parma, where he received news of Laura's death. That year the Black Death (an epidemic, or widespread outbreak, of the plague; see "Black Death" in Chapter 1) deprived Petrarch of several of his close friends, among them Colonna. Petrarch wrote several letters reflecting on the ravages of the plague. In 1350 he began to make the formal collection of his Latin prose letters, titled *Familiares*. Since 1350 was a Year of Jubilee (special spiritual celebration held every twenty-five years by the Catholic Church), Petrarch also made a pilgrimage, or religious journey, to Rome. On his way he stopped in Florence, where he made new friends, among them humanist author Giovanni Boccaccio. In 1351 he returned to Avignon, but two years later he left France and settled in Milan. He had become increasingly troubled by the presence of the papacy in Avignon. Arguing that the Catholic Church was being held hostage in France much as the ancient Jews were held captive in Babylon, he called the Avignon papacy the "Babylonian captivity" (see "Crisis in the papacy" in Chapter 1).

In 1361 Petrarch went to Padua because the plague, which took the lives of his son and several friends, had broken out in Milan. In Padua he completed the *Familiares* and initiated a new collection, *Seniles*. The following year Petrarch settled in Venice, where he had been given a house in exchange for the bequest (gift in a will) of his library to the city. In 1370 he retired to Arquà, near Padua, where he devoted his time to receiving friends, studying, and revising his works. Except for a few brief absences, Petrarch spent his last years at Arquà.

Although Petrarch promoted writing in the Italian language, he regarded *Canzoniere* and his other Italian poems as less important than his Latin works. He had mastered Latin as a living language, producing the great epic, or long poem, *Africa,* which de-scribed the virtues of the Roman Republic. Among his other important Latin works were *Metrical Epistles, On Contempt for the Worldly Life, On Solitude, Ecologues,* and *Letters.* Petrarch's sense of himself as an individual and his desire for personal earthly immortality had an impact on other humanists, who realized they were living at the end of a long dark age. The influence of Petrarch's art and his reflective approach was felt for more than three centuries in all European literatures.

Salutati founds civic humanism After Petrarch, Coluccio Salutati (1331–1406) was the most important Italian humanist. He originated the concept of civic humanism, which emphasized a humanist education for government officials and supported republican values, meaning a government that represents the people. Salutati began his career in 1339 as a private notary in the area around his hometown of Stignano. For the next sixteen years he held a number of short-term appointments as secretary of communal governments in the region. By 1358 he was the leading political figure in his local commune, a district governed by a group of leaders called a corporation. Early in 1374 Salutati was summoned to Florence to take up the newly created position of secretary of the Tratte, which supervised the republic's elaborate procedures for electing government officials by lot, or random chance. He was probably involved with the group that removed the chancellor (head official), Niccolò Monachi, from office the following

Giovanni Boccaccio

The Italian author Giovanni Boccaccio (pronounced bohk-KHAT-choh; 1313–1375) is considered one of the early humanists. He was the illegitimate son of Boccaccio di Chellino, a merchant from the small town of Certaldo. At first the young Boccaccio apprenticed as a merchant, then he abandoned that career for the study of canon law (official regulations and doctrines of the church). Through his father, who was a financial adviser to King Robert of Anjou, he gained contacts to the cultivated society of the court at Naples. There he mingled with scientists, theologians, scholars, and lawyers. He studied astronomy, mythology, classical literature, French adventure romances, and Italian poets. He also became a writer of love poems and allegories.

Boccaccio's most famous work is the *Decameron,* which he completed by 1353. The *Decameron* consists of one hundred stories, written in Italian, that are set in Florence during the Black Death. Seven young ladies and three young men meet by chance in the church Santa Maria Novella and agree to flee from the city to their country villas during the epidemic. Against the somber background of death and desolation, which Boccaccio portrayed in vivid detail, the group lives a carefree yet well-ordered life in the pleasant countryside for fifteen days, avoiding all thoughts of death. They meet daily in the cool shade, where each one tells a story on a specific subject, and the day ends with a ballad. Each day a king or queen is named to govern the happy assembly and to prescribe occupations and determine a theme for the stories. The storytelling continues for ten days, hence the title *Decameron* (*deca* is the Latin word for ten).

The tales have an abundance of subjects—comic, tragic, adventurous, ancient, and contemporary. Boccaccio portrayed a multitude of characters, from ridiculous fools to noble figures, from all eras and social conditions. He depicted human nature in its weakness and heroic virtue, particularly as revealed in comic or dramatic situations. The *Decameron* became the model of Italian literary prose. It also served as a model for the *Heptameron,* the famous novel by the French writer Margaret of Navarre.

year. Salutati then combined the position of chancellor with that of secretary of the Tratte and became the new leader of the Republic of Florence. At that time Florence was at war with the papacy over control of the republic. Salutati became internationally famous through the brilliance of his *missive,* or public letters, which he wrote to defend Florence's cause. Over the next thirty-one years he may have produced tens of thousands of letters, of which about five thousand remain. Despite the turbulent political life of the republic, Salutati successfully maintained a position of neutrality.

Although Salutati showed an interest in ancient literature and history, his approach to the ancients was different from that of Petrarch. Petrarch felt nostalgia for the ancient world, whereas Salutati was comfortable in the fourteenth century and did not accept Petrarch's notion of the "dark ages." For Salutati the centuries between antiquity and the present had witnessed only a gradual decay in learning. Petrarch preferred to study and translate Greek and Roman texts in scholarly seclusion, but Salutati promoted humanist ideals in public life. Another difference between Salutati and Petrarch was that Petrarch had roamed throughout Italy, whereas Salutati remained in Florence. In his letters he revived and perfected the *stilus rhetoricus* (rhetorical style) developed by the offices of the pope and the Holy Roman Emperor in the first half of the thirteenth century. Salutati argued that a political leader should have a knowledge of history and obtain a humanist education. As chancellor he had a corps of government messengers to carry his personal writings along with public correspondence to the corners of western Europe. He also produced significant studies in classical languages and literature as well as history, theology, and philosophy.

Largely through Salutati's efforts, Florence thus became the capital of the humanist movement in the first half of the fifteenth century. Over the decades Salutati nurtured a group of followers who included future humanist scholars Leonardo Bruni and Poggio Bracciolini. Particularly important was Salutati's role in reintroducing Greek learning to western Europe. In 1397 he was instrumental in bringing the Greek scholar Manuel Chrysoloras (1350–1415) to Florence. When Chrysoloras went on to Padua three years later, he left behind students who could work in the Greek language on their own. Salutati was therefore an immensely influential figure in the development of Italian humanism and in the establishment of Florence as the capital of the movement. His classical studies, his civic position, his influence on younger humanists, and the scholarly projects that he supported enabled the humanist movement to continue unchallenged throughout the next generation.

Bruni is best-selling author Leonardo Bruni (c. 1370-1444) was the best-known Italian humanist in the generation after Salutati. In the early 1390s Bruni went to the University of Florence to prepare for a law career. He joined Salutati's humanist circle and later wrote *Dialogi ad Petrum Histrum* (Dialogues dedicated to Pier Paolo Vergerio; 1405–06), which gave a brilliant picture of the group's literary discussions. Bruni was among the first Italian humanists to acquire a command of the Greek language, and he was recognized as one of the finest fifteenth-century writers in Latin.

In 1405 Bruni abandoned his legal studies and went to Rome, where, on Salutati's recommendation, he was appointed apostolic secretary to Pope Innocent VII (1336–1406; reigned 1404–06). With the exception of a brief period in 1411, when he held the post of chancellor of Florence, Bruni stayed with the papal office in Rome for nearly a decade. He then returned to Florence to take up the life of a private citizen and scholar. In 1416 he was granted Florentine citizenship and a tax privilege in recognition of his work on the *Historiarum Florentini populi libri XII* (Histories of the Florentine people in twelve books;1415–44). Bruni also undertook numerous translation projects and composed his most important treatises, including *De recta interpretatione* (On correct translation; c. 1420), *De militia* (On knighthood; 1421), *De studiis et literis* (On literary study; 1422–29), and *Isagogicon moralis philosophiae* (Introduction to moral philosophy; 1424–25).

In 1427 the Florentine Signoria, or senate, appointed Bruni chancellor of Florence for a second time. By this date he had become quite wealthy. To his professional and economic successes, he added numerous civic honors and his fame extended beyond Florence. He was undoubtedly the best-known literary man of his day and the best-selling author of the fifteenth century. More than thirty-two hundred books of manuscripts (unpublished works) and nearly two hundred editions containing his works survive from this period.

Valla is greatest Italian humanist
Many historians regard the philosopher and literary critic Lorenzo Valla (1407–1457) as the greatest humanist of the Italian Renaissance. He was born in Rome to a family of the lesser nobility. His father and his maternal uncles were lawyers employed by the curia, or papal court. Valla received a private education and was given guidance from a number of Greek and Latin scholars in the employ of Pope Martin V (1368–1431; reigned 1417–31). Despite this papal influence, Valla showed independence in his studies and judgment. For instance, in 1427, when he was only twenty years old, he conducted his own analysis of *Institutio oratoria* (Institutes of oratory) by the Roman orator and teacher Quintilian (pronounced qwin-TIL-yen; A.D. c. 35–c. 100). This work was the major ancient Roman handbook of rhetoric, which the humanist scholar Poggio Bracciolini (pronounced POHD-joh braht-choh-LEE-nee;1380–1459) had discovered and made available for study ten years earlier. In response to Quintilian's work Valla wrote *De comparatione Ciceronis et Quintilianus* (A comparison of Cicero and Quinitilian). He concluded that Quintilian should be the proper Latin guide to humanistic study. Valla was taking a controversial position because leading humanists in the papal court favored Cicero's ideas on rhetoric. Bracciolini became a lifelong critic of Valla and, in 1430, was instrumental in convincing the pope not to appoint Valla to the Roman Curia. Valla then left Rome and went to his family estate in Piacenza.

In 1431 Valla joined the faculty of the University of Pavia, where he taught rhetoric. At Pavia he made public his provocative work, *De volupate* (On pleasure), a dialogue on the nature of true goodness. He defended the Greek philosopher Epicurus (341–270 B.C.), who stated that a wise person who attains virtue may avoid a life of pain by prudently pursuing pleasure. Valla also attacked stoicism, the ancient Greek philosophy embraced by humanists, which advocated control of the emotions through reason and the pursuit of a simple life. His views shocked humanists, and he was finally forced to leave Padua in 1433 when he criticized the Latin translations of Bartolus of Sassoferrato, a late-medieval legal scholar who was highly esteemed by humanists.

In 1435, after teaching in Milan, Genoa, and Florence, Valla became secretary and historian at the court of Alfonso V of Aragon (1396–1458; ruled 1416–58), king of Naples and Sicily. During the naval battle of Ponza, Valla was captured along with Alfonso and taken to Milan. There he wrote a letter to his friend Pier Candido Decembrio (1392–1477), the Milanese humanist, in which he denounced Leonardo Bruni's history of Florence. Valla claimed that Florence was founded during the regime of the dictator Lucius Cornelius Sulla (138–78 B.C.) and thus was not a true heir to the Roman Republic. This position caused further controversy because Bruni and other humanists argued that the revival of classical culture in Florence represented a continuation of the achievements of the Roman Republic. In 1437 Valla returned with Alfonso to Naples. He served at the king's court for thirteen years. During this time he wrote many important

works, such as *De elegantiis linguae lattinae* (The elegances of the Latin language), which was the first great Renaissance study of language.

Convicted of heresy In 1440 Valla issued two works attacking powerful church institutions. The first was *De falso credita et ementitia Constantini donatione declamatio* (On the falsely believed and fictitious donation of Constantine), which questioned the legitimacy of the pope. According to church legend, when Constantine was on his deathbed he transferred rule of the Roman Empire to Pope Sylvester (died 335; reigned 314–35). Valla demonstrated that the document that supposedly recorded Constantine's gift to Sylvester was in fact a forgery concocted in the eighth century to support the power of the papacy during its struggle with emperors. (In fact, Sylvester died in 335, two years before Constantine's death in 337.) Valla produced his attack at a time when Alfonso was engaged in a similar war with Pope Eugenius IV (c. 1383–1447; reigned 1431–47) over territory. Valla's second challenge to the church was *De professione religiosorum* (On the profession of the religious). He criticized the vow taken by the regular (ordained) clergy that gave them the special title of *religiosi* (religious) and designated them as being more entitled to salvation (forgiveness of sin) than lay Christians. (The regular clergy are monks, nuns, friars, and members of other official church groups.) Both of these works aroused indignation among the clergy at the time Valla was seeking permission from Eugenius to return to Rome.

Valla caused even more furor with *Dialectical Disputations,* known as *Dialectica,* in which he defended the doctrine of the Orthodox Eastern Church, a separate division of the Catholic Church established in 1054 and based at Constantinople in present-day Turkey (see "Pope's authority challenged" in Chapter 1). According to Orthodox belief, the Holy Spirit comes only from the Father (God), not from the Son (Jesus Christ), as is held by the Roman Catholic Church. In 1444 Valla was brought before the Inquisition in Naples and charged with questioning church authority. (The Inquisition was a church court established to find and punish heretics, those who committed heresy, or violation of the laws of the church). After he was found guilty on eight counts of heresy, he saved himself from execution by writing an apology to Eugenius. Valla finally negotiated a permanent return to Rome. Eugenius died in 1448, and when Valla arrived in Rome later that year he received a warm welcome from the new pope, Nicholas V (1397–1455; reigned 1447–55), who was himself a humanist. Nicholas gave Valla a teaching position at the University of Rome, appointed him to the curia, and named him a canon of the Basilica of Saint John Lateran. In 1455 Valla became the apostolic secretary. In all of these roles he received generous financial rewards. During the last years of his life he continued publishing translations and histories.

Pico is Renaissance ideal The Italian philosopher Giovanni Pico della Mirandola (pronounced PEE-koh day-lah mee-RAHN-doh-lah; 1463–1494) expanded the concept of humanism, becoming the Renaissance ideal of a learned man. Described as being physically attractive, Pico combined physique, intellect, and spirituality in a way that captivated both humanists and Christian reformers. His career coincided with the last phase of humanism in Italy.

Pico was the youngest son of a princely family in the Lombardy region of Italy. He received a church benefice (land estate) when he was ten years old and was expected to pursue a career in the church or government. From 1480 to 1482 Pico attended the University of Padua. At that time the city of Padua and the university were under the patronage of Venice, which had become the center of humanism in Italy. Pico studied the works of Aristotle, the Hebrew language, Islam (a religion founded by the prophet Mohammad), philosophy, and science. By 1487 he had traveled to Florence and Paris, France, and had obtained a broad education. Disappointed by weaknesses he had found in the humanists' study of classical culture, he began searching for a common truth that would unite all knowledge.

Pico's first and most famous venture was a challenge to Europe's scholars to hold a public disputation (formal debate) at Rome in 1487. He prepared to defend 900 *conclusiones* (theses, or statements offered for proof), drawing 402 from other philosophers such as the scholastics (medieval scholars who sought to integrate ancient philosophy with Christian teachings), the Greek philosopher Plato (c. 428–c. 348 B.C.), and Arabic thinkers. The remaining 498 *conclusiones* were his own. Pico wrote *De hominis dignitate* (Of human dignity) to introduce the Roman disputation. In this thesis he argued that God had granted the power of free will to Adam (the first man on Earth, according to the Bible). That is, humans have free will (the ability to choose their own actions), an idea that contradicted the traditional church view that all human actions are controlled by God. According to Pico, each person is capable of making a distinction between right and wrong and can separate truth from illusion. The human intellect is therefore free to guide the soul and achieve union with the creator. A papal commission became suspicious of Pico's ideas and condemned thirteen of his theses. The assembly was canceled and Pico fled to Paris, where he was briefly imprisoned before settling in Florence late in 1487. His writings for the disputation were banned until 1493.

In Florence, Pico joined the Platonic Academy at the court of Lorenzo de' Medici (called the Magnificent; 1449–1492). The academy was formulating a doctrine of the soul that would combine Plato's philosophy with Christian beliefs. Pico took this process a step further by seeking to harmonize Plato and Aristotle and to link their philosophies with the teachings of Judaism (the Jewish religion),

Christianity, and Islam. His first works on this subject included the *Heptaplus* (1489), a commentary on Genesis, the first book in the Old Testament of the Bible. Pico stressed the connection between Genesis and sacred Jewish texts. He also wrote *De ente et uno* (On being and the one; 1492), in which he reflected on the nature of God and creation. One of Pico's later works, *Disputationes in astrologiam* (Disputations on astrology), was an unfinished attack on astrology (the study of the influence of celestial bodies on human events). He rejected occultism, the belief in or study of the influence of supernatural powers on human actions. Pico gradually renounced the splendor of the Medici court and supported the efforts of church reformer Girolamo Savonarola (1452–1498). Pico also purchased manuscripts, eventually accumulating one of Europe's great private scholarly collections. He died of fever in 1494, during the French occupation of Florence.

Machiavelli defines art of politics The Italian author and statesman Niccolò Machiavelli (pronounced mahk-yah-VEL-lee; 1469–1527) is best known for *The Prince*. In this book he enunciated his political philosophy, which remains controversial even today.

Machiavelli began his political career in 1498 when he was named chancellor and secretary of the Florentine republic. He also went on some twenty-three missions to foreign states. In 1503 he described his most memorable mission in a report titled "Description of the Manner Employed by Duke Valentino [Cesare Borgia] in Slaying Vitellozzo Vitelli, Oliverotto da Fermo, Signor Pagolo and the Duke of Gravina, Orsini." In great detail he described a series of political murders the notorious Spanish-born Italian nobleman Cesare Borgia (c. 1475–1507) ordered to eliminate his rivals. Machiavelli intended this work as a lesson in the art of politics for Florence's weak and indecisive leader, Pier Soderini. In 1510 Machiavelli was instrumental in organizing a militia (citizens' army) in Florence. In August 1512 a Spanish army entered Tuscany and raided the commune of Prato. The Florentines removed Soderini, and the Medicis, who had previously ruled Florence, were able to return to power (see "Florence" in Chapter 2). Three months later Machiavelli was dismissed. Soon afterward he was arrested, imprisoned, and subjected to torture as an alleged conspirator against the Medicis. Although innocent, he remained a suspect for years to come. When he was unable to secure an appointment from the reinstated Medicis, he turned to writing political treatises, plays, and verse. In 1513 he wrote *The Prince*.

The Prince is an influential work Machiavelli shared with Renaissance humanists a passion for classical antiquity. He had a fierce desire for political and moral renewal according to the ideals of the Roman Republic. Although a republican at heart, he saw the need for a strong prince, a political and military leader who could eliminate the French and Spanish presence in northern Italy by forming a unified state. When he wrote *The Prince* he envisioned such a possibility while the restored Medicis ruled both Florence and the papacy. In the final chapter of the book he issued a plea to the Medicis to set Italy free from the "barbarians" (the French and Spanish). It concludes with a quotation from Petrarch's patriotic poem "Italia mia": "Virtue will take arms against fury, and the battle will be brief; for the ancient valor in Italian hearts is not yet dead."

Machiavelli's chief innovation in *The Prince* was to view politics as a separate field. Since ancient times scholars and historians, including the humanists, had treated politics as a branch of moral philosophy. Fundamental to Machiavelli's theory were the concepts of *fortuna* (fortune) and *virtù* (virtue). Fortune, or chance, often determines a political leader's opportunity for decisive action. Yet Machiavelli, like others in the Renaissance, believed in *virtù*, the human capacity to shape destiny. This view contrasted sharply with the medieval concept of an all-powerful God and the ancient Greek belief that humans are powerless against fate. Machiavelli stressed the importance of *virtù*, which is unlike Christian virtue (goodness) in that it is a combination of force and shrewdness—somewhat like a combination of the lion and the fox—with a touch of greatness. According to Machiavelli, the inborn immorality of human beings requires that the prince instill fear rather than love in his subjects. When necessary the prince must also break his pledge with other princes, who will be no more honest than he. Machiavelli was attempting to describe rather than to invent the rules of political success. For him the needs of the state are greater than the individual interests of its citizens.

Many historians suggest that Machiavelli's reputation as a sinister and ruthless politician is largely undeserved. They point out that he lived by his own philosophy that a servant of government must be loyal and self-sacrificing. Furthermore, he never suggested that the political dealings of princes should be a model for day-to-day interactions among ordinary citizens. The main source of the misrepresentation of Machiavelli's ideas was the English translation, in 1577, of a work called *Contre-Machiavel* by the French Huguenot (Protestant) writer Gentillet. Gentillet distorted Machiavelli's teachings, which he blamed for the Saint Bartholomew's Day Massacre, the killing of Huguenots in Paris on a Catholic religious holiday, in 1572 (see "France" in Chapter 6). Many of Machiavelli's positive values were adopted in the nineteenth century. Among them were the supremacy of the state over religion, the drafting of soldiers for citizen armies, and the preference for a republican government rather than a monarchy. Machiavelli was also instrumental in reviving the Roman ideals of honesty, hard work, and civic responsibility.

Castiglione promotes humanist ideals The Italian author, courtier, and diplomat Baldassare Castiglione (pronounced kehs-steel-YOH-nay; 1478–1529) is known primarily for *Libro del cortegiano,* or *Book of the Courtier.* This work, which portrays the ideal courtier—a person who makes up part of a royal court—was instrumental in spreading Italian humanism into England and France.

After receiving a classical education in Mantua and in Milan, Castiglione served at the court of Lodovico Sforza (1452–1508), the duke of Milan, from 1496 to 1499. Castiglione then entered the service of Francesco II Gonzaga (1466–1519), the duke of Mantua. In 1503 he joined Gonzaga's forces in the fight against the Spanish in Naples. On his way north he visited Rome and then Urbino. He liked Urbino, and in 1504 he convinced Gonzaga to transfer him to the court of Duke Guidobaldo da Montefeltro (1472–1508). At Urbino, Castiglione participated in intellectual discussions headed by Guidobaldo's wife, Elizabetta. He decided to depict these discussions in a book, which he began writing in 1507. Titled *Book of the Courtier,* the work was published in 1528. It consists of four sections, or books, in which Castiglione blended classical learning into the format of polite conversation among courtiers and their ladies. He featured real-life figures as participants in the conversations.

The perfect courtier and lady In Book One the assembled courtiers and ladies propose games for their entertainment and decide to "portray in words a perfect courtier." All participants "will be permitted to contradict the speaker as in the schools of the [ancient] philosophers." Discussions are led by Ludovico da Canossa (1476–1532), a diplomat from Verona and a relative of Castiglione. The participants decide that the courtier should be noble, witty, and pleasant. He should be an accomplished horseman and a warrior (his principal profession) who is devoted to his prince. He should know Greek, Latin, French, and Spanish, and he should be skilled in literature, music, painting, and dancing. The courtier's behavior should be characterized by grace and ease, and he should carefully avoid any affectation.

Book Two treats the ways and circumstances in which the ideal courtier might demonstrate his qualities. It stresses decorum, or proper behavior, and conversational skills. At first Federico Fregoso (died 1541), cardinal and archbishop of Salerno, presides over the discussion. When the topic turns to humorous language, the famous comic author Bernardo Dovizi (da Bibbiena; 1470–1520) takes over. The participants then engage in humorous stories, pleasantries, and practical jokes. Book Three defines the qualities of a suitable female companion for the perfect courtier. Leading the discussions and defending women against attack is Giuliano de' Medici (1479–1516), son of Lorenzo the Magnificent and brother of Pope Leo X (1475–1521; reigned 1513–21). The participants discuss the virtues of women, giving ancient and contemporary examples and telling entertaining stories. They give the lady of the palace many of the same qualities as the courtier. Physical beauty is more important to her, however, and she

The perfect courtier and lady were expected to be skilled in literature, music, painting, and dancing. *Reproduced by permission of Hulton Archive.*

must always be more discreet in order to preserve her good reputation. In this book the voices of the assembled ladies are heard more often, but here, as in the other three books, women only ask questions. Although they lead the discussions, they are never active participants.

Book Four begins with a long discussion of the courtier's primary role as an adviser to his prince. The participants conclude that the courtier must earn the favor of the prince through his accomplishments. He must win his master's trust so completely that he can always speak truthfully without fear. He can even correct the prince if necessary. This subject leads to a debate of the merits of republics and monarchies. The topic of conversation finally turns to love, picking up a theme introduced in Book Three. Here the discussion centers on how the courtier, who is no longer young, should love. Pietro Bembo (1470–1547), a noted authority on the subject, instructs the assembled party on a humanist theory of love based on the works of Plato. Bembo explains, step by step, the way to rise from a vision of human beauty to an understanding of ideal beauty, and from there to God. As he speaks he seems to lose touch with his surroundings, and one of the participants tugs at his shirt to awaken him from his reverie.

Book of the Courtier was an immediate success, quickly becoming a book of etiquette (rules for proper manners) for both the bourgeoisie (middle class) and the aristocracy in Europe. Translated into Spanish (1534), French (1537), English (1561), and German (1566), the work went into forty editions in the sixteenth century alone and one hundred more by 1900. Through *Book of the Courtier,* the values of Italian humanism as they would be embodied in a learned, well-rounded man were spread throughout western Europe. The book also shaped the image of noblewomen who headed salons, literary gatherings that made important contributions to Renaissance culture. *Book of the Courtier* exalts humanist qualities not for themselves but as tools of self-advancement. Nevertheless, Castiglione gave a lofty concept of human personality, dignity, and capacity for creativity.

Women humanists

Women were active in the earliest stages of the humanist movement, which created an environment for the free expression of their ideas. Among the most prominent were Christine de Pisan, Isotta Nogarola, Cassandra Fedele, and Laura Cereta.

Pisan writes classic poem The Italian-born French writer Christine de Pisan (also Pizan; 1364–c. 1430) was among the first to view the status of women in the light of humanist ideas. As a young child Pisan moved with her family from Venice, Italy, to Paris, France, where her father had been appointed astrological and medical adviser to the French king, Charles V (1337–1380; ruled 1364–80). In 1380, at the age of fifteen, Christine married Étienne du Castel, a royal secretary at the French court. The couple had three children before Étienne died in an epidemic in 1390. After a period of struggle and mourning, Christine began to create a new life for herself through reading and eventually through writing. Her work attracted attention in 1399, when she became involved in a literary debate about *Roman de la rose,* or *Romance of the*

Salons

The *Book of the Courtier* was instrumental in shaping the image of noblewomen who headed salons, which contributed significantly to Renaissance culture. A salon was an intellectual and literary discussion held in the home of a socially prominent woman, which became popular in the 1600s, especially in France. It was held at a royal or noble court and headed by an aristocratic or high-born woman called a *salonnière*. The terms "salon" and "salonnière" were introduced in the nineteenth century. During the Renaissance salons were known as *ruelles* (companies). Many women who headed and attended these gatherings exchanged ideas, then published their views in books and pamphlets.

Early forms of the salon could be found in northern Italy in the 1400s. Examples were literary gatherings in Brescia, where the humanist scholar Laura Cereta presented her essays, and discussions headed by Marchioness Isabella d'Este (1474–1539) at her famous court in Mantua. Similar events were held in convents, where women could more easily express their views without the fear of ruining their reputations. The salon attracted a diverse range of participants and featured a varied program. It was held at the home of the *salonnière*. She presided over the conversation and set standards of etiquette to prevent disruptions and rivalries during the discussion. For the *salonnière*, the salon might serve as a means of education or a way to gain influence in society. The image of a *salonnière* was influenced by The *Book of the Courtier*. Castiglione portrayed women as delicate, sensitive, beauteous, and selfless, and the *salonnière* was expected to possess these qualities. Nevertheless, the prominence of women was one of the most criticized aspects of salons because many people objected to women taking an active role in society.

Rose, a popular medieval poem originally written in 1265 by Guillaume de Lorris (died c. 1240). The issue was a continuation of the poem written by Jean de Meun (Jean Chopinel; c. 1240–before 1305), in which Meun presented negative images of women. In 1402 Pisan became more publicly involved in a discussion of this question with young men at the royal court, who were embracing early humanist ideas coming from Italy.

Pisan's participation in the debate about *Roman de la rose* inspired her to write her most famous poem, *Le livre de la cité des dames* (The book of the city of ladies; 1405), which has become a classic of women's literature. Her ideas were influenced by *De claris mulieribus* (On famous women), a work by the Italian writer Giovanni Boccaccio that had recently been translated into French. In her own poem Pisan of-

Manuscript illumination showing Christine de Pisan presenting her manuscript to Isabel, queen of France, in a bedroom of the Royal Palace. *©Historical Picture Archive/Corbis. Reproduced by permission of the Corbis Corporation.*

fered a new interpretation of the historical role of women. She described a city built especially for women, which was placed under the supervision of three allegorical, or symbolic, assistants: Reason, Rectitude (righteousness), and Justice.

In the 1520s the French political situation began to deteriorate as

France and England struggled for control of the French throne (see "France" in Chapter 3). Pisan withdrew to the Abbey of Poissy, where her daughter was a member of the Dominican community. Pisan did not disappear completely from view, however. In 1429 she expressed her joy at the appearance of the teenage mystic Joan of Arc (c. 1412–1431), who led the French in military victories against the English. Pisan composed *Le ditié de Jeanne d'Arc* (The tale of Joan of Arc). It was the first literary tribute to France's heroine. Pisan is now considered the first independent professional woman writer.

Nogarola defends Eve The first major female humanist was Isotta Nogarola (1418–1466), who produced a large number of works. Born into a literary family in Verona, Italy, Nogarola received a humanist education along with her older sister Ginevra. While they were teenagers both girls won the attention of northern Italian humanists and courtiers. With these learned men they exchanged books and letters that showed their classical training and lively intelligence. In 1438 Ginevra married and ceased her involvement in the discussions of humanist ideas. Isotta continued to participate until 1441, when she became discouraged by attacks on her character. Historians believe these attacks came from men who did not approve of learned women. Isotta Nogarola withdrew from humanist circles to join her mother in her brother's house. She lived, as she put it, in a "book-lined cell" where, like medieval holy women, she continued her studies in solitude. For thirty-two years she exchanged letters with humanist friends on current political events and the historical tradition of heroic women.

Of special interest is the letter exchange between Nogarola and the Italian humanist Ludovico Foscarini, a Venetian statesman and governor of Verona. In 1451 Nogarola composed a dialogue titled "On the Equal and Unequal Sin of Eve and Adam," which was addressed to Foscarini. In the dialogue she explored the question of whether Adam or Eve committed the greater sin in the Garden of Eden. According to the story in the book of Genesis in the Old Testament (the first part of the Bible), Adam and Eve were the first two people on Earth, and they lived in the Garden of Eden. They had no awareness of evil because they had been forbidden by God to eat apples from the tree of knowledge. One day an evil serpent appeared in the tree and tempted Adam and Eve to eat an apple. Eve took a bite and then persuaded Adam to do the same. God later expelled them from the garden for committing the first sin. This story was used by Christian leaders to prove that Eve (representing womankind) was responsible for the fact that all humans are born with original sin—that is, sin is a part of human nature at birth—because she had tempted Adam (representing mankind) into an awareness of evil.

On the question of who had committed the greater sin, Foscarini took Adam's side, presenting the traditional argument for Eve's guilt. He pointed out that Eve's moral weakness, not the serpent (representing evil), was the temptation that made Adam surrender to a sinful act. Nogarola defended Eve, saying that Eve was incapable of choosing between good and evil and therefore should not be held accountable. At the time Foscarini was considered to be the winner of the argument because Nogarola had admitted that Eve was inferior to Adam in being unable to choose between right and wrong. "On the Equal and Unequal Sin of Eve and Adam" was the first contribution to feminist rethinking of the Adam and Eve story.

Fedele is child prodigy Cassandra Fedele (1465–1558) left a quite different legacy. Although she was active in humanist circles and was one of the most acclaimed women of her day, she accepted the traditional view of women. She believed in the "natural" inferiority of the female sex, and she routinely presented herself as being less important than men. Fedele was born in Venice and received a classical education through the efforts of her father, Angelo Fedele. When Cassandra was a young teenager Angelo represented her as a child prodigy (an exceptionally talented young person). She delivered orations, or formal speeches, standing before the assembled faculty at the University of Padua, the Venetian Senate, and the doge (duke of Venice) himself. Fedele's first book was published when she was twenty-two, and before she reached the age of thirty lists of her works were featured in encyclopedias of fa-

mous men and women. Her main professional achievement was the letters, perhaps thousands of them, that she exchanged with some of the most celebrated men and women of the day. Although Fedele never held an academic appointment, she corresponded with Niccolò Leonico Tomei, a scholar at the University of Padua, and she met regularly with prominent humanists at Padua. Fedele came close to accepting an academic appointment with Isabella I and Ferdinand II in Spain. For eight years Fedele corresponded with the queen and her representatives, but she canceled her plans in 1495 after the outbreak of the Italian Wars.

Fedele married in 1498 and was widowed in 1520. Childless and almost penniless, she shared cramped quarters with her sister's family until 1547, when Pope Paul III (1468–1549; reigned 1534–49) responded to her plea for assistance. He secured an appointment for her as prioress (supervisor) at the orphanage of San Domenico di Castello. In 1556 Fedele made her last public appearance when she delivered an oration welcoming the queen of Poland to Venice. Only two of her published writings survive. One is the small volume she wrote as a girl and the other is *Casandrae Fidelis epistolae et orationes* (Letters and orations of Cassandra Fedele; 1636), which contains 123 letters and 3 orations.

Cereta challenges gender roles The writer Laura Cereta (1469–1499) was one of the foremost female humanists of the Italian Renaissance. She participated in one of the early forerunners of the salon, a literary gathering held in a convent or an urban home. During Cereta's day, in the late fifteenth century, this setting enabled women writers to enter the public arena without injuring their reputations.

Born in Brescia (a province in northern Italy), Cereta was educated at home and at the nearby convent in Chiara. She married at age fifteen, but her husband died of the plague eighteen months later. Widowed and childless, Cereta spent her time alone writing essays in letter form to prominent churchmen, scholars, and citizens. In Brescia and Chiara she frequently attended gatherings with humanist scholars to whom she presented her essays. Although she failed in her attempts to befriend Cassandra Fedele, she did have friendships with a number of learned women. Among them were the nuns Nazaria Olympica, Vernanda (the abbess at the Chiari convent), and Santa Pelegrina.

Cereta was only thirty years old when she died. She left behind a single unpublished volume containing a dialogue and eighty-two Latin letters, many of which were autobiographical. In these letters Cereta portrayed herself as a compliant daughter of demanding parents, a war protester, a frustrated bride, a woman humanist in search of fame in a man's world, and a widow considering a life of religious seclusion. Her most important legacy to the women who followed her was the stating of concerns that affected women as a class. For instance, she challenged the traditional views of gender roles, she portrayed housework as a barrier to women's intellectual aspirations, and she described marriage as slavery. So widespread was her fame as a writer at the time of her death that all of Brescia was said to have mourned her passing.

Poetry

Classical poetry was revived during the Italian Renaissance. All scholars and writers knew the works of ancient Roman and Greek poets, primarily as a result of being educated in Latin grammar schools. Students were required to keep commonplace books, in which they copied passages from classical poetry. They were then required to memorize the passages for recitation in class and for use as models in writing their own poetry (see "Commonplace books" in Chapter 13). This practice eventually spread throughout Europe. Consequently, much early Renaissance poetry was written in Latin and based on classical themes such as love and mythological stories.

The first Italian to compose in his native language was the poet Dante (Dante Alighieri; 1265–1321). Dante lived at the end of the Middle Ages, yet his work influenced Renaissance poets. His best-known poem is the epic *Commedia,* or the *Divine comedy* (composed 1308–21), which is considered one of the masterpieces of Western literature. It consists of one hundred cantos, or sections, written in a complex verse form called terza rima, which utilizes three-line stanzas (lines arranged together) and various rhyming patterns. Divided into three parts, the *Divine comedy* tells the story of the poet's imaginary journey through Hell (*Inferno*), Purgatory (*Purgatorio*), and Heaven (*Paradiso*). Dante influenced later poets not only because he wrote in his own language but also because he addressed philosophical and religious themes with great imagination. Equally important was his creation of the character Beatrice, who guides him through Heaven. She was based on a real-life woman, thought to have been Beatrice Portinari, whom Dante loved and who died in 1290. She was the inspiration for Dante's work, and the *Divine comedy* was a memorial to her. Through this masterpiece Dante established Tuscan (a dialect spoken in Tuscany) as the literary language of Italy. Beatrice was also used as a model for the unattainable woman that became a popular theme in European poetry.

Petrarch perfects sonnet After Dante, Petrarch was the next Italian poet to make a major contribution to Western literature. He perfected the verse form called the sonnet in his *Canzoniere*. During the Renaissance, poets throughout Europe adapted the Petrarchan sonnet to their own traditions.

The sonnet was not original to Petrarch. It was invented in the first half of the thirteenth century by Giacomo da Lentino, a notary (one who records legal documents) at the court of Holy Roman Emperor Frederick II (1194–1250; reigned 1212–50). It was probably derived from the eight-line Sicilian peasant song, the *canzuna*, or

the eight-line literary verse called the *strambotto*. To the eight-line form Giacoma added six lines to create what is now known as the sonnet. He wrote a total of fifteen sonnets. The form was imitated through a poetic debate involving a sonnet by Jacopo Mostacci (died after 1277), a sonnet by Pier della Vigna (c. 1190–1249), and two sonnets by the abbot (head of an abbey) of Tivoli. These nineteen sonnets are considered the beginning of the tradition of writing sonnets.

Inspired by Dante's writing the *Divine comedy* in Tuscan, Petrarch realized that he might surpass Dante in writing sonnets in Italian. He then began composing *Canzoniere*. It was a collection of 366 sonnets and other poetic forms that celebrate his unrequited love for Laura, the woman he had seen in a Florence church (see "Petrarch studies classics" section previously in this chapter). *Canzionere* was first printed in 1470, after Petrarch's death, and by 1600 there were 170 editions. The name of Petrarch became an adjective to denote sonnet literature that depicted love for a reluctant lady. Petrarchan sonnets were immediately imitated by numerous Italian poets, and by the first half of the sixteenth century the sonnet had arrived in England, France, Spain, and Portugal. It was especially popular in England, where writers developed the English sonnet, the form that is best known today (see "Literature" in Chapter 9).

Ariosto writes classic epic The Italian poet Ludovico Ariosto (1474–1533) wrote *Orlando furioso* (Mad Roland), one of the masterpieces of Renaissance poetry that is most often associated with the period.

Ariosto was born at Reggio Emilia. When he was fourteen, his family moved to Ferrara, where his father, Niccolò, was in service at the ducal court of the Este family. Five years later his father gave him permission to stop preparing for a law career and study literature. Ariosto was first employed at the Este court in 1498. Two years later his father died, leaving him to provide for nine younger brothers and sisters. During this time he began writing neoclassical comedies (comic plays composed in the form of poetry and based on ancient Roman and Greek models). In 1503 Ariosto entered the service of Cardinal Ippolito I d'Este (1479–1520), who sponsored performances of his comedies, *La cassaria* (The coffer comedy) in 1508 and *I suppositi* (The pretenders) in 1509. His most successful later comedy, *La Lena,* (Lena) was performed under his direction in 1529.

In 1513 Ariosto met the beautiful Alessandra Benucci, whom he married secretly in 1528 to avoid the loss of his church benefices (church offices that provide a source of income). In 1518 he entered the service of the cardinal's brother, Duke Alfonso I d'Este (1486–1534). Except for a three-year period (1522–25) when he governed the bandit-ridden Garfagnana region for the duke, Ariosto was allowed more time for writing than he had been by Cardinal Ippolito. Among his works was *Satire,* in which he used irony (criticism implied by saying one thing but meaning another) to depict his problems in Ferrara, where the Este brothers failed to recognize his worth. He also described his experiences in Garfagnana and his missions to the papal court.

In 1516, while working for Ippolita, Ariosto completed the first version of *Orlando furioso.* It was a continuation of the popular epic poem *Orlando innamorato,* by Matteo Maria Boiardo (c. 1441–1494), about the medieval French hero Roland. Ariosto used Charlemagne's war against the Saracens (nomadic peoples of the deserts between Syria and Arabia) as a backdrop to explore Renaissance themes such as love, madness, and fidelity. In an elaborate subplot he dramatized how these themes affected the fortunes of the house of Este. The poem is recited by a *cantastorie* (minstrel) before his patron, Ippolito. Among numerous episodes about brave knights and enchanting women, the narrative has three main plots. The first is the Saracens' siege of Paris and their final defeat. Within this action Ariosto portrayed his second plot, the insanity of Orlando, who was driven mad by unrequited love for Angelica, Princess of Cathay. The third story line is the love of the warrior woman Bradamante for a man named Ruggiero. Orlando gradually loses his mind as he drifts from frightening dreams to hallucination to total madness. Ariosto's insight into the intricacies of human nature in so fantastic a world—which includes even a moon journey—is considered a remarkable feat of poetry. *Orlando furioso* portrays

"Scourge of Princes"

Pietro Aretino (1492–1556) was one of the most colorful and controversial poets of the late Renaissance. He flattered his patrons, attacked their adversaries, and wrote outspoken letters to popes, kings, and emperors. His works ranged from devotional literature to outright pornography. For his scathing writings directed at important people, the Italian poet Ludovico Ariosto called Aretino the "Scourge [whip] of Princes," a nickname that has stuck with him ever since.

Aretino rose from humble origins in Arezzo. Through friends of his mother he gained employment at the papal court in Rome. He stayed there until 1525, then settled in Venice. Aretino became quite wealthy through his writings, which enabled him to live in a luxurious home on the Grand Canal in Venice. Much of his income came from patrons who paid him to write attacks on their enemies and from others who paid him not to write about themselves. In spite of the questionable nature of his works, Aretino was known for a witty and dramatic style. He composed many successful comedies and an outstanding tragedy (drama that portrays the rise and fall of an honorable man) titled *Orazio* (Horace; 1546). It was based on a story by the Roman historian Livy (59 B.C.–A.D.17) about the conflict between love and honor in ancient Rome. *Orazio* is considered the best tragic drama written in Italian during the sixteenth century. Aretino's reputation was so bad by 1600, however, that his comedies were issued in a slightly rewritten form, under different titles and the names of other authors.

many values of the world of chivalry, such as love and fidelity. (Chivalry was a complex code of honor upheld by knights in the Middle Ages; see "Feudalism" in Chapter 1). It influenced the Spanish novelist Miguel Cervantes, the English poet Edmund Spenser, and the English playwright William Shakespeare (see "Literature" in Chapter 9). Ariosto died in 1533 after completing the last version of *Orlando furioso*.

Veronica Franco is "honest courtesan"
Contributions to Italian poetry were also made by women. Among them were courtesans such as the poet Veronica Franco (1546–1591), who had access to the intellectual life of the court. A courtesan was a prostitute, a woman who is paid to engage in sexual intercourse, whose clients were courtiers and other wealthy or upper-class men. Franco was the daughter of a procuress (one who obtains prostitutes for clients), Paola Fracassa, and a merchant, Francesco Franco. Her family had a coat of arms (emblem signifying noble rank) because they were native-born citizens who belonged to a professional class that made up the

government bureaucracy and Venetian confraternities (religious charitable organizations). In the early 1560s she was married to a man named Paolo Panizza in what was probably an arranged marriage, but she separated from him soon after. She bore six children from different men but only three survived beyond infancy. In the mid- to late 1560s, Franco became a *cortigiana onesta* (honest courtesan), meaning that she provided men with intellectual and cultural pleasures as well as physical ones.

Franco and her brothers were educated by private tutors at home, and she frequented literary gatherings in Venice during the 1570s and 1580s. She captured the interest of Domenico Venier (1517–1582), a Venetian poet and head of the most renowned Italian literary academy in Venice. Venier read her poetry and became her protector. Frequently visiting his private literary salon (gathering of nobles for discussion of literature and ideas), Franco composed sonnets and poems to exchange with male poets. By her mid-twenties, she was requesting sonnets for publication from these poets for anthologies that she assembled to commemorate men of the Venetian elite. In 1575 she published *Terze rime,* a volume of her own poetry. In these poems, which were often erotic and sexually explicit, Franco was forthright about her profession. Her frankness challenged the literary poses adopted by male poets, who praised an unattainable woman who rarely spoke in her own voice. Franco's verse form, terza rima, was often used for poetic debate. She used it to challenge her male opponents, revealing her verbal skills and sexual independence.

In 1580 Franco published a volume of fifty letters, *Lettere familiari a diversi* (Familiar letters to diverse persons). The first was written to King Henry III (1551–1589; ruled 1574–89) of France and the twenty-first was addressed to Jacopo Tintoretto, the Venetian painter (see "Painting" section later in this chapter). The letters detail Franco engaged in a variety of daily activities such as playing music, sitting for a portrait, organizing a dinner party, and participating in literary activities. The letters were inspired by those of ancient authors, which were translated into Italian by members of the Venier academy. Writing letters allowed Franco to position herself as judge and adviser, writing as a courtesan-secretary to noblemen who had been led astray by their passions.

In 1580 Franco was brought to trial by the Inquisition in Venice. She had to answer the accusation of Ridolfo Vannitelli, her sons' tutor, that she practiced magical incantation (worked magic spells) in her home. Through her own defense, the help of Venier, and probably the opinion of the inquisitor, she was found not guilty of the charges. Franco was impoverished when she died in Venice at age forty-five. The trial had damaged her reputation and she experienced grave financial losses during the plague that struck Venice from 1575 through 1577.

Colonna is ideal woman Italian noblewoman Vittoria Colonna (1492–1547)

Italian noblewoman Vittoria Colonna became one of the most important women of the Renaissance era. *Photograph courtesy of The Library of Congress.*

emerged as a prominent Renaissance figure. Noted for her intellect, piety, and charm, she became one of the most important women of the sixteenth century.

In 1509, at age seventeen, Colonna married the Spanish soldier Ferrante Francesco de Avalos (1490–1525), marquis of Pescara. While her husband was away at war, Colonna held court for intellectuals and artists at her home in Naples. She befriended notable Italian poets such as Jacopo Sannazaro (1458–1530), Bemardo Tasso

(1493–1569), and Benedetto Gareth Cariteo (c. 1450–1514). After her husband's death in 1525, the childless Colonna turned to intellectual pursuits and religious matters.

Colonna was drawn to Roman Catholic reformers and the intellectuals who flocked to her gatherings in the Roman convent of San Silvestro. She associated with reformers usually called the "Spirituali," who stressed renewed Christian spirituality. Among them were Spanish humanist Juan de Valdés (c. 1490–1541), Italian theologian Bernardino Ochino (1487–1564), English cardinal Reginald Pole (1500–1558), and Venetian cardinal Gasparo Contarini (1483–1542). In the 1530s Colonna and the artist Michelangelo Buonarroti (see "Painting" section later in this chapter) formed a friendship based on shared artistic and spiritual interests. Colonna's association with religious reformers brought her to the attention of the Inquisition in the 1540s. Suspected of heresy, Colonna was demoralized during her final years. She suffered a debilitating illness and died in 1547, with Michelangelo at her side.

Colonna's work, like the poet herself, ideally suited Renaissance taste. Although few of her compositions were issued with her consent, an unauthorized edition of her works appeared in 1538. It was followed by twenty more editions in the sixteenth century alone. Since 1547, her poetry has been divided into two sections: love compositions for her deceased husband and spiritual poems. Other works include epistolary sonnets (poems in the form of letters) and letters. A 1982 edition titled *Rime* (Rhymes) contains almost four hundred compositions by Colonna.

Renaissance art

The great era of Renaissance art (painting, sculpture, and architecture) lasted for nearly two hundred years. It is divided into three periods: early Renaissance (1420–95), High Renaissance (1495–1520), and mannerism (also called the late Renaissance; 1520s–1600). These periods overlapped, depending on the artists and the places where they worked. The Renaissance art movement began in the early fifteenth century when humanist ideas were put into practice by painters, sculptors, and architects in Florence. Using a human-centered approach, they started a revolution that quickly spread throughout Europe. During the Middle Ages, art had a religious theme and the artist was an anonymous vehicle for glorifying God. In the Renaissance, however, human beings became the central focus of artistic expression in painting, sculpture, and architecture. In the first decade of the sixteenth century, at the height of the High Renaissance, Rome become the artistic capital of Europe. The patronage of Pope Julius II (1443–1513; reigned 1503–13) attracted all the leading Italian artists to that city. Three artists in particular—Leonardo, Michelangelo, and Raphael—dominated the High Renaissance, and their influence overwhelmed the following generations. During the late Renaissance, artists developed mannerism as a reaction against the bal-

The Baroque Period

The "baroque period" is generally used to describe the music, art, literature, and philosophy of the seventeenth century. The concept of the baroque emerged in the eighteenth century to describe an exuberant, sensuous, expressive, and dynamic style that was different from the classical style of the Renaissance. For advocates of Renaissance ideals, this era was an age of decline. Its manners, morals, and arts—and architecture above all—were considered absurd, grotesque, corrupt, and contrary to good (that is, classical) principles. The word "baroque" may have come from the Portuguese *barroco* and the Spanish *barrueco,* terms for a misshapen pearl. Another origin may have been a nonsensical word created by medieval logicians (scholars who study logic, or the use of reason in thinking) for an excessively complicated argument. Whatever the origin of the word, the eighteenth century carried on its negative connotations to condemn the baroque for not being the Renaissance.

anced and majestic classical forms utilized in the High Renaissance. Their art emphasized bizarre effects, emotionalism, elegant forms, sense of movement, and personal expression. The end of the Renaissance merged into the "baroque" period, the term used to refer to the art, literature, music, and philosophy of the seventeenth century.

Painting

The early Renaissance was a time of experimentation, which started among painters in Florence and then spread to other Italian city-states such as Urbino, Ferrara, Padua, Mantua, Venice, and Milan. During this period each artist had an individual style—major artistic trends did not develop until the High Renaissance—but they all viewed the world in human terms. This trend began in the fourteenth century with the Florentine painter, architect, and sculptor Giotto di Bondone (c. 1266–1337), who "imitated nature" in fresco murals with the use of tempera in vivid colors. (A fresco is a wall painting made by first spreading moist lime plaster on the wall and then applying paint. Tempera is a water-based paint made with egg yolks and color pigments, that is, substances containing color derived from plant or animal matter.) Giotto's powerful figures, his use of light, and his ability to give a spatial depth to his compositions made his paintings seem lifelike. The realistic approach was fully utilized about a century later in the works of the Florentine painter Masaccio (pronounced mah-ZAHT-choh; 1401–1428).

Masaccio considered father of Renaissance painting Masaccio is considered by many to be the father of Renaissance painting. There is no evidence that he was influenced by Giotto but, like the earlier artist, he depicted figures that seemed to come to life. One major difference between Masaccio and Giotto was that Masaccio used linear perspective (also known as one-point perspective). Invented by the Florentine architect Filippo Brunelleschi (see "Architecture" section later in this chapter), linear perspective is a system derived from mathematics in which all elements of a composition are measured and arranged from a single point of view, or perspective. Masaccio was a friend of Brunelleschi and may have learned linear perspective from him. Masaccio used the technique to achieve the effect of light coming from one direction and illuminating figures. Through the interplay of light and shadow, these figures seem to have three dimensions and exist in actual space. An equally important feature of this technique is that it gives the viewer a sense of looking at a scene along with the painter. Masaccio's most celebrated work, dated 1425–27, is a series of frescoes in the Brancacci Chapel in the Church of Santa Maria del Camine in Florence. One scene, the *Expulsion from Paradise,* depicts Adam and Eve as they are cast out of the Garden of Eden. The painting vividly portrays their profound remorse and anguish through their body language and facial expressions. Masaccio achieved this sense of human drama in all of his works. Although he died at age twenty-seven, he had a profound impact on the art world. Generations of important artists throughout the fifteenth and sixteenth centuries in Florence studied Masaccio's murals.

As the Renaissance gained momentum, artists achieved new status as creators. Prior to this time the only creator was God, but now religious paintings were dominated by human concerns and emotions. Portraits of prominent people and their families also became increasingly popular, reflecting a dramatic shift from the idea that heavenly figures or saints were the only worthy subjects of art. In addition, landscape painting was emerging as a new genre, or form of art. This was another important change because, in medieval art, nature was simply the environment of human beings and therefore had little significance.

Alberti develops theory of painting In the early fifteenth century the theory of painting became a field of study. The first book on the theory of painting was *De pictura,* by Leon Battista Alberti (1404–1472), which appeared in Florence in 1436. *De pictura* represented yet another significant innovation in thinking about art. Throughout the Middle Ages artists were artisans, or technicians, who belonged to craft guilds (organizations that trained apprentices and supervised the quality of products) along with other workers in such industries as shoemaking, textiles (making of fabrics), and building (construction). The main function of artists was to produce decorative items for the trade in luxury goods.

In stark contrast to this tradition, Alberti stressed the creative role of the painter, pointing out that the artist is not merely a technician who prepares paint and applies colors to an object. Instead, Alberti argued, the painter uses his or her intellect to measure, arrange, and harmonize

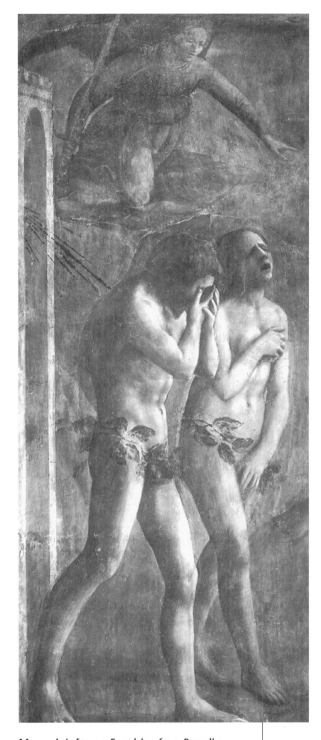

Masaccio's fresco *Expulsion from Paradise.*

a distinctive creation—a work of art. Alberti believed that painting should be considered equal to the liberal arts (grammar, dialectic, rhetoric, music, arithmetic, geometry, and astronomy), subjects identified by classical authors and considered necessary to a civilized life by humanists. Alberti's book prompted a reevaluation of the artist, and soon the rulers of Europe were bringing painters to their courts and starting collections of works by well-known artists. This flurry of activity led to the productive period that is known as the High Renaissance. Literally hundreds of artists were commissioned to do paintings and portraits that decorated grand palaces and public buildings. In fact, the artists are too numerous to name individually, but a few figures—Leonardo da Vinci, Michelangelo, Raphael, and Titian—stand out as the great masters, not only in the Renaissance but also in the history of Western art.

Leonardo depicts human drama One of the greatest figures of High Renaissance art was Leonardo da Vinci (1452–1519), a painter, sculptor, architect, engineer, and scientist. He had an enormous influence on the painting of future artists. At the age of fifteen Leonardo was apprenticed to Andrea del Verrocchio (pronounced vayr-RAHK-yoh; 1435–1488), the leading artist in Florence. Verrocchio was a sculptor, painter, and goldsmith noted for his remarkable craftsmanship. Leonardo stayed on as an assistant in Verrocchio's shop after completing his apprenticeship. His earliest known painting is a product of his collaboration with the master. Collaboration on a major project by a master artist and his assistant was standard procedure in the Italian Renaissance.

Around 1478 Leonardo set up his own studio. Three years later he received a church commission for an altarpiece (a work of art that decorates the space above an altar, a table used as the center of a worship service), the *Adoration of the Magi.* This unfinished painting depicts the story of the three Magi (kings), also known as the Wise Men of the East, told in the book of Matthew in the Bible. The Magi traveled to Bethlehem from the East (ancient Persia; present-day Iran) to pay respect to the newborn Jesus Christ. The adoration of the Magi was a popular subject in medieval and Renaissance art. In his painting Leonardo showed a new approach with the depiction of human drama through a sense of continuing movement. A crowd of spectators, with odd and varied faces, flutters around and peers at the Virgin Mary (mother of Jesus) who is holding the baby Jesus. In the background the three Magi are mounted on horses that prance among intricate architectural ruins. The painting also illustrates a strong sense of order. Traditionally, in paintings of this story, Mary and Jesus had appeared at one side of the picture and the Magi approached from the other side. Leonardo departed from tradition by placing Mary and Jesus in the center of the composition. He also used linear perspective to depict the ruins in the background.

Produces his greatest works Leonardo left Florence in 1482 to accept the post of court artist to Ludovico Sforza (1452–1508), duke of Milan. His first Milanese painting was the altarpiece *Virgin of the Rocks*. Although the *Virgin of the Rocks* was highly original, Leonardo adhered to tradition by showing Mary and Jesus in a cave. This composition gave him the opportunity to experiment with dimmed light, which is coming from two sources, one behind the cave and the other in front of it. (Leonardo once commented that an artist should practice drawing at dusk and in courtyards with walls painted black.) The technique highlights the four figures—Mary and Jesus and another woman and infant—in a soft, shadowy atmosphere. The distinctive feature of the painting is the pyramidal grouping of the figures, which unifies the composition and focuses the eye of the viewer on the central scene.

The other surviving painting of Leonardo's years in Milan is the *Last Supper* (1495–97). It was commissioned by the duke for a wall in the refectory (dining hall) of the convent of Santa Maria delle Grazie. For this painting Leonardo decided not to use fresco, which makes areas of color appear distinct and does not allow for shading. Instead, he experimented with oil-based paint, which is more easily blended. While his efforts resulted in a magnificent work, his experiment with oil-based paint proved less than successful. The paint did not adhere well to the wall, and within fifty years the scene had deteriorated

The Virgin of the Rocks by Renaissance artist **Leonardo da Vinci.** ©*National Gallery Collection, Nation Gallery, London/Corbis. Reproduced by permission of the Corbis Corporation.*

significantly. Attempts to restore the painting in the centuries since have been only partially successful. When the government of Milan was overthrown by the French invasion in 1499, Leonardo left Milan and returned to Florence.

Leonardo was received as a great man in Florence. During his years in the city (1500–06), he completed more projects than in any other period of his life. In 1503 he was invited to paint a large-scale fresco that celebrated the Battle of Anghiara, in which Florence defeated Milan in 1440. The fresco was to be painted on the walls of the newly built Council Chamber of the Republic in the Palazzo della Signoria. For the *Battle of Anghiara* Leonardo experimented with an oil-based paint on a primed (prepared with a sealing substance) wall surface. This process proved to be ineffective because the paint did not dry. The central section of the composition, which was destroyed during a restoration project in 1565, is now known through numerous copies made in the sixteenth and seventeenth centuries. As indicated in a copy made by the Flemish painter Peter Paul Rubens (see "Painting" in Chapter 9) in 1615, Leonardo presented the extreme physical exertion of men and horses engaged in furious battle. The group of central figures displays faces distorted by rage or pain. Even the heads of the horses, with flaring nostrils and gnashing teeth, were treated in this expressive manner. Shortly after Leonardo began the *Battle of Anghiara* his younger rival, Michelangelo, was commissioned to paint *Battle of Cascina,* another celebrated Florentine victory, for the same room in the Palazzo della Signoria.

In 1503, while working on the *Battle of Anghiara,* Leonardo started painting the *Mona Lisa.* Also called *La Gioconda,* it is a portrait of Lisa di Anton Giocondo, the young wife of the prominent Florentine citizen Francesco del Giocondo. The *Mona Lisa* became one of the most famous portraits in the Western world because of Lisa's mysterious smile, which is in the process of either appearing or disappearing. Leonardo had abandoned the *Battle of Anghiara* project by 1508, when he was called back to Milan by Charles Amboise, the French governor. Leonardo worked on an equestrian (rider mounted on a horse) statue, but he produced no new paintings. Instead he turned more and more to scientific observation. In 1513 the French were temporarily driven out of Milan and Leonardo moved to Rome. He received no other commissions, however, and at the end of 1516 he left Italy forever. He spent the last three years of his life at Amboise, France, in the small residence of Cloux (later called Clos-Lucé), near the summer palace of King Francis I (1494–1547; ruled 1515–47). Given the title of *Premier peintre, architecte et méchanicien du Roi* (first painter, architect, and mechanic of the King), Leonardo lived as an honored guest of Francis I. Leonardo produced no other major works, and he spent his time on his notebooks until his death in 1519.

Leonardo had considerable influence on artists of his own day and later times. Some of his views on art, which had been circulating since the sixteenth century, were published in

Leonardo Studies Science

For Leonardo da Vinci art theory was closely related to scientific investigation. Throughout most of his life he was immersed in the study of science. He was especially interested in studying anatomy in order to understand the human form. In fact, he dissected cadavers (human corpses) so he could examine the function of muscles or determine how the vocal cords produce sound. From the 1490s until 1515 Leonardo made extensive notes on his observations, including analytical drawings for illustrations in a treatise on anatomy, which he never completed.

Leonardo also worked on several inventions. He designed many mechanical devices, such as a screw jack, a two-wheeled hoist (both designed for lifting objects), an "armored car," a gun with three racks of barrels, and even a submarine. He refused to share his ideas for a submarine, however, because he feared it would be used for destructive purposes. Leonardo's best-known invention was a flying machine, which he designed by observing bird flight and the motions of air. He also mastered mathematics. For instance, he applied geometry and proportion to create a new sense of order in his drawings and paintings. He translated his study of optics and many of his theories of vision into mathematical terms. Leonardo used his knowledge of physical geography to investigate the origin of fossils and the utilization of water power.

1651 in *Trattato della pittura* (Treatise on painting), a collection of his writings taken from numerous manuscripts. The small number of Leonardo's surviving paintings show his achievements as an artist. He made contributions to every artistic form, from portraits to religious narratives. He gave new insights into figure grouping, space, individual characterization, and light and shade. Many of his works inspired copies, especially by Milanese artists such as Andrea Solari (after 1495–1514) and Bernardo Luini (died 1532). In Florence his compositions were carefully studied by Raphael. Even in the nineteenth century, long after *Battle of Anghiari* had disappeared, aspects of its design continued to intrigue artists throughout Europe.

Michelangelo: from sculptor to painter

Along with Leonardo and Raphael, Michelangelo Buonarroti (known as Michelangelo; 1475–1564) dominated the High Renaissance. First gaining fame as a sculptor (see "Sculpture" section later in this chapter), he also made many contributions to Renaissance painting and architecture (see "Architecture" section later in this chapter).

Michelangelo was apprenticed at the age of thirteen to Domenico

Ghirlandaio (also known as Domenico di Tommaso Bigordi; 1449–1494), the most fashionable painter in Florence. After a year the apprenticeship was broken off, and Michelangelo was given access to the collection of ancient Roman sculpture owned by the duke of Florence. In 1492, at age seventeen, Michelangelo began working as a sculptor. During the next sixteen years he produced many of the best-known sculptures of the Italian Renaissance. Then, in 1504, he received a commission to paint a fresco in the new Council Chamber of the Republic in the Palazzo della Signoria. The building was to have vast patriotic murals that would also show the special skills of Florence's leading artists: Leonardo da Vinci and Michelangelo.

The subject of Michelangelo's fresco was the Battle of Cascina, a celebrated Florentine military victory. Although the *Battle of Cascina* was never completed, several sketches and a copy of the cartoon exist. (At that time a cartoon had not yet come to mean a satirical or humorous drawing. Instead, it was a preparatory design or drawing for a fresco.) The central scene shows a group of muscular nude soldiers climbing from a river where they had been swimming to answer a military alarm. Michelangelo clearly felt the influence of Leonardo and his depiction of a continuous flowing motion through living forms. This combination of throbbing life with colossal grandeur became the special quality of Michelangelo's art.

Michelangelo's career took another direction in 1508, when Pope Julius II offered him a commission to decorate the ceiling of the Sistine Chapel at the Vatican in Rome. At first he protested that he was a sculptor, not a painter. Finally he accepted the job and devoted all of his creative energies to the project. The theme of the ceiling painting is the nine stories from the book of Genesis in the Bible. Interspersed with figures of the male biblical prophets are the female sibyls (prophetesses) of antiquity, a series of nude youths, lunettes (crescent-shaped decorative objects) with representations of the ancestors of Jesus Christ, and a host of other figures and decoration.

Sistine ceiling sets standard Four years later, when the Sistine Chapel project was completed, Michelangelo had made a major innovation in ceiling painting. Traditionally, artists had depicted only single figures, but Michelangelo introduced the portrayal of dramatic scenes. The concept was so successful that it set the standard for future painters. The painting is also considered one of the most awe-inspiring works of Western art. The German poet Johann Wolfgang von Goethe (1749–1832) reportedly remarked that one cannot fully appreciate human achievement without first seeing the Sistine Chapel. Nevertheless, the process had been a physically grueling one for Michelangelo, who was required to lie on a scaffold with arms outstretched for hours at a time. An accomplished and prolific poet, he composed a sonnet in which he described the ways he had to contort his body in order to paint the ceiling.

"My Beard Toward Heaven"

Michelangelo's painting on the ceiling of the Sistine Chapel at the Vatican is considered one of the most awe-inspiring works of Western art. It was the first major painting completed by Michelangelo, who was a renowned sculptor when he reluctantly accepted the Sistine commission in 1508. The four-year project was a physically demanding one for the artist, who painted much of the work while lying on his back on a scaffold. An accomplished and prolific poet, Michelangelo composed the following sonnet while working on the Sistine ceiling. He described the ways he had to contort his body in order to do the work, concluding "I'm not in a good place, and I'm no painter."

"Sonnet to John of Pistoia on the Sistine Ceiling"

I've got myself a goiter [swelling on the front of the neck] from this strain,

As water gives the cats in Lombardy

Or maybe it is in some other country;

My belly's pushed by force beneath my chin

My beard toward Heaven, I feel the back of my brain

Upon my neck, I grow the breast of a Harpy [Greek mythological creature that is part woman and part man];

My brush, above my face continually,

Makes it a splendid floor by dripping down.

My loins have penetrated to my paunch [stomach],

My rump's a crupper [part of a horse's saddle], as a counterweight,

And pointless the unseeing steps I go.

In front of me my skin is being stretched

While it folds up behind and forms a knot,

And I am bending like a Syrian bow.

And judgment, hence, must grow,

Borne in the mind, peculiar and untrue;

You cannot shoot well when the gun's askew [not aimed correctly].

John, come to the rescue

Of my dead painting now, and of my honor;

I'm not in a good place, and I'm no painter.

The Complete Poems of Michelangelo. *John Frederick Nims, translator. Chicago, Ill.: University of Chicago Press, 1998, pp. 5–6.*

In 1534 Michelangelo settled in Rome. For the next ten years he produced paintings for Pope Paul III (1468–1549; reigned 1534–49). Paul III convened the Council of Trent, which initiated the Catholic Reformation, a wide-ranging effort to revitalize the Roman Catholic Church. The first project Michelangelo executed for the pope was the *Last Judgment* (1536–41), a vast painting on the end wall of the Sistine Chapel. The design functions like a pair of scales, with some angels pushing the damned down to hell on one side and some pulling up the saved on the other side. Angels on both sides are directed by Jesus Christ, who "conducts" with both arms. In the two top corners are the cross and other symbols of the Passion (the crucifixion of Christ), which serve as Christ's credentials to be judge.

In the *Last Judgment* Michelangelo used simple colors, blue and brown. The somber tone seems to parallel the ideas of the Catholic Reformation, which called for a renewed emphasis on spirituality. Michelangelo had contact with reform leaders through the poet Vittoria Colonna (see "Poetry" section previously in this chapter), a close friend and supporter to whom he addressed many of his poems. From 1541 until 1545 Michelangelo painted two large frescoes—the *Conversion of Saul* and the *Crucifixion of Peter*—for the Pauline Chapel in the Vatican. They are similar to the *Last Judgment,* but in these works he expressed movement through perspective and used subtle colors in a more expressive way. He may have turned to these techniques because the Pauline Chapel frescoes were the first ones he executed on a normal scale and at eye level. After 1545 Michelangelo devoted himself almost entirely to architecture and poetry. Dying in 1564 at the age of eighty-nine, he lived nearly twice the average Renaissance life span.

Raphael represents High Renaissance
The Italian painter and architect Raffaello Sanzio, called Raphael (1483–1520), is considered the supreme representative of the High Renaissance. He was born in Urbino, the son of Giovan-

ni Santi, a painter. He was trained by his father, who died in 1494. Sometime thereafter he joined the workshop of Perugino (also known as Pietro Vannucci; c. 1450–1523), the most renowned painter in central Italy at the time. Raphael adopted Perugino's style and received several commissions before moving to Florence in 1504. When he arrived he discovered that his style was unsophisticated compared with the recent innovations of Michelangelo and Leonardo. Raphael was especially attracted to Leonardo's work. During the next four years he painted a series of Madonnas that incorporated Leonardo's techniques. One technique was sfumato, which involves defining a form by blending one color into another rather than using distinct outlines. He was also commissioned to do several portraits.

In 1508 Raphael went to Rome to decorate Pope Julius's apartment, the Stanza della Segnatura, at the Vatican. This work, which Raphael completed in 1511, consists of panels that represent the four areas of divinely inspired human intellect: theology, poetry, philosophy, and law. The panel on philosophy, titled *The School of Athens,* is considered one of Raphael's greatest achievements. The two central figures are the idealist Plato, who points heavenward, and the realist Aristotle, who gestures toward the ground. Around them are grouped many other classical philosophers and scientists, each indicating clearly by expression and gesture the character of his intellect. Raphael's painting technique is so precise that every detail in the *School of Athens* contributes to a balanced effect and conveys a sense of quiet grandeur.

After Raphael completed the Stanza della Segnatura, Julius commissioned him to decorate the adjacent room, the Stanza d'Elidoro (the audience chamber). Julius died before it was finished, but his successor, Pope Leo X, told Raphael to continue and eventually assigned him two more rooms, the Stanza dell'Incendio (the meeting room of the Catholic Church's supreme court) and the Sala di Constantino. Very quickly, Raphael became popular with Roman patrons. Commissions of all sorts poured into his workshop during the last six years of his life. By this time he was relying on assistants. For instance, frescoes in the Stanza dell'Incendio (1514–17) were based on his design but executed almost entirely by assistants, as was the fresco decoration of the Vatican loggias (1517–19). Many of his assistants were more collaborators than apprentices, and some were older than he. In 1515 he had what was probably the largest painting workshop that had ever been assembled.

Raphael also was much in demand by aristocrats who wanted him to paint their portraits. He was influenced by Leonardo's *Mona Lisa*. In 1517 Raphael adapted Leonardo's majestic design in the portrait of Baldassare Castiglione, author of *Book of the Courtier*. Like most of Raphael's finest portraits, it is the depiction of a close friend. Castiglione is portrayed with great psychological insight, his gentle, scholarly face perfectly suited to the man who, in *Book of the Courtier,* defined the qualities of the ideal gentleman. Descriptions of Raphael's own pleasant disposition and courteous manner indicate that he himself possessed the qualities Castiglione wished to find in the perfect courtier.

Invents new techniques Raphael had by now developed his own style, which consisted of a distinctive use of color and an emphasis on gesture and movement. This style is evident in such works as cartoons that depict the lives of Saints Peter and Paul. Other typical works were the decoration (begun in 1519) of the Villa Farnesina in Rome and Raphael's largest canvas painting, the *Transfiguration,* which was commissioned in 1517 but remained incomplete at his death. The Peter and Paul cartoons were sent to Flanders to be worked into tapestries (large embroidered wall hangings) for the Sistine Chapel and were partly responsible for the adoption of Raphael's style throughout Europe. His work was also spread through engravings. The market for art prints was just then getting established and Raphael was one of the first to take advantage of it. Raphael supplied unused drawings and designs to engravers, who were required to follow his instructions regarding the production of images. He collaborated with the engraver Marcantonio Raimondi (c.1480–c. 1534) and then allied himself with a businessman known as Il Bavieri, who was responsible for selling the engravings. Raphael appears to have set certain conditions with engravers to control quality and his copyright (exclusive legal right to the sale and reproduction of a work), and he received most of the profits.

When Raphael died in Rome at age thirty-seven his art was developing in new directions. The High Renaissance, which had reached its peak around 1510, had passed. Raphael's pupils began incorporating characteristics of the mannerist style in the last works of their great master. Raphael had made major contributions to painting. He invented new modes of composing a picture and new techniques for using color, which were much imitated. Although he often developed the methods of other painters such as Leonardo, his own style had the most influence. Raphael was a master of linear perspective, which was evolving throughout the High Renaissance. He also invented the concept of modes of coloring, in that he was the first to select a color style to match a project. This was an innovation because, in the traditional workshop of the fifteenth century, a master typically had only one color style, which he taught to his apprentices. As a result of Raphael's experimentations with color, the next generation of painters felt liberated to vary their choice of colors with each commission and to develop new modes.

Raphael's reputation suffered in the twentieth century because his style was adopted as the model for academic art, beginning in the French Academy of the sixteenth century. Elements of his methods were taught to young painters as strict rules. This practice contradicted the freedom that Raphael allowed his own students and collaborators. It was also inconsistent with his experimental approach, in which he never repeated himself. Nevertheless, Raphael has been recognized as one of the greatest European painters, not only of the Renaissance but of all time.

Titian emphasizes drama Titian (also known as Tiziano Vecellio; c. 1488–1576) was a great master of religious art, a portraitist in demand all over Europe, and the creator of mythological compositions.

At the age of nine Titian set out with his brother Francesco for Venice to enter the workshop of Sebastiano Zuccati, a mosaic artist. Not long thereafter Titian began to study painting with Giovanni Bellini (c. 1430–1516). Soon Titian met Bellini's other pupil, Giorgione da Castelfranco; c. 1477–1511), with whom he started collaborating in 1507. The two painters worked so closely at this time that their styles are virtually indistinguishable. Around 1510 Titian began producing his own work. He achieved fame as an interpreter of classical mythology with three paintings—*Andrians,* the *Worship of Venus,* and *Bacchus and Ariadne*—which he composed for the castle of Alfonso d'Este in Ferrara between 1518 and 1523. One of his best-known early works is the *Assumption of the Virgin* (1516–18), which marked the triumph of the High Renaissance in Venice. It shows the Virgin Mary soaring with arms outstretched to heaven.

During the 1520s Titian produced masterpieces such as the *Madonna and Child with Saints Francis and Aloysius* (1520), the *Resurrection* (1522), and the *Pesaro Madonna* (1519–26). In the *Pesaro Madonna* he used color, light, and atmosphere to establish a new formula for Venetian altars that continued into the following century. The *Martyrdom of St. Peter Martyr* (c. 1526–30; destroyed 1867), once regarded as Titian's greatest masterpiece, depicted a new feeling for heroic and dramatic action. It was influenced by the art of Michelangelo and central Italian painters.

Paints innovative portraits An important event in Titian's career was his trip to Bologna in 1530 to attend the coronation of Holy Roman Emperor Charles V (1500–1558; ruled 1519–56). At this time the artist painted his first portrait of the emperor in armor. In 1545 Titian traveled to Rome at the invitation of Pope Paul III. For the first time the artist saw the glories of ancient Rome as well as the masterpieces of Raphael and Michelangelo. Among the numerous works he produced during his brief stay in the city was *Paul III and His Grandsons,* which depicts a dramatic encounter between the aged pope and his scheming grandsons. It is considered one of the most psychologically revealing works in the history of portraiture.

In 1548 Charles V called Titian to Augsburg, Germany. The artist painted the celebrated equestrian portrait, *Charles V at Mühlberg,* which commemorated the emperor's victory over the German Protestants in the Battle of Mühlberg in 1547 (see "The Augsburg Confession" in Chapter 5). In this work Titian established a type of equestrian portrait that presents the ruler as a symbol of power. Titian also produced portraits of members of the emperor's court. The most important is that of Charles's son, Prince Philip (later King Philip II of Spain) in armor, which set a standard for state portraits. In the 1550s Philip II commissioned Titian to paint religious pictures for the monastery of the Escorial, the king's palace in Spain, which was designed by the Spanish architect Juan de Herrera (see "Architecture" in Chapter 9). Among them was the *Last Supper* (1557–64). During the same period Titian also executed mythological works for the Escorial, such as the *Rape of Europa*. Titian continued to explore the depths of human character in his portraits until the end of his life. His late religious pictures convey a mood of universal tragedy, as in the *Annunciation* (c. 1565) and *Christ Crowned with Thorns*. The *Pietà* which was unfinished at his death, was intended for his own tomb chapel. When Titian died at his spacious palace in Venice, he was universally recognized as one of the great masters.

Tintoretto follows great masters The Venetian painter Tintoretto (1518–1594) excelled in grand history paintings and dignified portraits of members of the Venetian aristocracy. His work represented the style of the mannerists, who rejected the classical ideals of proportion, balance, and refined images.

The real name of Tintoretto was Jacopo Robusti, but he is better known by his nickname, which means the "little dyer," so given because his father was a silk dyer. The artist was born in Venice, where he spent his entire life. Even though his painting is distinguished by great daring, he seems to have lived quietly and was concerned only with his work and the well-being of his family. His daughter Marietta and his sons Domenico and Marco also became painters. Domenico eventually took over the direction of Tintoretto's large workshop, turning out uninspired pictures in the manner of his father. Some of them are, on occasion, mistaken for works of the elder Tintoretto.

Tintoretto admired the paintings of Titian. Tintoretto combined the master's techniques with his own fiery and quick imagination, creating an effect of restlessness in his work. Tintoretto was primarily a figure painter and delighted in showing his figures in daring poses. His master in this aspect of his art was Michelangelo. Tintoretto is supposed to have inscribed on the wall of his studio the motto: "The drawing of Michelangelo and the color of Titian."

Tintoretto's earliest documented work, *Apollo and Marsyas* (1545), was painted for the poet Pietro Aretino (see "Poetry" section previously in this chapter). In a letter written for publication, Aretino noted the quickness of its execution and recommended the artist to the world as a genius of note. At about the same time Tintoretto painted *Christ Washing the Feet of the Apostles*. The picture is so arranged that the viewer sees Jesus Christ and Saint Peter last, even though they matter most in the story the picture brings to life. The action that binds these key figures together is dramatized chiefly by an exchange of glances between Christ and Peter.

Work becomes more elaborate Tintoretto's later works were even more elaborate than his early ones. As before, the actions of his figures are quite daring and majestic, yet they serve their function in dramatizing the story. The triumph of Tintoretto's art is his paintings for the Scuola di San Rocco in Venice, which he executed between 1564 and 1587. The walls and the ceilings are almost completely covered with depictions of great events of the Old and New Testaments and the lives of the saints. The focus of the work is the vast *Crucifixion* (1565), which captures the moment when a sponge is being dipped in vinegar to be lifted up on a stick to Jesus Christ. The cross is surrounded by a crowd of people—soldiers, followers of Christ, mockers, pagans, and contemporaries of Tintoretto—who behold the sacred scene as if it were taking place before the eyes of the viewer.

The majority of Tintoretto's large canvases were history paintings with religious subjects. Among his late works is the representation of Paradise in the Sala del Gran Consiglio of the Doges' Palace (1588). In this painting the Virgin Mary and saints, led by Saint Mark, recommend the Great Council of Venice and its decisions to the grace of Jesus Christ. The countless figures are bathed in a strange, phosphorescent light. Another late work is the *Last Supper* (1592–94), in which Tintoretto fills the air of a great hall with a rush of adoring angels. Their presence is made visible by subtle highlights accentuating the darkness of the room. Tintoretto also produced allegorical works and scenes from ancient and modern history, and he was much sought after as a portraitist. His figures are almost always elegant and proper. The women are gentle and the men are impressive, but they appear lonely. In 1588 Tintoretto painted his own self-portrait as an old man in a simple pose, looking resigned and wise.

Caravaggio revolts against trends Caravaggio (1573–1610) was among the most innovative mannerist painters. Born Michelangelo Merisi, he was called Caravaggio after the tiny town in Lombardy where he was born. After serving an apprenticeship and studying painting in Milan, he appeared in Rome around 1590. In his works he depicted insolent boys and rough peasants in the guise of Roman gods and Christian saints. Using a technique known as chiaroscuro (contrasts of light and dark), he often portrayed these figures as if they were emerging out of darkness, with part of their faces and bodies illuminated by a bright light.

The early works of Caravaggio show him in full revolt against both mannerism and classicism. He rejected the elongated figures and curvilinear

Caravaggio's painting *Boy Bitten by a Lizard.*
©*National Gallery Collection, National Gallery, London/Corbis. Reproduced by permission of the Corbis Corporation.*

shapes of the mannerists. He also ridiculed the concept of the classicists that the subject of a painting should be idealized and carry a moral message. In *Bacchus with a Wine Glass* (c. 1595), Caravaggio showed not a Roman god but instead a pudgy, half-naked boy draped in a bedsheet; he is identified as Bacchus only by the vine leaves in his hair. Sometimes the subject is a scene from everyday life. *The Fortune Teller* (c. 1595) shows an elegant young dandy with a sword at his side having his palm read by a Gypsy

Caravaggio's Turbulent Life

Caravaggio was an innovative, productive painter, yet he had a brief and turbulent life. It is easy to follow Caravaggio's career after1600, since his name regularly appeared in police records. After several brushes with the law over relatively minor offenses, Caravaggio was involved in a murder. In 1606 he was playing tennis with one Ranuccio Tomassoni. There seems to have been an argument over the score, which turned into a brawl and then into a sword fight. Tomassoni was killed, and Caravaggio was badly wounded. Aided by friends, Caravaggio fled Rome, then hid in the nearby Sabine Mountains. From there he set out for Naples, and by 1607 his friends were at work in Rome trying to obtain a pardon so he could return. Early in 1608 Caravaggio was on the small Mediterranean island of Malta, then ruled by the Knights of Malta, an aristocratic military order. Because he painted a portrait of Alof de Wignacourt, the head of the order, Caravaggio was made a knight of Malta. This honor was most unusual for a person of his modest background. A few months later he was again involved in a sword fight, this time with his superior officer, and

girl. He looks away with almost haughty boredom as she slips a ring off his finger. Many of the paintings of this period have a momentary quality, as if Caravaggio had isolated a single instant in time. An example is *Boy Bitten by a Lizard* (c. 1593), which portrays an affected young man with a small girlish mouth and a rose behind one ear. He squeals with fright as a lizard comes out from behind a flower and bites him on the finger.

When Caravaggio did paint religious subjects in the first decade of the 1600s, he employed a sense of immediacy and directness. For instance, in the *Calling of St. Matthew,* the saint, who was a tax collector in the ancient Roman Empire, is shown in contemporary Italian dress sitting at a table counting money. Around him at the table, as if in a gambling den, are a group of young swordsmen. Caravaggio's religious works are filled with deep shadows that absorb and conceal parts of the figures. At the same time the figures remain solid and powerfully three-dimensional where the light strikes them. Caravaggio was able to make a scene look as if it is taking place before the viewer's eyes. In his *Crucifixion of St. Peter,* for example, the saint is depicted at the moment when the executioners are beginning to raise up the cross to which he has been nailed upside down. His bare feet are thrust toward the viewer and the aged but powerful apostle lifts his head up from the cross in defiance. Scenes such as these reflect the efforts of the Catholic Reformation to was jailed. In some way that is still not explained, Caravaggio escaped from prison.

By October 1608 Caravaggio had reached Syracuse in Sicily. From this point on he was pursued by agents of the Knights of Malta, who sought to avenge what they considered an insult to their order. Caravaggio fled to Messina and then to Palermo. Somehow through it all he continued to paint. By fall 1609 he was back in Naples, where the Maltese agents trapped him and beat him so badly that he was disfigured almost beyond recognition.

By summer 1610 a papal pardon appeared imminent. For this reason Caravaggio took a boat to Port' Ercole, a small Spanish outpost north of Rome, where he was arrested in a case of mistaken identity. The Spaniards released him from jail after a few days, but the boat had sailed and took with it, so Caravaggio mistakenly thought, all of his possessions and one of his paintings. Raging along the shore under the hot sun, Caravaggio came down with a fever and died on July 18, 1610, at age thirty-six. Three days later a pardon came from the pope.

appeal directly to the masses through their emotions.

Caravaggio painted his last works when he was fleeing from one southern Italian town to another. During this time his style changed. The modeling is softer, the paint is thinner and applied more rapidly, and the shadows are less profound. The expressive content is deeper. All this can be seen in the *Resurrection of Lazarus,* painted in 1609 at the end of the artist's life. In it a small crowd huddles around the dim figure of Jesus Christ, which is almost phosphorescent where the light strikes it. The whole upper half of the picture is left dark and empty, capturing the shadowy moments between death and rebirth. Although Caravaggio was never truly famous in his own lifetime, many who knew his work realized they were seeing something amazingly new. His style spread rapidly throughout Europe. Without Caravaggio it is not possible to understand the works of the countless artists who followed in the seventeenth century.

Women painters achieve fame

A number of women artists emerged during the sixteenth and seventeenth centuries in Italy. Among them were the painters Sofonisba Anguissola and Artemisia Gentileschi, both of whom broke out of the tradition that discouraged achievement by women and gained equal stature with male artists.

Anguissola's innovative portraits Italian painter Sofonisba Anguissola (pronounced ahn-GWEE-so-lah; 1532–1625) was the first woman to establish an artistic identity and produce a substantial body of work. Her narrative portraits, each of them telling a story, proved to be ahead of their time at the end of the sixteenth century, when nature scenes and genre scenes (such as crucifixion, Resurrection, still life) were the main interests of Italian art.

Born in Cremona, Italy, Anguissola was the eldest child in a family of six daughters and a son. She and her sisters all received a humanist education. Four became artists (Sofonisba, Lucia, Europa, Anna Maria); another (Minerva) was noted for literary studies. Sofonisba's artistic emergence in the humanistic atmosphere was unusual in a period when women artists were typically trained by their fathers. She studied painting with a local artist and she taught her younger sisters. Sofonisba's specialization in portraits and self-portraits were shaped by the restraints placed on women at the time. Women artists were not allowed to study anatomy or male models, thereby preventing them from gaining access to large-scale history paintings. Her depiction of animated faces, firmly drawn within a delicate surrounding, is her trademark style. Her earliest known works are the *Portrait of a Nun* (1515) and the *Self-Portrait* of 1554. Other early portraits include those of the artist Guilio Clovio and the young Massimiliano Stampa.

Encouraged by Michelangelo Anguissola's paintings were admired by contemporaries such as the Roman nobleman Tommaso Cavalieri, who disregarded the popular belief that painting was a masculine art. She was encouraged by Michelangelo, who said of her drawing of a smiling girl teaching her nurse to read that a weeping boy would have been more difficult to draw. This comment caused her to draw a boy (her brother Asdrubale) being bitten by a crayfish. This drawing was probably the model for Caravaggio's painting *Boy Bitten by Lizard,* which shows her influence on the important artists of her time.

Portrait painting did not receive much respect at the time, but Anguissola used it as a metaphor for artistic achievement. In *The Chess Game* (1555), she depicted her sisters Lucia, Europa, and Minerva at the chess board. This painting was meant to demonstrate female excellence at an intellectual game. It also hinted at the sisters' shared history as aspiring artists who competed with and learned from one another. In Anguissola's works of the late 1550s, such as *Bernardino Campi Painting Sofonisba Anguissola* and *The Family Group*, the expression of pride in female achievement is reversed to become a commentary on the male-dominated society, values, and norms.

Anguissola spent the years 1559 through 1573 in Madrid, Spain, as court painter and lady-in-waiting to Queen Isabella of Valois, whom she taught to paint. Anguissola's Spanish paintings are not well documented and have been confused with the works of other painters. Among the few certain portraits are *Philip II* and

Sofonisba Anguissola's painting *The Chess Game* was meant to show female excellence at an intellectual game. ©*Ali Meyer/Corbis. Reproduced by permission of the Corbis Corporation.*

Isabella of Valois. Anguissola's marriage in 1573 to a Sicilian nobleman, Don Fabrizio de Moncada, ended with her husband's death in 1579. Her marriage in 1580 to the Genoese nobleman Orazio Lomellini took her to Genoa, Italy. For the next four decades she developed a new baroque (elaborate) style. She spent her final years in Palermo, Italy. Her eyesight began to fail in her twilight years, which prevented her from painting. In 1624, one year before her death, Flemish artist Anthony Van Dyck visited her and sketched her portrait in his note-books. He noted that she had a clear memory, told good stories, and gave him advice on his own paintings. Anguissola was an important figure, especially for women, in the tradition of Renaissance art.

Gentileschi portrays emotions The modern perception of Artemisia Gentileschi (pronounced jahn-tee-LES-kee; 1592–1653) has been colored by the legend surrounding her. She was born in Rome and trained as a painter by her father, Orazio Gentileschi. When she was seventeen she was allegedly raped (forced to have sexual intercourse) by Orazio's colleague, the painter Agostino Tassi. In 1611 Orazio brought legal action against Tassi. After a seven-month trial Tassi was convicted and given light punishment. Gentileschi's family quickly arranged her marriage to a Florentine artist in 1612 and she moved to Florence. She had a daughter with her husband, but eventually she separated from him and led an unusually independent life for a woman of her time. As a result of these events, she was portrayed as a sexual libertine (one who freely engages in sexual relations) in the eighteenth century, though there is no firm evidence to support this view.

During her eight-year stay in Florence, Gentileschi received many commissions from Michelangelo and Duke Cosimo II de' Medici (1590–1621). By the time of her marriage she had already become an accomplished artist. Nearly all of her pictures portray women in the central role. The characterizations are emotional without being sentimental, concentrating on psychology and action. Her earliest surviving work may be *Madonna and Child* (1609). A clearer idea of her early style can be seen in two other pictures, both dated 1610: *Judith and Her Maidservant with the Head of Holofernes* and *Susanna and the Elders*. These works feature attractive figures and sparkling costumes painted in a crisp style. Scholars note that Orazio may have contributed to the paintings, which also reflect the influence of the Caravaggio school in the use of sharp contrasts between light and shadow. Nevertheless, the pictures show some distinctive traits of Gentileschi's own style, such as the depiction of authentic emotions as evidenced by the alert stare of Judith and the startled gaze of Susanna.

Paints her masterpieces Gentileschi returned to Rome around 1620. Among her masterpieces from this period are *The Penitent Magdalen* (c. 1617–20), *Lucretia* (c. 1621), and a second version of *Judith and Her Maidservant with the Head of Holofernes* (1625). Around 1628 Gentileschi moved to Naples, where she gained commissions for religious pictures. She began hiring assistants to paint architectural and landscape backgrounds in her works. From 1638 until 1641 she worked in England with her aging father at the court of King Charles I (1600–1649; ruled 1625–49) and Queen Henrietta (1600–1669). The Gentileschis decorated the ceiling of the Great Hall of the Queen's House at Greenwich. Artemisia spent her final years in Naples. In the 1640s she painted *Bathsheba*, a second *Susanna*, and *Lot and His Daughters*.

Gentileschi's letters reveal her determination to excel in the male-dominated art world. Her success is seen in her influence on other European artists working during the transition between the late Renaissance and the era that later became known as the Baroque period. Among them were Simon Vouet (1590–1649) in France, Giovanni Barbieri (called Il Guercino; 1591–1666) in Italy, Rembrandt (Rembrandt Harmensz; 1606–1669) in Holland, and possibly Diego Velázquez

(1599–1660) in Spain. Many of Gentileschi's works were attributed to her father until the twentieth century, when art historians began identifying her paintings.

Sculpture

The development of Italian Renaissance sculpture can be divided into three periods. The first covers the transition from the later Middle Ages, ending around 1400. At this time sculptors were incorporating numerous trends that began emerging in the late medieval period, such as more realistic figures, dramatic expression, and intense movement. As the humanist movement gained momentum in Florence, sculptors were also becoming more aware of ancient Roman art. Most historians agree that Renaissance sculpture really began during the second phase, which took place in the 1400s and was dominated by the activity of artists in Florence. Many outstanding sculptors were at work in Florence during the first half of the fifteenth century. The single event that many consider the beginning of the Renaissance sculpture is the competition for a second set of bronze doors for the Baptistery of Florence in 1402 (a baptistery is a building used for baptism). The winner was the prominent sculptor Lorenzo Ghiberti, but his student, Donatello, is regarded as the first true Renaissance sculptor.

Intense artistic activity took place during the career of Donatello, marking the peak of the High Renaissance in sculpture. This period reflects the civic pride of Florence, which was linked to the democratic values of the Roman Republic. Sculpture was used as a display of wealth by autocratic leaders who were strengthening their rule. Soon cities throughout Italy were being decorated with sculptures. The third phase covers the sixteenth century, beginning with the High Renaissance and Michelangelo. The depiction of grandeur and power increasingly assumed a major role, influencing sculptors' interpretations of human bodies and actions. This approach is known as the mannerist style, which often featured free-standing statues with elongated bodies depicting dramatic movement.

Donatello The Italian sculptor Donatello (also known as Donato di Niccolò Bardi; c. 1386–1466) was the most influential Florentine sculptor before Michelangelo. Nearly every later sculptor, as well as numerous Florentine and Paduan painters, was indebted to him.

Little biographical information about Donatello is available. It is known that he was apprenticed to Lorenzo Ghiberti (pronounced ghee-BEHR-tee; c. 1378–1455), the most prominent sculptor in Florence at that time. In 1403, at the age of seventeen, Donatello was working for Ghiberti on the bronze reliefs of the doors of the Baptistery of Florence. By 1407 he had left Ghiberti and the workshops of the cathedral in Florence. One of Donatello's earliest known works is the life-sized marble statue *David* (1408), which was set up in the Palazzo Vecchio, the city hall, in 1414 as a symbol of the Florentine republic.

Rapidly maturing as a sculptor, Donatello produced two works that established his reputation. The first is the large marble figure *St. Mark,* located in a niche on the exterior of Or San Michele (a Florentine cathedral), which Donatello completed between 1411 and 1413. The other is the seated *St. John the Evangelist,* which he created for the facade (outside of the front wall) of the cathedral and completed in 1415. The *St. Mark* broke with tradition in such details as its classical stance and realistically modeled drapery. Donatello's new style was evident in the famous *St. George,* which he carved in marble in 1416 and 1417 for the exterior of Or San Michele. The Christian saint has the face not of an ideal hero but of a real one. Even more significant is the small marble relief *St. George and the Dragon* that decorates the base of the niche. The marble was ordered in 1417, and the relief was completed shortly afterward. This is an important date, for the relief is the earliest example in art of the new science of perspective used to create a measurable space for sculpted figures. Up to this time artists had placed figures on a flat background. In Donatello's work the forms seemed to emerge from atmosphere and light. Donatello was probably influenced by the one-point perspective studies of the architect Filippo Brunelleschi (see Architecture" section later in this chapter).

Perfects his style Between 1415 and 1435 Donatello and his pupils com-pleted eight life-sized marble representations of the Hebrew prophets (wise men in the Old Testament) for the cathedral in Florence. The most impressive of the group are the so-called *Zuccone* ("big squash" or "baldy"), perhaps representing Habakkuk (c. seventh century B.C.), and the figure of Jeremiah (c. 650–c. 570 B.C.). In both of these figures Donatello portrayed psychological tension and deliberately emphasized physical ugliness. About 1425 Donatello entered into partnership with the sculptor and architect Michelozzo di Bartolomeo (1396– 1472), with whom he made a trip to Rome after 1429. They produced a series of works, including the tomb of antipope John XXIII (died 1419; reigned 1410–15) in the Baptistery in Florence and the tomb of Cardinal Brancacci in Santa Angelo a Nilo in Naples. These tombs served as models for later Florentine sculptors. Possibly just after the trip to Rome, Donatello created the well-known gilded limestone *Annunciation,* depicting Gabriel (one of four archangels named in Hebrew tradition) and the Virgin Mary, in Sta Croce, Florence.

Much of Donatello's later work revealed his understanding of classical art. An example is the bronze statue *David* in the Bargello, featuring a young boy clothed only in boots and a pointed hat. This enigmatic figure is in all probability the earliest existing free-standing nude since antiquity. From 1443 to 1453 Donatello was in Padua, where he created the colossal bronze equestrian monument to the Venetian condottiere (leader of a band of mercenaries, or hired soldiers) called Gattamelata, in the Piazza del Santo. Donatello portrayed Gattamelata as the ideal man of the Renaissance. Another major commission in Padua was the high altar of Saint Antonio. It was decorated with four large reliefs representing the life of Saint Anthony. Surrounding the central figures are smaller reliefs and seven life-sized statues in bronze, including a seated Madonna and Child and a bronze Crucifixion. These reliefs presented an explosive conception of space with sketchy figures worked into a unified surface design. They had a lasting influence on painters in northern Italy.

After returning to Florence, the aged Donatello carved the statue *Mary Magdalen.* Mary Magdalen (A.D. first century) was a Galilean woman who was cleansed of evil spirits by Jesus Christ. She was also the first person to see Christ after his resurrection (rising after death). Donatello made the figure from poplar wood for the Baptistery (1454–55). Depicted in extreme ugliness, the emaciated figure of the penitent Mary Magdalen in the wilderness originally had sun-tanned skin and gilding (gold tints) on her long, straggly hair. When Donatello died in 1466 he left two unfinished bronze pulpits in Saint Lorenzo, Florence. On one are relief panels, showing the torture and murder of Christ by means of distorted forms and wildly emotional actions. Finished by his pupil Bertoldo di Giovanni (c. 1420–1491), the pulpit scenes reveal the great master's insight into human suffering and his pioneering exploration of the dark realms of human experience.

Michelangelo introduces new style

Michelangelo began his career as a sculptor, but he also became a renowned artist and architect. Michelangelo's earliest sculpture was a stone relief he made when he was about seventeen. Resembling the Roman sarcophagi (coffins) in the Medici collection, it had simple, solid forms and squarish figures. Soon after Lorenzo de' Medici died in 1492, the Medicis fell from power and Michelangelo fled from Florence to Bologna. In 1494 he obtained a commission to carve three saints needed to complete the tomb of Saint Dominic in the church of San Domenico. The tomb had been started by the sculptor Nicola Pisano (c. 1220–c. 1278) around 1265. Michelangelo's figures are again squarish, in contrast with the linear forms that were then dominant in sculpture.

After settling in Rome in 1496, Michelangelo executed a statue of Bacchus for the garden of ancient sculpture owned by a banker. His earliest surviving large-scale work, the *Bacchus,* shows the god in a teetering stance, either because he is drunk or dancing. His other works were generally set in front of walls and to some extent resemble reliefs. In 1498, through the same banker, Michelangelo obtained his first important commission, the larger-than-life *Pietà,* which is now in Saint Peter's Basilica. The term *pietà* refers to a popular image in which Mary supports the dead Jesus Christ across her knees.

Michelangelo's version of this scene is the most famous one. In both the *Pietà* and the *Bacchus* he made hard polished marble resemble soft flesh.

When Michelangelo returned to Florence in 1501 he was recognized as the most talented sculptor in central Italy. That year he was commissioned to do the marble sculpture *David,* one of his best-known works, for cathedral in Florence. After he completed the project in 1504, the magnificent sculpture was placed in front of the Palazzo Vecchio. Immediately thereafter Michelangelo accepted the job of painting the *Battle of Cascina,* a huge fresco for the Council Chamber of the Republic in the Palazzo della Signoria (see "Painting" section previously in this chapter). He never completed the fresco, and from then on his work consisted mainly of very large projects that he never finished. Because he preferred to work on a grand scale, he could not turn down commissions from great clients. For instance, he contracted to make statues of the Twelve Apostles (Jesus's disciples) for cathedral in Florence, yet he started only the *St. Matthew.*

Michelangelo stopped working on the Apostle statues when Pope Julius II called him to Rome in 1505. He accepted a commission to design the pope's tomb, which was to include about forty life-size statues. This project occupied Michelangelo off and on for the next forty years. In 1506 a dispute over funds for the tomb led Michelangelo, who had spent almost a year at the quarries in Carrara, to flee to Florence. A reconciliation between Julius II and Michelangelo took place in Bologna, which Julius had just conquered. In 1508 Michelangelo began working on the Julius's tomb, but he set that project aside when the pope asked him to decorate the ceiling of the Sistine Chapel in the Vatican in Rome (see "Painting" section previously in this chapter).

Medici Chapel is Renaissance model

In 1520 Michelangelo was commissioned to execute a tomb chapel for two young Medici dukes. The Medici Chapel (1520–34), an annex to Saint Lorenzo, is the most nearly complete large sculptural project of Michelangelo's career. The two tombs, each with an image of the deceased and two allegorical figures, are placed against elaborately decorated walls. These six statues and a seventh, the *Madonna,* on a third wall are by Michelangelo's own hand. The two saints flanking the *Madonna* were made by assistants from his clay sketches. On the tomb titled *Day and Night* the figures of day and night recline on a curved lid, as do the figures of morning and evening on the tomb titled *Morning and Evening.* Political leaders were becoming more powerful at the time, and Michelangelo's statues were often used as models for portraits that depicted emperors, popes, kings, and dukes.

In 1534 Michelangelo left Florence for the last time and settled in Rome. For the next ten years he produced paintings for Pope Paul III. After 1545 he devoted himself almost entirely to architecture and poetry. Michelangelo's sculpture during this period was limited to two pietàs that he executed for himself. The first one (1550–55, unfinished), which is in the cathedral in Florence, was meant for his own tomb. His last sculpture was the *Rondanini Pietà* in Milan, which he started in 1555. He was working on it just six days prior to his death on February 18, 1564.

Other sculptors gain prominence Of the outstanding sculptors active in the middle of the sixteenth century, more is known about Benvenuto Cellini (1500–1571) than about many others because he left behind an autobiography. Trained as a goldsmith, he also made monumental sculptures such as the gigantic bronze *Perseus* (completed 1554), which stands in the Loggia dei Lanzi in Florence. In the latter part of the century the French-born sculptor Giovanni da Bologna (Giambologna; 1529–1608), who worked in Italy, created monumental figure groups. The most famous are *Rape of the Sabines* (completed 1583) and *Hercules Fighting a Centaur* (completed 1599), both of which are in the Loggia dei Lanzi.

As the sixteenth century progressed, autocratic leaders made effective use of sculpture to promote themselves and their luxurious way of life. Bologna's equestrian bronze portrait of Duke Cosimo I de' Medici (1519–1574) was completed in 1595 and placed in the Piazza della Signoria in Florence. Allegorical stories from classical literature were quite popular. Among them were grand fountain sculptures of the mythological figures Orion (Greek giant hunter) and Neptune (Roman god of the sea) by Gio-

Renaissance artist Michelangelo's sculpture *Pietà* was his first important commission. The sculpture is now housed in Saint Peter's Basilica.

vanni Angelo Montorsoli (c. 1507–1563), which were completed in the 1550s and installed in Messina. Bartolomeo Ammanati (1511–1592) created the *Fountain of Neptune* (completed 1575), which features many bronze figures of sea divinities, for the Piazza della Signoria.

Sculptural decorations of buildings also became prominent. Jacopo Sansovino, the architect for the city of Venice (see "Architecture" section later in this chapter), made his architecture appear more luxurious by freely integrating sculpture into the design. This style can be seen in Venice in the library of Saint Mark, which was begun in 1537. The relief decoration along the attic of the library features putti (figures of infant boys) carrying festoons (decorative chains), and the balustrade, or railing, rising from the roof is decorated with sculptures. Sansovino also richly adorned the facade beneath the bell tower in the Piazza San Marco (completed 1540) with reliefs and niche statues of virtues (statues of women representing various virtues) and ancient gods. Sixteenth-century Italian sculpture influenced the baroque style of the seventeenth century and had an impact on the rest of Europe.

Architecture

Many architects were active in Italy during the Renaissance as part of the humanist-influenced effort to revive classical culture. They were involved in refurbishing old buildings and constructing new ones according to the style found in Roman ruins. Features of this style included simple but impressive building shapes, columns from the three basic classical orders (Corinthian, Doric, and Ionic), porticos (entrance porches), and loggias (roofed open galleries overlooking courtyards). In addition to reviving the glories of the ancient Roman Republic, architects designed structures to sym-

bolize the growing power of their wealthy patrons, primarily political leaders and popes from prominent families. Cities throughout Italy were crowded with buildings dedicated to rich and influential people. The rebirth of classical architecture took place during the fifteenth century. In the sixteenth century there was an increasing trend toward mannerism in the late Renaissance. Mannerist architects rejected the classical style and emphasized unusual treatment of space, wall surfaces, and decorative details. Among the most prominent Renaissance architects were Filippo Brunelleschi in the early Renaissance, Bramante in the High Renaissance, and Michelangelo in the mannerist period. One of the best-known Renaissance architects was Andrea Palladio, who worked during the mannerist period but sought to restore the style of the High Renaissance.

Brunelleschi introduces perspective Filippo Brunelleschi (pronounced broo-nail-LAYS-kee; 1377–1446) was an architect, goldsmith, and sculptor. Considered the first Renaissance architect, he formulated the concept of linear perspective, which influenced the depiction of space in painting and sculpture until the late nineteenth century. His refined classical style was inspired by twelfth-century Tuscan architecture and by the buildings of ancient Rome. He used the Corinthian style, the most ornate of the three ancient Greek architectural orders, almost exclusively. It is characterized by large capitals (caps on the tops of columns) decorated with acanthus (a prickly herb) leaves.

Brunelleschi was born in Florence and began his career as a goldsmith. In 1401 he entered the competition for a new set of doors for the Baptistery of the cathedral in Florence, but the commission was awarded to Lorenzo Ghiberti (see "Sculpture" section previously in this chapter). Details of Brunelleschi's life during the next several years are vague, though he probably made trips to Rome to survey its ancient monuments. In 1417 he and other master goldsmiths presented opinions on the design and construction of the great dome that was to be built atop the cathedral in Florence. It was perhaps at this time that Brunelleschi devised the method of constructing linear perspective, which he illustrated in two panels (now lost): one depicted the Baptistery as viewed from the cathedral entrance, and the other illustrated the Palazzo Vecchio.

Beginning in 1418 Brunelleschi concentrated on architecture. That same year he began the church of San Lorenzo. It is a Latin-cross basilica, an early Christian church building consisting of a nave (main part) with three arcaded aisles (passageways lined on each side with pillars supporting high arches), side chapels, and a dome over the crossing (the center point of the cross). In 1419 he designed the loggia of the Ospedale degli Innocenti, a hospital for orphans. This hospital is usually considered the first Renaissance building. In 1420 Brunelleschi began to erect the magnificent dome of the cathedral in Florence dome in collaboration with Ghiberti, who eventually withdrew from the project. In the meantime Brunelleschi was consulted on projects in Pisa, Mantua, and Ferrara, and in 1433 he was again in Rome to study the antiquities.

After returning to Florence in 1434 Brunelleschi worked on central-plan churches. Considered the ideal design during the Renaissance, this type of church is in the shape of a Greek cross, with four equal wings extending from a central circle. Brunelleschi designed Santa Maria degli Angeli, which would have been the first central plan of the Renaissance, but it was never completed. In 1436 Brunelleschi designed another basilican church in Florence, Santo Spirito (constructed 1444–82), which shows a much greater concern for a unified composition than San Lorenzo does. The interior is carefully organized to create a very harmonious space that is the ideal of Renaissance architecture. In 1440 Brunelleschi returned to Pisa for further work on the Citadel, which he had started in 1426. He died at Florence in 1446 and received the unusual honor of being buried in the cathedral in Florence. Brunelleschi's architecture remained influential in Florence through the sixteenth century.

Bramante introduces monumental style
Bramante (also known as Donato di Pascuccio d'Antonio; 1444–1514) was the first High Renaissance architect. He transformed the classical architecture initiated by Brunelleschi into a grave

and monumental style that represented the ideal for later architects.

Bramante was born at Monte Asdruvaldo near Urbino. Nothing is known of the first thirty years of his life. The first notice of Bramante dates from 1477, when he decorated the facade of the Palazzo del Podestà at Bergamo with a fresco depicting philosophers. Around 1481 he became the court architect for the Sforza family, the rulers of Lombardy (the region that includes Milan). His first important commission began in 1482 with the reconstruction of the church of Santa Maria presso San Satiro in Milan. He encountered a challenge with this project because it was a basilica church with transept (part that crosses the nave) and dome over the crossing. It therefore did not allow enough space for a deep choir (the part of the church where the service is performed). Through the ingenious use of perspective in sculptural and painted relief, Bramante gave the illusion of a deep choir space when in fact the area was quite shallow. In 1492 Bramante began the design for the Canons' Cloister (monastery) of Sant'Ambrogio in Milan, but only the southern wing was built at that time. In 1497 he planned four more cloisters (walkways with an arched open side supported by columns) for the monastery, but only two were completed in the sixteenth century.

When the French captured Milan in 1499, Bramante fled to Rome. In preparation for the Jubilee Year of 1500 he painted a fresco featuring the arms of Pope Alexander VI (1431–1503; reigned 1492–1503) at Saint John Lateran Basilica. He also explored ancient Roman monuments. The impact of Roman architecture is evident in his cloister of Santa Maria della Pace in Rome (1500–04). The simple but monumental style of the small square court reflects the classical style adopted during the High Renaissance in Rome. Bramante's Roman style is also represented in the tiny circular Tempietto at San Pietro in Montorio, in Rome (1502).

Appointed papal architect After the election of Pope Julius II in 1503 Bramante became the official papal architect. He did extensive work in the Vatican Palace. The tremendous Belvedere Court of the Palace (begun in 1503) was terraced up a hillside on three levels joined by monumental stairs. The lower terrace was to serve as a theater. Completed with many revisions in the late sixteenth century, it is now altered almost beyond recognition. Nearby is a spiral, ramped staircase (begun before 1512) that provides access to the statue court beyond the Belvedere Court. As a new facade for the Vatican Palace, Bramante designed a series of superimposed (added to an existing structure) loggias (1509–18), later converted into the Court of San Damaso. Completed by the painter and architect Raphael (see "Painting" section previously in this chapter), the building features two superimposed arcades with Tuscan and Ionic pilasters (column-like structures that extend from a wall). Above them is a colonnade of the Composite order. (The Ionic order is a style of ancient Greek architecture that features fluted, or grooved, columns set on bases and topped with capitals decorated with scroll designs. The Composite order is a combination of the Ionic order and the Corinthian order, featuring grooved columns topped by capitals with leaf designs.)

In 1505 Pope Julius II decided that Saint Peter's Basilica should be completely rebuilt, and he commissioned Bramante to prepare a plan for the new church. Bramante based his plan on a central Greek cross design. It called for a large dome sitting atop a drum (open circular base) supported by colonnades at the crossing. It also featured four smaller domes and corner towers. When the Greek-cross design was not accepted, he planned to lengthen one arm of the cross to form a nave. He then added ambulatories (walkways) in the wings that projected outward from the crossing. The foundation stone was laid in 1506, but at the time of his death Bramante had erected only the four main piers (bases) and the arches that were to support the dome.

In 1513 the pope bestowed the office of *Piombatore,* or sealer of the papal briefs, on Bramante. The architect's last work was probably the Palazzo Caprini, which he started after 1510. It had a rusticated ground floor with shops and an upper story with coupled Doric half columns. Owned later by Raphael, the Palazzo Caprini became the model for numerous palaces, especially in northern Italy. Bramante died in 1514 and was buried in Old Saint Peter's Basilica.

Michelangelo the architect The great Renaissance painter and sculptor Michelangelo was an equally accomplished architect. In 1547 Pope Paul III appointed him to direct construction of Saint Peter's Basilica, the largest church in the Christian world and the symbol of papal authority. It is now considered the crowning achievement of Renaissance architecture, yet the project was beset by problems from the very beginning. In 1506 Pope Julius II decided that Saint Peter's should be entirely rebuilt, and he appointed Bramante to draft the design of the new church. Records show that Bramante originally planned the building in the shape of a Greek cross topped by a great dome at the center. This design caused considerable controversy throughout the sixteenth century, since many people wanted the church to be built in the shape of a Latin cross (a long shaft crossed with a shorter shaft above the middle).

By the time Michelangelo took over the project, two other architects—Raphael and Antonio da Sangallo (1583–1446)—had changed the design, and construction was delayed. When Michelangelo died in 1564 the building was completed in its present form up to the dome. Giacomo della Porta (c. 1537–1602) then altered the design again (he may have used a model made by Michelangelo) and completed the dome in 1590. Finally, supporters of the Latin cross design won, and Carlo Maderna (1556–1629) added a nave and facade, which were completed in 1614.

An illustration of Saint Peter's Square and Basilica from the 1500s. Pope Paul III appointed Michelangelo to direct construction of the Basilica in 1547. *Reproduced by permission of the Corbis Corporation.*

In 1538 Pope Paul III also commissioned Michelangelo to redesign and refurbish Capitoline Hill, the geographical and ceremonial center of ancient Rome. As with many of Michelangelo's other commissions, the project was completed after his death. At the direction of Paul III, Michelangelo also directed construction of the Farnese Palace in 1546. During the reign of Pope Pius IV (1499–1565; reigned 1559–65) Michelangelo designed the Porta Pia, converted the Roman Baths of Diocletion into the Christian church of Santa Maria segli Angeli, and designed the Sforza Chapel in Santa Maria Maggiore. Thus, Michelangelo became an urban planner as well as an architect, helping to transform the appearance of Rome.

Palladio influenced by Roman ruins

Andrea Palladio (also known as Andrea di Pietro della Gondola; 1508–1580) is one of the architects most closely associated with the Renaissance. A native of Padua, he apprenticed as a stonemason in Vicenza. By 1537 he had joined the circle of Gian Giorgio Trissino (1478–1550), a humanist and aristocrat. Trissino gathered in his villa an academy of intellectually promising young men from Vicenza. Trissino's impact on Palladio was great: through Trissino he was first exposed to humanist education, learned Latin, and was introduced to the treatise on architecture by Marcellus Vitruvius Pollio (called Vitruvius; first century B.C.), the ancient Roman architect and engineer. Through Trissino, Palladio also became acquainted with many important intellectuals. The name Palladio, which he adopted in about 1545, came from Trissino's circle. In the 1540s Palladio visited Rome at least five times, often in the company of Trissino. During a trip in 1546–47 he met Michelangelo. Preserved drawings show that Palladio spent much of his time in Rome studying and surveying the Roman ruins.

Palladio's study of Roman ruins led him to pursue a career as an architect in the late 1530s. The breakthrough in his career came in the late 1540s, when the city council of Vicenza commissioned him to complete the facade of the Basilica, the city's public palace. The Basilica is actually a complex of medieval buildings that were reorganized into a single structure during the fifteenth century. The entire structure had been surrounded by arcades in a medieval style called Gothic. The arcades collapsed soon after they were completed in 1496. Over the next fifty years city leaders looked for an architect to design a new facade in the Renaissance style. Palladio resolved the structural problems by adapting Bramante's fifteenth-century classical designs rather than the mannerist style that was then in fashion.

Popularizes classical villa Palladio's contribution to Renaissance architecture was the villa, or large country house, which became popular throughout Europe. A series of villas built during the 1550s and 1560s represent the model that is associated with Palladio. All these villas have a vaulted *sala,* or central hall, that can be square or rectangular, or in the shape of a cross or the letter "T." A row of rooms lines each side of the *sala,* and the facade has a Greco-Roman temple portico (a Roman style influenced by the Greeks). A few villas have an upper story, in which the same design is repeated. The popularity of the villa resulted from changes in the Venetian economy and an increasing trend toward agriculture. Villas functioned as homes for noblemen on agricultural estates. Palladio's most famous structure was the Villa Rotonda, known also as Villa Capra, which was built in the late 1560s for the retired papal secretary Paolo Almerico. Located on a hill near Vicenza, the villa had a central hall covered by a dome with four big rooms in the corners and four smaller rooms next to them. Four identical porticoes open on all four facades. Over the centuries, the Rotonda became the prime example of Palladio's

architecture and has been copied many times in various parts of the world.

Throughout his career Palladio maintained contacts with humanists. Among them was Daniele Barbaro (1513–1570), a scholar and member of the Venetian high nobility. The patron of several artists, Barbaro helped Palladio establish his reputation and introduced him to prospective Venetian clients. Palladio also designed a villa for Barbaro and Barbaro's brother Marcantonio. By the mid-1550s Palladio was working on *Four Books on Architecture,* which he published in 1570. Book one of this work discusses elements of architecture and the theory of the classical orders. Book two presents plans for residential buildings Palladio designed. Book three describes a number of bridges Palladio designed and gives an account of his work on the Basilica in Vicenza. Book four contains Palladio's surveys of Roman temples. During the latter part of his career he began working on churches. His greatest ecclesiastical building was the church of San Giorgio Maggiore, which was started in 1566. In 1570 Palladio succeeded Jacopo Sansovino (1486–1570) as the main architectural adviser for the Venetian republic. The ten years from this appointment until his death in 1580 were marked by one grand project, the votive church of Redentore.

Many scholars consider Palladio to be the foremost Renaissance architect. The influence of his *Four Books on Architecture* is second only to that of *Regola delli cinque ordini d'archittura* (Canon of the five orders of architecture; 1563) by the architectural theo-

The Villa Rotonda by Andrea Palladio. Over the centuries, the Rotonda became the prime example of Palladio's architecture. *©Sandro Vannini/Corbis. Reproduced by permission of the Corbis Corporation.*

rist Giacomo Barozzi da Vignola (1507–1573). Vignola's work was a detailed description of classical architecture and served as a manual for the education of Renaissance architects. Palladio's book shifted the focus from theory to practice by showing how classical ideas were used in Renaissance buildings. His designs were often copied, and his innovative use of classical architecture became common practice. Palladio had an immense influence on architects in Italy. By the seventeenth century his ideas had also arrived in England through the efforts of the English designer Inigo Jones (see "Architecture" in Chapter 9). Soon Palladio's style was spreading across Europe. Interest in his work did not wane even in the twentieth century, when architects were again focusing on Palladio's use of details from the classical orders.

Performing arts

Not only was the Renaissance known for advances in poetry, painting, sculpture, and architecture, it was also an important era in the development of the performing arts. Both

Mounted Imperial trumpeters of the Holy Roman Empire. Musicians were in great demand by wealthy patrons during the Renaissance. *Reproduced by permission of Hulton Archive.*

music and theater underwent substantial changes during the Renaissance period.

Music

A major turning point occurred in European music at the beginning of the Renaissance, in the first half of the fifteenth century. Increasing commercial activity and economic prosperity contributed to a thriving cultural life at princely courts. Musicians were in great demand, both as composers and performers, by wealthy patrons. Most musicians came from the Low Countries (called the Netherlands school) and from France and Flanders (called the Franco-Flemish school). They traveled throughout Europe and lived at the courts of noblemen, civic leaders, popes, and cardinals. In northern Italy the most prominent courts were those of the Medici family in Florence and the Sforzas in Milan. Popes and cardinals in Rome were also important patrons of composers, choirmasters, and singers. A typical musician was Josquin des Prez (c. 1440–1521), the most influential composer of his day. A native of Flanders (a region in what is now

Belgium), he served the Sforza family in Milan, the papal choir in Rome, and Duke Hercules I of Ferrara. He also served at the court of King Louis XII of France before returning to Flanders in 1516. Josquin des Prez and other composers developed musical techniques that became the basis of later innovations. The invention of the printing press, which was perfected in the 1450s by the German inventor Johannes Gutenberg, facilitated the spread of knowledge about the latest musical trends. Now music could be mass produced and distributed beyond the region where it was composed.

Vocal music Extensive creative and experimental activity took place in vocal music during the late fifteenth century and into the sixteenth century. In the early 1400s, at the end of the Middle Ages, polyphonic music consisted of three singing parts. (Polyphonic music is sung by voices in two or more separate parts, or melodic lines, to produce harmony.) In the late fifteenth century a fourth part was added to produce a fuller sound. This development led to the duet style, a feature of Josquin's music, in which the two upper parts might sing a passage and then be echoed by the two lower parts. Soon another technique called imitation (one voice repeating a figure sung by another voice) gave more equality to the parts. Along with imitation came the "familiar style," in which all parts are sung together in chords. In northern Italy the familiar style gave rise to the frottola, a three- or four-part song based on a poem.

The emergence of the frottola led to the development of the Renaissance madrigal.

The origin of the term "madrigal" is uncertain, but it probably comes from the Latin *matricale* (in the mother tongue; in this case Italian). The madrigal was based on a poem and consisted of two or three stanzas of three lines each, with seven or eleven syllables per line. It was sung by four voices in two parts that reflected the structure of the poem. Until the late fifteenth century, music masters from northern France and the Netherlands used poems from their own regions. By the beginning of the sixteenth century, the Renaissance madrigal was emerging in Florence and Mantua. It was based on traditional Italian music, such as the Florentine carnival song as well as the Mantuan frottola. The sixteenth-century madrigal also utilized various types of poems. It comprised a five- to fourteen-line stanza of seven or eleven syllables per line. The last two lines formed a rhyming couplet. Sung by four or five voices, the Renaissance madrigal had a more complex musical structure involving interwoven melodies that expressed certain emotions. Dramatic effect therefore became as important as the music and the text. As in the Middle Ages, the mass and the motet (choral composition based on a sacred text) were the main forms of sacred, or religious, vocal music during the Renaissance. Although sacred music style remained conservative, some of the newer techniques of secular, or nonreligious, music were introduced during the Catholic Reformation.

Instrumental music New ways of using musical instruments were emerging along with the development of vocal music. Instruments had been commonly used throughout the Middle Ages, but they were usually played along with or substituted for voices in polyphonic pieces. Instruments also provided music for dancing. As the Renaissance progressed, instrumentalists began experimenting with rhythms, tones, phrasing, and ornamentation of melodies. The invention of music printing helped spread information about new techniques.

The major instruments were the lute, the organ, and stringed keyboard instruments. The most popular and versatile was the lute. The two main classes of keyboard instruments, which resemble the modern-day piano, were the clavichord and the harpsichord. There were many types of harpsichord, such the virginal, spinet, clavecin, and clavicembalo. Instrumental ensembles, or groups, were called consorts, and many consorts consisted of only one type of instrument, such as viols, woodwinds, recorders, and shawms (loud oboes). Consorts of brass instruments such as the cornet (a type of trumpet) and sackbut (an early trombone) were also common. Mixed consorts of various types of instruments were more popular, though the combinations depended on the players available. Organs were used as accompaniment for sacred music.

Two styles of music By the seventeenth century, two distinct musical styles had been established. The first, called *prima prattica,* was the style of the sixteenth century, which had evolved from the Franco-Flemish music of the late Middle Ages. The other, called *seconda prattica,* was a more theatrical, dramatic style that was practiced primarily in Italy. It is usually associated with the baroque period, which came after the Renaissance but is nevertheless considered a continuation of the music of that era. The *seconda prattica* led to a distinction between sacred and secular music and between vocal and instrumental music. There were also distinctions between music of different countries. The medieval forms of melody and harmony were gradually replaced by a system known as tonality. This system was based on contrasting keys, or sets of interrelated notes and chords derived from a major or minor scale. It gave rise to the concertato, which involved the contrast, combination, and alternation of voices and instruments. The concertato was based on the basso continuo, an accompaniment consisting of a low-pitched instrument, such as a violoncello or a bassoon, combined with a keyboard instrument or lute. Tonality remained a standard part of Western music until the twentieth century.

A prominent Italian composer is associated with each of these styles. Giovanni Palestrina represented the achievement of Renaissance music, or *prima prattica*, of the sixteenth century. Claudio Monteverdi is considered the greatest innovator of *seconda prattica* in the baroque era of the seventeenth century.

Palestrina known for sacred works
Giovanni Pierluigi da Palestrina (c. 1525–1594) was the foremost composer of the sixteenth century. His sacred works represent one of the great achievements of Renaissance music.

Born Giovanni Pierluigi, the composer adopted the name of his native town, Palestrina, which is located near Rome. Little is known about his early life, though it is assumed that at the age of seven he was a choir singer at the church of Saint Agapit in Palestrina. Records show that he was a member of the choir at the basilica of Santa Maria Maggiore in Rome in 1537. Palestrina served at the basilica until his nineteenth birthday. During this time he probably received musical training from Jacques Arcadelt (c. 1505–1568). In 1544 Palestrina returned to his native town as organist and singing master at the local church. Over the next six years he married, fathered the first of his three sons, and began composing. Most important for his future career was the attention given his music by the new bishop of Palestrina, Cardinal del Monte. Del Monte became Pope Julius III in 1550, and the following year he appointed Palestrina choirmaster of the Julian Chapel at Saint Peter's Basilica in Rome.

All singers in this choir traditionally were unmarried, and they were admitted only after rigorous examination. Since the pope had ignored these requirements, Palestrina's appointment was viewed with little enthusiasm. In 1554 Palestrina published his first book of masses and dedicated it to Julius. The following year he was promoted to singer in the pontifical choir. When Julius died the following year, Pope Paul IV (1476–1559; reigned 1555–59) enforced the celibacy rule as part of the Catholic Reformation and dismissed Palestrina from Julian Chapel. The pope then appointed Palestrina choirmaster at the Basilica of Saint John Lateran, where he remained until 1560. For the next eleven years he held posts at various other churches. In 1571 he was reappointed choirmaster at the Julian Chapel. Seven years later he was given the title of master of music at Saint Peter's, a position he held for the rest of his life.

The "Prince of Music" Palestrina's works included the major types of late Renaissance music: masses, motets, and madrigals. He wrote 105 masses and 250 motets, but madrigals played a small role in his compositions because he was primarily interested in sacred music. Using original techniques, he frequently adapted polyphony to such traditional forms as plainsong (early Christian chants), hymns, and biblical texts. He often created as many as eight interwoven parts in counterpoint (separate melodies sung above or below a main melody). Yet Palestrina had a carefully controlled, sensitive style that adhered closely to his chosen text and lacked the drama of music by other composers at the time. His religious compositions, especially the masses, were of such high quality that he was called the "Prince of Music." Palestrina's most famous mass was *Missa Papae Marcelli*, which he dedicated to Pope Marcellus II (1501–1555; reigned 1555).

Palestrina wrote his works during a period of change in the Roman Catholic Church. For twenty years, from 1545 to 1565, the church held a series of meetings called the Council of Trent (see "Council of Trent" in Chapter 7). The purpose of the council was to initiate reforms at every level of religious life. A frequent topic of discussion was simplifying the music used in the liturgy, or church service. Some officials even suggested totally eliminating polyphonic music because it was too elaborate and secular and distracted from the solemnity of the worship service. In 1562 the council issued a canon, or church law, stating that all secular matter must be removed from liturgical music. While music should be pleasing to the ear, it must also be simple and direct, having no embellishments that would interfere with an understanding of the text. Historians have speculated that Palestrina composed his masses to fit the requirements of the Council of Trent. An example is the *Missa Papae Marcelli.* According to one story, Palestrina saved the art of music with this work by dedicating it to Marcellus, who advocated reform. There seems to be no evidence that Palestrina deliberately modified his compositions, for scholars point out that he never showed any real interest in highly dramatic or experimental sacred music. It is known, however, that Palestrina's works were performed for, and approved by, Cardinal Carlo Borromeo. Borromeo was charged with

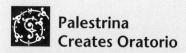

Palestrina Creates Oratorio

Giovanni Palestrina is credited with creating the oratorio, a lengthy religious choral work that features recitatives (singing that resembles speaking), arias, and choruses without action or scenery. He composed oratorios for a Catholic group called the Oratorian congregation in Rome. The organization was founded by the Italian priest and reformer Philip Neri (1515–1595). Philip made friends easily, and in the late 1550s he began meeting regularly with some of them in his room, the "Oratory," at the church of San Girolamo della Carità. Philip disliked formality and loved spontaneity. He gave his little groups a definite character with Scripture readings, short commentaries, brief prayers, and hymns. Palestrina set many of the scriptural texts to music, creating the "oratorio"—named for Philip's room—a form of musical presentation that is still popular today.

making certain that liturgical music was free of secular tunes and unintelligible texts.

Palestrina also was consulted on musical matters by church officials. In a papal order of 1577 Palestrina and a colleague, Annibale Zoilo, were directed to revise the *Graduale Romanum,* the list of liturgical music used by the church. Their job was to purge all of the secular tunes that had accumulated during the centuries.

Palestrina never did complete this laborious task. A new list, the *Medicean Gradual*, was released in the early seventeenth century. Although it is sometimes thought to be Palestrina's work, it was actually compiled by others. Since the Renaissance, Palestrina has been regarded as one of the foremost composers of sacred music. Yet his reputation suffered somewhat at the end of the nineteenth century, when his works were reduced to a set of composition "rules" by music teachers at academies and universities. Subsequent generations of young composers thus produced "Palestrinian" music that failed to meet the standards of free expression that the master achieved in his own compositions.

Monteverdi known for innovation
Claudio Giovanni Antonio Monteverdi (1567–1643) was the foremost Italian composer of the seventeenth century. During his long career he mastered the main forms of Renaissance music, such as motets and madrigals, but he is best known for his operas. Monteverdi now ranks as one of the major European composers of all time.

A native of Cremona, Monteverdi studied composition with Marc' Antonio Ingegneri (c. 1547–1592), the music director at the cathedral in Cremona. Around 1590 Monteverdi became a string player at the court of Duke Vincenzo Gonzaga (1562–1612) in Mantua. By this time he had already published three books of madrigals and two books of songs. In 1602 he was promoted to *maestro*

della cappella (chorus master). Within the next five years he published two more madrigal books and the first set of compositions called *Scherzi musicali,* a form of vocal chamber music. (Chamber music is composed for performance in a private room or small auditorium, usually with one performer for each part.) Until 1605 his musical compositions consisted mainly of madrigals for five voices. Thereafter he experimented with *seconda practtica,* new combinations of voices and instruments.

In 1607 Monteverdi's first opera, *La favola d'Orfeo,* was performed in Mantua. *Orfeo* tells the story of the Greek god Orpheus who makes a journey to Hades (the underworld) to rescue his wife Euridyce by charming Pluto (Greek god of the underworld) and Persephone (daughter of Zeus and Demeter, abducted by Pluto) with his lyre, or harp. The opera represented a cross section of musical forms of the early seventeenth century—including choruses in complex harmony, solo ensembles, arias (elaborate melodies sung by one voice), dances, and independent instrumental pieces. The orchestra consisted of more than forty instruments, including harpsichords, organs, strings, woodwind, and brass. The music director mainly decided which instruments were played when, though in certain instances Monteverdi specified the instrumentation. For example, the spirits of Hades are accompanied by two organs, five trombones, two bass gambas, and a violone. The combination of these instruments produces a strikingly dark sound. In fact, as a result of this opera, trombones have traditionally been associated with anything "infernal" (related to hell or the underworld).

Composes great operas Vincenzo died in 1612, and Monteverdi was dismissed from his position by Vincenzo's successor, Ferdinand. For more than a year Monteverdi tried to find employment that would match his fame as a composer. Finally, in 1613, he was appointed to one of the most prestigious musical positions in Italy, that of *maestro di cappella* at the famous basilica of Saint Mark's in Venice. Monteverdi spent the rest of his life in Venice, dying there in 1643. He had a highly productive career during his thirty years at Saint Mark's. In addition to completely reorganizing the whole musical setup and raising the standards of the singers and instrumentalists, he composed a quantity of music, both sacred and secular. Most of Monteverdi's sacred music consisted of masses, though he also composed songs, litanies (repetitive chants), and magnificats (songs of praise). His secular music can be divided into two types: chamber and dramatic. The chamber category includes madrigals and the second set of *Scherzi musicali* (1632). The dramatic category includes nine operas, three ballets, and the dramatic cantata *Il combattimento di Tancredi e Clorinda* (1624). This work is still performed today, as are the ballets *Tirisi e Clori* (1616) and *Volgendo il ciel* (1637). Monteverdi's last two operas, *Il ritorno d'Ulisse in patria* (1641) and *L'incoronazione di Pop-*

pea (1642), have also survived. *Poppea* is now considered one of the masterpieces of Western music.

Poppea was the first opera on a historical subject (as opposed to mythological, biblical, or poetical subjects). It is based on the true story of the Roman emperor Nero (A.D. 37–68) and his infatuation with the beautiful courtier, Poppaea Sabina (died A.D. 65). Nero's obsession led him to repudiate the rightful empress of Rome, his wife Ottavia, and to crown his lover, Poppaea, as the true empress. This ill-fated union ended in Poppaea's murder at the hands of Nero. (According to one account, Nero kicked or stomped Poppaea to death.) Monteverdi's opera, however, deals only with Nero's early obsession, his repudiation of Ottavia, and the coronation of Poppaea. In composing *Poppea* Monteverdi largely rejected spectacular effects and relied more on characterization of the leading figures. He balanced music and drama, making the music seem to spring directly from the actions of the characters.

Monteverdi's influence, both before and after his death, was not equal to his achievement. He was not part of a "school" (a group of musicians following similar styles and practices) and therefore had no followers. One reason was that musical taste and fashion were changing rapidly during the last phase of the Renaissance and the beginning of the baroque period. Nevertheless, today Monteverdi is regarded as one of the outstanding composers of all time. He used music as a vehicle for drama, portraying a wide range of human emotions and personalities.

Theater

In the mid-1500s a distinctive form of theater appeared in northern Italy. It differed from all other kinds of entertainment available in the Italian peninsula from antiquity through the Middle Ages. Later called commedia dell'arte (pronounced kuh-MAY-dee-uh dell ahr-tee), this type of theater was performed by companies of professional actors who played specific characters. They improvised plots and the characters took on various identities, depending on the materials at hand as well as the talents and knowledge of the actors. Commedia dell'arte troupes (companies) became immensely popular with their colorful, antic plays, which incorporated many aspects of the culture and society of the day. Several troupes toured throughout Italy and eventually into most parts of Europe between the sixteenth and eighteenth centuries.

Commedia dell'arte Scholars have attempted to determine the origins of commedia dell'arte. Many speculate that it can be traced to mime and farce, forms of theater that were passed down through the ages from ancient times. (Mime is an ancient dramatic entertainment that depicts scenes from life, usually in a ridiculous manner. Farce is an entertaining dramatic composition that uses satire, or criticism through humor, and an improbable plot.) Scholars do know that farces were performed in local di-alects (versions of a language spoken in particular places) throughout Italy during the Middle Ages. The name "commedia dell'arte" itself remains ambiguous. "Arte" refers to a professional guild, though the companies never organized as one; it also refers to skill in theatrical craft. "Commedia" usually indicates commercial acting and the improvisation on a three-act scenario (called *soggetto*), for which the troupes were famous.

According to historical records, the first commedia dell'arte company appeared in Padua in 1545. Eight men signed a contract agreeing to perform comedies as a traveling troupe. The roaming players set up trestle tables in piazzas (public squares) and earned money by passing a hat to collect donations. In the 1560s the informal bands of players gave way to prosperous companies like the Gelosi, the Accesi, the Dsiosi, the Confidenti, and the Fideli. These companies boasted popular leading ladies and performed scripted comedies, tragedies, and pastorals before private audiences. Typically, commedia dell'arte was improvised using skeletal scripts of accomplished literary plots such as urban domestic conflicts between generations and love affairs encouraged by shrewd, bawdy servants. These plots involved tricks and high jinks, deceits and errors, disguises, cross-dressing (one gender wearing the clothes of the opposite gender), and disappearance—all ending happily in marriages and family reunions.

The companies recruited strolling players, acrobats, street enter-

A print depicting actors performing a commedia dell'arte. *©Gianni Dagli Orti/Corbis. Reproduced by permission of the Corbis Corporation.*

tainers, and actors. Adapting to the tastes of their audiences, they experimented with dialects, comic action, exaggeration, and parody. With little scenery and minimal costumes, the actors used their wit and inventiveness to create atmosphere and depict characters. The scenarios changed frequently, and companies used ten to twelve actors who specialized in stock characters (fixed types), who performed with or without masks.

Stock characters Commedia dell'arte ensembles included several stock characters. Every company found it neces-sary to feature fashionable young lovers who spoke in an elegant Tuscan dialect. The lovers performed without masks, as did maidservants, another set of stock characters. A standard maidservant role, the middle-aged Franceschina, was often played by a man. Fathers of the two young lovers were Pantalone (Pantaloon) and Dottore Gratiano, who were masked or had facial disguises. Pantalone was a serious-minded Venetian merchant, rarely played as a comic figure, who gave good advice and launched into long tirades. Dottore (doctor) Gratiano was a gullible and lecherous Bolognese lawyer who affect-ed great learning by speaking in a mixture of Italian and Latin. Commedia dell'arte also relied heavily on clowns, or *zanni,* often played by acrobats. *Zanni* were clever or buffoonish servants who varied their identities and dialects depending on the company or the actors' individual talents.

The *zanni* had various names, such as Panzanino, Buratino, Scapino, Fritellino, Trappolino, Arlecchino, Pedrolino, Pulcinella, and Brighella. The most famous were Arlecchino (now known as Harlequin), Pedrolino, and Pulcinella. Harlequin was a childlike, amorous (prone to falling in love) acrobat and a wit. He wore a catlike mask and multicolored clothes and carried a bat or wooden sword (the origin of the modern comedy form slapstick). Harlequin's sidekick was Brighella, a more sophisticated and scheming character who would do anything for money. Pedrolino was a white-faced dreamer, who became Pierrot in French theater. The character Pulcinella was adapted as Punchinello, or Punch, in the popular English Punch and Judy puppet shows. He was a dwarfish character with a large crooked nose. A cruel bachelor, he liked to chase pretty girls.

Other important figures were the Capitano and Columbina. The Capitano was a swaggering mustached captain who often had a terrifying name like Matamoros, Cardone, Spavento da Vall' Inferna, Cocodrille, and Sbranaleoni. Columbina was a maidservant who was often paired in love matches with Arlecchino, Pedrolino, or the Capitano. With Harlequin she became a main character in the English pantomime, the harlequinade. The many lesser characters called for in commedia dell'arte scenarios—Gypsies, drunken innkeepers, and peasants—could be played by actors doubling in roles. When pastorals or tragedies were improvised, the troupe would add nymphs, shepherds, satyrs, magicians, kings, queens, warriors, spirits, and wild animals to the evening's performance.

Commedia dell'arte was despised by cultivated writers, who considered it plagiarized (copied from other works), obscene, and shapeless. The comic players did indeed steal material from established dramatic forms. Nevertheless, the literary playwrights also learned from the *comici* (commedia dell'arte actors) how to enliven their scripts with variety, physical action, and more complete female roles. Acting was not yet a respectable profession, but successful troupes benefited from patrons like the Gonzagas in Mantua and the Medicis in Florence and their royal relatives in France. In the late 1500s commedia dell'arte troupes began foreign tours, traveling to France and Spain, crossing the English Channel, and going as far east as Poland. The Italian troupes had a special rapport with French audiences, and commedia dell'arte humor had a direct influence on the works of the French actor and playwright Molière (1622–1673).

Commedia dell'arte began to decline when foreign audiences could not understand the humor of Italian dialects. The comic antics of the characters also became too predictable as actors stopped improvising their roles. By the late 1600s commedia dell'arte no longer reflected the conditions of real life, and an important function of the comedy was lost. Nevertheless, the traveling troupes had already made a strong impact on all European theater.

Commedia dell'arte received scholarly attention in the 1800s, and in the twentieth century it was once again being performed.

Northern Renaissance Culture

During the 1400s commerce and trade flourished in northern Europe, around the coast of the Baltic Sea and in the Rhine River region of Germany. These areas were linked with trade routes to Italy and the region around the Mediterranean Sea in the south. Often accompanying traders, Italian humanist scholars journeyed north to work as diplomats (official representatives of governments), secretaries, and university lecturers. They took with them the ideas of the Italian Renaissance, which was flourishing in city-states such as Florence, Milan, and Venice. The scholars were soon followed by artists and artisans, who received commissions from northern European monarchs and noblemen. Inspired by the innovations of the Italian Renaissance, thinkers and artists from the north then traveled to Italy to study with prominent figures. Soon northern European scholars and artists began making their own cultural contributions, which became known as the northern Renaissance. (For purposes here, northern Europe is defined as Germany, the Low Countries—present-day Netherlands, Belgium, and Luxembourg—France, England, and Spain.

Italian Renaissance ideas adopted

During the northern Renaissance, advances took place in literature, painting, sculpture, architecture, and music. Many northern European artists gained international reputations, especially in Germany and the Low Countries, which was also the center of humanism in northern Europe. Most of the art was religious, reflecting a society in which religious images indicated personal piety (religious devotion) as well as heavenly and earthly aspirations. The invention of the printing press greatly facilitated the spreading of the latest scholarly studies, novels, stories, poems, plays, artworks, and musical compositions. The Protestant Reformation, a movement to reform the Roman Catholic Church, dealt a severe blow to the Renaissance in Germany and the Low Countries. Protestant reformers did not approve of most Renaissance culture. They prohibited the display of paintings and sculpture in churches, and they frowned on the performance of music during worship services. The Protestants claimed that art and music detracted from the glorification of God. Germany and the Low Countries were at the center of reform activity, but the impact was also felt in France, England, and Spain.

The Renaissance in France is often thought to begin with the reign of King Francis I (1494–1547), who ruled from 1515 to 1547. Nevertheless, strong medieval traditions in the arts continued during this period. They gradually gave way to the influence of Italian writers and artists and artisans who brought fashionable new styles to France. By the mid-sixteenth century the French had developed their own version of the Renaissance, particularly in literature and architecture. During the latter part of the sixteenth century, however, the cultural world was devastated by the Wars of Religion (1562–98), a bloody conflict between Catholics and Protestants.

The course of the Renaissance in England followed the history of the Tudors, the royal family who gained control of the throne in 1485. Renaissance ideas were only beginning to reach England at that time and gradually emerged over the next century. The English Renaissance was firmly established when Queen Elizabeth I (1533–1603; ruled 1558–1603), the last Tudor monarch, died in 1603. The Elizabethan era produced some of the greatest literature in Western history, and Britain became a major world power by expanding its empire into the New World (the European term for the Americas). Renaissance ideals continued to flourish during the reign of King James I (1566–1625; ruled 1603–25), but lost importance under his son Charles I (1600–1649; ruled 1625–49). Charles's attention was diverted to government crises and the English civil war (1642–49), which led to the fall of the monarchy.

Spain's limited involvement with Italian Renaissance culture began in 1442, when King Alfonso V of Aragon (1396–1458; ruled 1416–58) conquered the Kingdom of Naples. He then moved his royal court from

Valencia to Italy. For more than sixty years Alfonso and his descendants sponsored Italian painters, sculptors, and architects who influenced art in Aragon. Elsewhere on the Iberian Peninsula (present-day Spain and Portugal), however, artists developed distinctive styles that reflected the existence of several independent kingdoms. Iberian culture was also shaped by Moorish (Muslim) traditions that were established after Muslims from Asia conquered most of the peninsula in the eighth century. For this reason, the Renaissance was not widespread throughout Spain. The greatest efforts to promote the Renaissance were made in the sixteenth century by Holy Roman Emperor Charles V (1500–1558; ruled 1519–56) and his son King Philip II (1527–1598; ruled 1556–98), who were active patrons of the arts. This era is known as Spain's golden age.

Humanism

Northern European humanist studies began in the Low Countries and Germany in the late 1400s. Like the Italian humanists, northern thinkers drew their inspiration from the languages and literature of ancient times, and they believed in the human potential for self-improvement. Scholars in the Low Countries and Germany expanded this philosophy to include religion. At that time they were facing the decline of scholasticism, which had been developed in the Middle Ages by such thinkers as Thomas Aquinas (1225–1274) and Albertus

Magnus (c. 1200–1280). The scholastics sought to combine Christian teachings with the concept of reason found in the works of ancient Greek philosophers such as Plato (c. 428–c. 348 B.C.) and Aristotle (384–322 B.C.). Scholasticism became the basis of education in Europe. By the fifteenth century, however, scholasticism was dominated by scholars called nominalists, who claimed that faith was beyond the reach of reason.

At the beginning of the Renaissance, a scholastic education consisted mainly of a series of exercises that subjected biblical texts to rational proof, or logical reasoning. This development displeased many religious people, who felt that such training failed to respond to the spiritual side of human experience. Humanists were instrumental in revealing the great ignorance of some scholastics and the inaccuracy of their work. At the same time, newly studied ancient texts and reinterpreted biblical texts seemed more and more to offer the inspiration that was lacking in scholasticism. One result was that the humanists started the Brethren of the Common Life, an educational movement that emphasized inner piety. The Brethren schools provided a training ground for an impressive number of northern European humanists.

Agricola introduces
studia humanitatis

Rudolf Agricola (also known as Roelof Huisman; 1444–1485) was the pioneer of humanistic learning in northern Europe. A native of the Netherlands, he studied in Italy in the late 1470s. He encountered the new educational curriculum *studia humanitatis* (humanist studies), which was then being introduced in Italy. In 1479 Agricola returned to the Netherlands and completed his major work, *De inventione dialectica libri tres* (Three books on dialectical invention). After serving as secretary to the city of Groningen for five years, he moved to Heidelberg, Germany. He went there on the invitation of his friend Johann von Dalberg, the bishop of Worms and the chancellor of Heidelberg University. Agricola became active in the intellectual community in Heidelberg, lecturing, delivering speeches, and participating in academic disputations, or formal debates. He also began to learn Hebrew. In 1485 he and Dalberg went to Rome to attend the consecration of Pope Innocent VIII (1432–1492; reigned 1484–92). Agricola wrote the speech that Dalberg delivered before the new pope. On the journey home Agricola fell ill, and he died a short time later in Heidelberg.

Although Agricola's career was brief, he had a strong influence on humanism in northern Europe. Among his numerous works were orations, poems, letters, and Latin translations of Greek texts, most of which were published after his death. Agricola's greatest achievement was *De inventione dialectica libri tres,* which was inspired by his discontent with current educational methods. He based *De inventione* on Aristotle's philosophy of rhetoric and dialectic, providing a

 Celtis starts sodalities

The German poet Conrad Celtis (1459–1508) played a major role in humanism by initiating societies called sodalities. He modeled these groups on Italian humanist academies he had visited in Florence and Rome. The best-known sodalities were located in Heidelberg, Germany, and in Vienna, Austria. Inspired by Celtis, other groups were formed in German cities such as Augsburg, Ingolstadt, and Olmütz. Members of these circles worked together on scholarly projects. Regardless of their social or professional background, they found a sense of belonging to a larger intellectual movement.

comprehensive theory of methodical thinking and reasoning. Agricola's book was highly influential as a statement of humanist rhetoric, partly because he illustrated rules with detailed examples from classical works. Printed in 1515, *De inventione* was widely read by advanced students, professors, and theoreticians during the sixteenth century. One of Agricola's letters, "De formando studio" (On the organization of the program of studies), also influenced humanists. This letter became popular because it included a brief description of making a commonplace book, a collection of excerpts from ancient texts that provided models for teaching writing and recitation. The commonplace book was used in Latin grammar schools throughout Europe until the eighteenth century (see "Commonplace books" in Chapter 12).

Erasmus is foremost humanist

The Dutch scholar Desiderius Erasmus (1466–1536) was the foremost humanist in northern Europe. Known as a "Christian humanist," he combined Christian teachings with classical ideals. Erasmus was born in Rotterdam, Holland, the illegitimate son of a priest and a physician's daughter. Throughout his life he was sensitive about the lowly circumstances of his birth. After receiving a classical education with the Brethren of the Common Life, Erasmus entered the monastery at Steyn in 1487. He was ordained a priest in 1492 and appointed secretary to the bishop of Cambrai the following year.

Erasmus's life took a significant turn in 1495, when he went to Paris, France, to study theology (religious philosophy). Paris was then the center of theological training in Europe. He lived at the Collège de Montaigu, a hostel, or lodging house, for poor students. During his stay in Paris he developed a strong distaste for the scholastic method. In letters to friends Erasmus made scathing comments about the Paris professors, whom he described as pseudotheologians (fake religious scholars) and obscurantists (those who make ideas unnecessarily complex). Finding the living conditions at the Collège de Montaigu unbearable, Erasmus struck out on his own and began to tutor the sons of wealthy families.

He never completed his degree in Paris. In 1499 he traveled to England with one of his pupils, William Blount, Lord Montjoy. During his stay in England he made lifelong friends, such as the humanists Thomas More and John Colet. In 1506 Erasmus moved to Turin, Italy, where he obtained a doctorate in theology without meeting the requirement of being a resident student at the university. He then established a connection with the printing house of Aldo Manuzio (1449–1515) in Venice, which later contributed to his productive career as a writer.

Writes *Praise of Folly* By the time Erasmus returned to England in 1509, he was disillusioned with the Catholic Church. He disapproved of the wars that popes were always waging, and he was critical of clergymen who failed live by the Christian teachings. As a result of this experience Erasmus wrote *Encomium moriae,* or *Praise of Folly,* a satire of the church and the clergy. (Satire is criticism through the use of humor.) In a famous passage a character named Dame Folly ridicules human folly—foolishness or lack of good sense—in general, but she focuses particularly on the self-importance and lack of spiritual values among theologians and clergymen. The book concludes with an appeal to Christians to embrace what appears to be folly in the eyes of the world—that is, the simple-hearted devotion to the teachings of Jesus Christ, which leads to the Kingdom of Heaven. *Praise of Folly* made Erasmus famous. In 1515 he was appointed councilor to Prince

Charles (later Emperor Charles V). To be near the royal court at Brussels in Belgium, Erasmus took up residence in Louvain, where he joined the theology faculty at the university. His relationship with other faculty members was an uneasy one from the outset because many of his writings drew criticism from theologians.

Publishes New Testament Erasmus was an unusually learned scholar and a highly productive writer. He published innumerable works on a wide variety of subjects, including biblical studies, education, and religious reform. During his career he also wrote more than three thousand letters to kings, popes, scholars, financiers, humanists, and reformers.

Erasmus was best known for his edition of the New Testament, the second part of the Bible that contains the teachings of Jesus Christ (called the gospels). Erasmus started his project in 1504, when he discovered a set of notes on the New Testament made by the Italian humanist Lorenzo Valla (1407–1457; see "Humanist literature" in Chapter 8). Following in Valla's footsteps, Erasmus began making notes on differences and errors he found when he compared Latin translations with the Greek biblical texts. In his New Testament he presented the original version of the biblical texts, which was written in the Greek language, and placed it alongside a Latin translation. Released in 1516, Erasmus's book was the first published Greek text. It provided a basis for further study of the New Testament by scholars and re-

Desiderius Erasmus was the foremost humanist in northern Europe during the Renaissance. *©Bettmann/Corbis. Reproduced by permission of the Corbis Corporation.*

formers. Erasmus also published *Enhiridion militis Christiani* (Handbook of a Christian soldier; 1503), in which he described a tightly structured patriarchal (headed by men) society built on Christian values. Although he held traditional views on the role of women, he advocated education for women and emphasized mutual respect and fellowship in marriage.

Erasmus stated his educational views in *De pueris instituendis* (On the education of children; 1529) and other works, which were typical of hu-

The Reuchlin affair

As Erasmus was expanding humanism in northern Europe, a controversy called the Reuchlin affair was taking place in Cologne, Germany. It began when Johannes Pfefferkorn (1469–c. 1522), a converted Jew, tried to convert other Jews to Christianity. Backed by members of the Dominican community (a Catholic religious order) in Cologne, Pfefferkorn claimed that Jewish religious literature encouraged Jews to resist conversion. In 1509 Holy Roman Emperor Maximilian I (1459–1519; ruled 1493–1519) authorized him to examine Jewish books and to destroy those that prevented conversion. In 1510, however, the archbishop of Mainz became involved. He had friendly relations with the Jewish community in Cologne, and he persuaded the emperor to authorize a group of experts to conduct a study of Jewish religious literature.

The German humanist Johann Reuchlin (1455–1522), the leading Christian expert on Hebrew, was one of those consulted. Other members of the study group decided that the Jewish literature should be destroyed, but Reuchlin opposed this move. He argued that destruction of Hebrew books would not only harm biblical scholarship but also violate property rights established by the laws of the Holy Roman Empire. Maximilian followed Reuchlin's advice and refused to seize the Jewish books. Pfefferkorn responded by writing *Handt spiegel* (Hand mirror; 1511), in which he

manist philosophy. He believed that parents had a duty to educate their children. If they could not give instruction themselves, they should select a teacher who could provide the necessary moral and intellectual guidance. Erasmus did not approve of physical punishment, and he recommended motivating learners with interesting material, a healthy challenge, and positive reinforcement. His ideal curriculum was based on language studies, the core subject of *studia humanitatis*. Another dimension to Erasmus's writing was *Querela pacis* (The complaint of peace; 1517), in which he condemned war as an instrument of tyranny and warned rulers to fulfill their obligation to preserve Christian harmony.

Drawn into Reformation debate In the 1520s Erasmus was drawn into the Reformation debate. His position at Louvain became increasingly difficult because he was considered a supporter of Martin Luther (1483–1546), the German priest who initiated the Protestant Reformation in 1517. To escape the hostile climate, Erasmus moved to Basel, Switzerland, where he became the center of a scholarly circle that included many prominent humanists. He remained charged that Reuchlin had been bribed by rich Jews. Reuchlin defended his position with *Augenspiegel* (Eye mirror; 1511).

Some Cologne theologians claimed that *Augenspiegel* had damaged Christianity by upholding the Jews. Although most German humanists respected Reuchlin and resented the attacks on him, few of them shared his enthusiasm for Hebrew. Even those who sympathized with his efforts and despised his critics thought *Augenspiegel* was unnecessarily controversial. One of those critics, Jacob Hoogstraeten, initiated an investigation of *Augenspiegel*. Reuchlin then appealed to the office of the pope. Pope Leo X sent the case to the bishop of Speyer, who ruled in 1514 that *Augenspiegel* was not heretical. The bishop ordered Hoogstraeten to abandon his attacks. Although the theologians appealed the decision to the pope, Leo X had no desire to condemn either Reuchlin or the Cologne theologians. In 1516 the pope imposed an order of silence on both sides, but Hoogstraeten continued his attacks and launched a new appeal. In the end, Reuchlin lost his legal case. The theologians renewed their appeal, and in 1520 the pope reacted against the religious revolution in Germany by condemning *Augenspeigel* as a scandalous book. Reuchlin quietly submitted to the pope's order that he make a public apology and pay the heavy costs of the appeals procedures.

in Basel from late 1521 until 1529, when the city formally turned Protestant. At that point he went to Freiburg, a Catholic city in Germany. During the last decade of his life, however, controversy continued to swirl around him.

At the beginning of the Reformation, Erasmus had given Luther limited support, but he also voiced disapproval of Luther's radical language. When Erasmus saw that the changes proposed by Luther and other reformers would lead to a split in the church, he distanced himself from the movement. Although he preferred to stay on the sidelines, he finally had to defend himself against Catholic charges that he was a Lutheran supporter. In 1524 he wrote *De libero arbirio diatribe* (Diatribe on free will), in which he quoted biblical passages for and against the concept of free will (humans' ability to choose their own actions). He argued that in cases where Scripture (religious writings) is not clear on the matter, the church should be the final authority. Luther issued a sharp reply in *De servo arbitrio* (The bondage of the will), stating that humans do not have free will and insisting that this fact is clearly stated in Scripture.

Condemned by the church Many Catholic theologians thought Erasmus's contribution to the debate came too late, even though he had taken the side of the church. By this time he had already made theologians angry with *Praise of Folly,* in which he held the church up to ridicule. But he had caused the most controversy with his edition of the New Testament. Although the book was welcomed by humanists, it was attacked by theologians. In the sixteenth century people believed that the Vulgate Bible, the official Latin version, was written by Saint Jerome, in Latin, under divine inspiration (directly from the word of God). Since Erasmus had found errors in the Latin translation, he was charged with blasphemy (insulting God) and accused of giving support to the reformers. From 1523 onward, Erasmus's works were investigated by the Paris theological faculty, whose judgment was considered the final word in religious matters. Numerous passages in his writings were censored. In 1531 the church issued a formal condemnation and Erasmus gave a lengthy apology. Until his death in 1536 he was the focus of attacks from both Catholics and Protestants. Catholics continued to question his faithfulness to the church and Protestants called him a hypocrite for his failure to support Luther.

More supports Christian humanism

The impact of humanism in England was greatly intensified after 1500, partly by Erasmus's first visit. His biblical interests spurred the work of Englishmen who had recently returned from Italy. They had studied Greek intensively and were eager to analyze the New Testament and the writings of the early church fathers. The most prominent English humanist was the statesman Sir Thomas More (1478–1535). He was joined by John Colet (c. 1466–1519), dean of Saint Paul's Cathedral and founder of its famous humanist school, in leading educational reform activities among English churchmen. The movement quickly gained momentum and spread to Cambridge, where Erasmus was periodically a faculty member. The focus on biblical scholarship made London a favored meeting place for Europe's men of letters.

More's life exemplifies the political and spiritual upheaval of the Protestant Reformation. Born into a well-to-do middle-class family in London, More was trained for a career in government at an early age. He studied law at Oxford and came under the influence of Colet, who had been to Italy. Colet had brought back to England the new Italian method of reading ancient texts from a historical perspective. In 1499 More met Erasmus, who increased his interest in humanism. In 1504, while pursuing a legal career, More entered Parliament, the main governing body of Britain. By this time he was active in the Christian humanist movement. In fact, he considered entering the priesthood. He was intrigued by the Italian philosopher Giovanni Pico della Mirandola (1463–1494), who had also become more religious as he approached the age of thirty a decade earlier (see "Humanist literature" in Chapter 8). More finally decided that he could fulfill a Christian vocation while remaining a layman. Throughout his life his household was filled with humanist visitors, such as his great friend Erasmus, and provided a model educational community for his children—More corresponded with his daughters in Latin, for instance—and servants.

Writes *Utopia* In 1511 More was appointed undersheriff of London. This job involved acting as an adviser at the court of King Henry VIII (1491–1547; reigned 1509–47) and as a negotiator with foreign merchants. Four years later More took his first official trip abroad, to Antwerp in present-day Belgium. When he returned to London he began his greatest work, *Utopia,* a fiction that he wrote in Latin and modeled on Plato's *Republic.* Published in 1516, *Utopia* describes an imaginary land that is free of ostentation (grand displays of wealth), greed, and violence. More's inspiration for the book was the discovery of the Americas.

In the first part of *Utopia* More recounts his meeting with a sunburned Portuguese mariner named Raphael Hythloday, who has been with the explorer Amerigo Vespucci in the New World. Hythloday is a philosophical traveler, both opinionated and virtuous. As Hythloday, More, and More's friend Peter Giles converse, Hythloday launches into a critique of the ills of European society. Every

Sir Thomas More was the most prominent English humanist. *Photograph courtesy of The Library of Congress.*

place he has seen in his voyages seems superior to Europe. He criticizes a legal system that allows a few to amass great wealth, while multitudes endure such poverty that they have to beg or steal to survive.

In the second part of *Utopia* Hythloday speaks enthusiastically of a republic on an island off the coast of Brazil where, 1,760 years before, a benign conqueror named Utopus established a constitution based on a system intended to make its citizens virtuous and its society secure. Hythloday then goes on to describe in great detail the structure of this society, noting that all the citizens converted to Christianity. By the end of the book, More had given a bleak picture of humanity, and he had portrayed European rulers as being inherently corrupt.

Named lord chancellor In the meantime, King Henry VIII had invited More to become a councilor in the royal court. More's deep suspicion of rulers and politics made him reluctant to accept the invitation. Nevertheless, he finally agreed to the appointment in 1517, and he went on to build a career in diplomacy, legal service, and finance. More eventually learned that his early doubts about serving Henry had been justified. By 1523 More had risen to the position of speaker of the House of Commons (lower branch of Parliament). Under the direction of the lord chancellor of England, Cardinal Thomas Wolsey (c. 1475–1530), he had to promote a highly unpopular war levy, or tax, that was ultimately discontinued. In negotiations with other European countries, More was constantly frustrated by Henry's belligerence and Wolsey's political ambition. More wanted to stop wars so that the Christian faith and culture could be preserved. In 1529 Henry appointed More lord chancellor of England, replacing Wolsey, who had failed to obtain the pope's approval of the annulment of the king's marriage to Catherine of Aragon (1485–1536; see "England" in Chapter 3). More now occupied the highest administrative office in the land. Yet he soon found

himself in a distressing role as Henry's chief agent in dealing with the pope.

Defies the king While serving as chancellor, More was deeply engaged in writings against Lutherans. In such works as *Dialogue Concernynge Heresyes* (1529) and *Apologye* (1533) he defended the Catholic Church, even though he was aware of its flaws. More steadfastly held that heretics—those who violate the laws of the church—should be burned for their blasphemy against God's true church. At the same time, Henry was drawing further away from the church because the pope still refused to grant him a divorce. In 1532 More resigned from office, primarily because of illness and distress over Henry's outright threat to break from the church. Finally, Henry simply announced that the pope had no authority in England. Statutes passed by the Reformation Parliament in 1533 and 1534 named the king supreme head of the church and cut all ties with the papacy. The Anglican Church thus became an independent national body.

More recognized the dangers posed by his pro-Catholic writings, so he tried to avoid political controversy. But Henry pressured him to repudiate the pope's jurisdiction in England. More refused Henry's order because he did not want to contribute to disharmony within the Christian world. In April 1534 More was summoned for interrogation by royal officials. When he did not change his position he was put on trial for treason and found guilty. He was beheaded on July 6, 1535. Although More is most often remembered as the man who defied Henry VIII, the significance of his life extends beyond the realm of English history. During the turbulent years of the early Reformation, he worked to revitalize Christianity within the church through his active involvement in humanism. In 1935 he was canonized as a saint in the Catholic Church. More's *Utopia* is still being read today as a classic work on the ideal society.

France

The leading humanists in Renaissance France were Guillaume Budé and Jacques Lefèvre d'Étaples. Budé was a strong advocate of French "genius" and often criticized the royal court for its excessive admiration of Italian culture. Lefèvre d'Étaples tried to bring reform to the Catholic Church through the study of the classic works of early Christianity.

Guillaume Budé Guillaume Budé (1467–1540) served as secretary to King Louis XII (1462–1515; ruled 1498–1515). In 1508 Budé published the first extensive humanist study of the *Digest* by Eastern Roman Emperor Justinian I (483–565; ruled 527–65). The *Digest* was the most important part of *Corpus iuris civilis* (Body of civil law), Justinian's compilation of Roman law. Budé applied new humanist philological methods (study of language as used in literature) to solve the problem of contradictory passages that had long been debated by medieval scholars. He revealed that Tribonian (died 545), Justinian's chief legal minister, had made errors. In his next work, *De asse* (On

the Roman penny; c. 1515), Budé studied ancient money systems and units of measure. This field was a major concern of humanists who wanted to reconstruct the life and society of Greece and Rome. Budé's project involved the innovative use of Roman coins as sources of historical information.

Budé's works were filled with glowing praise for France and the French king, whom he compared with Roman emperors. When Francis I took the throne in 1515, Budé encouraged the king to become an active patron of humanist projects. In 1530 Francis created the Royal Lectureships, which were professorships in Greek, Hebrew, Latin, and mathematics. The Royal Lectureships led directly to the founding of the College of France. Budé was also rewarded with several royal appointments. His last major work was *De transitu Hellenismi ad Christianismum* (The passage from Hellenism to Christianity; 1535), an attempt to distance humanism from Protestantism. Although Budé had been a critic of the excesses and corrupt practices of the Catholic clergy, he staunchly opposed Luther and other reformers. He rebuked many of his fellow humanists for giving Greek and Roman philosophy a status equal or superior to that of the Christian faith. At the same time, he viewed classical mythology, classical Latin, humanism, and philology as being compatible with Christian theology.

Jacques Lefèvre d'Étaples Jacques Lefèvre d'Étaples (also known as Jacobus

Faber Stapulensis; c. 1455–1536) began his career as a professor in the Collège du Cardinal Lemoine in the University of Paris. In 1508 he joined a monastery (religious house for men), the Abbey of Saint-Germain-des-Prés, which was headed by abbot Guillaume Briçonnet (c. 1472–1534). Lefèvre d'Étaples found the religious life of the monks to be lacking in spirituality, and he felt they did not know how to pray with devotion. They were using a popular version of the Book of Psalms from the Old Testament, which had been issued a century and a half earlier by Nicolaus of Lyra (c. 1270–1349). Nicolaus had given a literal interpretation of the psalms, and Lefèvre d'Étaples claimed this was the reason for the absence of spirituality in the monks. In 1509 he published *Quincuplex psalterium* (Fivefold psalter). In this work he contrasted five versions of the Book of Psalms, providing brief statements of the spiritual meaning of each psalm.

Briçonnet was named bishop of the diocese (church district) of Meaux, and in 1521 he put Lefèvre d'Étaples in charge of reforming the clergy and the laity (unordained members of a church) in the region. Lefèvre d'Étaples was part of a group of scholars involved in publishing works aimed at educating the secular clergy (unordained members of religious orders) and lay members of the church. Another goal was to engage parish priests once again in their roles as spiritual leaders. In 1522 Lefèvre d'Étaples published a French translation of the Gospels, the books of the New Testament that contain the teachings of Jesus Christ. Two years later he translated the Catholic Epistles, which comprise the New Testament books James; 1 and 2 Peter; 1, 2, and 3 John; and Jude. Lefèvre d'Étaples had published a French New Testament in 1523, and in 1530 he followed it with a translation of the entire Bible.

The reform efforts were successful, but the Franciscans (members of the order of Saint Francis) in Meaux became upset. They had previously been fulfilling the roles now being taken over by parish priests. At the urging of the Franciscans, the faculty of theology at the University of Paris accused Lefèvre d'Étaples and his colleagues of supporting the Lutherans and thus committing heresy. Their reform activities and their insistence on making scripture available in the French language seemed similar to Luther's work in Germany. Lefèvre d'Étaples' group was split up because of the charges brought against them. Lefèvre d'Étaples fled to the protection of the queen, Margaret of Navarre, in Nérac (see "Margaret of Navarre" section later in this chapter). Although the reform movement had royal support, it was never able to complete its work in Meaux or extend its influence throughout France.

Spain

The leading humanist in Spain was Juan Luis Vives, a friend of Desiderius Erasmus, Thomas More, and Guillaume Budé. Vives became a prominent humanist in Europe, contributing ideas on educational and social reform that influenced modern-day thinking.

Juan Luis Vives Juan Luis Vives (1492–1540) was born into a prominent merchant family in the Jewish community of Valencia. His parents and relatives on both sides of the family had been persecuted by the Inquisition because they were Jews. After a long trial in 1525, his father was executed by burning, and his mother's remains were exhumed (dug up) and burned in 1528. Vives left Spain at age seventeen and never returned. In 1509 he entered the University of Paris, where he studied for three years. Although he did not complete his degree, he gained respect as a humanist while serving in various positions in Bruges, Belgium, and Louvain, France. In 1519 he was granted permission to deliver public lectures without holding an academic appointment at the University of Louvain. The following year he published the anti-scholastic work *In pseudodialecticos* (Against the pseudodialecticians), which brought him to the attention of Thomas More and initiated his career as a leading European humanist.

At the request of Erasmus, Vives wrote a commentary on Augustine's *De civitate Dei* (The city of God). Augustine (354–430) was an early champion of Christianity; Vives's commentary on his work was published in 1522 and dedicated to King Henry VIII of England. In this work Vives made comments on such Christian beliefs as the Immaculate Conception (the Virgin Mary gave birth to Jesus without having had sexual inter-course) and predestination (the fate of all humans is determined by God before birth). He also criticized the gluttony and lustfulness of the clergy and popes. Vives's royal patrons and other scholars did not respond favorably to his ideas. Nevertheless, in 1523 Cardinal Thomas Wolsey, the chancellor of England, appointed Vives to a lectureship at Corpus Christi College at Oxford University and supported educational reforms that Vives initiated at the college. For the next five years he divided his time between England and the Low Countries.

In 1526 Vives wrote *De subventione pauperum* (On aid to the poor), a proposal that war refugees throughout Europe be treated like native citizens. Vives eventually lost his position at Oxford and fell out of favor with the king for taking controversial positions. First, he advocated European unity against the threat of the troops of Ottoman Sultan Süleyman (c. 1494–1566, ruled 1520–66; see "Ottoman Empire" in Chapter 1). Then he tried to intervene on behalf of Queen Catherine of Aragon when King Henry VIII was seeking a divorce from her (see "England" in Chapter 3). In 1528 he was banned from England.

Introduces modern ideas Vives returned to Bruges in 1529. Although he had to sever his ties with England, two of his most important works on education were connected with his earlier visits to that country. The first was *De institutione feminae Christianae* (Education of the Christian woman), which he wrote in 1523 and dedicated to Catherine of Aragon. The other, also written in 1523, was *De ratione studii puerilis epsitolae duae* (On the right method of instruction of children). It was a guide for the education of Princess Mary, the future Queen Mary I (1515–1558; ruled 1553–58) of England. In *De institutione feminae Christianae* Vives advocated an ascetic, or spiritually disciplined, life for women, but he also argued that education was compatible with female virtue. This work was so successful that in 1528 he wrote a sequel on the duties of the husband, *De officio mariti*. Vives's other educational works supported methods of education devoted to social and moral reform. They were widely translated and used in schools throughout Europe.

Historians note that Vives's interpretation of Christian charity was far ahead of its time. During his final years he continued to contribute to the discussion of moral and social improvement. In 1529 he wrote *De concordia et discordia in humano genere* (Peace and conflict in human society). With this work Vives intended to inspire Holy Roman Emperor Charles V to meet the challenge of moral as well as political leadership. Two years later Vives published *De disciplinis libri xx* (Twenty books on education), which offered not only a revolutionary program of education but also a plan for reforming corrupt human culture. The last book published during his lifetime, *De anima et vita libra tres* (Three books on the soul and on life; 1538), contributed to the development of modern concepts of psychology. Vives based his ideas on observation and experience rather than the works of Aristotle, which were central to the scholastics' view of human behavior.

Literature

During the Renaissance, literature throughout Europe was directly influenced by the humanist emphasis on reviving ancient and traditional literary forms, exploring human creativity, and writing in native languages. Humanism had also produced widespread scrutiny of traditional values, especially scholasticism and the role of religion in people's everyday lives. In France this influence took the form of scathing satires of scholastic traditions, invention of the essay, and refinement of the Italian novella. In England, drama and poetry reached a level of refinement never before witnessed in Western (that is, non-Asian) literary history. Spain was the birthplace of the modern novel and a Spanish novelist provided one of the most memorable characters in world literature.

Writers in most European countries were immensely prolific, producing works in every imaginable literary form. It is therefore impossible to give a complete overview of Renaissance literature. Instead, the sections below focus on a few figures in France, England, and Spain, countries where the major literary contributions were made during the Renaissance period.

France

The comic writer François Rabelais and the essayist Michel de Montaigne have traditionally been considered the most important writers in

France during the sixteenth century, the height of the Renaissance era. In the twentieth century, however, Margaret of Navarre was given equal status with these authors because she perfected the novella.

François Rabelais The French humanist, physician, and author François Rabelais (pronounced rah-bleh; c. 1494–c. 1553) is acclaimed as a comic genius. He published several works, but he is best known for *Gargantua and Pantagruel.* There are gaps in information about Rabelais's life. It is known that he came from the province of Touraine, where he may have had a scholastic education. This type of education would explain the disdain for overly learned, self-important scholars that he expressed in his writings. During the 1530s and 1540s Rabelais made three trips to Rome, where he absorbed humanist ideas. In 1532, after receiving a medical degree in Montpellier, he settled in Lyons as a physician at the hospital Hôtel-Dieu. Shortly thereafter he began his career as a writer.

Publishes *Gargantua and Pantagruel*
Gargantua and Pantagruel consists of a collection of four books released separately, and out of sequence, over a period of twenty years (1532–52); a fifth book was published in two parts (1562 and 1564) after Rabelais's death. Scholars are still disputing whether he wrote book five, as it was published under the pseudonym (pen name) Master Alcofibras, which contains the letters of Rabelais's name.

Gustave Doré's illustration from "The Life of Gargantua and Pantagruel," written by François Rabelais. *©Leonard de Selva/Corbis. Reproduced by permission of the Corbis Corporation.*

Rabelais based *Pantagruel* (book two) on a popular collection of fanciful tales of giants set against a background of the Arthurian legend (medieval stories about the legendary English hero King Arthur). These tales were called *Les grands et insetimables chroniques du géant Gargantua* (Chronicles of Gargantua). Rabelais presented his own work as a sequel to the tales. He depicted the birth, education, and adventures of Gargantua and his son Pantagruel, both of whom are giants.

Two other characters play prominent roles in the stories. In *Gargantua* (book one), Friar Jean represents a new type of monk, a worldly and dynamic one, who tills the earth and performs heroic feats against the army attacking his vineyards (grape vines). In *Pantagruel,* Panurge is a comic prankster who becomes Pantagruel's companion. The author was also influenced by classical writers of a literary form called Menippean satire, which is a loose collection of parodies (comic imitations) of intellectual and religious figures.

Influences other writers Rabelais wrote *Gargantua and Pantagruel* during the religious and intellectual turmoil of the Protestant Reformation. He rejected rigid ideologies, which he attacked with outrageous scenes and excessive language. Rabelais drew his words from both the highest and lowest elements of his world. He also gave conflicting points of view. For instance, in *Gargantua* the narrator presents himself as a wise philosopher and then as a carnival barker selling his wares. Rabelais calls for an excess of eating and drinking, and he incessantly mocks the seriousness of clerics, intellectuals, and ideologues (those who adhere to rigid ideals) of every variety. An example is an English scholar who appears and seeks a debate in which only hand signals can be used since words cannot express the mysteries of truth. Panurge responds with a series of mostly obscene gestures that mock this learned fool.

Although Paris theologians routinely condemned *Gargantua and Pantagruel,* the work was an immediate popular success. Scholars note that it most certainly influenced *Don Quixote,* the novel by Spanish author Miguel de Cervantes (see "Spain" section later in this chapter). Rabelais also had an impact on modern writers, and the adjective "Rabelaisian" has come to mean any text that is characterized by extravagant and coarse humor.

Michel de Montaigne The French author Michel Eyquem de Montaigne (1533–1592) created a new literary genre (form), the essay, in which he used self-portrayal as a mirror of humanity in general.

Montaigne was born into a noble family in Périgord near Bordeaux. His father, Pierre Eyquem, was a Bordeaux merchant and municipal official whose grandfather was the first nobleman of the line. His mother, Antoinette de Louppes (Lopez), was descended from Spanish Jews, called Marranos, who had converted to Catholicism. He was educated at the Collège de Guyenne, in Bordeaux. In 1557 Montaigne obtained the position of councilor in the Bordeaux Parliament (the law-making body), where he met his closest friend, Étienne de La Boétie (1530–1563). The two men shared many interests, especially a passion for classical antiquity. La Boétie died from dysentery (infectious disease causing extreme diarrhea) in 1563. The loss of his friend was a serious emotional blow that Montaigne later described in his essay "On Friendship." Two years later he married Françoise de la Chassaigne, daughter of a co-councilor in the Bordeaux Parliament. Montaigne and his wife were apparently compatible but the marriage was sometimes cool—he believed that marriage ranked somewhat lower than friendship.

In 1568 Montaigne's father died, and Montaigne inherited the rank of lord. Before his death, Pierre Montaigne had persuaded his son to translate into French the *Book of Creatures or Natural Theology* by the fifteenth-century Spanish theologian Raymond of Sabunde (died 1436). The work was an apologia—an apology for, or defense of, the Christian religion based on proofs from the natural world. From his work on this translation, which he published in 1569, Montaigne later developed the longest of his many essays, "The Apology for Raymond Sebond." In this essay, Montaigne presented his philosophy of skepticism (attitude of doubt), attacked human knowledge as presumptuous and arrogant, and suggested that self-knowledge could result only from awareness of ignorance.

"What do I know?" In 1570 Montaigne resigned from the Bordeaux Parliament and retired to his country estate, where he began writing *Essais,* or *Essays.* Ten years later books One and Two were published in Bordeaux. In *Essais* Montaigne used self-portrayal as a method for reaching conclusions about human experience in general. He was not a systematic thinker, however, and he did not maintain a single point of view. Instead, he preferred to show the randomness of his own

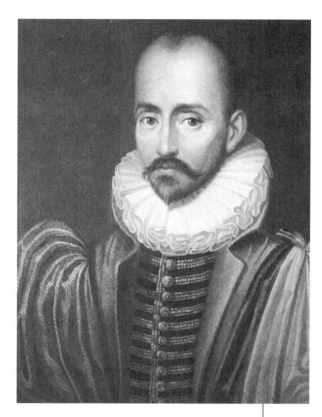

Michel de Montaigne is credited with creating the new literary genre known as the essay. *Photograph courtesy of The Library of Congress.*

thought as representative of the self-contradiction to which all people are prone. Montaigne's characteristic motto was "Que sais-je?" ("What do I know?"). Although he was skeptical about the power of human reason, he argued that each person should have self-knowledge in order to live happily.

Since Montaigne believed that "each man bears the complete stamp of the human condition," his essays can also be seen as portraits of humankind in all its diversity. He constantly attacked the presumption, arrogance, and pride of human beings, yet he held the highest view of human dignity. As a skeptic, Montaigne opposed intolerance and fanaticism, saying that truth is never one-sided. He championed individual freedom but held that even repressive laws should be obeyed. He feared violence and anarchy (lawlessness, or political disorder) and was suspicious of any radical proposals that might jeopardize the existing order. Acceptance and detachment were for him the keys to happiness.

From 1580 until 1584 Montaigne served as mayor of Bordeaux, and he indirectly defended his regime in the essay "Of Husbanding Your Will." He was in failing health during his last years, so his young admirer Marie de Gournay (1565–1645), worked on the expanded edition of his works. Drawing mainly from annotations made by Montaigne, Gournay published the edition in 1595, three years after his death. It was the basis of the 1603 English-language edition by John Florio, which was a source for Shakespeare's play *Tempest* (see "William Shakespeare" section later in this chapter) as well as the works of other playwrights.

Margaret of Navarre Margaret of Navarre (1492–1549), duchess of Angoulême, was the sister of King Francis I of France. She became an important political and social figure when Francis took the throne in 1515. In 1527, two years after the death of her first husband, Margaret married Henry II, king of Navarre (1503–1555; ruled 1517–55). Interested in philosophical and religious matters, she was familiar with the works of Italian poets Dante (1265–1321) and Petrarch (1304–1374; see "Poetry" in Chapter 8) and with the Bible. She set the intellectual and cultural tone at court, especially in the 1530s and early 1540s. An early supporter of reform in the French church, she remained outwardly obedient to Catholicism. At the same time, however, she protected leading humanist reformers such as Guillaume Briçonnet and Jacques Lefèvre d'Étaples (see "Humanism" section previously in this chapter), who were suspected of Lutheran leanings.

A prolific writer, Margaret produced many works, though few were published during her lifetime. In 1531 she published the long poem *Le miroir de l'âme pécheresse* (Mirror of the sinful soul), which was followed two years later by *Dialogue en forme de vision nocturne* (Dialogue in the form of a nocturnal vision). These works were condemned by the theology faculty of the Sorbonne because of Margaret's reformist views concerning grace, faith, and free will. In 1547 she published a collection of her poetry under the title of *Les marguerites de la marguerite des princesses* (Pearls from the pearl of princesses ["marguerite" means pearl]).

Writes *Heptaméron* Margaret's most famous work, which was incomplete at her death, is the *Heptaméron*. The book is a collection of novellas (a form, originating in Italy, of short fictitious stories) modeled on the *Decameron* by the Italian writer Giovanni Boccaccio (1313–1375; see "Giovanni Boccaccio" box in "Humanism" in Chapter 8). The narrative centers on ten aristocrats—five men and five women—who are stranded by a flood. They tell stories while waiting for a bridge to be built. After each story, they comment on the tale just told, drawing from it moral lessons that usually present contradictions and have no neat conclusions. Complex relationships are established among the speakers. They focus on the difficulties of meeting the demands of a worldly life while trying to live according to the Christian message of charity. Because of the frank and stark depiction of sexual desire, many sixteenth-century readers were perplexed by the book and tended to view it as a collection of indecent tales. Late-twentieth-century scholars reevaluated the *Heptaméron,* however, stressing its complex narrative and the prominence of women in the tales. The *Heptaméron* is now ranked alongside the books of François Rabelais and Michel de Montaigne as one of the greatest prose works of the French Renaissance.

England

Three great figures emerged during the English Renaissance—the playwrights William Shakespeare and Ben Jonson and the poet Edmund Spenser. Shakespeare and Jonson wrote some of the most brilliant dramas in Western literature. (Although plays were created for performance, they are now considered part of the literary tradition.) Spenser invented new poetic forms that influenced the work of later poets.

William Shakespeare The playwright, poet, and actor William Shakespeare (1564–1616) is generally acknowledged to be the greatest of English writers and one of the most extraordinary creators in human history. Shakespeare's career coincided with the height of the English Renaissance, and his plays were immensely popular. Theater in London was just coming into its own, and audiences from a wide range of social classes were eager to reward his talents. He devoted his entire life to the public theater, creating works alongside other great playwrights such as Christopher Marlowe and Ben Jonson. Most of Shakespeare's plays are still read and performed throughout the world today.

Perfects dramatic forms Shakespeare came from the small town of Stratford-upon-Avon in Warwickshire, England. Although no documents survive from his school years, his literary work shows that he attended the Stratford grammar school. At age eighteen he married Ann Hathaway, with whom he had three children. Shakespeare began his career in London by writing comedies and historical dramas called "chronicles." In the early comedies—including *The Comedy of Errors* (c. 1590), *The Two Gentlemen of Verona* (1591), and *Love's Labour's Lost* (1593)—he showed his talent for using intricate plots, dazzling language, and a wide range of characters. His first chronicle plays were *Henry VI* (1592) and *Richard III* (1594). These dramas dealt with the tumultuous events of English history between the death of

Shakespeare's sonnets

During much of 1593 and 1594 English theaters were closed down because of an epidemic known as the plague (a widespread outbreak of disease). Shakespeare therefore turned to writing nondramatic poetry to make a living. Again he excelled in his chosen craft by producing two masterpieces, the serious-comic *Venus and Adonis* and the tragic *Rape of Lucrece,* for a wealthy patron, the earl of Southampton. Both poems carry the sophisticated techniques of Elizabethan narrative verse to their highest point, drawing on Renaissance mythological and symbolic traditions. Shakespeare's most famous poems were his 154 sonnets (published in 1609). They are considered the supreme English examples of the sonnet form, which was in vogue in Europe during the Renaissance. Shakespeare used the fourteen-line sonnet with its fixed rhyme scheme to express emotions and ideas ranging from the frivolous to the tragic. The sonnets are dedicated to "Mr. W. H.," whose identity remains a mystery. Scholars also cannot determine whether there was a real-life "dark lady," or an unfaithful friend, who are the subjects of a number of the poems.

King Henry V in 1422 and the accession of Henry VII in 1485. At the time they marked the most ambitious attempt in English theater to present epic drama. Shakespeare's first tragedy, *Titus Andronicus* (1593), reveals similar ambition. Although the play may seem to be a chamber of horrors—the plot is full of mutilations and murders—Shakespeare succeeded in outdoing other English playwrights in the lurid tradition of the revenge play. For twenty more years he continued to master and perfect all of these forms—comedy, history, and tragedy—as one of the most productive and brilliant playwrights in history.

By 1594 Shakespeare was established as a prominent playwright. In that year he became principal writer for the successful Lord Chamberlain's Men, one of the two leading companies of actors in London. In addition to performing as a regular actor in the company, he was a "sharer," or partner, in the group of artist-managers who ran the entire operation. The Lord Chamberlain's Men performed in unroofed but elaborate theaters. Required by law to be set outside the city limits, these theaters were the pride of London. They were among the first places shown to visiting foreigners and seated up to three thousand people. The actors played on a huge platform stage equipped with additional playing levels and surrounded on three sides by the audience. The absence of scenery made possible a flow of scenes comparable to that of modern-day movies. Music, costumes, and ingenious stage machinery created successful illusions under the afternoon sun. In 1599 the company had the Globe Theater built on the south bank of the Thames River.

For the Lord Chamberlain's Men, Shakespeare produced a steady outpouring of plays. Among them were the comedies *The Taming of the Shrew* (1594), *A Midsummer Night's Dream* (1595), *The Merchant of Venice* (1596), *Much Ado about Nothing* (1598), and *The Merry Wives of Windsor* (1599). In the year 1600 alone he wrote *As You Like It,* and *Twelfth Night. Twelfth Night* is often described as the perfect comedy. Shakespeare's only tragedies of the period are among his most familiar plays: *Romeo and Juliet* (1596), *Julius Caesar* (1599), and *Hamlet* (1601). Continuing his interest in the chronicle, Shakespeare wrote *King John* (1596), *Richard II* (1595), the two-part *Henry IV* (1597), and *Henry V* (1599). At the end of Queen Elizabeth's reign he wrote works that are often called his "problem plays." *All's Well That Ends Well* (1602) is a romantic comedy that presents sexual relations between men and women in a harsh light. *Troilus and Cressida* (1602) is a sardonic and disillusioned piece on the Trojan War. The tragicomic *Measure for Measure* (1604) suggests that modern urban hopelessness was settling on London.

Writes great tragedies

When King James I took the throne in 1603, he became the patron of the Lord Chamberlain's Men. The flag of the King's Men now flew over the Globe. During the next five years Shakespeare wrote fewer but perhaps even finer plays: *Othello* (1604), *King Lear* (1605), *Macbeth* (1606), *Antony and Cleopatra* (1607–08), *Coriolanus* (1607–08). Each in its own way is a drama of alienation, works that con-

tinue to be relevant to the lives of people in the twenty-first century. These tragedies present an astonishing series of worlds different from one another, in language that exceeds anything Shakespeare had done before. He also created some of his most complex and vivid characters and used a variety of new structural techniques.

A final group of plays took a turn in a new direction. Commonly called the "romances," *Pericles* (1607), *Cymbeline* (1609), *The Winter's Tale* (1611), and *The Tempest* (1611) were tragicomedies, a form that had been growing increasingly popular since the early years of the century. Shakespeare turned this fashionable mode into high art. *The Winter's Tale* is considered one of his best plays, while *The Tempest* is perhaps the most popular. After completing *The Tempest,* Shakespeare retired to Stratford. In 1613 he returned to London to compose *Henry VIII* and *The Two Noble Kinsmen.* He died in 1616, at age fifty-two. Shakespeare's reputation grew quickly, and his work has continued to seem to each generation like its own most precious discovery. His value to his own age is suggested by the fact that, in 1623, two fellow actors gathered his plays together and published them in the Folio edition. Without their efforts, since Shakespeare was apparently not interested in publication, many of the plays would not have survived.

Ben Jonson The English playwright and poet Ben Jonson (1572–1637) is best known for his satiric comedies.

Christopher Marlowe

The English dramatist and poet Christopher Marlowe (1564–1593) died tragically at age twenty-seven. Scholars speculate that if he had lived longer he would certainly have rivaled the dramatic genius of Shakespeare and Ben Jonson. Marlowe was the first English playwright to make significant advances in tragic drama. Marlowe's best-known tragedies are *Tamburlaine the Great* (printed 1590), *The Jew of Malta* (printed 1633) and *Doctor Faustus*. In each of these plays he focused on a single character who dominates the action with his extraordinary strength of will. Shakespeare later perfected this form in his famous tragedies.

Marlowe was killed in a tavern fight on May 30, 1593. He was dining in the town of Deptford with a man named Ingram Frizer and two other men. In the course of an argument over the tavern bill, Marlowe wounded Frizer with a dagger. Frizer then seized the same dagger and stabbed Marlowe over the right eye. According to the coroner's inquest, Marlowe died instantly. Despite the unusual wealth of detail surrounding this fatal episode, there has been much speculation about the affair. It has been suggested, for example, that the deed was politically motivated and that Frizer (who was subsequently judged to have acted in self-defense) was simply acting as an agent for a more prominent person.

An immensely learned man with an irritable and domineering personality, he was, next to Shakespeare, the greatest dramatic genius of the English Renaissance.

Jonson was probably born in or near London and received his formal education at Westminster School. He did not continue his schooling, probably because his stepfather forced him to engage in the more practical business of bricklaying. Nevertheless, Jonson continued to study the classics throughout his active life. He began his theatrical career as a strolling player in the provinces. By 1597 he was in London and had begun writing plays. His first piece of dramatic writing, *The Isle of Dogs,* was judged to be indecent, seditious (inciting resistance to the government), and slanderous (making false charges against someone). Jonson was imprisoned for this offense. In 1598 he was in more serious trouble. He narrowly escaped being hanged after he killed a fellow actor in a duel (formal combat fought by two persons with guns).

Reveals dramatic genius In the same year, Jonson's first major work, *Every Man in His Humour,* was performed by the Lord Chamberlain's Men, with Shakespeare taking the lead role. Called a "comedy of humors," the play features characters whose behavior is dictated by a dominating whim or affectation. It was followed by *Every Man out of His Humour* (1599 or 1600), *Cynthia's Revels* (1601), and *Poetaster* (1601). These three "comical satires" represent Jonson's contribution to the so-called war of the theaters—a short-lived feud between rival theatrical companies. Jonson then wrote one of his most important works, the tragedy *Sejanus His Fall* (1603), which was admired by intellectuals but considered boring by average playgoers.

By 1604, before he had written his most famous works, Jonson had become known as the foremost writer of masques, a popular form of theatrical entertainment, in England. He continued writing masques throughout his career, frequently in cooperation with the famous architect Inigo Jones (see "Architecture" section later in this chapter), who designed the stage sets and machinery. Jonson's dramatic genius was fully revealed for the first time in *Volpone, or the Fox* (1606), a satiric comedy that contains the playwright's harshest and most unrelenting criticism of human vice. All the principal figures are named (in Italian) after animals suggestive of their characters: for example, Volpone, the cunning fox, and Voltore, the ravenous vulture. The main action turns on Volpone's clever scheme to cheat those who are as greedy as he but not nearly so clever. Volpone is too clever for his own good, however, and the punishment imposed on him is unusually severe for a comedy.

Next to William Shakespeare, Ben Jonson was the greatest dramatic genius of the English Renaissance. *Photograph courtesy of The Library of Congress.*

Career declines The satire of Jonson's next three comedies is less harsh. *Epicoene, or the Silent Woman* (1609) is an elaborate intrigue built around a farcical character with an insane hatred of noise. In *The Alchemist* (1610) the characters are activated more by vice than folly—particularly the vices of hypocrisy and greed. Their punishment consists largely in their humiliating self-exposure. *Bartholomew Fair* (1614) has a relatively thin plot featuring a rich and varied collection of unusual characters. After *Bartholomew*

Fair Jonson's dramatic powers suffered a decline. Nonetheless, he remained an impressive and respected figure, especially in literary and intellectual circles. He was also idolized by a group of younger poets and playwrights who styled themselves as the "tribe of Ben."

Jonson's nondramatic writings included a grammar (rules for using language) of the English language (1640), a collection of notes and reflections titled *Timber, or Discoveries* (1640), and a large number of poems. After the death of King James I in 1625, Jonson suffered a number of setbacks. His talents as a masque writer were not fully appreciated by the new king, so he was less in demand and frequently short of money. After becoming paralyzed in 1628, Jonson was confined to his home in Westminster. When he died nine years later, he was buried with great ceremony in Westminster Abbey.

Edmund Spenser Edmund Spenser (c. 1552–1599) ranks as the foremost English poet of the sixteenth century. His best-known work was the unfinished epic poem *The Faerie Queene.*

Spenser was working as a government official when he began writing poetry. In 1579 he met Philip Sidney, the poet and courtier. Spenser had written a considerable quantity of poetry by this time, but he had published nothing. Upon the advice of friends he decided to make his literary debut with *The Shepherd's Calendar* (1579), which he dedicated to Sidney.

In this work he adopted a variety of poetic forms—dirges, complaints, paeans—and attempted to enrich the English poetic vocabulary with foreign terms and archaic and dialect words. Spenser continued writing poetry while studying law. In 1580 he was named secretary to Arthur Grey de Wilton (1536–1593), the new lord deputy of Ireland. Spenser moved to Ireland, where he remained for the rest of his life. In 1588 he settled at a castle in County Cork, where he remained for the rest of his life, except for trips to London.

Publishes *The Fairie Queene* For some years Spenser had been working on *The Faerie Queene.* He had completed three books in 1589, when the English courtier Walter Raleigh paid him a visit. Raleigh was so impressed with this work that he took Spenser with him back to England. Early the next year the first three books of *The Faerie Queene* were published, with an elaborate dedication to Queen Elizabeth I. Spenser's ambition was to write the great English epic. His plan was to compose twelve books, each concerned with one of the twelve moral virtues as classified by Aristotle. In turn, each of these virtues was to be embodied in a knight. Thus the poem would combine elements of the romance of chivalry, the handbook of manners and morals, and the national epic.

Spenser's style is distinctively his own in *The Fairie Queene.* For his verse form he created the Spenserian stanza, which has since been often imitated in English literature. Composed

Philip Sidney

The English poet Philip Sidney (1554–1586) is sometimes ranked with William Shakespeare and Edmund Spenser as one of the great figures of English Renaissance literature. Sidney is best known for three major works—*The Defense of Poetry, The Countess of Pembroke's Arcadia* (known as *Arcadia*), and *Astrophil and Stella.*

The Defense of Poetry (1595) is a statement of Renaissance ideals that Sidney wrote in the form of an autobiographical essay. By poetry he meant imaginative literature, which he claimed has the power to bring about moral improvement in the reader. In this work Sidney reviewed the course of English poetry and challenged his peers to write English literature that emulates the achievements of the Greek and Roman poets.

Arcadia (1590) is considered the first English novel. It is written in the form of letters and stories within stories, from various points of view. The narrative includes plot devices that became common in English fiction: near drowning at sea, near rape of the lead female character, crowd scenes, court-of-law scenes, and royal court scenes. All are colored by a female sensibility. Sidney wrote *Arcadia* for his sister, Mary Sidney, countess of Pembroke (1561–1621). Mary Sidney was herself an accomplished writer and literary patron, who supervised the publication of *Arcadia.*

In *Astrophil and Stella* (1591), a series of sonnets, Sidney tells the story of Astrophil, a brilliant young man who pursues an adulterous affair with Stella, an unhappily married woman. The real-life model for Stella was possibly Penelope Rich, whose father wanted her to marry Sidney. Although Sidney married Francis Walsingham, some scholars suggest that he was in love with Rich. *Astrophil and Stella* is a psychological study of the vanity of human wishes and the joys of poetic ambition, all capped with a visit to the tortuous world of melancholy love.

of nine lines, the Spenserian stanza contains eight lines of iambic pentameter (five units, called feet, consisting of one short, or unstressed, syllable followed by one long, or stressed, syllable) and concludes with a line of iambic hexameter (six metrical feet) called the Alexandrine. *The Faerie Queene* met with much acclaim. Although he enjoyed great success in London, he returned to Ireland. He wanted a government post in England, but in courtly circles he was considered a minor figure.

In 1595 Spenser published a collection of poems dedicated to the memory of Sidney. It contains "Colin Clout's Come Home Again," which he dedicated to Raleigh. Considered one of Spenser's most charming poems, "Colin Clout" tells the story of the poet's reception in London and his impressions (mostly negative) of court life. The collection also includes the first elegy (poem expressing sorrow), "Astrophel." A year earlier Spenser had married Elizabeth Boyle, an Anglo-Irish woman from a well-connected family. His sonnet series "Amoretti" and the love poem "Epithalamion" give a poetic account of his courtship and marriage. "Epithalamion" is regarded as one of the greatest love poems in English. In this poem a lover's passion blends with a deeply religious spirit, combining both classical myth and medieval legend. During a trip to London in 1595 Spenser published three more books of *The Faerie Queene*. He also worked on *View of the Present State of Ireland* (published 1633). In this prose tract he proposed a program for subjugating (governing and controlling) the Irish people and then establishing an English form of government in the country.

After returning to Ireland in 1597 Spenser continued writing *The Faerie Queene*. Two more cantos (parts) of a seventh book were published in 1609, but most of what he wrote in these years has been lost. In October 1598 Spenser was named sheriff of Cork. Shortly after he took office, Tyrone's Rebellion, a revolt against English rule in Ireland, broke out in Munster. Spenser's castle was burned, and the poet was forced to flee with his wife and four young children. In December the provincial governor sent Spenser to London as a messenger to Elizabeth I. Weakened by the hardships of the preceding months, Spenser died in London the following January. He was buried near other poets in Westminster Abbey.

Spain

Spain was somewhat culturally isolated from mainstream Renaissance literature, yet the author Miguel de Cervantes produced *Don Quixote,* one of the great masterpieces of world literature, during this period. This work was largely responsible for creating the modern novel, a fictional story that depicts the motivations and actions of several characters in complex plots. One of Cervantes's contemporaries, the prolific playwright Lope de Vega, introduced the concept of "new theater" to Spain.

Miguel de Cervantes Miguel de Cervantes Saavedra (known as Cervantes; 1547–1616) was a native of Alcalá de Henares, Spain. He lived at the end of the glorious years of the Spanish empire and his own experiences paralleled those he described in *Don Quixote.* Moving to Italy in 1570, Cervantes served in the Spanish army in Naples. At that time Spain had the most powerful army in the world. Some of its bases were located in Italy for better access to the Mediterranean Sea, where Spain could fight the Ottoman Empire, which posed a major threat to European countries. The following year he fought heroically and was wounded at the Battle of Lepanto, a naval conflict in which an alliance of European nations defeated the Ot-

EL INGENIOSO
HIDALGO DON QVI-
XOTE DE LA MANCHA,

*Compuesto por Miguel de Ceruantes
Saauedra.*

DIRIGIDO AL DVQVE DE BEIAR,
Marques de Gibraleon, Conde de Benalcaçar, y Baña-
res, Vizconde de la Puebla de Alcozer, Señor de
las villas de Capilla, Curiel, y
Burguilios.

Año,   1605.

CON PRIVILEGIO,
EN MADRID, Por Iuan de la Cuesta.

Véndese en casa de Francisco de Robles, librero del Rey nro señor.

The title page from *Don Quixote.* ©Bettmann/Corbis. Reproduced by permission of the Corbis Corporation.

toman Empire. Cervantes remained in Italy until 1575, when he boarded a ship headed for Spain. Off the coast of France the ship was seized by Turks, and Cervantes and several other passengers were taken captive. They were held in Algeria until 1580. Cervantes's military service in Italy and his subsequent years of captivity did not win him any privileges upon his return to Spain. Throughout his life he existed on the margins of society in a continuous struggle for economic survival.

In 1585 Cervantes wrote his first novel, *La Galatea,* which gave him some prestige but not much financial relief. Two years later he was appointed commissary (officer in charge of supplies) for the Spanish Armada, a fleet of heavily armored ships built to defeat the British navy. The Armada expedition ended in catastrophe in 1588, when it was defeated by the British during a dramatic battle in the English Channel (see "Spain" in Chapter 3). Spain then fell upon hard times. When municipalities and local churches refused to pay support for the Armada, Cervantes was accused of mismanagement. He was held in Spanish prisons in 1592 and 1597. It was probably during his last imprisonment that he conceived the idea of writing *Don Quixote.* In the 1590s Cervantes wrote a collection of stories titled *The Exemplary Novels* (published 1612). In the prologue (introduction) he declared himself the first person ever to write novellas in Spanish. In one story, "El Licenciado Vidriera" ("The Glass Licentiate"), the main character is much like the madman

Cervantes later portrayed in *Don Quixote*: a scholar who becomes insane and believes that he is made out of brittle glass. His temporary insanity gives him remarkable understanding of the problems of his society.

Achieves fame In 1605 Cervantes published the first part of *Don Quixote.* It was an immediate success and established him, at age fifty-eight, as an important writer. The novel contains a number of the popular literary styles and subjects of the time, such as the romantic novel focusing on tales of chivalry, and such subjects as religion and faith. (Chivalry was a medieval tradition that required knights, or nobleman soldiers, to pledge themselves to a complex code of honor. Knights frequently dedicated their military adventures to ladies, whose virtue they vowed to protect.) Cervantes intended to mock the popular chivalric romances and the adventure stories of traveling knights. He created the character of Don Quixote, an elderly gentleman who becomes insane due to his excessive passion for reading chivalric romances. Don Quixote leaves his home, having decided to revive heroic times by reenacting knightly feats. Later, with the promise of fabulous rewards, he convinces the poor peasant, Sancho Panza, to be his squire, or shield bearer. The novel narrates in a descriptive and majestic manner the absurd adventures of knight and squire as they travel through Spain. Using a satiric approach, Cervantes depicted characters who reflected their society, thus making a commentary on the social customs of the day. The book was an immediate success and was edited several times in subsequent years. It was translated into English as early as 1612 and appeared in French and other European languages.

The popularity of *Don Quixote* was so extraordinary that in 1614 a man named Avellaneda attempted to write a sequel without the permission of Cervantes. This unauthorized work so enraged Cervantes that he decided to write the second part of *Don Quixote,* which was published in 1615. The continuation is considered to be as good as, if not better than, the first installment. The second part is more reflective and possesses greater structural unity. At the conclusion Don Quixote dies after recovering his sanity, much to the distress of a transformed Sancho who is eager to engage in more adventures. With Don Quixote's death Cervantes ended the possibility of further adventures for his character.

Fails as playwright In addition to writing novels, Cervantes tried to become a playwright. At that time in Madrid, theater-going had become a popular form of entertainment, much like going to the movies today. There were several open-air theaters in the city, and people were eager to see new plays. Cervantes decided to try his fortune in the thriving market of comedies. He wrote several plays, but only two have survived from this period: *El cerco de Numancia* and *El trato de Argel* (The traffic of Algiers). The public's fa-

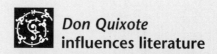

Don Quixote influences literature

Don Quixote has been translated into more languages than many works of Western literature. The literary influence of the novel has been immense. Direct traces can be identified in the work of countless other authors of various nationalities. In addition, thinkers and philosophers have dedicated essays to the myth of Don Quixote. Such twentieth-century musical productions as *The Man of La Mancha,* as well as several movies, have been inspired by *Don Quixote.* Modern artists like the Spanish painter Pablo Picasso (1881–1973) have immortalized the image of the errant knight escorted by his faithful squire.

vorite playwright, and Cervantes's main rival, was Lope de Vega. Cervantes eventually failed as a writer of plays, but he did not abandon the theater entirely. In 1615, at a bookseller's request, he collected some of his plays and published them under the title of *Ocho comedies y ocho entremeses* (Eight plays and eight interludes). The plays were published in the three-act *comedia* form, with the interludes (short plays between acts of longer plays) in the traditional form of farce (obvious humor). These plays were never performed in Cervantes's lifetime.

Cervantes's achievements as a novelist did not guarantee him the economic security that best-selling works bring their authors today. In the seventeenth century writers lost the rights to their work after selling it to a merchant. Therefore, Cervantes had no access to the profits made from his books. Before he died in 1616, he was trying to finish what would be his last novel, *Los trabajos de Persiles y Segismunda* (The Labors of Persiles and Segismunda). The book was published by his widow after his death. Cervantes was proud of this novel and thought its success would exceed that of *Don Quixote*. *Los trabajos de Persiles y Segismunda* was not well received, however, and Cervantes's fame rests on his creation of the traveling knight and his faithful squire.

Lope de Vega The Spanish playwright, poet, and novelist Lope Félix de Vega Carpio (known as Lope de Vega; 1562–1635) was an immensely productive writer. He produced so many works—reportedly eighteen-hundred-plays alone—that he was called "monstruo de la naturaleza" (prodigious monster of nature) and "fénix de los ingenios" (intellectual phoenix; a phoenix is a mythical bird that rose to life again after being burned). Lope wrote in nearly all the literary genres of his time—sonnet, ballad, epic, Byzantine (pertaining to the Byzantine Empire) and pastoral (rural) romance, Italian-style novella, and prose fiction mixed with poetry. Today he is known mainly as a playwright.

The son of a master embroider-er, Lope was a child prodigy (unusually talented child or youth) who composed verses before he could write. He was able to read Latin as well as Castil-ian (form of Spanish spoken in the Castile province) by age five, and he claimed he wrote his first play when he was twelve. In 1588 Lope was banished for eight years from Madrid and for two years from the entire kingdom of Castile. He was being punished for malicious libel against the family of Elena Osorio, a married woman with whom he had an affair. This incident was the basis for numerous sonnets and ballads featuring Elena.

Introduces "new theater" Lope spent his exile in the province of Valencia, where he became acquainted with dramatists. Upon his return to Madrid he introduced several theatrical innovations that challenged current practices based on classical Greek and Roman forms. He later described these innovations in *Arte nuevo de hacer comedias en este reino* (New art of playwriting in this kingdom; 1609). For instance, he advocated using comedy in serious dramatic works, and he reduced the number of acts from the traditional four to three. He also used different rhyme schemes to make the language of a play more lively and interesting. Lope drew his plots from history, legend, mythology, and religion. Introducing subplots involving lower-class characters, he developed the comic figure of the *gracioso*, who was usually a witty servant. Other popular features of his plays were the figures of the peasant protagonist, or hero, and the *mujer varonil*, a woman dressed as a man. Lope was recognized for his role in transforming Spanish theater into the popular *comedia nueva* (new theater) that drew crowds to open-air patios adapted for theatrical use in Madrid.

Lope wrote many kinds of theatrical works. Among them are "peasant honor" plays and *capa y espada* (cloak-and-sword) plays. A typical peasant honor play is *Fuenteovejuna* (The sheep-well; 1612–14), which is based on an actual fourteenth-century uprising of peasants against a tyrannical overlord. Lope set the plot in the fifteenth century and justified the peasants' actions by making them loyal to Ferdinand of Aragon (1452–1516) and Isabella I of Castile (1451–1504). At the time the Spanish monarchs were symbols of stability against rebellious nobles. In another of Lope's peasant play, *Los comendadores de Córdoba* (The commanders of Córdoba), an outraged husband kills his wife when he learns she has had an affair. He then kills all of the servants and even the animals in his household who might have witnessed his dishonor. Lope's *capa y espada* plays ridiculed the customs, taboos (forbidden behavior), and prejudices of Spanish society of his day. For instance, *La vengadora se las mujeres* (The avenger of women; 1621) features a *dama docta* (learned woman) who protests the injustice of historical accounts written by men. She is determined to write her own defense of women's virtue.

Many of Lope's plays have been translated into English, as has *La Dorotea* (1632), a dramatic dialogue narrating his youthful affair with Elena Osorio. In 1627 Lope wrote the poem *La corona trágica* (The tragic crown) about the life of Mary Stuart.

Mary was the Catholic queen of Scotland who was beheaded by order of her cousin Elizabeth I, the Protestant queen of England. This poem earned Lope the title of doctor of theology and the Order of Saint John. Thereafter he signed his works Fra Lope de Vega.("Fra" is a term for a priest.) Thirteen years earlier Lope had in fact been ordained a Roman Catholic priest, perhaps in response to the death of his second wife. He did not observe the rules of celibacy, however, and continued to have love affairs. Lope's humble family origins and his ability to write with great ease were criticized by his more learned rivals. Some of them could claim a noble heritage, but none could challenge his theatrical and literary success. His death in 1635 was the occasion of public mourning.

Northern Renaissance art

Art flourished in northern Europe, especially in Germany and the Low Countries, in the fifteenth century. Italian Renaissance theories of art had begun to influence painting, sculpture, and architecture around the mid-1400s. In each country Renaissance concepts were adapted to existing art forms to produce distinctive versions of Renaissance classicism.

More than ever before art was available as well as affordable. For instance, a simple woodcut cost only pennies. Wealthy merchants filled churches with altarpieces, statues, stained-glass windows, and tombs.

They decorated their homes with portraits, goldsmith wares, and small collectible objects. Most of the art was religious, reflecting a society in which religious images indicated personal religious devotion as well as heavenly and earthly aspirations: a patron might commission an altarpiece as a sign of his desire for salvation and as a reminder to fellow citizens of his prominent social or financial status. Unlike Italy, there were no great cultural centers to which large numbers of artists gravitated. Most artists in northern Europe, therefore, created their works in a certain town or region, rather than moving from one artistic haven to another. Only a few of the biggest towns were able to attract a group of artists who received commissions from patrons in other countries.

The Protestant Reformation dealt a severe blow to Renaissance art, and many artists' careers were damaged. Protestants objected to the presence of statues of saints and other religious figures in churches because, they said, the artwork detracted from direct communication with God. Many charged that the statues themselves were being worshiped as a replacement for God. These complaints resulted in widespread destruction of religious art throughout northern Europe in the 1520s and 1530s. Even in Catholic regions, the demand for religious art waned dramatically. Since moving was not an option for most artists, many failed to adapt to the changing times. Others branched out into portraiture, notably in the form of small medals, or specializations such as landscapes, small-scale reliefs, and statuettes.

Painting

Innovations in painting emerged primarily in Germany and the Low Countries and then spread to other parts of northern Europe. An early pioneer was the Dutch painter Jan van Eyck (c. 1390–1441), who rediscovered the ancient art of oil painting practiced by Apelles (fourth century B.C.), court artist of the Macedonian king Alexander the Great (356–323 B.C.; ruled 336–323 B.C.). Although mixing pigments in an oil base was not new to the fifteenth century, van Eyck was the first to use thin pigmented oil glazes and varnishes in all of his works. He created an enamel-like surface by applying several layers of thin oil glaze. Brush strokes can hardly be seen in van Eyck's paintings, and colors are so luminous and clear that the passage of five hundred years has not dimmed them. His techniques had a direct impact on painters working in the mid-1400s.

Van Eyck perfects oil painting Van Eyck's paintings display astounding visual beauty and virtuosity. Neither microscope nor telescope—both inventions of a later age—can match the precision with which van Eyck captured the individual hairs of a fur collar, the texture of an Oriental carpet, or the minute reflection on the polished surface of a single pearl. An example is the rich attention to detail in the *Madonna with Canon George van der Paolo*. At the same time, he enjoyed depicting things seen at great distances. The faraway cityscapes and country vistas glimpsed through the windows and archways of van Eyck's richly appointed interiors are, upon close inspection, actually comprised of a multitude of individual elements— each paving stone, flower, and tree is painted with as much care as if it were meant to be placed in the foreground before our very eyes. An example is the background vista of the *Madonna with Chancellor Nicolas Rolin*. Van Eyck also focused upon human subjects. His painted portraits combine realistic detail with what eventually became the accepted formula for Netherlandish portraits. Each sitter appears in three-quarter facial view against a blank background, eyes gazing outward and directly engaging those of the viewer. The result is an eerie sense that the face in the portrait is communicating wordlessly with the living viewer. An example is *Man in a Red Turban* (1433), which some art historians consider to be a self-portrait of the artist.

Dürer introduces Renaissance The German painter and graphic artist Albrecht Dürer (1471–1528) introduced the achievements of the Italian Renaissance into northern European art. His influence was greater than that of any other northern artist of his time and was most widely felt through his woodcuts and engravings.

The young Dürer received training as an engraver in his father's workshop in Nuremberg. He executed his first self-portrait, a drawing in silver-point, at the age of thirteen. After serving an apprenticeship with a local painter and woodcut illustrator, Dürer traveled in the Low Countries, then worked as a woodcut designer in Basel, Switzerland. In 1494 he journeyed to Venice, Padua, and Mantua, where he copied works by the leading contemporary Italian masters. While in Italy, Dürer became interested in the art of the ancients. He also gained an appreciation of art theory, to which he later devoted much of his time. Dürer's travels opened his eyes not only to the marvels of ancient art but also to the variety to be found in nature, which he captured in landscape drawings and watercolors of Alpine views.

In 1498 Dürer published a series of fifteen woodcuts, titled *Apocalypse,* which was based on the fantastic images described in the Book of Revelation. It is considered the highest achievement in German woodcut art. Dürer's self-portrait of 1498 marked the turning point of his art. He represented himself as a humanist scholar and an elegant young man, asserting that the artist is a member of the cultural elite instead of being merely a craftsman. This new concept of the artist was widely accepted in Italy (see Painting" in Chapter 8), but it had not yet reached northern Europe.

Dürer revealed humanist influences in other works. He used perspective (artistic technique of depicting an object from a single point of view) in the Paumgartner Altarpiece (1504), and his portraits, such as *Oswolt Krell* (1499), were characterized by sharp psychological insight. He depicted mythological and allegorical subjects

Printmaking

During the fifteenth century the Rhineland and southern Germany were the foremost centers for the early printing and publishing industry. The industry was based on the technology of printmaking, which involved reproducing text and images from woodcuts and engravings.

Woodcuts could be created with a minimum of technological expertise. To make a woodcut, an image was drawn onto a flat plank of fairly hard wood, such as pearwood. The wood was cut away from the sides of the lines, leaving the image in relief (raised above the surface). Ink was then applied onto the woodcut, which was then pressed onto a piece of paper. Woodcuts were probably being printed on paper by 1400. The great majority of early woodcuts depicted a saint or a religious scene, often accompanied by a prayer. After the invention of movable type in the mid-1400s, woodcuts were used for illustrating books that were produced on the printing press. By 1500 illustrated books were issued in great numbers north of the Alps (a mountain range between France and Italy). In the 1490s Albrecht Dürer singlehandedly raised the woodcut to the level of high art.

An engraving is made by cutting lines into a metal plate (usually copper). The cutting tool, called a burin, creates grooves of varying width and depth depending on the pressure applied to it. Ink is spread onto the plate, and the surface is then wiped clean. A dampened piece of paper is put on top of the plate. Next the paper is covered with a piece of felt or blanket, and the two are run through a roller press, resulting in the transfer of the ink in the plate's grooves to the paper. A much more complex technology was needed to manufacture a flat, smooth metal plate than to prepare a plank of wood. For that reason the production of engravings was more expensive, so it was usually confined to a local area. Engraving seems to have begun in the upper region of the Rhine River valley, near Lake Constance. Again it was Dürer who brought the Renaissance to the north by using engravings to reproduce fine art.

in engravings on metal, such as the *Dream of the Doctor* (after 1497) and *Sea Monster* (c. 1498). He also used that technique for one of his most popular prints, the *Prodigal Son* (c. 1496); this work is based on a biblical story, but Dürer represented the hero in a new way. Dürer chose to depict neither the prodigal son's sinful life nor the happy ending of his return to his father, but instead captured the moment when the son becomes aware of his sinful life and begins his repentance. The print *Nemesis* (1502) shows Dürer's knowledge of human anatomy and his interest in humanistic allego-

Albrecht Dürer's painting titled *St. Jerome in His Study.* *Reproduced by permission of Mary Evans Picture Library.*

ry (story featuring characters with symbolic significance), which appears in several of his prints of that period.

Dürer went to Venice again in 1505, and the paintings being pro-

duced in the city at that time strongly influenced his work. In 1506 he painted *Feast of the Rose Garlands* for the church of the German merchants in Venice, San Bartolomeo. After returning to Nuremberg the artist painted several large altarpieces (works hung above altars in churches) that combined colorful Italian features with the traditional northern style. Among them are *Martyrdom of the Ten Thousand* (1508) and *Adoration of the Trinity* (1511), which show little figures in vast landscapes. Dürer then left painting and returned to printmaking. Perhaps his most important works of the period from 1513 to 1520 were his engravings, which show the influence of his friendships with distinguished German humanists. The three so-called Master Engravings—*Knight, Death, and the Devil* (1513), *St. Jerome in His Study* (1514), and *Melencolia I* (1514)—represent the height of Dürer's engraving style and also express his thoughts on life, man, and art. These engravings are allegories of the three kinds of virtue associated with the three realms of human activity—action, contemplation, and intellectual pursuit. The active realm is depicted in *Knight;* the contemplative, in *St. Jerome;* and the intellectual, in *Melencolia I.*

Dürer gave equal attention to the world around him. Throughout his life he drew and engraved simple motifs studied from life, as in the dramatic drawing of his aging mother, who is emaciated and ill (1514). Until 1519 Dürer worked for Emperor Maximilian I. He was involved in various allegorical and decorative projects, most of them prints, such as *Triumphal Arch* and *Triumphal Procession of Maximilian I.* Dürer also did some miniatures, such as drawings in the *Maximilian I Prayer Book* (1515).

In 1520 Dürer left Nuremberg for Antwerp, Belgium, to collect his yearly salary from Charles V, the new Holy Roman Emperor. This trip was a triumph for the artist and proved that he was held in high esteem. In his travel journal Dürer left a daily record of his stay in Antwerp and of his visits to various Dutch, Belgian, and German towns. He met princes, rich merchants, and great artists. He drew portraits, landscapes, townscapes, and curiosities in his sketchbook. He met Erasmus, whom he admired and of whom he made a portrait drawing; in 1526 he made an engraving of this drawing.

During the final decade of his life Dürer supported the reform ideas of Martin Luther. Dürer's last great work was a two-panel painting, often called *Four Apostles* (1526). The monumental, sculpture-like figures represent Saints John and Peter (left panel) and Saints Mark and Paul (right panel). The paintings were probably intended as the wings of a triptych (three-panel artwork), but Dürer did not paint the central panel. He gave *Four Apostles* to the Town Council of Nuremberg. In the panels he included quotations from the writings of the saints, which contained accusations against "false prophets." Dürer's work proclaimed the unity of the new Protestant faith against the different sects arising at that time. In 1525 Dürer published a book on perspective *Instruction in Measurement,* and his treatise on fortifications appeared in 1527. He died in 1528, a few months before the publication of *The Four*

Books on Proportions, his last and most important theoretical work.

Hans Holbein is popular portraitist

The German painter Hans Holbein the Younger (c. 1497–1543) was one of the best-known portraitists of the northern Renaissance. He still ranks among the great portrait painters in European art history.

A native of Augsburg, Holbein was the son of Hans Holbein the Elder (c. 1465–1524). The elder Holbein was noted for his silver-point (drawn with a pencil of silver) portrait drawings that showed mastery of the art of characterization. The younger Holbein's natural gift for drawing and for satire was recognized by Erasmus while the artist was still a teen-aged journeyman in the publishing capital of Basel, Switzerland. Erasmus's heir, Bonifacius Amerbach,was instrumental in collecting Holbein's early paintings and drawings in the Basel Museum. Among these works is *Christ in the Tomb,* a depiction of the dead Jesus of Nazareth as a stiffened and sightless cadaver. The image was so shocking that many critics accused Holbein of being an atheist (one who does not believe in God). There is virtually no evidence as to what Holbein's religious views may or may not have been, though some point to the mocking tone of his *Dance of Death* woodcut series as an indication of his feelings about religion. In one scene Death attacks a mendicant (begging) friar who tries to save his money-box, and in another Death snuffs out a nun's candle as she is entertained by

German artist Hans Holbein is still considered one of the greatest portrait painters in European art history. *Photograph courtesy of The Library of Congress.*

her secret lover. Modern scholars have noted that this famous series is the last of a long line of medieval depictions of Death as the unwelcome force that robs every class and profession of its status symbols.

Although Holbein designed weapons, jewelry, tableware, biblical illustrations, and mantelpieces, and painted several murals, he is best known as a portrait artist. He is particularly famous as court painter for King Henry VIII of England. He painted portraits of Henry; works depicting two of the king's wives, Jane Seymour and Anne of Cleves; and a portrait of Princess Christina of Denmark, to whom Henry unsuccessfully proposed. Holbein also did portrait paintings, drawings, and miniatures of various members of the court, including the French ambassador and his house guest, the Bishop of Lavour. Painted in 1533 and titled *The Ambassadors,* the double portrait includes the haunting image of a skull that serves as a contrast to youth, intellect, and good health. Other portrait subjects were the humanist Thomas More and young German merchants of the Hansa (trading organization) headquarters, or of the "Steelyard" in London.

Holbein's portraits were cherished by their owners. Yet before the advent of color photography in the twentieth century, when copies of his works were widely reproduced, he was relatively unknown. Holbein was not honored in Germany primarily because he moved first to Switzerland and later to England. Beginning in the twentieth century, however, exhibitions of the painter's works were held in Europe and the United States.

Pieter Bruegel the Elder The Dutch painter and engraving designer Pieter Bruegel the Elder (pronounced BROO-gehl; c. 1525–1569) is considered one of the foremost late northern Renaissance artists. His works provide insight into humans and their relationship with nature. He lived and worked in Antwerp and Brussels at a time when northern European art was strongly influenced by the late Italian

Renaissance style called mannerism, which was characterized by distortion of space and elongation of human forms (see "Painting" in Chapter 8). Yet he chose to develop his own style, often adapting the themes and techniques of earlier artists.

After studying and working with artists in Antwerp, Bruegel traveled extensively in France, Italy, and the Alps in the early 1550s. Returning to Antwerp in 1555, he embarked on a successful career. Bruegel was a remarkably versatile painter. He produced landscapes, religious and allegorical subjects, scenes of peasant festivities, depictions of Flemish proverbs (brief statements of truth), and compositions in the manner of Hieronymus Bosch. Bruegel's career falls into two major phases—the first in Antwerp, the second in Brussels. In Antwerp he produced many designs for the print publisher Hieronymous Cock. Bruegel's earliest known paintings were also done in Antwerp. Among them were *Parable of the Sower* (1557), *Children's Games* (1560), and *Carnival and Lent* (1559). All were inspired by Flemish speech and folk life, but with allegorical content. In Brussels, Bruegel continued producing designs for Cock, but he concentrated on painting.

Bruegel's art represents the culmination of the Flemish realistic tradition, often reviving styles and compositions of earlier generations. In *Procession to Calvary* (1564), his largest surviving painting, he drew upon a traditional composition, possibly invented by Jan van Eyck, and adapted the holy figures from the Flemish painter Rogier van der Weyden (c. 1399–1464). Bruegel's interest in Bosch appears in some of his earliest print designs, such as *Big Fish Eat the Little Fish* and especially *Triumph of Death*. The latter painting is closest to Bosch in its apocalyptic (expectation of catastrophe) view of human destiny. Bruegel's landscapes range from depictions of the Flemish countryside to grand vistas. Vast space and heroic scale distinguish his two famous paintings of the *Tower of Babel,* one dated 1563 and the other probably done later. Bruegel's allegorical works are often satires of human folly, presented with a biting wit that reflects his interest in humanist themes (see "Humanism" section previously in this chapter). His peasant scenes also contain acute observations of the human form and psychology. Among the best-known are *Wedding Dance* (1566), *Peasant Dance,* and *Peasant Wedding.*

Although Bruegel studied in Italy in the early 1550s, he showed little interest in Italian art until he moved to Brussels in 1565. Many of his works from that time on show closer attention to composition and feature larger-scale figures. He was possibly influenced by the Italian painter Raphael (1483–1520; see "Painting" in Chapter 8). Most notable in this regard is *Christ and the Woman Taken in Adultery* (1567). Some of his later paintings may be comments on the troubled times that led to the Eighty Years' War (1568–1648), the conflict in which the Netherlands sought independence from Spain. Among them are *Census at Bethlehem*

Hieronymous Bosch

Hieronymous Bosch (Jheronimus or Jeroen van Aken; 1450–1516) was a Dutch painter who developed a distinctive, often disturbing style. Although Bosch depicted traditional subjects—folk tales, stories about Christ, images of saints—his paintings are filled with bizarre plants and animals, distorted human figures, and amusing cartoon-like creatures. Paying close attention to small details, he used brilliant colors that gave a nightmarish, grotesque effect to his pictures. One of his best-known works, *Garden of Earthly Delights,* seems to be an elaborate morality tale (story with a lesson on good and evil) about the punishment of sinners, yet art scholars have been unable to agree on an exact interpretation of the painting. After Bosch died, Pieter Bruegel the Elder and other artists made copies of his paintings and produced new works that imitated his style. Some modern scholars believe Bosch's art was an expression of his disturbed mental state, while others think it was inspired by witchcraft or alchemy (science devoted to turning base metal into gold) and astrology (prediction of future events according to the positions of the planets and stars).

(1566), *Parable of the Blind* (1568), and *Misanthrope* (1568). Before his death Bruegel destroyed a number of his satirical drawings to save his wife from persecution. Bruegel's paintings and prints were endlessly copied and imitated. His peasant subjects and landscapes influenced later Netherlandish painters, including the great baroque artist Peter Paul Rubens (1577–1640). Bruegel's legacy was most directly transmitted through his two painter sons: Pieter the Younger (1564–1638) and Jan (1568–1625).

Foreign artists dominate Spain and Portugal For most of the Renaissance, painting in Spain and Portugal was dominated by foreign masters—artists from Flanders and Burgundy in the fifteenth century and artists from Italy in the sixteenth century. Bridging these two influences was the Spanish painter Pedro Berruguete (c. 1450–c. 1504). From about 1475 to 1482 Berruguete worked in Italy at the court of Federigo da Montefeltro, duke of Urbino (1422–1482), where he created his own distinctive style. The artist's return to his native land in about 1483 marked an important point in the Spanish Renaissance. Working in Ávila and Toledo, Berruguete incorporated Italian and northern European influences into his paintings. Equally important was King Philip II, an avid art collector who was particularly interested in the works of the Italian mannerist Titian (c. 1488–1576; see "Painting" in Chapter 8). Philip covered the walls of his study in the Alcázar, the royal castle at Madrid, with Titian's paintings of nude figures. Beginning in the 1560s, the king erected the famous Escorial, an enormous complex of buildings north of Madrid (see "Architecture" section later in this chapter). To impress the elite in the Italian cultural centers of Florence and Rome, Philip invited a team of Italian painters to decorate the interiors of the rooms. Collaborating with them was the Spanish painter Juan Fernandez de Navarrete (1526–1579), who was called "El Mudo" (the mute). Philip also commissioned the Flemish-trained Spanish painter Alonso Sánchez Coello (c. 1531–1588) to paint formal portraits to hang on the walls. These portraits provided a striking contrast to the exuberant, colorful Italian style of the rooms. Philip's efforts to promote Renaissance culture ensured significant artistic advances in Spain. Yet his commission of a painting by the Greek-born painter El Greco proved to be a disappointment for both the king and the artist.

El Greco displeases king El Greco (1541–1614) began his career in Venice in the 1560s. Born Doménikos Theotokópoulos (pronounced tay-oh-toh-KOH-poo-los) in Crete, he is said to have been a pupil of Titian. During his stay in Italy he became known as Il Greco ("the Greek") because his name was too difficult to pronounce. Later, in Spain, he was called El Greco. Various reasons have been suggested for El Greco's move to Spain. According to one theory, he could no longer find patrons in Italy and he hoped for commissions to work at the Escorial. He knew Philip had been a patron of Titian, who provided several religious compositions for the Escorial as well as mythological pictures and portraits for Philip's art collection.

In 1577 El Greco moved to Toledo in Castile, where he was

Wedding Dance **by Pieter Bruegel the Elder.** *©Francis G. Mayer/Corbis. Reproduced by permission of the Corbis Corporation.*

awarded a commission to paint the *Disrobing of Christ* for the city's cathedral. El Greco merged episodes from different accounts of Christ's Passion (death on the cross) in this picture, and he used a vivid, somewhat abstract painting technique (a technique not based in reality). *Disrobing of Christ* met with much criticism. One complaint was that El Greco had raised the heads of secondary figures above the head of Christ. Refusing to make changes, the painter filed a lawsuit to obtain full payment for his work. Eventually he had to settle for much less money than he had antici-

pated. The main problem was that El Greco embraced the Italian Renaissance concept of the artist as a creative genius who must be given complete freedom. The Spanish audience deemed such an idea unacceptable.

El Greco finally received a commission from King Philip, who selected him as one of the artists to provide altarpieces for the royal church at the Escorial. In 1582 El Greco completed *Martyrdom of St. Maurice and the Theban Legion.* (Martyrdom is defined as suffering death for one's religion.) Philip was displeased with this painting, but he kept it, paying El Greco less than he had requested. The king then ordered a new picture of the same subject from the Italian painter Romulo Cincinnato. Scholars have concluded that Philip was disturbed because El Greco had put portraits of contemporary people in an event from early Christian history. He had also placed the martyrdom scene in the distance and to the left, instead of featuring it as the central focus of the picture. As a result of his innovative methods, El Greco succeeded in alienating two of the most powerful patrons in Spain—the Catholic Church and the king himself—in less than five years.

Promotes Catholic Reformation El Greco returned to Toledo, and by 1585 he had established a successful workshop that produced copies based on his paintings, as well as picture frames and statues. In 1586 he obtained the important commission for *The Burial of the Count of Orgaz* for a chapel in Santo Tome, Toledo. This monumental picture depicts the moment when the heavens opened, and Saints Augustine and Stephen suddenly appeared in order to lower the corpse of the prominent Toledo citizen Gonzalo de Ruiz into his tomb. The fourteenth-century scene is witnessed by late sixteenth-century Toledan aristocrats and church officials. They watch as Gonzalo's soul is lifted by an angel toward God in heaven, which hovers just above them. Gonzalo was renowned for his gifts to the church. The painting declares that good works are needed to

obtain salvation and reveals the power of saints to deliver the soul to God. Both of these doctrines were vigorously disputed by Protestants, who declared that salvation can be gained through faith alone and that saints are false idols. El Greco thus contributed to the Catholic Reformation, which was underway at the time, by asserting the validity of church teachings. He was also known as a great portrait painter with a gift for achieving psychological insights into his subjects. Examples are *Gentleman with His Hand on His Breast* (1579) and the famous *Cardinal Fernando Nino de Guevara* (c. 1600).

El Greco was a learned, well-read, and highly inventive artist who advanced Renaissance ideals in Spain. Yet he had no talented followers, and his style fell out of fashion after his death in 1614. By that time the Renaissance period had come to a close, and the baroque movement, with its emphasis on sensuality and expressiveness, was gaining momentum in Europe.

Sculpture

Germany was the major center for the production of sculpture in northern Europe. Sculptors created religious works such as statues, altarpieces, and tombs to be placed in a growing number of churches. The most popular form of religious art was the altarpiece (a large sculptural work placed above the altar, or the center of worship, in a church). As the number of churches continued to grow, so did the quantity and variety of altarpieces.

Riemenschneider is foremost sculptor

Prior to the Reformation the foremost sculptor in northern Europe was Tilman Riemenschneider (REE-men-shnigh-der; c. 1460–1531), a native of Heilgenstadt, Germany. Little is known about his artistic training, except that he moved to Würzburg around 1479 and joined the Guild of Saint Luke four years later. Riemenschneider enjoyed great success as an artist, especially in Würzburg. Between 1501 and 1517 Riemenschneider supervised twelve apprentices (people being trained), producing mainly altarpieces for churches in the region. Riemenschneider controlled all aspects of altarpiece production, so his large workshop included joiners (artisans who join pieces of wood), sculptors, and painters.

Working in both wood and stone, Riemenschnieder carved large altarpieces, tombs, and epitaphs (inscriptions on tombs), and statues. He chose to stain (apply dye or other pigment) his pieces rather than decorate them with bright-colored paint, a process called polychrome, which had been a tradition during the Middle Ages. Many of Riemenschnieder's creations were destroyed or damaged in the Peasants' War (1524–26) and other upheavals. Riemenschnieder's best-known altarpieces are *Holy Blood* at Saint Jacob's Church in Rothenburg (completed 1505) and *Assumption of the Virgin* (completed 1510) at the Herrgottskirche in Crenlingen. In both works, which stand about thirty feet (nine meters) high, the artist pierced the back wall of the altarpiece to make effective use of light from nearby windows. For instance, in *Holy Blood,* light streaming through the windows behind the Last Supper section heightens the moment when Jesus Christ stares at Judas, the disciple who betrayed him. The brighter illumination also enabled Riemenschneider to draw attention to the apostles' expressions and poses.

Riemenschneider produced at least ten known altarpieces and possibly eleven others that were done in his style. Riemenschneider was quite influential within the Würzburg diocese until 1525, but the future impact of his work was severely limited by the Protestant Reformation and its political upheaval. Virtually no important sculpture was created in Germany between 1520 and 1555 because the Protestant Reformation brought an end to the Renaissance. Protestant reformers did not approve of most Renaissance art, and they prohibited the display of paintings and sculptures in churches. They claimed that such works detracted from the glorification of God. Martin Luther took a moderate position on religious art, and gradually sculptors began depicting images of him.

France and Spain dominated by Italians

Sculpture in France was dominated by Italians. Among the most influential was Francesco Primaticcio (1504–1570). In 1545 he completed stucco statues of elegant nude figures in the room of Anne de Pisseleu, duchesse d'Estampes (1508–c. 1580) at the royal château Fontainebleau. (For a description of Fontainebleau, see "Architecture" section later in this chapter). Important early French sculptors were Jean Goujon (c. 1510–1568) and Germain Pilon (1535–1590). Goujon made reliefs (raised images on a flat surface) of nymphs for the Fountain of the Innocents, which can now be viewed in the Louvre Museum in Paris. Pilon used images that were characteristic of Italian Renaissance style. For instance, in *Gisants* (the term for the deceased reclining just after death), which decorated the tomb of King Henry II (1519–1559; ruled 1547–59) and Queen Catherine de Médicis (1519–1589), he depicted idealized likenesses of the French monarchs. This portrayal was a contrast to the late Gothic (early fifteenth century) style, which showed the dead in a state of decay. Italian influences can be seen in the rich sculptural decor of the upper story of French architect Pierre Lescot's Louvre Court (see "Architecture" section later in this chapter).

As in France, Spanish sculpture was dominated by foreign masters for most of the Renaissance. During the fifteenth century masters came mainly from Flanders and Burgundy. When Spanish artists began returning from Italy in the sixteenth century, Italian influences became stronger. Sculptors worked closely with architects in designing columns, doorjambs, and window frames, and especially the retablo, an ornamental high altar that is the most distinctive Iberian (the Spanish and Portuguese peoples) feature of church architecture. The Spanish sculptors Bartolomé Ordoñez (died 1520) and Diego de Siloé (c. 1495–1563) first

collaborated in the early 1500s in Naples, which was ruled by Spain at the time. They created the decorative details for the church of San Giovanni a Carbonara, which was completed in 1516. Siloé and Ordoñez then took their innovative style back to Spain. From 1517 to 1520 Ordoñez produced the spectacular tombs of the Capilla Real, the royal chapel in the Cathedral of Granada. He also created monuments for Spanish monarchs Ferdinand II of Aragon, Isabella I of Castile, Philip I (1478–1506), and Joan I (1479–1555). The free-standing figures in these works reflect the influence of the great Italian sculptor Michelangelo (see "Sculpture" in Chapter 8). Siloé and Juan de Juni (c. 1507–1577) continued using Italian techniques for the rest of the century. Alonso Berruguete (1488–1561) worked as both a painter and a sculptor in the elaborate and highly expressive mannerist (late Renaissance) style introduced by Italian artists (see "Renaissance art" in Chapter 8). He had adopted these techniques during his visit to Italy from about 1504 to 1518, when he met Michelangelo and the art historian Giorgio Vasari (1511–1574).

Architecture

The French château was the major contribution to northern Euorpean architecture during the Renaissance. A château is a large country house, or mansion, that was the residence of the royalty and the nobility. Many châteaux had been built as fortified castles in the Gothic style from the twelfth century into the sixteenth century. During the reign of King Louis XII the châteaux of Blois, Amboise, and Gallion were remodeled. Under King Francis I more châteaux, both royal and noble, were built—Chambord, Azay-le-Rideay, Écouen, and Madrid (now destroyed)—and Blois was further renovated. Chambord, which was completed in 1540, was built on the plan of a medieval castle, with an elaborate roof that features dormers (projecting windows on sloping roofs), towers, and turrets (small towers).

King Francis imports Italian Renaissance Francis's most famous project was the expansion and renovation of the château of Fontainebleau, located outside of Paris. Starting in 1528, the king attempted to use Fontainebleau as a way to bring the Italian Renaissance into France. He was motivated by his defeat in a crucial phase of the Italian Wars (1494–1559), a conflict between France and Spain over control of Italy (see "Italian Wars dominate Renaissance" in Chapter 2). Francis had had some initial successes in the war, but in 1525 he lost the Battle of Pavia in Italy and was taken captive. After being imprisoned in Spain for about a year, he returned to Paris and decided to "conquer" Italy by bringing its culture into France. He had already made a start earlier, in 1517, when he persuaded the great Italian artist Leonardo da Vinci (1452–1519) to retire to France (see "Painting" in Chapter 8). The king also had agents in Italy collecting books, medals, antiquities, modern paintings and sculptures, and reproductions of numerous pieces of antique sculpture.

Francis was given an opportunity to promote his cultural campaign in 1527, when the army of Holy Roman Emperor Charles V sacked, or raided, Rome. Italian artists, who had been part of the flourishing culture of Rome, no longer had jobs, and they were quite willing to travel to France. Francis therefore set out to incorporate Italian style into French culture by employing Italian artists for the Fontainebleau project. Many of the workers were also French and Flemish. The Italian artists brought with them the highly ornamental mannerist style, which was then popular in Italy. It was easily adapted to the flamboyant Gothic features of Fontainebleau. The most influential artists were the painters Giovanni Battista di Jacopo Rosso (known as Il Rosso Fiorentino) and Francesco Primaticcio. They were responsible for decorating the apartments of Fontainebleau with frescoes (wall paintings made by applying paint over a thin layer of damp lime plaster).

Fontainebleau promotes king's image The most notable accomplishment at Fontainebleau was the Galerie François I, which was completed in the 1530s by numerous artists working under Rosso's direction. It is considered one of the finest works of mannerist art outside Italy. The gallery was decorated with large narrative frescoes and other details such as fresco medallions and friezes, stucco reliefs (raised images on a flat background), and woodwork. The frescoes depict mythological stories and allegories (symbolic stories) featuring Francis himself in both violent action and solemn rituals. For the gallery Rosso invented stucco "strapwork," a curving, leather-like ornamental detail. Strapwork had a strong influence on art when engravers made copies of Rosso's designs and distributed prints throughout northern Europe.

The abundant ornamentation of Fontainebleau promoted Francis's image of himself as a powerful and cultured monarch. This abundance was also evident in Primaticcio's stucco decorations for the chamber of the duchess of Étampes, the king's mistress (a woman who has a sexual relationship with a married man). The chamber is decorated with delicate female forms, fruits, and putti (figures of small children). Primaticcio used similar decorations elsewhere at Fontainebleau, including the Galerie d'Ulysse, the ballroom, and the baths—most of which have been destroyed. The use of stucco by both Rosso and Primaticcio had an influence on Italian interior design.

French classicism emerges Gradually, French architecture began to incorporate Italian classical features such as columns, arcaded loggias (open porches called galleries with roofs supported by arches), and squared windows and doorways. This led to the style called French classical. In the 1540s the Italian architect Sebastiano Serlio (1475–1554) visited Fontainebleau and developed a new kind of column. Spaced at intervals along the length of the column were rusticated (roughened)

stone rings, a style that was widely imitated in France. Other characteristics of the French style were experiments with staircases and with ornamental brickwork.

The height of sixteenth-century French classicism was reached with the remodeling of the Cour Carrée (square court) château during the reign of King Henry II. The building was renamed the Louvre, which is now a museum and the remodeling was designed by the French architect Pierre Lescot (c. 1515–1578). Lescot expanded the original structure by adding new wings (extensions) that had classical features as well as typical French slate-covered roofing. He also used a pitched roof, large windows, double-columned pavilions, and abundant decorative detail. These became standard design elements in later châteaux.

Along with Lescot, France's most important architect of the period was Philibert de l'Orme (also known as Delorme; c. 1515–1570). His most famous work was the château of Anet, which is still standing today. Anet was built for Diane de Poitiers (1499–1566), mistress of Henry II, after she fell from favor upon the king's death in 1559. De l'Orme is also known for his writings on architecture, *Nouvelles inventions pour bien bastir à petits frais* (New inventions for building well at little cost; 1561) and *Architecture* (1567). In these works he sought to develop a French style of architecture based on classical theories and practical building techniques.

The Retablo

The Iberian Renaissance was characterized by a close relationship between architecture and sculpture. This union can be seen in the most distinctively Iberian feature of church architecture, the retablo, or ornamental high altar. Originating in the Middle Ages, the retablo was a huge construction that often included paintings, sculpture, and architecture depicting up to sixty sacred scenes. By the time of the Renaissance, retablos could extend all the way from floor to ceiling and had become extremely ornate, covered with intricate carvings and loaded with paintings and statues. As tastes shifted from elaborate Gothic detail to simpler Renaissance forms, retablos were adapted to the plasteresco style. The most beautiful examples, both in Spain and Portugal, were plasteresco altars created for cathedrals. Even though these high altars were considerably less ornate, they still provided a riot of decoration. An example was the retablo of San Lorenzo at the Escorial, which was constructed according to a severely proper design by the great Spanish architect Juan de Herrera. It features brilliantly colored paintings by Italian artists, gilded statues, and colored marble columns. The popularity of the retablo tempted painters like El Greco to try their hand at sculpture with trained stonecarvers and metalsmiths.

Spain and Portugal introduce new styles The first Renaissance buildings appeared on the Iberian Peninsula in the late fifteenth century. Many Spanish buildings were constructed in a style called *plasteresco*. Plasteresco combined Gothic features, such as spires, decorated window frames, and pointed arches, with Renaissance classical details, such as portals (entryways) with columns and rounded arches. Examples are the Medinaceli Palace in Cogolludo (completed 1409), the Palacio de Cogolludo, and the University of Salamanca (completed 1494). In Portugal the architect Diogo Boytac (died before 1528) developed the style known as "Manuelino," named for King Manuel I (1469–1521; ruled 1495–1521). Like Spanish architecture, Manuelino combined decorative Gothic elements with simple Renaissance classical lines. A distinctive feature of Portuguese Renaissance architecture was the use of ornamental tiles known as azulejos to decorate facades, floors, and fountains. Two spectacular sixteenth-century tiled buildings can still be seen today. They are the Quinta de Bacalhoa at Azeitão (1565) and the church of São Roque by Francisco de Matos (1584) at Coimbra.

Herrera completes Escorial The most famous architect of sixteenth-century Spain was Juan de Herrera (c. 1530–1597). He had no formal training, but he probably acquired practical knowledge of architecture while serving in the army in the mid-1550s. Herrera began his architectural career as an assistant to Juan Bautista de Toledo (died 1567). Toledo was the architect who designed San Lorenzo el Real del Escorial (called the Escorial) for King Philip II. The Escorial contained a mausoleum (building that houses tombs) for the Habsburgs (Philip's family line), a monastery and church, and a royal residence. Soon after Toledo's death in 1463, Herrera took over construction of the Escorial, which he completed in 1584. Herrera's main contribution to the project was the church, the Basilica of San Lorenzo el Real.

Herrera was involved in a number of other architectural projects. Among them were the royal palaces at Aranjuez, the Alcázar in Toledo, and the palace of Emperor Charles V in the Alhambra at Granada. He also created designs for the rebuilding of the cathedral at Valladolid, considered one of his greatest achievements. In addition, he was involved in designing town halls in Toledo and Valladolid, and he planned the Merchant's Exchange in Seville. He constructed water systems for the Escorial and Valladolid, built bridges, and worked as a city planner. Herrera was a true Renaissance man, excelling in numerous professions—architecture, engineering, writing, philosophy, and mathematics. He gained favor with King Philip, with whom he shared a preference for architecture that eliminated ornament and emphasized simple geometry. Nevertheless, Herrera's

designs had little influence in other countries because Spanish architecture was still culturally isolated from the rest of Europe.

Jones brings Renaissance to England
English architecture was strongly influenced by the designer Inigo Jones (1573–1652). Considered the first professional architect in England, he was responsible for introducing Italian Renaissance architecture into the country. During a stay in Italy in the early 1600s he observed the buildings of Andrea Palladio (1508–1580), one of the major architects of the late Renaissance (see "Architecture" in Chapter 8). A series of villas (country houses) built in Italy during the 1550s and 1560s represent the model that is associated with Palladio. All of these villas have a vaulted *sala,* or central hall, that can be square, rectangular, or in the shape of a cross or the letter "T." A row of rooms lines each side of the *sala,* and the facade (front) has a Greco-Roman temple portico (a portico is a type of porch, in this case designed in a Roman style influenced by the Greeks). Palladio's theories and designs had a profound effect on Jones. In 1615 King James I appointed Jones surveyor of the king's works, which was essentially chief architect to the king. Jones also held this position under Charles I until 1642, when the outbreak of the civil war between the Puritans and supporters of the monarchy disrupted court life. During the reigns of both monarchs Jones also designed and produced elaborate theatrical festivals called court masques. The

masques allowed him to use his imagination in ways that were not possible with his sober architectural designs.

Jones designed many architectural projects, some of them vast in scale. Only seven buildings actually executed from his designs remain, and most of them have been altered or restored. The earliest of Jones's surviving buildings is the Queen's House at Greenwich, a project he undertook for Queen Anne, wife of James I, in 1616. The lower floor was completed at the time the Queen died in 1619. Work then stopped but was resumed in 1630 for Queen Henrietta Maria, Charles I's wife, and was completed in 1635. The building is marked by a symmetrical plan, simplicity of classical detail, harmonious proportions, and severe purity of line. All of these elements reflect Italian Renaissance influences and at the time represented significant architectural innovation to the English.

Designs Banqueting House The building now most associated with Jones is the Banqueting House at Whitehall (completed 1622), which was intended to serve as a setting for state functions. The building clearly shows the influence of Palladio. The main facade consists of seven bays (main divisions) and two stories gracefully unified in an elegant, rational pattern of classical columns and pilasters, lightly rusticated stone, and understated carved ornamentation. The interior is simply designed. In 1635 the ceiling was decorated with rich paintings by the Flemish artist Peter Paul Rubens,

English architecture was strongly influenced by designer Inigo Jones. *Engraving after the painting by Anthony Van Dyck. Photograph courtesy of The Library of Congress.*

which provide a dramatic contrast to the classical style of the interior.

Jones also developed the design for the Queen's Chapel, Marlborough Gate (completed 1627), the first church structure in England in the classical style. In 1631 Jones became associated with a city planning project in the Covent Garden district of London. He designed Saint Paul's Church, which still exists in a restored condition. It was built in the form of a classical temple with a deep portico and severe Tuscan columns. Between 1634 and 1642

Jones was occupied with extensive restoration of the old Saint Paul's Cathedral (now destroyed). From about 1638 he was also involved in preparing designs for a vast palace planned by Charles I, but it was not built.

In 1642 the conflict between Parliament and the king erupted in open warfare that swept away the elegant court of Charles I. Jones's world disappeared along with it. He undertook his last important work in 1649, when he and his assistant, John Webb (1611–1672), provided designs for the Double- and Single-Cube Rooms at Wilton House. Wilton House was completed in 1652, the year of Jones's death.

Entertainment

During the Renaissance the most popular forms of entertainment among the upper classes were music and the court masque.

Music

Throughout the Renaissance, the Low Countries were the birthplace of many major composers as well as a vast number of lesser-known musicians who wrote works that were performed in the chapels, churches, and cathedrals of Europe, particularly in France and Italy. No single reason can fully explain the large number of composers and musicians originating in the Low Countries, but several factors contributed to it. The Low Countries had choir schools associated with churches and large cathedrals. Comparable institutions were not nearly so prevalent elsewhere in Europe. In these schools choirboys learned the art of singing, and the more talented ones received their first lessons in music composition. Music masters from the Low Countries traveled throughout Europe training musicians and composers. For instance, the great Italian composers Giovanni Palestrina (c. 1525–1594) and Claudio Monteverdi (1567–1643) were trained by masters from the Low Countries (see "Music" in Chapter 8). Another important factor was patronage. The dukes of Burgundy and later the Habsburg emperors were important patrons of music who spent large sums of money on singers, composers, instrumentalists, and music books. As the Low Countries grew in prosperity, smaller churches were able to support modest chapels. Towns hired trumpeters and wind bands, and the increasingly larger middle class could afford to promote music through guilds (professional trade and artisan organizations) and confraternities (religious organizations for lay people).

Equally significant was the printing of music. Many of the large cities of the Low Countries had a room called a scriptorium where manuscripts were produced. The most important were such rooms in the court of Margaret of Austria in the Netherlands and Holy Roman Emperor Charles V in Brussels and Mechlin. The first successful music press in the Low Countries was founded by Tylman Susato (c. 1500–1564) in Antwerp in 1543. Over a period of eighteen years

Susato published at least fifty-seven books of music, including chansons (types of French songs), motets (choral music based on sacred texts), masses (music for Catholic worship services), psalms (sacred songs), and dances. During the Reformation the singing of psalms in native languages became important in all Protestant countries. The first Dutch psalter (psalm book) was published in 1540 by Symon Cock in Antwerp. Known as *Souterliedekens,* these psalms were set to popular tunes, mostly Dutch folk songs but also some French and German folk songs. They were meant for singing at home. Later composers produced polyphonic (music with harmonizing parts) versions of the *Souterliedekens.*

Composers set trends Several major composers emerged in the Low Countries during the early Renaissance period. Among them were Johannes Cicona and Guillaume Dufay. Cicona was probably born in the 1370s and was a choirboy in Liège (in present-day Belgium), but he spent most of his adult career in northern Italy. He thus set a precedent followed by many other Renaissance composers who were trained in one country and pursued careers in other countries. Cicona combined aspects of the complex musical styles of fourteenth-century France and Italy. The principal forms at this time were motets, masses, and three types of chansons: ballade, rondeau, and virelai. Dufay was a choirboy at Cambrai (in present-day France) from 1409 until at least 1414, then spent much of his early career in Italy. He served at the papal court and the court of Savoy before returning to Cambrai in 1439. Dufay integrated Cicona's music with three-part works of English composers Leonal Power (died 1445) and John Dustable (c. 1390–1453). Dufay's innovations became the standard in Europe for the rest of the fifteenth century. It was the starting point for other composers, who transformed his style to suit their own purposes. Among them was Johannes Ockeghem (c. 1410–1497), who spent part of his career in Antwerp and Moulins before joining the French royal court. He expanded the concept of music by giving nearly equal prominence to each voice in a polyphonic work.

Josquin des Prez (c. 1450–1521) was one of the most important musical figures of the Renaissance. He may have been born in Condé-sur-l'Escaut in Hainault, where he retired after a career at courts in France and Italy between the late 1470s and 1504. Some of his technical innovations include a closer relationship between words and music and the use of imitation (repetition by one voice of a melody sung by another voice). He and his contemporaries in the Low Countries were sought after in courts and churches throughout Europe. During this generation the mass and motet were of greater interest to composers, and chansons ceased to be limited to the ballade, rondeau, and virelai.

The so-called post-Josquin generation was also dominated by composers from the Low Countries. Adrian Willaert (c. 1490–1562), born in Bruges or Roulaers, spent most of his career in

Orlando di Lasso

Orlando di Lasso (1532–1594) was a Franco-Flemish composer who wrote more than one thousand compositions. Although he did not compose instrumental music, he excelled in all musical forms of his day—motets, masses, magnificats (music based on the song of the Virgin Mary in the book of Luke), madrigals, and songs (short compositions of words and music). The most famous and admired composer in Europe in the late sixteenth century, Lasso was hailed early in his career as "prince of music" and "le divin Orlande" (divine Orlando). He was known for his talent for expressing the meaning of words in music. In fact, his music can be understood only in the context of the words that it so vividly presents. He accomplished this by a variety of means, sometimes through sudden changes in rhythm, melody, or harmony. Lasso rarely experimented with the latest musical trends, so by the end of his life his style was overtaken by newer techniques. Nevertheless, he was the first great composer whose fame was spread by printed music. During his lifetime and soon after his death more than six hundred publications featured his music. That is, between 1555 and 1595 a composition by Lasso appeared in print on the average of once a month in France, Italy, the Low Countries, or the German empire.

Italy. He worked in Ferrara and then as choirmaster at Saint Mark's in Venice. Nicolas Gombert (c. 1495–1560), a native of Flanders, served at the chapel of Emperor Charles V. Thomas Crecquillon (c. 1480–1557) also worked for the emperor and served in Béthune and Louvain. These composers and their contemporaries continued the innovations of Josquin, particularly his use of imitation and his attention to the relationship between text and music. The madrigal, an Italian vocal music form that first appeared in the 1520s, was dominated for some time by composers from the Low Countries working in Italy.

Although there were several important composers from the Low Countries during the Renaissance, their dominance had essentially passed by the end of the sixteenth century. The most prominent, Orlando di Lasso (1532–1594), was born in Mons, but he spent most of his career in Italy and at the chapel of Charles V. A far more dramatic composer than his Italian contemporary Palestrina, Lasso wrote in every musical form and in a wide variety of styles. He was committed to the idea that music should heighten and convey the meaning of a text.

Court masque

The masque was a popular form of court entertainment, especially in Italy, France, and England, during the Renaissance. Sovereigns and courtiers wearing masks participated in this dazzling spectacle, which was organized around allegorical or mythological themes. The performance usually took place in the evening and involved music, ballet, and spoken parts. It required fantastic costumes, complex stage machinery, and brilliant stage settings. The masque was customarily performed as part of Christmas festivities, or else staged to mark significant state occasions. Today the masque is most closely associated with the reign of King James I of England and is often called the Jacobean court masque.

The premier English masque designer and producer was Inigo Jones (see "Architecture" section previously in this chapter), who served as surveyor of the king's works during the reigns of both James and Charles I. Between 1605 and 1640 Jones worked on at least twenty-five of these productions. James's queen, Anne of Denmark (1574–1619), was devoted to lavish entertainment and to the masques, and the tradition was continued in the reign of Charles I. Hundreds of Jones's drawings for the costumes and stage designs still exist. None would have been possible without his knowledge of Italian art and draftsmanship.

Scripts for masques were written by playwrights such as Ben Jonson (see "Literature" section previously in this chapter), Thomas Campion (1587–1620), and George Chapman (c. 1559–1634). The script writers faced a complex task. Central to all masques was the entry of disguised courtiers who performed a series of choreographed (composed and arranged) dances. After this formal presentation the courtiers selected members of the audience to participate in social dances, called "revels," that occupied most of the evening. The first step, then, was to construct a narrative that might explain the masquers' arrival. Consequently, the masque "plot" often referred to visitors arriving to pay homage to, or show respect for, the monarch. At the same time, this device had to be appropriate to the particular occasion of the performance or meet the demands of a certain patron. Masques also provided a way of displaying the magnificence of the court to an audience that frequently included foreign ambassadors (representatives of governments). Above all, it was essential that the masque praise the monarch, who was the most important spectator.

An example of a playwright's response to such demands was *The Masque of Queens,* which Jonson wrote in 1609. For this masque Queen Anne suggested that her entrance be preceded by a "false masque," called an antimasque. Jonson then provided an antimasque of witches to set against the "good Fame" that was represented by the queen and her ladies. After 1609 the antimasque, usually performed by professional actors, became a permanent part of the masque. Thus masques presented a moral debate by having the antimasque figures of evil, deceit, or trickery symbolize the opposite of the heroic virtues embodied by the principal masquers. For Jonson the masque was a learned, moral, and instructive form of drama. Although not everyone shared his view. To many critics the masque seemed to symbolize the extravagance rather than the magnificence of the court. Nevertheless, the masque made a significant contribution to theater by adopting the latest musical fashions and introducing complex stage machinery and elaborate sets.

Science |

A scientific revolution occurred during the Renaissance and Reformation when humanist scholars took a renewed interest in the work of ancient philosophers. Greek texts in particular were given updated translations and interpretations. Scientists then developed new theories that eventually replaced the Greek concepts that had dominated science for almost two thousand years. Science became a separate field from philosophy (a search to define values and reality through reason and thought rather than scientific observation) and technology (the application of practical knowledge, such as engineering), which had been the major areas of thought in ancient times. An even more important development was that science now had a practical function. For instance, scientists were asking *how* things happened in nature, whereas the ancients were mainly concerned with *why* things happened. This shift in thinking had a profound impact on all aspects of life, and by the end of the 1600s science had replaced Christianity as the center of European civilization.

Aristotle influences science

The works of the Greek philosopher Aristotle (384–322 B.C.) were especially popular among fifteenth- and sixteenth-century scientists. Aristotle was a student of the Greek philosopher Plato (c. 428–c. 348 B.C.), whose academy he attended for twenty years. Aristotle then founded his own school of philosophy, the Lyceum, near Athens, a Greek city-state. Aristotle preferred to teach while strolling around the school, and his students followed along. For this reason members of the Lyceum were called Peripatetics, a name that came from the Greek word for "walking about."

Both Plato and Aristotle had a strong influence on European culture in the Middle Ages. Plato was favored by early Christians because of his teachings on the human soul (eternal spirit) and creation. Aristotle surpassed Plato in the twelfth and thirteenth centuries when his long-lost works on the arts and sciences became available in Latin translations. Aristotle's writings filled several hundred scrolls (rolls of long strips of parchment), which were divided into three classes. The first were notes to aid the memory and prepare for further work, but all of these have been lost. The second were written for the general reading public, in dialogue (question and answer, or conversation) form. They included titles such as *On Philosophy, On Justice,* and *On Ideas.* Only fragments of these works survive, though some idea of their contents can be gained from comments made by later Greek and Roman scholars.

The third class consisted of treatises written in a brief, direct style meant for school use. The surviving works of Aristotle belong to this class.

Pioneered classification Aristotle was a pioneer in the systematic classification of all fields of knowledge. He considered the ideal form of knowledge to be science, which he defined as universal and necessary knowledge gained through analyzing the causes of things. According to Aristotle, one type of science starts with things that are known and its only aim is to acquire knowledge. He called this theoretical science and gave it three divisions: natural, mathematical, and divine. For Aristotle, another kind of science starts with the person who gains knowledge, and it is aimed at either taking action or making something. If the goal involves human action or conduct, he called it practical science. If the goal involves something to be made, he called it productive science.

For Aristotle the first theoretical science is natural philosophy, which is concerned with the examination of nature. He investigated topics such as chance, motion, the infinite, place, the void, and time. He also studied the soul and its powers. For Aristotle the second theoretical science is mathematics. It is concerned with numbers, lines, surfaces, and solids, which can be understood through a process of abstraction (formulation of ideas). He also described "mixed sciences," which apply mathematics to the study of natural things.

Among the mixed sciences are optics (geometric study of light), astronomy (study of celestial bodies, such as planets, stars, the Sun, and the Moon), and mechanics. The third theoretical science is metaphysics, or the study of the nature of reality and existence.

Aristotle's practical sciences, also called moral philosophy, include ethics (a field that tries to define good and bad behavior) and politics (guiding or influencing government policy). The subject matter of the practical sciences is human conduct, and the aim is to achieve the good, which can be described as the mean, or midpoint, between excessive behavior and lax behavior. The good can be achieved through sound judgment of the prudent person. To be prudent, a person needs the moral virtues of moderation, courage, and justice. Such virtues, in Aristotle's view, have to be instilled in young children through correct education. Good laws and customs are all-important for this process. Also essential are good health, good fortune, sufficient riches, and friends, all of which make possible a life of contemplation (concentration on spiritual matters). For Aristotle, the life of contemplation is the highest human activity, for it alone produces happiness. According to his view, the best form of government aims at the common good of all people, not the needs of a particular class, and provides conditions in which happiness can be achieved.

Aristotle discussed productive sciences in his treatises on poetics (theory of poetry) and rhetoric (effective speaking and writing). In a work titled *Poetics* he stated that the role of the poet (artist) is to create a representation of nature (humans and their world) through a process he called *mimesis* (the Greek word for imitation). To explain the function of mimesis Aristotle focused on tragedy, an ancient form of dramatic presentation that traces the rise and fall of a great man. According to Aristotle, tragedy is the ideal imitation of human experience because it enables spectators to release their own emotions of pity and fear by vicariously (through imagination or sympathy) participating in the events of the drama. In his *Rhetoric* he examined the nature of a persuasive argument in terms of appeals to logic (thought or argument based on reason), the emotions, and ethics. He then showed how to present a persuasive argument through proper delivery, style, and composition.

Almagest is basis of astronomy

Renaissance science was also influenced by the Egyptian scholar Ptolemy (Claudius Ptolemaeus; A.D. c. 100–c. 170), who wrote on astronomy, geography (study of the physical and cultural features of Earth's surface), optics, and related sciences. Little is known about Ptolemy's life. Most of what is known about him comes from his own works and some ancient texts. Since his name was derived from both Latin (Claudius) and Egyptian (Ptolemy), he probably came from a mixed family. He wrote his best-known work, the *Almagest,* around 150. Since he produced several other major works after the *Almagest,* he probably lived into the reign of Roman emperor Marcus Aurelius (died 180). Ptolemy appears to have spent his whole life in Alexandria, Egypt.

Ptolemy's views on the heavens are developed primarily in the *Almagest,* his masterpiece of mathematical astronomy. Originally called the *Mathematical Syntaxis* (Mathematical compilation) in Greek, the work was given the medieval Arabic title *al-majisti,* which became *almagesti* or *almagestum* in medieval Latin. The Latin form produced the title *Almagest.*

The *Almagest* is written in thirteen books, covering all aspects of mathematical astronomy as it was understood in antiquity. To attain knowledge of the universe, Ptolemy argued, one must study astronomy because it leads to the Prime Mover, the first cause of all heavenly motions—that is, God. Ptolemy followed earlier Greek thinkers such as Aristotle, who believed that Earth is the center of a perfectly balanced universe. Ptolemy argued that the universe has a spherical shape and that stars and planets move in spherical patterns. He also contended that Earth is spherical and remains in a fixed position at the center of the universe. However, its size is insignificant in comparison to the heavens.

Revived ancient theory In the *Almagest* Ptolemy also dealt with problems that had been puzzling mathematical astronomers. For instance, he discarded Aristotle's idea that Earth is at the exact center of the orbits (paths)

of all heavenly bodies. Instead, he adopted the ancient Greek concept that heavenly bodies revolve around Earth in eccentric (not exactly centered) circles. Early Greek astronomers had introduced this idea to explain why the seasons of the year are not of the same length. Thinking that the Sun revolved around Earth, they drew diagrams of the universe that showed the Sun moving in a circle that was not exactly centered on Earth. Thus they were able to determine that some seasons were longer than others because the Sun was farther away from Earth at certain times of the year. Another problem was that the planets appeared to stop at some point as they move around Earth and then go backward before proceeding once again on their circular orbits. To account for this, the early astronomers drew diagrams that placed the planets on little circles known as epicycles, which they then placed on big circles called deferents. As the deferents moved, they carried the epicycles with them. Consequently, from the vantage point of Earth, during this process a planet would appear to stop and go backward for a time before continuing in its proper circular orbit.

In the *Almagest,* Ptolemy introduced the concept of the equant point, which he combined with eccentric circles, epicycles, and deferents. The equant point was located at the exact center of an eccentric circle, which was also a deferent—that is, it was a large circle on which epicycles, or small circles, moved around Earth. By combining all these devices, Ptolemy managed to create mathematical models that fit very well with observations of heavenly bodies. His system was the basis for mathematical astronomy until the publication of Nicolaus Copernicus's *On the Revolutiom of the Heavenly Spheres* in 1543 (see "Astronomy" section later in this chapter).

Scientific method

The ancient Greeks introduced the concept of following a particular order, or method, to study nature or solve an abstract problem. Interest in method was revived during the Renaissance, when it was combined with the new science to produce the idea of the "scientific method."

The Greek teaching on method originated with the medical writer Hippocrates of Cos (c. 460–c. 377 B.C.). It is described in Plato's *Phaedrus* as a technique of dividing and collecting ideas or things that are observed. Out of this grew Plato's "dialectical method," which consisted of four stages: analysis, definition, division, and probative. These stages were closely associated with art. Aristotle extended Plato's idea to all rational investigation, not merely that of the arts. For the sciences, which aimed at precise and certain knowledge, Aristotle wrote the *Analytics* to provide detailed methods of analysis and definition. A further influence came from the Greek physician Galen (129–c. 199), who accepted Aristotle's ideas but took inspiration also from Hippocrates and Plato. Galen focused first on analysis, then on synthesis (combination), and associated both with definition and division. The Egyptian mathematician Pappus (after 300–350) likewise wrote on methods, though he confined his attention to geometry. His account influenced Renaissance mathematicians. Finally, Greek scholars who studied Aristotle were a major source of renewed interest in method. Many of them also accepted the views of Plato, so they set out to incorporate the four dialectical methods of Plato with Aristotle's various logical teachings.

Galileo expands method

Renaissance writers of texts in classical Latin never stressed method to the same extent as the Greeks. Instead, they concentrated on order. For instance, the Italian philosopher Jacopo Zabarella (1533–1589) stated that order means simply that one thing should be learned before another. In contrast, method means that what is known first will lead to or produce a second stage of scientific knowledge. Zabarella influenced the great Italian astronomer Galileo Galilei (called Galileo;1564–1642; see "Astronomy" section later in this chapter), who expanded on Zabarella's concepts. The clearest account of Galileo's ideas is found in *Logical Treatises*. Drawing upon Zabarella's work, Galileo developed a twofold process of scientific investigation. The first part involves using reason to determine the cause of something. The second part goes in reverse to determine the effect of a specific action (cause). Operating between these two processes is the intellect (rational thought), also

English philosopher Frances Bacon stressed the practical aspects of science in his book titled *Novum organum*.

bodies. He also went beyond Zabarella's theory to cover probable reasoning—the conclusion that, on the basis of specific observations, certain conditions must exist. Using this form of reasoning, Galileo concluded that the tides (regular rising and falling of oceans and other bodies of water) are a probable cause of the motion of Earth.

Practical science stressed

Scientific method in the Renaissance also was influenced by the French philosopher Petrus Ramus (Pierre de La Ramée; 1515–1572) and the English philosopher Francis Bacon (1561–1626). Ramus was an educational reformer and humanist who reacted against the Aristotelian logic he had been taught at the University of Paris. Ramus especially wished to revive the mathematical arts of arithmetic, geometry, astronomy, and physics (the science that deals with energy and matter and their interactions). He wanted to show that they could be put to practical uses. He thought Aristotle's theories on physics were too complicated for educational purposes. Ramus recommended starting with Aristotle's works on mechanical problems and meteorology (study of weather patterns) and biology (study of living organisms and their processes). He also thought classical texts on mathematics and natural history should be part of the university curriculum. He placed great emphasis on method, but what he meant by this was more a method of teaching than of conducting scientific study.

mentioned by Zabarella, which will assure that the proper conclusions about cause and effect are reached. As explained by Zabarella, the result of this third step is a unique form of knowledge called *scientia* (science).

Galileo expanded Zabarella's third stage by including geometrical reasoning and experimentation. Galileo claimed he achieved scientific results in this third stage by making the first detailed observations of the mountains on the Moon, the satellites (celestial bodies that orbit a larger body) of Jupiter, and the laws of falling

Bacon was also interested in educational reform, and he stressed the practical aspects of science. Despite being a contemporary of Galileo and other founders of modern science, he knew little of their achievements. Instead, he based his ideas on classical sources and his contributions to science were limited to theories he described in his books. Bacon himself did not make scientific observations or conduct experiments. Like Ramus, he felt that Aristotle's system was not suited to discovery of new truth. Bacon also rejected Plato's ideas because they turned the mind inward upon itself, "away from observation and away from things." Bacon proposed a new method that emphasized "the commerce of the mind with things." Science was to be experimental, to take note of how human activity produces changes in things and not merely to record what happens independently of what men do. Bacon called this "active science." In addition, science should be a practical instrument for human betterment. His views are best summed up in the section of *Novum organum* (New method) titled "The New Philosophy or Active Science." Bacon stated that a scientist must make observations of the natural world and then base reports and interpretations only upon these feelings. A scientist cannot know anything more about nature than what he or she discovers through direct observation.

Bacon introduces new method The most important work by Bacon was *Novum organum* published in 1620.

The foundation of Bacon's science was to be natural history, which would serve as the base of a "ladder of axioms." (An axiom is a statement accepted as being true.) At the top of the ladder would be physics, which in turn would lead to metaphysics, or a form of physics that could be applied to all aspects of nature. Both physics and metaphysics would then provide explanations for causes of things in the natural world. To explain his theories, Bacon developed a set of tables that would assist in a process known as "Baconian induction," which involved observing specific facts of nature and reaching general conclusions based on those facts. Bacon's new method was never completely successful. However, his emphasis on experimentation set an ideal for the Royal Society—founded in England in 1660—one of the most prestigious scientific institutions in the world.

Astronomy

At the beginning of the Renaissance astronomy was linked, as it had been since ancient times, with cosmology and astrology. It did not develop into a separate scientific field until the late seventeenth century. Cosmology is the study of the nature of the universe as an ordered structure. Cosmology is closely allied with philosophy and theology (the study of religious faith, practice, and experience). Astrology is the "science" of the influences of heavenly bodies on earthly matters, including the lives and fortunes of humans. Astronomy is the study of the number, size, and motions of heavenly bodies. Some of the most famous Renaissance views of the universe, such as infinity (unlimited time and space), were developed not by astronomers but by philosophers and theologians. These ideas were then incorporated into astronomy.

Copernicus starts scientific revolution

The scientific revolution began in astronomy, with the work of Polish theologian Nicolaus Copernicus (1473–1543), Danish astronomer Tycho Brahe (1546–1601), German mathematician Johannes Kepler (1571–1630), and Galileo.

Copernicus had a life-long career as a canon (clergyman at a cathedral) in the Roman Catholic Church, pursuing the study of astronomy in his spare time. He graduated from the University of Cracow in Poland in 1494. Although he did not attend any classes in astronomy, he began to collect books on astronomy and mathematics during his student years. In 1496 Copernicus was appointed a canon in Frauenburg (now Frombork), Germany. Shortly after arriving at Frauenburg, he set out for Bologna, Italy, to study canon (church) law. In Bologna, he came under the influence of the astronomer Domenico Maria de Novara and recorded the positions of some planets. He did the same in Rome, where he spent the Jubilee Year of 1500. (A jubilee, occurring every twenty-five years, is a time of special

solemnity declared by the pope, head of the Roman Catholic Church.)

In 1503 Copernicus earned the degree of doctor in canon law, then studied medicine in Padua until 1506. After returning to Frauenburg, Copernicus began mulling over the problems of astronomy, and the concept of the heliocentric (Sun-centered) system of planets in particular. He outlined the system in a short manuscript, known as the *Commentariolus* (Small commentary), which he completed in about 1512. At the outset of this work Copernicus listed seven axioms, each of which stated a feature of the heliocentric system. The third and most controversial axiom stated that since all planets revolve on orbits around the Sun, the Sun must therefore be the center of the universe. This idea was controversial because all astronomers at the time accepted Ptolemy's theory that the Sun revolved around Earth, a view that was enforced by the church, which found evidence for it in the Bible.

Copernicus's fame began to spread. In 1514 he received an invitation to be present as an astronomer at the Lateran Council, a church conference that had as one of its aims the reform of the calendar. He did not attend. His secretiveness only seemed to enhance his reputation. In 1522 the secretary to the king of Poland asked Copernicus to give an opinion on *De motu octavae spherae* (On the motion of the eighth sphere), which had just been published by Johann Werner, a respected mathematician. This time Copernicus responded in a letter expressing a rather low regard for Werner's work. In the letter Copernicus also stated that he was writing his own study on the motion of the stars. He could pursue his study only in his spare time, however, because his responsibilities as a canon kept him busy. Although he did not publish anything about astronomy, rumors continued to circulate about the revolutionary nature of his theory.

Turns world upside down Not all the comments about Copernicus were flattering. The Protestant reformer Martin Luther (1483–1546) denounced Copernicus for foolishly trying to overturn established theories on astronomy. In 1531 a satirical play was produced about Copernicus in Elbing, Prussia, by a local schoolmaster. In Rome things went better. In 1533 John Widmanstad, a secretary of the pope, lectured on Copernicus's theory before Pope Clement VII (1478–1534; reigned 1523–34) and several cardinals (church officials who rank directly below the pope). Three years later Cardinal Schönberg wrote Copernicus a letter, urging him to publish his thoughts. It was a useless request. Probably nobody knew exactly how far Copernicus had progressed with his work until Georg Joachim Rheticus (1514–1576), a young scholar from Wittenberg, Germany, arrived in Frauenburg in 1539.

When Rheticus returned to Wittenberg, he had already printed an account, known as the *Narratio prima,* (First report) of Copernicus's nearly completed book. Rheticus was also instrumental in having the book published in Nuremberg. Andreas Osian-

der (1498–1552), a Lutheran clergyman, was also involved in the publication process. Osiander might have been the one who gave the work its title, *De revolutionibus orbium coelestium* (On the revolution of the heavenly spheres), which is not found in the manuscript. The printed copy of the six-volume work reached Copernicus only a few hours before his death on May 24, 1543. The thousand copies of the first edition of the book did not sell out, and the work was reprinted only three times prior to the twentieth century. Nevertheless, Copernicus gave important information about the orbits of the planets. His book began a revolution in human thought by serving as the cornerstone of modern astronomy.

Brahe changes observation methods

The next significant advance in astronomy was made later in the sixteenth century by Tycho Brahe, one of the most colorful figures in scientific history. Rejecting the theories of both Ptolemy and Copernicus, he made major changes in observations of the stars and planets. The son of a Swedish nobleman, Brahe was "adopted" (some say kidnapped) at age one by his childless uncle. He received an excellent education. When he was thirteen he entered the University of Copenhagen to study rhetoric and philosophy. He was well on his way toward a career in politics when he witnessed an eclipse of the Sun (a circumstance when the Moon passes in front of and temporarily blocks out the Sun) on August 21, 1560. Brahe spent the next two years studying mathematics and astronomy, then he moved on to the University of Leipzig. In August 1563, when he was not quite seventeen, Brahe made his first recorded observation, a close grouping of stars between the planets Jupiter and Saturn. He also developed interests in alchemy (science devoted to converting base metals into gold) and in astrology (see "Alchemy" and "Astrology" sections later in this chapter), which he mistakenly considered scientific disciplines. He began to cast horoscopes, or predictions of a person's future based on the positions of heavenly bodies.

In November 1572 a supernova (explosion of a very large star) burst into view in the constellation of Cassiopeia, and Brahe was enthralled. The new star became brighter than the planet Venus and was visible for eighteen months. He described it in such detail in a book that the new star became known as "Tycho's star." This book accomplished three things. First, the title, *De Nova Stella* (Concerning the new star), linked the term "nova" to all exploding stars. Second, it made clear that Brahe had been unable to make a parallax measurement (angular distance in the direction of a celestial body as measured from two points on Earth's orbit) for the nova, revealing that it was much more distant than the Moon. This conclusion was a crushing blow to Aristotle's teachings that the heavens were perfect and unchanging. Since Aristotle stated that all bodies in the universe were fixed (unchanging), they could therefore be measured. However, Brahe was not able to get a measurement for the nova, so this means the nova did not remain in the same location. Consequently, it would suggest that other bodies in the universe also changed positions, thus disproving Aristotle's theory of an unchanging universe. The third achievement of Brahe's book was to establish his reputation as an astronomer.

Builds first observatory Brahe was quite arrogant, and he managed to anger nearly every person with whom he came into contact. At the age of nineteen he was involved in a dispute over a mathematical point. He and his opponent had a duel (a form of combat with weapons between two persons in the presence of witnesses), during which the opponent shot off Brahe's nose. Brahe spent the rest of his life wearing an artificial nose made of silver. Fortunately for Brahe, one of the few people who were not alienated by him was Frederick II (1534–1588; ruled 1559–88), the king of Denmark and a great patron of science. In 1576 Frederick provided Brahe with an annual income and gave him a small island called Hveen (now Ven) off the southwest coast of Sweden. The king funded the building of an observatory, which was the first real astronomical observatory in history. Brahe was always mindful of his noble background, so he made sure that no expense was spared. The principal building, Uraniborg (Castle of the Heavens), was the main residence.

Next to it was built the main observatory, Stjerneborg (Castle of the Stars).

In 1577 a bright comet (a celestial body consisting of a fuzzy head surrounding a bright nucleus) was visible in the skies, and Brahe observed it with great care. Measurements showed that it, too, was farther away from Earth than the Moon and therefore did not conform to Aristotle's teachings. Brahe reluctantly came to the conclusion that the path of the comet was not circular but elongated. This conclusion meant it would have to pass through the "spheres" that carried the planets around the sky, which would be impossible; one possible explanation for the comet's movement was that these spheres did not exist. This concept was personally troubling to Brahe, who rejected Copernicus's Sun-centered theory because it violated Scripture (text of the Bible). It also contradicted the teachings of Ptolemy, who contended that Earth is spherical and remains in a fixed position at the center of the universe.

Astronomer Tycho Brahe is credited with building the first real astronomical observatory. *Reproduced by permission of Archive Photos, Inc.*

Makes accurate observations Brahe spent twenty years at Hveen, recording exceptionally accurate observations. He used many scientific instruments. Among them was a huge quadrant, an instrument used for measuring altitudes. It is in the shape of a quarter part of a circle, much like a wedge of pie. Each of the two straight edges of a quadrant is called a radius (plural of radii). Radius is a term in geometry (mathematical study of surfaces and angles) for the distance of a line from the center of a circle to the perimeter, or outer curved edge. The two radii of Brahe's quadrant measured 6 feet (1.83 meters). Other devices were sextants (instruments used for measuring angular distances), a bipartite arc (two-part half circle), astrolabes (instruments to observe and calculate the distance of celestial bodies), and various armillae (instruments composed of rings showing positions of celestial spheres). Brahe's measurements were the most precise that could be made without the aid of a telescope (a tube-shaped instrument

Gregorian Calendar

The Gregorian calendar, approved by Pope Gregory XIII in 1582, was a revision of the Julian calendar. The Julian calendar was introduced by Roman Emperor Julius Caesar in 46 B.C. It was used in Europe until the Gregorian calendar was officially adopted by the Catholic Church.

Julius Caesar had devised his calendar in order to make up for accumulated slippage in the Egyptian Calendar, which was used in ancient times. He added two extra months as well as twenty-three days to February, thus making the year 46 B.C.

455 days long. Gregory XIII issued his new calendar to make up for the accumulated error in the Julian calendar. The pope decreed that October 5, 1582, would be October 15, thus eliminating ten days. Not everyone changed over to the Gregorian calendar at once. Catholic Europe adopted it within two years, and many Protestant countries did so by 1700. England imposed it on its colonies in 1752, and Sweden accepted it in 1753. Many non-European countries adopted it in the nineteenth century, with China doing so in 1912, Turkey in 1917, and Russia in 1918.

---

with a lens or mirror used for viewing distant objects). He corrected nearly every known astronomical measurement and made possible the calendar reform approved by Pope Gregory XIII (1502–1585; reigned 1572–85) in 1582. Brahe himself did not adopt the new calendar until 1599.

Frederick II died in 1588. His son, Christian IV (1577–1648; ruled 1588–1648), was only eleven, so the country was ruled by regents (interim rulers), who let Brahe do whatever he wanted. When Christian took the throne in 1596, he quickly lost patience with the expensive, haughty astronomer. Brahe was relieved of his royal duties the following year. He moved to Prague, the capital of Bohemia (now Czech Republic), where

he resumed his observations as the mathematician-astronomer to Holy Roman Emperor Rudolf II (1552–1612; ruled 1576–1612). Brahe employed a young German assistant named Johannes Kepler, to whom he gave all his observations on the planet Mars. He assigned Kepler the task of preparing tables of planetary motion. This decision would turn out to be among the most significant of Brahe's life, since Kepler went on to use Brahe's data to discover the three laws of the motions of planets.

Kepler discovers laws of universe

Kepler was originally trained as a theologian (scholar of religion) at the University of Tübingen in Germany, where he received a bachelor of arts degree in 1591. But he was also interested in astronomy, and in 1594 he accepted the post of the mathematician of the province in Graz. One of his duties was composing an almanac, in which the main events of the coming year were to be predicted. Kepler's first almanac was a great success. Two of his predictions—an invasion by the Turks and a severe winter—came true and established his reputation as an astrologer. He also spent his time studying problems in astronomy, working out theories of the circular orbits of planets.

In 1600 Kepler accepted the position of assistant to Brahe and moved to Prague. When Brahe died the following year, Kepler was appointed his successor. Kepler's first task was to prepare Brahe's collection of astronomical studies for publication. The outstanding feature of Brahe's work was that he surpassed all other astronomers before him in making precise observations of the positions of stars and planets. Kepler tried to utilize Brahe's data in support of the circular orbits of planets. He was therefore forced to make one of the most revolutionary assumptions in the history of astronomy. He found that there was a difference of eight minutes of arc between his own calculations and Brahe's data about Mars. (An arc is the path of a celestial body above and below the horizon of Earth. Minutes of arc is the length of time required for the body to move along its path.) This difference could be explained only if the orbit of Mars was not circular but elliptical (oval-shaped), which indicat-

ed that the orbits of all planets were elliptical, a theory that became known as Kepler's first law. Kepler then developed his second law, which states that the imaginary line joining Mars to the Sun sweeps over equal areas in equal times in an elliptical orbit. He published these two laws in his lengthy discussion of the orbit of the planet Mars, the *Astronomia nova* (New astronomy; 1609).

Introduces theory of "magnetic arms"
In 1611 Rudolf stepped down from the throne, and Kepler immediately looked for a new job. He took the post of provincial mathematician in Linz (in present-day Austria). While he was in Linz he published *Harmonice mundi* (Harmony of the world; 1618), in which he stated his third law. According to Kepler's third law, a planet's revolution (the time it takes to make one complete circle) is proportional to the cube of its average distance from the Sun. In other words, once one knows how long it takes a planet to complete an orbit, one can calculate its relative distance from the Sun. Kepler based this theory on his conviction that God created a balanced universe. Later he wrote, "Since God established everything in the universe along quantitative norms, he endowed man with a mind to comprehend them. For just as the eye is fitted for the perception of colors, the ear for sounds, so is man's mind created not for anything but for the grasping of quantities."

While living in Linz, Kepler also wrote *Epitome astronomiae Copernicanae,* (Epitome of Copernican astronomy) which was published in parts between 1618 and 1621. It was the first astronomical study that abandoned the idea of circles carrying the various planets in their orbits. Kepler thus raised the question of what kind of force was holding the planets in their paths. He concluded that it was a physical force consisting of "magnetic arms" that stretched out from the Sun. By identifying a physical force in the universe, Kepler laid the foundation for a relationship between physics and astronomy. In 1628, two years before his death, he published *Tabulae Rudolphinae* (Rudolfine tables; 1628), a catalog of stars. This work added 223 stars to the 777 stars that had been observed by Brahe. The tables were used by astronomers for the next century.

Galileo proves Copernican theory

The most revolutionary contribution to the field of astronomy was made by Galileo. In 1581 Galileo entered the University of Pisa to study medicine, but two years later he became interested in mathematics and the physical sciences. Financial difficulties forced him to leave the university in 1585 before he completed his degree. Returning to his home city of Florence, Galileo spent three years vainly searching for a suitable teaching position. During that time he wrote works that gained him a reputation as a mathematician and natural philosopher (natural scientist; one who specializes in such fields as physics, chemistry, and biology). He then secured a teaching post at the

University of Pisa in 1589. From the beginning of his academic career, he was an eager participant in disputes and controversies. For instance, he made fun of the custom of wearing academic gowns. He was willing to condone ordinary clothes, he said, but the best thing was to go naked.

When Galileo's father died in 1591, Galileo was left with the responsibility for his mother, brothers, and sisters. He had to look for a better position, which he found in 1592 at the University of Padua in the Republic of Venice. In 1604 Galileo publicly declared that he supported Copernicus's theory of a Sun-centered universe. He then gave three public lectures before large audiences in Venice. He argued that a new star, which had appeared earlier that year, was major evidence in support of Copernicus's views. More important was a letter Galileo wrote that year, in which he stated his theory of natural motion. By natural motion Galileo meant that a body will fall freely in space, and he proposed the law of free fall to account for this phenomenon.

Comes into conflict with church In 1609 Galileo learned about the success of some Dutch eyeglass makers in combining lenses into what later came to be called the telescope. He feverishly set to work, and on August 25 he presented to the Venetian Senate a telescope as his own invention. The success was tremendous. He obtained a lifelong contract at the University of Padua, but he also stirred up resentment when it was learned that he was

Galileo's telescope. Although not the original inventor of the device, he presented it as his own invention to the Venetian Senate in 1609. ©*Jim Sugar Photography/Corbis. Reproduced by permission of the Corbis Corporation.*

not the original inventor. Within a few months, however, Galileo had gathered astonishing evidence about mountains on Earth's Moon and about moons circling Jupiter. He also identified a large number of stars, especially in the belt of the Milky Way (a galaxy, or very large group of stars, of which Earth's solar system is a part). On March 12, 1610, all these sensational items were printed in Venice under the title *Sidereus nuncius* (The starry messenger), a booklet that took the world of science by storm. The view of the heavens drastically changed, and so did Galileo's life.

In 1610 Galileo accepted the position of mathematician in Florence, Italy, at the court of Duke Cosimo II de' Medici (1590–1621). In the beginning everything was pure bliss. He made a triumphal visit to Rome in 1611, and the next year his *Discourse on Bodies in Water* was published. In this work he disclosed his discovery of the phases of the planet Venus, which proved the truth of the Copernican theory that celestial bodies travel around the Sun.

Galileo's aim was to make a detailed description of the universe according to the theories of Copernicus and to develop a new form of physics. A major obstacle was the traditional belief, stated in the Bible, that Earth is the center of the universe. To deal with the difficulties raised by the Scripture, Galileo addressed theological issues. He was assisted by church leaders, such as Monsignor Piero Dini and Father Benedetto Castelli, who was his best scientific pupil. In letters to Dini and Castelli, Galileo produced essays that now rank among the best writings of biblical analysis of those times. His longest letter was addressed to Grand Duchess Christina of Tuscany. In all of the letters he discarded the idea of an Earth-centered universe in favor of the theory that Earth revolves around the Sun. As the letters circulated, a confrontation with church authorities became inevitable. In 1616 Cardinal Robert Bellarmine issued an order that forbade Galileo to continue teaching or writing about the Copernican doctrine of the motion of Earth.

Galileo agreed not to promote Copernicus's views, saying he wanted to serve the long-range interest of the church in the world of science. Nevertheless, he was determined to have the order overturned. The next year Galileo had six audiences (formal meetings) with Pope Urban VIII (1568–1644; reigned 1623–44). Urban promised a pension for Galileo's son, Vincenzio, but he did not grant Galileo permission to resume his work on a new description of the universe. Before departing for Florence, Galileo was informed that the pope had re-marked that he did not believe the Roman Catholic Church would ever declare the Copernican theory to be heretical, but he was also certain the theory could never be proven. This news gave Galileo encouragement to go ahead with the great undertaking of his life, the *Dialogue concerning the Two Chief World Systems.*

Church officials were outraged by the *Dialogue,* which proved without doubt that Galileo supported Copernicus's ideas. Galileo was summoned to Rome to appear before the Inquisition, a church court set up to punish heretics (see "Popes implement Roman Inquisition" in Chapter 7). The proceedings dragged on from the fall of 1632 to the summer of 1633. During that time Galileo was allowed to stay at the home of the Florentine ambassador in Rome. He was never subjected to physical force, but he suffered the frustration and humiliation of having to publicly reject the doctrine that Earth moved around the Sun. On his way back to Florence, Galileo enjoyed the hospitality of the archbishop of Siena for nearly five months and then received permission in December to live in his own villa at Arcetri. He was not supposed to have any visitors, but this order was not obeyed. The church was also unable to prevent the printing of Galileo's works outside Italy. During the next five years translations of his writings were published in France and Holland. But the most important publishing event took place in 1638, when Galileo's *Two New Sciences* was printed in Leiden, Holland.

Galileo's *Dialogue*

Galileo's *Dialogue concerning the Two Chief World Systems* was published in 1632. The book features four main topics discussed by three speakers in dialogue form on four consecutive days. The speakers are Simplicius, Salviati, and Sagredo. Simplicius represents Aristotle, Salviati is a spokesman for Galileo, and Sagredo plays the role of an arbiter (one who makes the final judgment on an issue) who leans heavily toward Galileo. The first day is devoted to the criticism of the alleged perfection of the universe, as claimed by Aristotle. Here Galileo made use of his discovery of the "imperfections" of the Moon, namely, its rugged surface as revealed by the telescope (Aristotle contended that the Moon's surface is perfectly smooth). The second day is a discussion of the rotation of Earth on its axis (an imaginary line extending through the center of Earth from north to south) as an explanation of various celestial phenomena.

During the third day the orbital motion of Earth around the Sun is debated. A main issue is the undisturbed nature of the surface of Earth in spite of its double motion—that is, its revolving on an axis while at the same time orbiting around the Sun. The discussion on the fourth day shows that the tides (the rhythmical rising and falling of oceans and other bodies of water) are proof of Earth's twofold motion. In this section Galileo seems to contradict the contention of the third day's discussion, that Earth's surface remains undisturbed by its double motion. The tides, which cause the regular movement of oceans, show that Earth's surface is in fact affected by the twofold motion.

Remains a Christian The *Two New Sciences* dated back to Galileo's days at Padua. Like the *Dialogue,* it is in dialogue form and the discussions are divided into four days. The first day focuses on the mechanical resistance of materials and includes speculations on the atomic composition of matter. There are also long discussions on the question of vacuum and on the vibrations of pendulums. During the second day these and other topics, such as the properties of levers, are discussed in a strictly mathematical manner. The third day's discussion is a mathematical analysis of uniform and accelerated motion. The topic of the fourth day is the projectile motion of a cannonball. There Galileo proved that the longest shot occurred when the cannon was set at an angle of 45 degrees.

Although Galileo proposed a radically new concept of the universe, he remained a Christian to the end of his life. He believed that the world was made by a rational creator (God) who gave order to everything according to weight, measure, and number. Galileo stated this faith in the closing pages of the first day of the *Dialogue*. He described the human mind as the most excellent product of the creator, because it could recognize mathematical truths. Galileo spent his last years partially blind, and he died in 1642. By the time of his death the Copernican doctrine of the universe was being accepted as scientific fact.

Mathematics

The flowering of mathematics in the Renaissance was stimulated by many social and economic changes of the time and by the recovery of Greek mathematical works. There were major breakthroughs in algebra, an abstract form of arithmetic in which letters, also called variables, represent numbers. The use of letters in algebra as known to us today is a Renaissance creation. Renaissance mathematicians adopted the Hindu-Arabic notation for base-10 arithmetic (the familiar numeral system in which all derived units are based on the number ten and the powers of ten). More important, they made advances in trigonometry (a branch of applied mathematics concerned with the relationship between angles and their sides and the calculations based on them) and used geometry (a branch of mathematics that deals with points, lines, angles, surfaces, and solids) to perfect perspective in painting. They also invented logarithms (or exponents; for example, in base-10 arithmetic, the logarithm of 100 is 2 because 10 to the second power is equal to 100).

Mathematicians were connected with humanists through networks of personal friendships and patronage (financial support given by wealthy people). Interest in the works of Plato helped encourage the view that mathematics was the key to understanding nature. Universities established professorships of mathematics, and new courses in mathematics and mathematical books were added for accountants, artisans, engineers, and navigators. This boom in mathematical awareness and sophistication set the stage for the scientific revolution of the sixteenth century.

The abacists and the rise of algebra

In the early fourteenth century a new class of professional mathematicians, called abacists, emerged in Italy and produced a set of practical mathematical texts. Abacists taught merchants how to use the Hindu-Arabic system of mathematics, introducing some abbreviations and symbols for operations. They also used algebra to solve problems arising from commerce, banking, and weights and measures. The abacists lectured in the languages people actually spoke and wrote understandable books that contained worked-out examples of problems with detailed instructions. The first printed Renaissance algebra book, *Summa de arithmetica, geometrica, proportioni et proportionalita* by Italian mathematician Luca Pacioli (1445–1514), was a summary of the work of abacists. It included not only arithmetic and the solving of equations but also elementary geometry and double-entry bookkeeping, which is a method

"Cardano's Solution"

In the sixteenth century, Italian mathematicians often engaged in problem-solving competitions. Winners received university positions and monetary rewards. In the 1530s one such competition produced the solution of the general cubic equation. Special cases had been treated earlier, but two important cubics equations had not yet been solved. The solutions to the cubic of the first form seems to have been discovered by Scipione del Ferro (1465–1526), professor of mathematics at Bologna. He told his student, Antonio Maria Fior, how to solve the problem. The Italian mathematician Niccolò Tartaglia (c. 1499–1557) claimed he could solve cubics of the second form. In 1535 Fior challenged Tartaglia to a public mathematical contest. Tartaglia worked out the solution to cubics of the first type and won the competition.

News of Tartaglia's victory reached Girolamo Cardano (1501–1576), who was then lecturing on mathematics in Milan. He was known as an astrologer, a physician, and a gambler. Around 1526 he had written the first treatise on applying mathematics to games of chance, the *Liber de ludo aleae* (Book on games of chance). Cardano talked Tartaglia into revealing the method of solving the cubic and swore that he would keep the solution a secret. Nevertheless, in 1545 Cardano published it in his *Ars magna* (Great art), the most famous of Renaissance algebra books. Although Cardano named Tartaglia as one of the discoverers of the solution, Tartaglia was outraged. He retaliated by publishing the text of the oath that Cardano had violated, but today the method is still known as "Cardano's solution." Cardano's *Ars magna* marked the first significant advance in algebra outside of the Islamic world.

of bookkeeping that keeps track of both expenses and income.

Interest in algebra soon spread to many other countries. Among the European mathematicians who made contributions to algebraic theory were Nicolas Chuquet (c. 1445–1500) in France, Pedro Nunes (1492–1577) in Portugal, and Cristoph Rudolff (c. 1500–c. 1545) and Michael Stifel (1487–1567) in Germany. In England, the royal physician Robert Recorde (1510–1558) published the first English-language algebra book, the *Whet-*

stone of Witte (1557), which introduced the equal sign (=).

Advances in trigonometry Significant advances in trigonometry also took place during the Renaissance. The German mathematician Johann Müller of Königsberg (1436–1476), better known as Regiomontanus (the Latin term for Königsberg), conceived a grand plan to translate and print Greek scientific work. Although he died before carrying out the project, he did complete a Latin version of Ptolemy's *Almagest*. In

1464 Regiomontanus also wrote *De triangulis omnimodis* (On triangles of all kinds), which drew on the work of Ptolemy and on Islamic plane and spherical trigonometry. (Plane geometry deals with straight lines and two-dimensional figures on flat surfaces. Spherical trigonometry, also called spherical geometry, deals with complex components of curves in multidimensional space.) *De triangulis omnimodis* was the first extensive European work on trigonometry. When the Polish astronomer Nicolaus Copernicus (see "Astronomy" section previously in this chapter) proposed the idea that Earth revolves around the Sun, he needed to use trigonometry to work out the details of his theory. Copernicus relied not only on the theories of Islamic mathematicians but also on Georg Joachim Rheticus, who was familiar with Regiomontanus's theories. Rheticus published an even more extensive treatise on trigonometry, which featured elaborate tables of all six trigonometric functions.

Meanwhile, the French mathematician François Viète (1540–1603) was drawing from his knowledge of Islamic and Greek mathematics to develop multi-angle formulas for trigonometry. He used them to solve algebraic equations. Viète's work helped broaden the scope of algebra and trigonometry, bringing together these two branches of mathematics, which had previously been separate.

Geometry and art

Many Renaissance artists used geometry to give the viewer the visual sense of three dimensions (a technique called perspective). Most notable were the Italian painter Piero della Francesca (c. 1412–1492) and the German painter Albrecht Dürer (1471–1528). Piero wrote *De prospectiva pingendi* (On perspective in painting), the first mathematical study on the use of perspective in painting. By constructing one point at a time, he showed how to depict objects in three dimensions on a flat surface. Even though *De prospectiva pingendi* was not printed, it influenced later theories on the geometry of perspective. In 1525 Dürer wrote *Underweysung der Messung* (Treatise on measurement), the first text on geometry written in German. Dürer is sometimes considered the inventor of descriptive geometry because he showed how to project three-dimensional curves onto two perpendicular planes. The methods of projection developed in the Renaissance helped direct attention to many of the key ideas of projective geometry, a subject initiated in the seventeenth century by the French mathematicians Gérard Desargues (1591–1661) and Blaise Pascal (1623–1662).

Rapid calculation

Trigonometric functions often needed to be multiplied or divided, but it is much harder to multiply or divide numbers that have many digits than it is to add or subtract them. The Scottish mathematician John Napier (1550–1617) resolved this problem by developing a system of numbers called "logarithms." Napier explained his

Napier Develops Logarithms

In the sixteenth century the Scottish mathematician John Napier developed a method of simplifying the process of multiplication and division, using exponents of 10. (Exponents are symbols written to the right of and above a mathematical expression to indicate the number by which it is to be multiplied by itself.) Napier called these exponents "logarithms," commonly abbreviated as "logs." Using this system, multiplication is reduced to addition and division is reduced to subtraction. For example, the log of 100 (10^2) is 2. The log of 1000 (10^3) is 3. The multiplication of 100 by 1000, or $100 \times 1000 = 100,000$, can be accomplished by adding their logs—in other words, log [(100)(1000)] = log (100) + log (1000) = 2 + 3 = 5 = log (100,000). Napier published his methodology in *Description of the marvelous table of logarithms* in 1614. In 1617 he published a method for using a device, made up of a series of rods in a frame that is marked with the digits 1 through 9, to multiply and divide using the principles of logarithms. This device was commonly called "Napier's bones" or "Napier's rods."

system with points that move on two lines of numbers. One point moves according to arithmetic numbers of increasing value. The other moves according to decreasing geometric values. He used this idea to calculate a table of logarithms, which he published in *Mirifici logarithmorum canonis descriptio* (Description of the marvelous table of logarithms) in 1614. It was translated into English in 1616 by the British navigator Edward Wright (1558–1615). Logarithms soon became widely used, especially in the simplified base-10 arithmetic devised by Henry Briggs (1561–1639). Furthermore, the development of the slide rule—basically a kind of "computer" that multiplies numbers by adding their logarithms—put fast calculation within the reach of people who worked with large numbers every day

(see "Scientific instruments" section later in this chapter).

Another influential writer on calculation was Simon Stevin (1548–1620), an engineer, mathematician, and physicist from Bruges, Belgium. In 1585 Stevin wrote *De thiende* (The tenth) on decimal fractions. A decimal fraction is a fraction, or mixed number, in which the denominator (the part of the number below the line in a fraction) is a power of 10, indicated with a dot called a decimal point. Although decimal fractions had been developed earlier in the Islamic world, they were commonly used in Europe only after Stevin published his work. If one uses decimals, said Stevin, arithmetic can be performed with fractions just the way it is with whole numbers.

Medicine

The love of all things Greek and Roman that characterized much Renaissance culture also profoundly affected medicine. By re-creating pure ancient medicine, scholars wanted to reform current knowledge and improve medical practice. Greek texts especially were seen as possessing the purest wisdom. At the beginning of the sixteenth century the translation and editing of classical texts was centered in Italy, then Paris led the way after the 1530s. Humanists focused on the two main sources of classical medical knowledge. The first was the Hippocratic works, which were composed by a variety of writers between 420 and 350 B.C. The second was the works of Galen, who created a comprehensive medical system that combined ancient medicine and philosophy with his own research. Between 1500 and 1600, around 590 separate editions of Galen texts were published. In 1525 the Aldine Press in Venice, Italy, published the complete works of Galen in Greek. The result of this activity was to clear up ambiguities in medical terminology and to substitute classical terms for Arabic words. Just as in religion, reform of medicine meant going back to the original Greek sources and discarding changes and additions that had been made during the Middle Ages.

The four humors

The Hippocratic treatises developed the humoral theory of health and illness, which was refined by Galen. Learned physicians of the Renaissance followed Galen's theory. According to Galen, the body is made up of four humors: blood, phlegm (mucus), yellow bile, and black bile. These humors reflected the four elements of the world—air, water, fire, and earth—that were identified by Aristotle. They were the product of hot, cold, dry, and wet, which Aristotle defined as the basic constituents of the world. The microcosm (little world) of the body was therefore linked to the macrocosm (world at large) and also to the seasons. Galen introduced the concept that each person has a temperament, or mix of humors, in which one humor is dominant. The dominant humor determined whether that person's physical and psychological nature would be sanguine (cheerful; relating to blood), phlegmatic (slow; relating to phlegm), melancholic (sad; relating to black bile), or choleric (angry; relating to yellow bile).

The temperament of the individual was supposed to be taken into account when devising rules for living healthily. Phlegmatic patients, for example, should avoid watery foods and eat dry and hot ingredients. Illnesses were also categorized in terms of humors. Medical treatment was based on the idea that opposites cure opposites, so that a cold illness was cured by a hot remedy. Until the early 1600s the determination of the degree of hot, cold, wet, and dry in a patient was usually based only on a physician's opinion. Then in 1612 Santorio Santorio (1561–1636), a professor of the theory of medicine at the University

Anatomy of Melancholy

Renaissance physicians relied on Galen's concept that each person has a temperament, or mix of humors, in which one humor is dominant. The dominant humor determined whether that person's physical and psychological nature would be phlegmatic, melancholic, sanguine, or choleric. The melancholic humor, or melancholy, was of special interest at the time. The English scholar and writer Robert Burton (1577–1640) wrote an entire work, *The Anatomy of Melancholy,* on the subject.

First published in 1621, *The Anatomy of Melancholy* eventually went through five editions by 1651. While some Renaissance writers and artists exalted melancholy as the affliction of gifted people, Burton saw it as a debilitating condition to which everyone was vulnerable. The *Anatomy of Melancholy* is divided into three parts. The first examines the causes and symptoms of melancholy, the second describes possible cures, and the third analyzes the two important types—those associated with love and with religion. Famous sections of the work include the "Digression on the Misery of Scholars" and the "Digression of Air." In "Digression of Air" Burton takes an imaginary flight through the heavens and gives often contradictory explanations for events on Earth and in the cosmos.

Burton devoted his life to the study of melancholy. The inscription on his tomb at Christ Church College, where he pursued his lifelong study of melancholy, states that melancholy gave him both his life and his death. This has caused some scholars to wonder if he committed suicide, but there is no evidence to support the theory.

of Padua, invented a thermometer for measuring body temperature (see "Scientific instruments" section later in this chapter).

Humors determine treatments The body was viewed as being interconnected by means of arteries, veins, and nerves. Humors could clog up these passages and cause disease. Putrefaction (rotting material) was an especially potent source of disease, whether located in the intestines, stomach, lungs, brain, or blood vessels. Highly communicable, or infectious, diseases like the plague and syphilis (a disease of the genital organs; see "Syphilis" section later in this chapter) were often seen as being caused by a contagious poison. Disease was thought to be able to travel from one part of the body to another. Headache, for instance, was sometimes viewed as resulting from smoky vapors (gases) that started in the stomach and traveled to the brain. Physicians used many methods to expel disease-producing humors from the body. Among them were bleeding, purging (evacuating the bowels), sweating, cupping (drawing blood to the surface of the body with a heated glass), vomiting, and blistering (placing extreme heat on the skin to create blisters, which were then drained). Physicians routinely used bleeding and purging to cure any illness.

This view of the body was also common among surgeons, who operated on broken limbs and treated wounds. In addition, they treated cancers and skin conditions, including syphilis. Like physicians, they saw the day-to-day progress of their patients in terms of the four humors and they used the same procedures. This technique was especially the case with surgeons who studied the medical and surgical texts of the Greeks, which were translated into the vernacular (language spoken in a particular region). In 1569 the French surgeon Jacques Daléchamps (1513–1588) brought together ancient learning in *Chirurgie française* (French surgery). Ambroise Paré (1510—1590), who wrote in French, was the most distinguished surgeon of the sixteenth century. He gained status through royal patronage and had immense knowledge of classical medicine. He made several innovations such as using salves (ointment) rather than boiling oil on gunshot wounds.

Trained physicians also gave advice on ways to prevent or treat illness in daily life. This advice was usually based on Galen's concept of "six nonnaturals": food and drink; air; sleep and waking; evacuation and repletion; motion and rest; and the passions of the soul or the emotions. A number of works on health were popular throughout the Renaissance. Among them were *Regimen sanitatis Salernitanum* (Guide to health) from the thirteenth century, *Castel of Health* (1536) by English scholar Thomas Elyot (c. 1490–1546), and *Trattato de la vita sobria* (Treatise on the temperament of life; 1558) by Italian nobleman Luigi Carnaro (1500–1558).

Herbal remedies developed

Since classical times, plants (their leaves, stalks, flowers, roots, and seeds), as well as animals and minerals, had been used to cure disease. Herbal (plant) remedies were of two types, simple and compound. Simples consisted of one ingredient, while compounds could involve a large number of ingredients. Advice on using herbal remedies could be found in classical texts such as the botanical works of Greek philosopher and naturalist Theophrastus (c. 372–288 B.C.) and *On Materia Medica* by the Greek physician Dioscorides (A.D. c. 40– c. 90). Galen's medical works also provided information on simples and compounds. Religious justification for herbal remedies was given by the often-quoted passage from Ecclesiastes (a book in the Old Testament of the Bible): "The Lord hath created medicines out of the earth."

During the Renaissance medical students were taught how to recognize plants that could be used as cures. Towns and universities built botanical gardens (gardens for the cultivation, study, and exhibition of special plants), and the holders of newly created chairs (top faculty positions) of medical botany took their students on field trips into the countryside to examine plants. Herbalists (plant specialists) produced large, realistically illustrated books that described northern European and western Mediterranean plants. There were also books on plants in the eastern Mediterranean and in Asia Minor, which had been described by classical writers. Herbalists also searched for the lost drugs of antiquity. Among these drugs was theriac (a treatment for poisons made from at least eighty-one ingredients). In the 1540s many of the drugs could not be found, but by the end of the sixteenth century physicians and pharmacists were confident that they had been recovered. The Italian herbalist Pier Andrea Mattioli (1500–1577) acted as a center for collection of information on the lost drugs. In several editions of *Di pedacio Discoride* (Commentaries of Dioscorides), he publicized the research of herbalists and travelers in Greece, the Mediterranean islands, and Asia Minor. They rediscovered balsam (an oily substance from many plants), myrrh (gum resin from a tree), petroselinum (a group of herbs including parsley), and other drugs known to the ancients.

Medicines brought from New World

The European view of the world greatly expanded during the Renaissance, looking not only backward to the classical era but also outward to new lands. The voyages of Portuguese explorers in the fourteenth and fifteenth centuries brought Africa, India, the East Indies, and even Japan and China into direct contact with Europe. The legendary Spice Islands (the Moluccas) had been discovered in the Pacific in 1512 and 1513 by the Portuguese. The spices and remedies of the East flowed more freely into Europe, and new medicines also traveled west. In 1563 the Portuguese physician and trader Garcia de Orta (c. 1501–1568) publicized some of India's medicines in *Coloquios dos simples, e drogas he cousas mediçinais da India* (Dialogues about simples and drugs and medical matters from India).

The New World (the European term for North and South America) also provided new medicines, which the Spanish physician Nicolás Monardes popularized in *Dos libros, El uno que trata de todas las cosas que traen de nuestras Indias Occidentales* (Two books, one which deals with all things that are brought from our West Indies; 1565, 1571, and 1574). Tobacco (a leafy plant cultivated for smoking), sarsaparilla (greenbrier root used for flavoring), sassafras (dried root bark of a laurel tree), and especially guaiac (evergreen tree) wood were welcomed by European physicians and patients, who were always eager for exotic remedies from faraway countries. These new drugs were easily adapted to the humoral system of medicine.

Syphilis: a new European disease

In addition to sharing medicines, Europeans also exchanged diseases with people in the New World. Native Americans suffered the most because they had not previously been exposed to the mix of diseases brought by settlers from the Old World (Europe); consequently they had no immunity, or resistance, to them. In the century after Christopher Columbus landed in the New World in 1492 (see "The age of European exploration," in Chapter 3), epidemics, or widespread outbreaks, of tuberculosis (a disease of the lungs) and infectious diseases such as measles, mumps, influenza, and scarlet fever contributed to the devastation of Native American populations. The only disease Europe reportedly received from the Americas was syphilis, though this fact is still being disputed by historians. Syphilis is a disease of the genital organs that is spread mainly through sexual contact, though it can be transmitted from an infected mother to her fetus. The disease becomes increasingly more serious over three stages, ending with infections of the eyes, bones, liver, heart, and central nervous system. Syphilis was the subject of a poem by Girolamo Fracastro (c. 1478–1553), titled *Syphilis sive morbus gallicus* (Syphilis, or the French disease; 1530). In the poem Fracastro argued that syphilis and other diseases were spread by "seeds of disease," which produced putrefaction (rotting) in a receptive body.

Syphilis was initially treated with mercury—a silver-colored, poisonous metallic element—but the chemical had severe side effects, such as excessive sweating and saliva and the rotting of bones. These effects were described by Ulrich von Hutten (1488–1523) in *De guaici medicina et morbo gallico* (On the guaiac remedy and the French disease; 1519). Hutten recommended using resin from the guaiac, an evergreen tree, instead of mercury to treat syphilis. The Spanish had seen Native Americans using guaiac to treat syphilis or yaws, a similar disease, and they made huge profits from importing the wood into Europe. Guaiac proved to be ineffective, however, and mercury came back into use. Eventually the severe form of syphilis changed to a less deadly type, and by the end of the sixteenth century Europeans were asserting that the disease had burned itself out.

Paracelsus brings radical change

In the early sixteenth century, Galen's humoral system was challenged by Paracelsus (also known as Philippus Bombast von Hohenheim; 1493–1541), the German physician and alchemist. Paracelsus and his followers claimed that Earth and human beings were made up of three basic chemicals: salt, sulfur, and mercury. According to their theory, the processes of the body involved chemicals, not humors, so chemicals should be used to treat disease. Although Paracelsus's view was in some respects similar to modern medicine, it had some highly mystical elements. He believed that the microcosm (human body) and macrocosm (larger world) were interconnected, and that events in the heavens could send disease to people. Paracelsus also believed that certain plants were created to cure particular parts of the body. For instance, the walnut could be used to treat brain disorders because a walnut looks like the brain. Similarly, the root of an orchid could cure disorders of the testicles because the root looks like a testicle. For Paracelsus the physician's ability was God-given and could not be taught. He therefore advocated learning from nature and not from books.

Paracelsus's ideas slowly spread after his death, first to the courts of German princes and then to France. The major center in France was the royal court at Montpellier, which was dominated by physicians. In the courts Paracelsus's radical political views were toned down because he had supported German peasants in their rebellions against their rulers (see "Peasants' War" in Chapter 5). Instead, the mystical, chemical aspect of his work was emphasized. In England during the Civil War (a movement to overthrow the monarchy; 1642–1649), reformers hoped to create a new medicine based on Christian principles and Paracelsus's theories. Some writers, like the German physician Gunther von Andernach, however, claimed that theories of Paracelsus and Galen could be combined. By the 1660s, chemistry was increasingly accepted within natural philosophy and medicine. Galen's humoral system was on the decline, but it continued to be practiced into the eighteenth century.

Anatomy

Although numerous changes were taking place in the medical field,

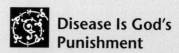

Disease Is God's Punishment

Syphilis linked sexual intercourse, disease, and death together for the first time. Surgeons like William Clowes (1544–1604), the English writer on syphilis, were concerned about preventing the disease. They did not hesitate to condemn prostitutes (people who charge money for sexual intercourse), the poor, and the sexually promiscuous. They also pointed out that the well-to-do respectable classes could acquire it by sitting on contaminated toilets. New diseases like syphilis and the "English sweat" (perhaps influenza) were viewed as part of God's continuing punishment of humans for their sins.

anatomy (study of the body) was the real success story of Renaissance medicine. In the Middle Ages anatomy was mainly taught to surgeons, and lecturers in anatomy held a low position. By the middle of the thirteenth century surgeons were conducting autopsies (dissection of a body to determine cause of death) in towns in France, Germany, and Italy. The first systematic human dissection for medical education was carried out in 1316 by Mondino dei Liuzzi in Bologna, Italy. In 1316 he published *Anatomia,* which helped gain respect for anatomy as a branch of medicine. In the sixteenth century the teaching of anatomy began to change into a more critical, research-oriented activity. Sixteenth-

Artists Study Anatomy

The emphasis on realism in Renaissance art helped to promote the study of anatomy. Scholars and sculptors urged artists to gain personal knowledge of the structure of the human body, rather than relying on past authorities. By the early sixteenth century the artists Raphael, Albrecht Dürer, and Michelangelo were integrating their knowledge of anatomy into their paintings. The painter Leonardo da Vinci even sought out cadavers (dead bodies used for study purposes) to dissect from the hospital of Santa Maria Nuova in Florence. With increasing naturalism and detail, he depicted parts of the body such as the hand, foot, shoulder, head, and internal organs. Leonardo wrote that pictures could say more than words, and he planned an anatomical atlas of the stages of man from fetus to death. Although he did not complete this work, his attitude was representative of both anatomists and artists: the body had to be drawn from nature, not from books.

century anatomists also emphasized anatomy's theological and philosophical roles, contending that it demonstrated God's marvelous workmanship in creating the body. The impact of anatomy upon medicine was so great that by the end of the century students at Padua, the center for study of the field, were asserting that anatomy and not philosophy was the foundation of medicine.

Anatomists looked back to ancients such as Galen. He wrote *On the Use of the Parts of the Body,* among other works, which became widely available with the advent of printing (it was too long to be frequently copied by hand in the Middle Ages). Galen's *On Anatomical Procedures* was discovered and translated in 1531. These works provided a wealth of information about the functioning of the body and also exemplified Galen's view of anatomical research, which was based on *autopsia,* or seeing for oneself.

Vesalius revolutionizes anatomy The most important contributions to the study of human anatomy were made by the Belgian scientist Andreas Vesalius (1514–1564). He was educated in France at Louvain and Paris, which were then the major centers for the study of Galen's theories of medicine. Vesalius gained a reputation as a medical scholar and in 1537 he was appointed a lecturer in anatomy and surgery at the University of Padua in Italy. The following year, after he published six anatomical charts designed for students, Vesalius became critical of Galen's anatomy. He realized that Galen had dissected animals, especially apes, rather than humans. Consequently, all of Galen's observations had to be compared to the actual human body.

In 1543 Vesalius published *De humani corporis fabrics* (On the structure of the human body). Vesalius contradicted Galen on a number of details. For instance, he established that the liver does not have five lobes as Galen contended, and he deter-

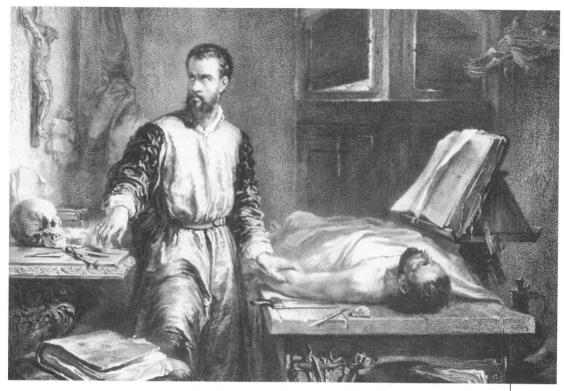

The "father of modern anatomy" Andreas Vesalius dissecting a cadaver. *Reproduced by permission of the Corbis Corporation.*

mined that the vena cava (large vein in which blood is returned to the right atrium of the heart) does not originate in the liver. Contrary to Galen's view, Vesalius also suggested that mental faculties are not located in particular parts of the ventricles of the brain. However, Vesalius was the first Renaissance anatomist to follow Galen's system of performing a dissection. That is, he began with the bones and proceeded to the muscles, vascular system, nervous system, abdominal organs, and organs of the thorax. He ended with the brain. Although Vesalius and the anatomists who followed him prided themselves on their obser-

vational accuracy, they did not challenge Galen's theories of how the body works. Some anatomists, like Gabriele Fallopio (1523–1562) and Caspar Bauhin (1560–1624), sought to surpass Vesalius in creating an even more precise anatomy of the body. Others produced detailed anatomical studies of particular parts of the body. Most significant was the move to studying many animals, including man, in order to create an overall picture of particular organs.

Harvey discovers circulatory system

The last great medical achievement of the period was the discovery of the systematic circulation of blood by the English anatomist William Harvey (1578–1657). He studied at the University of Padua, where he relied upon the past work of his colleagues. Among them was Matteo Realdo Colombo (c. 1516–1559), who used the bodies of dogs to show that blood travels through veins from the pulmonary artery to the lungs. In the lungs blood mixes with air to become arterial blood (blood that flows to the heart). It is then conveyed through the pulmonary vein to the heart. This description of the transit of blood through the lungs replaced Galen's theory that blood moves through invisible pores in the membrane of the heart. But Colombo held that the blood is replaced as it moves through the body, for he believed in Galen's theory about blood. According to Galen, blood—which he thought was made from chyle, a product of digested food, in the liver—is used up by the parts of the body as needed. Colombo also prepared the ground for Harvey by showing that the arteries fill with blood after the heart constricts, acting in systole (rhythmic contraction) and not in diastole (rhythmic expansion) as Galen had thought.

Harvey's notes for the anatomy lectures he gave to the College of Physicians in London, England, indicate that by 1616 he agreed with Colombo. In 1628 Harvey announced his discovery of the circulatory system in *Exercitatio anatomica de motu cordis et sanguinis in animalibus* (An anatomical exercise concerning the movement of the heart and blood in animals). In this work he established that the heart acts like a muscle when it contracts. He also pointed out flaws in Galen's description of the cardiovascular (heart and veins) system. For instance, Galen incorrectly believed that air and sooty vapors flowed two ways in the pulmonary vein. According to Galen, sooty vapors were the by-product of blood in the left ventricle (chamber) of the heart. Harvey went on to state that blood is not continually produced and used up by the body. Instead, the same blood constantly circulates throughout the body. He calculated the amount of blood that is ejected from the heart in a given time and concluded that the quantity is so great that it has to move in a circle; otherwise, the body would burst.

For this theory Harvey relied on the work of the Italian surgeon Girolamo Fabrici (1537–1619), who discovered the valves of the veins. Fabrici thought the valves were designed to keep the extremities of the body from being flooded with blood. Harvey showed that the valves in the veins actually lead the blood back from the body's extremities to the heart. Although he could not show how the arteries are joined to the veins, Harvey was able to conclude that there is a connection by loosening and tightening a light ligature (string or cord) and observing the flow of blood with a simple magnifying glass. When the ligature was tight the blood was prevented from going down through the artery. When it was moderately tight it allowed blood to travel down the artery and then up along the vein until it was stopped below the ligature. In 1661 the Italian anatomist Marcello Malpighi (1628–1694) used a microscope to discover that arteries are joined to veins by small blood vessels called capillaries.

Geography and cartography

During the Renaissance, Europeans became increasingly interested in understanding their world. Both geography (the study of the features of Earth) and cartography (the study of maps and mapmaking) became more popular and more important in trade, politics, and exploration.

Geography

During the sixteenth and seventeenth centuries geography was developing into a field separate from the older study of cosmography. The subject of cosmography was the globe and its relationship with the heavens as a whole. Cosmographers pictured Earth as an inseparable part of the universe, while geography concentrated primarily on Earth itself. Geography developed into three related branches: mathematical, descriptive, and chorographical geography.

Mathematical geography Mathematical geography had its roots in *Geographia,* a text written by the Egyptian scientist Ptolemy. Translated into Latin in 1410, *Geographia* provided many types of information to Renaissance thinkers. It contained mathematical

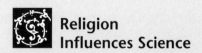

Religion Influences Science

Michael Servetus (1511–1553), the Spanish physician and theologian, was among the scientists in the sixteenth century who proposed that blood flows through the pulmonary artery. In his *Christianismi restititutio* (The restitution of Christianity; 1553) he argued that God breathed the divine spirit or soul into the blood. The best place for this to happen is in the lungs, as its area is larger than the left ventricle of the heart. Servetus used his anatomical experience to develop this argument.

In 1553 Servetus was burned as a heretic in Geneva, Switzerland, on orders of the Protestant reformer John Calvin. Most of the copies of *Christianismi restititutio* were also burned. Servetus's work had no influence upon William Harvey. Nevertheless, it illustrates that anatomists were accepting the pulmonary theory, as well as showing how religion could influence medicine.

formulas, called projections, that could be used to determine the exact positions of points on Earth. It also gave the size of large portions of Earth's surface, the shape and size of the planet itself, and the variations in Earth's magnetism (electrical force). Renaissance scholars who contributed to this branch of geography included two of the most popular authors of the early sixteenth century, the German geographers Peter Bennewitz (also known as Petrus Apianus; 1495–1552) and Sebastian Münster (1489–1552). Bennewitz's *Cosmographia,* first published in 1529, contained Ptolemy's method and theory of map projection. It also provided observation charts of longitude (imaginary lines passing through the center of Earth from the North Pole to the South Pole) and latitude (imaginary lines that are parallel to Earth's equator), as well as maps of the world inspired by Ptolemy's work. Münster's popular work, also titled *Cosmographia,* was published in 1544. It began with Ptolemy's maps of the Old World, and continued with more recent maps of the New World, based on Ptolemy's techniques. In fact, by the mid-sixteenth century, all major geographical treatises began with information from Ptolemy (also see "Cartography" section later in this chapter).

Descriptive geography Descriptive geography developed separately from mathematical geography. Based on the work of the ancient geographer Strabo of Amaseia (c. 63 B.C.–c. A.D. 20), descriptive geography portrayed the physical and political structures of other lands. It encompassed everything from descriptions of European road conditions to outlandish stories about exotic places. This form of geography helped people establish their own national and local identities apart from those of other European and non-European nations. Descriptive geographers included Giovanni Battista Ramusio (1485–1557) in Italy, José de Acosta (c. 1539–1598) in Spain, Jan Huygen van Linschoten (1563–1611) in the Netherlands, Theodore de Bry

(1528–1598) and Johann T. de Bry (1561–c. 1623), and Richard Hakluyt (c. 1552–1616) in England.

Chorographical geography The final type of geography, chorography, was a combination of the medieval chronicle (account of events in chronological order) and the Italian Renaissance study of descriptions of local places. Chorography was the most wide-ranging branch of geography. It included an interest in genealogy (study of family lines), chronology, and antiquities, as well as local history and topography (study of natural and man-made features of a place). Two famous Renaissance chorographers were Joseph Justus Scaliger (1540–1609) in Italy and William Camden (1551–1623) in England.

Cartography

Beginning in the fifteenth century cartography underwent a revolutionary transformation as new types of maps were developed through the use of geometry. During the Middle Ages, pictorial representations of Earth were called *mappae mundi* (maps of the world). They were of various types, but more than half were known as the "T-O" map, which was in the shape of a wheel. On the "T-O" map the Don River, the Nile River, and the Mediterranean Sea formed a "T," which divided the world into three continents. Jerusalem, a city in Israel that is considered holy by many religions, was often featured in the center. At the top, which was considered the east, was pictured an earthly paradise. The "T-O" map was not intended to depict the world as it actually appeared. Instead, it represented God's orderly plan, as well as the relationship between the microcosm of Earth and the macrocosm of the universe.

Geometry applied to maps The translation of Ptolemy's *Geographia* began to change the concept of mapping. In this work Ptolemy constructed a geometric grid of longitude and latitude, then established methods for determining the exact location of geographical points on that grid. Renaissance interest in the geometrical representation of the world was the result of a new emphasis on geometry (see "Geometry" section previously in this chapter). In the drive to create a measurable world, the *Geographia* was extremely important. The book rapidly became popular and was published in Latin six times between 1462 and 1490. The French cartographer Pierre d'Ailly (1350–1420) incorporated Ptolemy's methods and maps into his *Comendium Cosmographiae* in 1413. The *Nürnberg Chronicles,* first published in 1493, contained a Ptolemaic map. By the sixteenth century, all cartographers were using Ptolemy's methods.

As maps based on Ptolemy's geometrical grid became increasingly popular with the general public, a separate development was occurring in more practical maps. Sea charts, and especially the portolan maps of Iberian navigators, had long been constructed according to observation of the sea, wind directions, and simple astronomical sightings. These maps were used first to sail on the Mediterranean and later to venture farther around Africa and to the New World. The charts were never published, and they were jealously guarded and shared by navigators. The firsthand knowledge represented in these charts did not find its way onto published maps and globes until the sixteenth century.

Maps popular during Renaissance Part of the revolution in cartography was the explosion of interest in purchasing maps and globes that occurred during the Renaissance. One of the earliest globes was made by the cartographer Martin Behaim (c. 1459–1506) in Nuremberg, Germany, in 1493. By the mid-1500s many prosperous merchants and noblemen could purchase globes, which were signs of a sophisticated knowledge of the world. Likewise, the atlas—a collection of maps in book form—developed as a completely new form of map ownership and one that achieved huge popularity in the sixteenth century. The geographers who took greatest advantage of this trend were the Flemish cartographers Gerard Mercator (also known as Gerhard Kremer; 1512–1594) and Ortelius (also known as Abraham Oertel; 1527–1598). In 1541 Mercator produced a globe that he claimed was based on objectivity, classical methods, and modern accuracy. In 1569 he developed a new world map with a projection that widened the latitudes of the north and created a sense that the world was dominated by northern Europe and the New

World. The first true atlas, *Theatrum orbis terrarum* (Theater of the world), was published by Ortelius in 1570. It served as a model for all future atlases.

The exploration of the world had a strong influence on the growing interest in geography and cartography. By the end of the seventeenth century, Europeans appreciated the social value of maps and understood the importance of geometry and objectivity. Yet maps also served to increase Europeans' sense of superiority (see "The idea of Europe" in Chapter 1). As they set out to conquer new territories, they usually dismissed maps of other cultures as being "non-objective" and therefore inferior or insignificant. Geography and cartography soon became tools for building future empires.

Scientific instruments

Scientific instruments, or devices used for the study of nature, were perfected throughout the Middle Ages. Renaissance scientists further improved these devices and invented instruments that facilitated new methods of observation and experimentation. Scientific instruments were used for observing, measuring, drawing, calculating, and teaching in various fields of study. The most active fields were astronomy, navigation, land surveying, physics, and medicine.

Astronomy instruments

Basic instruments for astronomy in the early Renaissance were the astrolabe, the quadrant, and the armillary sphere. Scientists later added the astronomical ring, the torquetum, and the equatorium. The astrolabe, a device used to sight the altitude, or distance from the ground, of a heavenly object, was very common and of various types. It was usually made in the form of a small brass disk that could be held in a vertical position on the thumb with a ring. It was known as a planespheric astrolabe because the markings on the disk showed various projections of a planet or star on a plane. Calibrated scales on the instrument then enabled an astronomer to read off the hour or the date in order to make accurate observations. Much rarer was the spherical astrolabe, which used the heavenly body itself as a measuring instrument. Quadrants were basically devices in the shape of a quarter circle that measured angles up to 90 degrees and likewise were used for determining altitudes. As with astrolabes, there were various types of quadrants.

The armillary sphere was a ball-shaped object made of rings. Scientists added various concentric and movable rings to show the supposed orbits of heavenly bodies. A similar but simpler device was the astronomical ring, which consisted of two circles, one representing the equator and the other representing the meridian (a longitudinal line running through the North and South Poles). A third ring, which pivoted on the imaginary Earth's axis, could be used to sight a star and find the angle between the star and the meridian. More complex was the torquetum, or "Turkish instrument." This three-dimensional teaching device could be used to demonstrate angles in different systems of celestial coordinates. The equatorium was a planar, or flat, instrument inscribed with various circles that could be used to find the positions of planets without having to make calculations.

Telescope is greatest advance An early instrument maker was Jean Fusorius (c. 1355–1436), a canon in Paris, who produced astrolabes, quadrants, "solid" spheres, and an equatorium. Early fifteenth-century craftsmen at Oxford and Cambridge universities in England also made instruments of these types. In Vienna, Austria, the Catholic priest Hans Dorn (c. 1430–1509) was particularly productive and innovative as an instrument maker. In the early sixteenth century Gemma Frisius (1508–1555) and Gerard Mercator had workshops in the Low Countries from which these instruments flowed constantly. At Nuremberg, Germany, Georg Hartmann (1489–1564) produced numerous astrolabes and other devices, in some cases making them in batches from identical molds. In London, English astronomers were similarly supplied by instrument makers Humphrey Cole (c. 1520–1591) and Elias Allen (after 1602–1653).

In the later Renaissance the most important observational astronomers were Bernard Walther (1430–1504) and Tycho Brahe (see "Astronomy" section previously in this chapter). Walther made precise measurements for thirty years. He used a cross staff, an instrument used

The frontispiece to Gerard Mercator's *Theatrum Orbis Terrarum,* **the first true atlas.** ©*Archivo Iconografico, S.A./Corbis. Reproduced by permission of the Corbis Corporation.*

to measure the altitude of stars, that was nine feet long and graduated in thirteen hundred equal divisions, as well as an armillary sphere three feet in diameter and graduated (marked to indicate intervals) to five minutes of arc (distance a celestial body travels in five minutes). While working at Wittenberg, Germany, in 1589, Brahe constructed a wooden quadrant with a nineteen-foot radius. It had a brass scale graduated to one minute of arc. Later he built an eight-foot equinoctial armillary sphere that read to fifteen seconds of arc (distance a celestial body travels in fifteen seconds), and a mural quadrant that read to ten seconds of arc. In his observatory at Uraniborg, Brahe consistently made angular measurements with an accuracy within one minute of arc. With the data supplied by Brahe's instruments, by 1609 Johannes Kepler (see "Astronomy" section previously in this chapter) was able to detect that the orbit of Mars is elliptical, not circular, as had previously been believed.

The greatest advance, however, came at the end of the Renaissance with the invention of the telescope. This device was first made sometime during 1608 by Zacharias Jansen (1580–c. 1638), an eyeglass maker in the Netherlands. During 1609 the news spread to Thomas Harriot (c. 1560–1621) in England and Galileo in Italy (see "Astronomy" section previously in this chapter). Harriot made the first recorded use of the telescope in July 1609, followed by Galileo later that year. Galileo revolutionized astronomy in 1610 with the publication of the *Sidereus nuncius*. In this work he gave an account of mountains on the Moon, the moons of Jupiter, and the many stars making up the Milky Way. Galileo's telescope had a small concave (hollowed inward) lens at the end and a single convex (curved outward) lens for its eyepiece. By 1611 Kepler had worked out the optics of the telescope, which were unknown to Galileo, and proposed a superior astro-

nomical instrument that employed concave lenses at both ends.

Navigation

Astronomical instruments were readily applied in navigation. The cross staff was equipped with sighting vanes (devices showing the direction of the wind) and gave direct readings in degrees. Usually made of wood and about three feet long, the cross staff was used to measure the Sun's midday altitude or the altitude of a star above the horizon. Later models had more than one crosspiece to increase the accuracy of the measurement. When the astrolabe was adapted for use on ships, its center portion was cut away to make it easier to hold in the wind. The mariner's astrolabe was made of metal so it would be more durable. It was usually equipped with an alidade, a device with vanes set close together to facilitate reading under conditions at sea.

The magnetic compass was readily adapted for nautical use. It is an instrument used to determine direction by utilizing the magnetic dipoles, or the attracting force between the two poles—north and south—at the extreme opposite ends of Earth's sphere. The device consists of a magnetic needle mounted on a compass card. The needle turns freely on a pivot and points to the magnetic north. During the Renaissance instrument makers developed a compass in which the compass card itself was pivoted and highly ornamented. The course of the ship was then indicated by the card's position relative to the ship's axis, or center. Speed was measured by a device called a log. It was a weighted rectangular plate attached to a long cord that, when thrown overboard, set itself crosswise and remained that way while the cord unwound. By the end of the sixteenth century, log cords were knotted at regular intervals so that the number of "knots" could be counted. Time was measured at half-minute intervals by a sandglass or log glass. The distance a ship traveled and its position could then be indicated on a peg compass, or "traverse board." The traverse board consisted of a board pierced with holes in which pegs could be inserted every half hour, thus providing a record of the ship's course.

Land surveying

Land surveying (measuring angles and lines on land with the use of geometry and trigonometry) was stimulated by the demand for new charts and maps, by military needs, and by changes in land ownership. Since both surveying and navigation involved the measurement of heights, bearings (position of one point in relation to another point), and distances, there was some similarity of methods. Surveyors and navigators also used some of the same instruments, such as the cross staff. The tendency, however, was toward developing specific instruments for specific purposes. Measuring rods and chains were inherited from the Middle Ages. During the Renaissance, triangulation (the process of finding a point in relation to two other points) became more common

and led to the development of new instruments. The Dutch instrument maker Gemma Frisius invented one of the first devices for measuring horizontal angles. This tool was a horizontal circular disk divided into four equal parts, called quadrants, of 90 degrees. At the center was an alidade that pivoted. A small compass was later added.

A further development was the geometrical square, a square-shaped board of wood or metal with a graduated scale running along the two sides opposite the corner where the alidade was located. It was used to measure right angles. A related instrument was the plane table, which was first described in the sixteenth century and quickly came into common use among surveyors. A plane table is an instrument consisting of a drawing board on a tripod (three-legged stand) with a ruler pointed to the object being observed. It was used to plot and measure lines. Surveyors also used hodometers and pedometers (instruments in the form of a watch that record the distance a person travels on foot), also known as way wisers, to provide quick estimates of distances.

Drawing

Drawing instruments were also improved during the Renaissance. Among them was the camera obscura, a dark chamber with a lens or pinhole through which an image is projected onto an opposite wall. The camera obscura has a long history, but from the fifteenth century onward it was used

Abacus

Although Renaissance mathematicians and merchants did most of their mathematical calculations on paper, using handbooks of mathematical problems, the abacus also continued to be used. The abacus grew out of early counting boards, which were boards with hollows holding pebbles or beads used to calculate. It has been dated to around 3500 B.C. in Mesopotamia. The abacus used in the Renaissance consisted of beads that slide on rods; it was developed in China in the fifteenth century. Before the use of decimal numbers, which allowed paper-and-pencil methods of calculation, the abacus was essential for almost all multiplication and division. The abacus is still used in many countries where modern calculators are not available. It also is still used in countries, such as Japan and China, with a long tradition of relying on this instrument.

as an aid by artists. As knowledge of optics increased, the pinhole was replaced by a lens to concentrate the image the camera produced. Dividers and compasses of various types were also produced, including the reduction compass and the proportional compass. The reduction compass was invented around 1554 and consisted of two legs attached at one end by a pivot and fitted with both fixed and adjustable points. It was used to divide straight lines or circles into integral parts and to find the proportions of unequal lines. The proportional compass was a further development proposed in 1568 by the Italian mathematician Federico Commandino (1509–1575). It consisted of two slotted arms with points at each end, held together by a cursor (a movable item used to mark a position) that acted as a pivot. A further improvement was the geometrical and military compass, which Galileo developed between 1595 and 1599. It may be described as the first mechanical mathematical calculator for general use—one that was not restricted to specific tasks. A similar device was invented around the same time by the English mathematician Thomas Hood (after 1582–1598), who called it a sector and described it in a work published in 1598.

Calculating

Although mathematicians and merchants did most of their mathematical calculations on paper with the aid of handbooks of mathematical problems, the frame counter or abacus also continued to be used. In 1617 John Napier, the discoverer of logarithms (see "Mathematical" section previously in this chapter), invented a calculating aid known as Napier's rods or Napier's bones. This device conveniently arranged the multiplication table to shorten the time of ordinary calculations. It consisted of a series of rods in a frame, marked with the digits 1 through 9, to multiply and divide using the principles of logarithms.

The next step was the slide rule, a device consisting of a ruler and

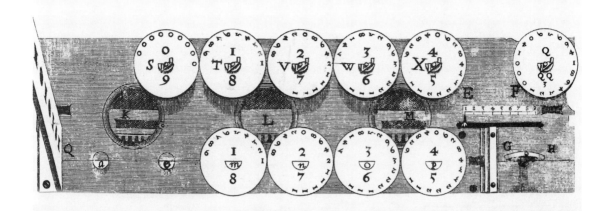

An illustration of John Napier's multiplying machine known as Napier's bones. *Photograph courtesy of The Library of Congress.*

a movable middle piece, which are marked with graduated logarithm scales. The concept of the slide rule was proposed in 1620 by English mathematician Edmund Gunter (1581–1626), who called it the "logarithmic line of numbers." The first slide rule was made by English mathematician William Oughtred (1575–1660) in 1621. Oughtred did not publish a description of his invention until 1632. In 1630 Richard Delamain (after 1610–1645), Oughtred's former pupil, published a description of a circular slide rule. Oughtred accused Delamain of stealing his idea, but evidence indicates that the two men worked on their inventions independently. Edmund Wingate (1596–1677) was credited with developing the modern straight slide rule, an instrument with a slider that moves on a fixed piece. A variety of specialized slide rules were developed by the end of the seventeenth century for trades such as masonry (brick and stone laying), carpentry, and tax collecting. While the slide rule was popular as a calculating tool for several centuries, it has largely been replaced by the electronic computer.

Precision in reading instruments was greatly improved by the invention of two devices, the nonius and the vernier. Each consists of a short graduated scale that slides along a longer graduated scale and enables one to make fractional divisions in units indicated on the longer scale. The nonius, which had more than thirty subdivisions, was the work of the Portuguese mathematician Pedro Nunes. It was improved by the Bavarian astronomer Christoph Clavius (1537–1612) and became the basis of the vernier, a simpler device that usually had only ten subdivisions to take into account. The vernier was perfected by French mathematician Pierre

Vernier (1584–1638) and is still used in the present day.

Physics and medicine

Other instruments of the Renaissance pertained mainly to the physical or natural sciences and to medicine. The microscope was less popular than the telescope, but medical scholars began to use the microscope and to make new discoveries in the middle of the seventeenth century. Historical records indicate that, prior to 1624, Galileo had adapted the telescope to make a compound microscope that would make a fly appear as large as a hen. Galileo also invented or experimented with other instruments, including the pusilogium (a pendulum type of pulse watch), the bilancetta (a small balance used to study fluids), the thermoscopium (in effect a thermometer without a scale), the giovilabio (a paper instrument that could be used to determine the positions of Jupiter's satellites), and an escapement (a device that controls wheelwork) for the pendulum clock.

In the field of magnetism, the English physician William Gilbert (1544–1603) was the major pioneer. Among the instruments with which he experimented was the terrera, or "earthkin," a small spherical magnet that simulated Earth. He also worked with the dipmeter, which measured magnetic dip and which he incorrectly thought could be used to determine latitude. In addition Gilbert developed the versorium, a pivoted needle that could be used for identifying "electrics."

In medicine the foremost instrument maker was the Venetian physician Santorio Santorio. Santorio perfected two devices that had already been anticipated by Galileo. The first was the thermometer, which Santorio equipped with a scale whose extreme points were determined by the temperatures of snow and a candle flame. The second was the pulsimeter, which measured blood pulse (the regular pulses caused by the beating of the heart) by the length of a pendulum whose swing matched the pulse's beat. He also invented a hygrometer for measuring humidity; the trocar, a special syringe for extracting bladder stones; and a bathing bed. Another significant invention was the weighing chair, which enabled Santorio to investigate variations in weight experienced by the human body as a result of ingestion (taking in food and liquids) and excretion (eliminating waste).

Alchemy

Alchemy was an ancient science that focused on changing base metals, such as lead, into silver and gold. Some scholars suggest that it was first practiced in early Egypt, while others believe it originated in the fifth or third century B.C. in China and moved westward. Alchemy often lapsed into mysticism and is no longer considered a science. Nevertheless, it was based on solid chemical knowledge and provided the foundation for the development of modern chemistry.

The alchemy of the Renaissance was based on ancient ideas,

Renaissance alchemists at work. Alchemy was an ancient science that focused on changing base metals into silver and gold. *Reproduced by permission of Hulton Archive.*

which passed from antiquity into the hands of Arab philosophers and scholars such as Geber (also known as Jābir ibn Hayyān; c. 721–c. 851). They drew together various ideas about the interaction of the two qualities of matter— the sulfuric (inflammable) quality and the mercurial (volatile) quality—with the four elements of matter: air, earth, fire, and water. As these ideas entered Christian Europe in the thirteenth century, they were again transformed by the translation of Arabic texts into Latin. Added to these texts were Christian concepts such as transubstantiation, or the belief that bread and wine actually turn into the body and blood of Jesus Christ during communion (a religious rite that commemorates the final meal, or Last Supper, that Christ had with his disciples). In the Middle Ages scholars also developed a complex system to explain alchemy. By the time of the Renaissance, alchemy was a practice that involved both the "life of the mind," associated with education and learning, and the "life of the hands," enjoyed by craftsmen and other members of the lower social classes.

Alchemists help metals "grow"

Renaissance alchemy was based on the idea that metals "grew" in the "womb of the earth." A metal underwent an organic process that was likened to the growth of any other living substance such as a plant or an animal. Metals where thus drawn into the "great chain of being" in which every aspect of the divinely created world was joined to everything else according to God's perfectly ordered scheme. The great chain of being was not only ordered, but it was also hierarchical (arranged according to levels of importance). The kingdom of metals was organized into a sequence that led from the crudest and most immature metals (lead, tin, iron, and copper) to the higher, more nearly perfect metals (mercury, silver, and gold). Through natural life-giving processes, all metals were literally growing and changing in the earth. They reached their peak in the most pure and perfect gold, which did not tarnish, corrode, or otherwise decay.

The art and practice of alchemy was supposed to hasten this natural, organic process. Alchemists argued that if the womb of Earth could serve as a vessel for the transformation of lead into gold, then a glass vessel containing lead could be subjected to heat and then led through the same growth process. Other metals and chemicals were added to speed the process further and facilitate a successful outcome. Alchemists worked over hot charcoal fires for weeks (and often years) as they attempted to nurture the metals into higher and higher levels of perfection. When substances were added to the glass vessels the process was often described as "feeding." The

substances in the vessels were then reduced through distillation (evaporation and condensation) and fed once more. This process often caused spectacular changes in the color of the substances. Alchemists believed that the changes in color reflected important transformations in the metals, so they carefully noted these changes.

The work of alchemy was risky, however. All too often the charcoal fires would burn too hot and the glass vessels would explode, spilling the contents onto the fire and releasing poisonous fumes. Alchemists who spent weeks tending the fires would often have singed eyebrows and eyelashes. Because there were no tests to determine the purity of metals, alchemists often unwittingly put toxic substances into their vessels. The free use of sulfur and mercury also endangered the health of the alchemists, who absorbed these substances through the skin. They sometimes even ate or drank the results of their experiments to determine what metals were present.

Quest for philosopher's stone For many alchemists the goal of this painstaking and dangerous work was gold and the lure of an unlimited supply of riches. For others, however, the goal was not gold but an elusive substance called the philosopher's stone. The philosopher's stone could supposedly be produced by subjecting alchemically purified metals to more refined processes. The stone would be an all-purpose medicine capable of both "healing" sick or imperfect metals and curing sick and imperfect human bodies. Some alchemists believed that the stone could make human beings immortal (live forever), redeeming their earthly bodies and transforming them into a spiritual and divine body. During the Renaissance alchemists interested in pursuing this more philosophical and metaphysical branch of alchemy kept their ideas and techniques as secret as possible. Although alchemists shared their texts on the philosopher's stone, they kept the contents cloaked in obscure symbolism. This technique was a way to contain full knowledge of the art within a tight-knit circle of alchemists and their apprentices (those who learn a craft from a master).

In the sixteenth century, many social changes began to threaten these well-guarded secrets. For instance, higher levels of literacy (the ability to read and write), along with a dramatic rise in the publication of books, made knowledge more available to the general public. As increasing numbers of popular alchemists went to fairs and markets, charlatans (those who engage in fraud) were investigated and imprisoned by state and local officials. In addition, the German alchemist and natural philosopher Paracelsus (see "Medicine" section previously in this chapter) introduced a new principle (salt, or the fixed principle) into alchemy for the first time in centuries. He challenged the ancient sulfur-mercury theory of metallic generation and transformation. Paracelsus's work was enormously influential in the sixteenth century. Alchemists, physicians, and apothecaries (pharmacists) began to experiment with his theories

and with a considerable body of chemical medicines attributed to him.

Monarchs hire alchemists

Despite the increase in the number of charlatans, alchemy retained its connections to royalty during the Renaissance. Many members of the nobility throughout Europe maintained alchemical laboratories and hired their own alchemists. The Medici family of Florence was interested in alchemy, as were Queen Elizabeth I of England (1533–1603; ruled 1558–1603) and King James I of England (1566–1625; ruled 1603–25). The leader most associated with alchemy, however, was Holy Roman Emperor Rudolf II (1552–1612; ruled 1576–1612). His court at Prague, Bohemia (now the Czech Republic), served as an intellectual center for many European alchemists in the sixteenth century. In addition to Paracelsus, many alchemists made significant contributions to understanding the structure of matter. Basil Valentine (born 1394) was a medieval author whose works were recovered and published during the Renaissance. Also important were Leonhard Thrumeysser (1531–1596), Andreas Libavius (c. 1560–1616), and Michael Sedzimir (also known as Sendigovius; 1566–1636). Robert Fludd (1574–1637) kept alchemical ideas alive in England well into the seventeenth century.

Astrology

Astrology is another field that was considered a science during the

Horoscope

Astrology enjoyed considerable popularity during the Renaissance. Monarchs and noblemen had astrologers create charts called horoscopes, which mapped the position of astronomical bodies at certain times and were used to predict future events. Although astrology eventually fell out of favor because of new theories of the universe, it remains popular even today. Most newspapers and magazines feature horoscope sections that are avidly consulted by readers.

A horoscope is a diagram in the shape of a circle, called the ecliptic, which represents Earth's orbit in its annual rotation around the Sun. The ecliptic is divided into twelve sections known as the signs of the Zodiac, and each sign is associated with a set of human characteristics. The twelve signs are Aries, Taurus, Gemini, Cancer, Leo, Virgo, Libra, Scorpio, Sagittarius, Capricorn, Aquarius, and Pisces. Each planet, including the Sun and the Moon, is associated with basic human drives. The ecliptic is also divided into twelve houses corresponding to the twenty-four-hour period during which Earth rotates once on its axis. Each house is related to certain aspects of a person's life.

In casting a horoscope, an astrologer chooses a date in the future and then assigns each planet a particular sign according to where the planet appears on the ecliptic for that time. The astrologer then makes a prediction about events that will take place by interpreting the position of the planets within the signs and the houses. Astrologers also give a person a certain sign, such as an Aquarius or a Taurus, according to the sign occupied by the Sun at the time of the person's birth. It is called the person's Sun sign.

early Renaissance period but has since been widely discredited. Closely related to astronomy, astrology is the study of how events on Earth are influenced by the positions and movements of the Sun, Moon, planets, and stars. Astrologers believe that the position of heavenly bodies at the exact moment of a person's birth reflect his or her character. Later movements of heavenly bodies determine that person's destiny.

Historians estimate that the earliest known form of astrology was practiced by the Chaldeans, who lived in Babylonia (now Iraq), in 3000 B.C. Astrology was also part of ancient cultures in China and India, and evidence of astrological practices has been found in Maya ruins in Central America. Astrology reached Greece by the fifth century B.C., and philosophers such as Pythagoras and Plato incorporated it into their study of religion and astronomy. Astrology was popular in Europe throughout the Middle Ages, though it had been condemned by church leaders since the early days of

Christianity. The reason for the church's dislike was because astrologers relied on readings of the positions of planets and stars, rather than on the Bible, to interpret and predict human events. Astrology also originated in the East, which was considered a heathen culture. Like alchemy, astrology eventually fell out of favor when Copernicus, Kepler, Galileo, and other scientists discovered new facts about Earth and the universe. Nevertheless, astrology enjoyed considerable popularity during the Renaissance. Monarchs and noblemen had astrologers create charts called horoscopes, which mapped the position of astronomical bodies at certain times and were used to predict future events. One of the most famous astrologers was Nostradamus (also known as Michel de Notredame; 1503–1566), whose prophesies attracted the attention of the French king Henry II (1519–1559; ruled 1547–59) and his wife, Catherine de Médicis (1519–1589).

The twelve signs of the Zodiac used by astrologers. Although considered a science during the early Renaissance, astrology has since been widely discredited. ©Bettmann/ Corbis; Reproduced by permission of the Corbis Corporation.

Nostradamus is famous doctor

Nostradamus was born in Provence, a region in southern France. His family was of Jewish heritage but they had converted to Catholicism during a period of religious intolerance. Jews were always outsiders in western Europe, and over the centuries many were forced to convert to Catholicism. Both of Nostradamus's grandfathers were esteemed scholars. One was a physician, and Nostradamus studied classical languages with the other. At the age of fourteen

Nostradamus left home to study in Avignon, the ecclesiastical (Roman Catholic Church) and academic center of Provence. In class, he sometimes voiced opposition to the teachings of the Catholic priests, who dismissed the study of astrology and the theories of the astronomer Nicolas Copernicus. Copernicus had recently gained fame with his theory that Earth and other planets revolved around the Sun—contrary to the Christian beliefs about the heavens (see "Astronomy" section previously in this chapter). Nostradamus's family warned him to hold his tongue, since he could be easily singled out for persecution because of his Jewish background in the anti-Jewish society of France. Earlier, from his grandfathers he had secretly become acquainted with some mystical areas of Jewish wisdom, including the Kabbalah (a Jewish body of knowledge studying divinity, creation, and many other subjects) and alchemy (see "Alchemy" section previously in this chapter).

In 1525 Nostradamus graduated from the University of Montpellier, where he had studied both medicine and astrology. During the first several years of his career as a doctor he traveled to towns and villages where people were dying of the bubonic plague (see "Black Death" in Chapter 1). Called "Le Charbon" (charcoal) because of the festering black sores it left on victims' bodies, the deadly epidemic had no cure. Doctors commonly "bled" their patients, and knew nothing of how to prevent further infection. They did not realize that unsanitary conditions contributed to the spread of the disease. Nostradamus would prescribe fresh air and water, a low-fat diet, and new bedding for the afflicted. He often administered an herbal remedy made from rosehips, later discovered to be rich in vitamin C. Entire towns recovered with these herbal remedies, which were common at the time, but Nostradamus's beliefs about infection control could have resulted in charges of heresy (violation of the laws of God and the Catholic Church) and death.

Begins foretelling future Word of Nostradamus's healing powers made him a celebrated figure in Provence. He wrote a book listing the doctors and pharmacists he had met in southern Europe, translated anatomical texts, developed recipes for gourmet foods, and received his doctorate from Montpellier in 1529. He also taught at the university for three years, but he left when his radical ideas about disease were censured. He chose a wife from among the many offered to him by wealthy and connected families and settled in the town of Agen. Then the plague killed his wife and two young children. Because the famed physician could not save his own family, citizens suddenly looked upon him with scorn. His in-laws sued for the return of the dowry given to him. His patron, a scholar and philosopher named Julius Caesar Scaliger (1484–1558), also broke ties with him. A chance remark Nostradamus had once made about a statue of the Virgin Mary (mother of Jesus Christ) landed him in court defending himself against charges of heresy. He fled the area when told he was to appear before the feared Inquisition, a church court set up to search out and punish heretics (see "Popes implement Roman Inquisition" in Chapter 7).

For the next several years Nostradamus traveled through southern Europe. Some modern scholars have suggested that this difficult period probably awakened his powers of clairvoyance (ability to predict the future). By 1544 torrential rains were bringing more disaster to southern France, which had already been devastated by the plague. Nostradamus appeared in Marseilles and then in Aix, where he managed to halt the spread of disease and was again celebrated for his skills. Moving to the town of Salon, he set up a medical practice, remarried, and began a new family. Although he was outwardly a practicing Catholic, he secretly spent the night hours in his study meditating over a brass bowl filled with water, a practice that would have caused suspicion among guardians of the Catholic faith. The meditation would put him into a trance. Scholars theorize that he may have used herbs to achieve such a state. In these trances Nostradamus would, according to his writings, have visions about events that were to happen during the coming year.

Predicts king's death Nostradamus wrote down his visions, and in 1550 he began publishing them in almanacs, which appeared annually for the next fifteen years. In the almanacs Nostradamus described astrological phases for the next year and he offered hints of upcoming events in rhymed four-line verses called quatrains. The almanacs became immensely popular, and soon Nostradamus was even more famous in France. By now his visions were such an integral part of his scholarship that he decided to compile them into one massive book for posterity. He would call this book *Centuries*. Each of the ten planned volumes would contain one hundred predictions in quatrain form, and the next two thousand years of humanity would be forecasted.

Nostradamus began working on *Centuries* in 1554. The first seven volumes were published in Lyon the following year. Although he completed volumes eight through ten by 1558, he would not allow them to be published until after his death. Yet the reception of the initial works made Nostradamus a celebrated figure. His writings attracted the interest of France's royal family. In 1556 he was invited to the Paris court of King Henry II and Queen Catherine de Médicis. Catherine belonged to the powerful Médici family of Florence, Italy, who were known for their political ambitions. The queen hoped that Nostradamus could give her guidance regarding the futures of her seven children. Nostradamus had also been summoned to explain Quatrain Thirty-Five of the first volume of *Centuries*, which apparently referred to Henry. It read: "The young lion will overcome the older one / On the field of combat in single battle / He will pierce his eyes through a golden cage / Two wounds made one, then he dies a cruel death."

Nostradamus told the king to avoid any ceremonial jousting during his forty-first year (1559), a warning that had also been given by Henry's own astrologer. Nostradamus spent the next three years sheltered in the luxury of the royal court. He drew up astrology charts for four of the royal couple's sons and predicted that they would all become kings. Then Nostradamus received word that Catholic authorities were again becoming suspicious of his foretelling and were about to investigate him. He returned to his wife and children in Salon. Finishing volumes eight through ten of *Centuries,* he began work on two additional volumes. On June 28, 1559—in his forty-first year—King Henry was injured in a jousting tournament celebrating two marriages in his family. With thousands watching, his opponent's lance penetrated the visor of his helmet and lodged in his brain. The blinded king died ten days later.

Remains popular today Already a celebrity in France, Nostradamus became a figure inspiring both awe and fright among the populace. His other prophecies regarding France's royal line were consulted, and most seemed to predict only death and tragedy. Catherine de Médicis visited Nostradamus in Salon during her royal tour of 1564, and he again told her that all four of her sons would become kings. Yet the children came to equally dismal ends: one son became king of Poland, but was murdered by a priest; another died before carrying out a plot

to kill another brother; two others died young as well; the three daughters also met tragic fates. The family's House of Valois came to an end with the death of one of the daughters, Queen Margaret (1553–1615), wife of King Henry IV (Henry of Navarre; 1553–1610; ruled 1572–89).

Nostradamus himself died in 1566, after many years of suffering from gout, a disease characterized by painful swelling of the joints. Naturally, he predicted his own end, though records show that he was off by a year. Many translations of his *Centuries* and treatises on their significance appeared in the generations following his death. For two centuries the Vatican (office of the pope) issued the Index of Prohibited Books, a list of forbidden publications (see "Popes implement Roman Inquisition" in Chapter 7). *Centuries* was always on the list. *Centuries* remains popular to the present day, and interpreters claim Nostradamus predicted many important twentieth-century events. For instance, he reportedly warned that the German Nazi leader Adolf Hitler (1889–1945) would rise to power in the 1930s. Another of Nostradamus's supposed predictions was the explosion of the U.S. space shuttle *Challenger* in 1986.

Social Status and Community

11

Social status was the basis of life in Europe during the Renaissance and Reformation. Since the early Middle Ages, people had been divided into three groups, called estates. Each of the Three Estates were further subdivided into many other levels. A person's rank on the social scale was determined by birth, gender, sources of wealth, occupation, political position, residency in town or country, and numerous other factors. The system was somewhat flexible, however, and people frequently moved up within their own social class, or even occasionally elevated themselves to a higher estate.

First Estate

The First Estate was comprised of the Roman Catholic clergy (church officials; also called clergymen). They were placed at the top of the social ladder because their involvement in spiritual matters was considered vital to the welfare of society. The clergy were divided into secular (unordained) and regular (ordained) branches. An ordained clergyman is one whom the church officially authorizes to perform priestly duties. These duties include holding worship services, hearing confession (church members' admissions of sin), and administering the sacraments (holy rituals) of the Catholic religion.

The secular clergy were high officials called prelates. Prelates were the pope (supreme head of the Roman Catholic Church), cardinals (officials ranking directly below the pope), and bishops (heads of church districts). Most prelates came from the ranks of the nobility, although some were from wealthy commoner families and a few had lower social origins. During the Middle Ages the secular clergy wielded extensive power, constantly coming into conflict with kings and emperors over the question of the proper authority of the church. These conflicts reached a crisis during the Renaissance and Reformation. Prelates enjoyed income from land estates, loans, taxes on clergy, and the wealth of their families of birth. Moreover, they formed the learned elite of late medieval society, until Renaissance education created a new class of scholars from the secular world.

Below the secular clergy were the regular clergy. Regular clergymen were urban priests (heads of local churches in cities), cathedral canons (heads of cathedrals, or large main churches, in cities), and parish priests (heads of town and village churches). All of these clergymen occupied a considerably lower position than the secular clergy, both within the church and in society. There was a wide gulf between high prelates and parish priests in terms of wealth and level of education. Prelates were well educated and had luxurious palaces (large homes), whereas parish priests tended to have minimal education and lived in near poverty. The regular clergy also included monks (men who live in religious houses called monasteries) and nuns (women who live in religious houses called convents or nunneries). Many monks and nuns came from noble families. In fact, unmarried sons and daughters of noblemen were able to secure powerful and lucrative positions in the church as abbots (heads of monasteries) and abbesses (heads of convents). Along with bishops, abbots and abbesses controlled vast amounts of land, received substantial donations from parishioners (church members), and made profitable investments. In addition, they had jurisdiction over many subjects and enjoyed important connections with powerful noble families.

Second Estate

The Second Estate was reserved for the nobility—emperors, kings, dukes, counts, and multiple ranks of knights. Membership in the Second Estate was originally limited to those who were born into noble families. For the most part, nobles were expected to live on the income from their land. Business, trade, and industry were considered degrading occupations. Yet there were stark contrasts among the nobility. Lords of large estates exercised considerable authority over neighboring villages and peasants, whereas some lesser noble families were barely able to maintain their social position. Noblemen were mainly concerned with exhibiting their elite status and staying in positions of power. From medieval chivalry and romance, which fascinated all European noblemen during the Renaissance, there evolved the arts of courtesy, heraldry (family insignia on armor), and emblems, as well as elaborate codes of honor. The nobility maintained elaborate courts, surrounding themselves with servants, advisers, and others who helped them create an aura of influence and prestige. They were devoted to armed combat, both for war and for leisure. They upheld the chivalric code, a complex set of social rules dating from the days of knighthood in the Middle Ages (see "Feudalism" in Chapter 1). The nobility paid great attention to manners. They cultivated body movements, facial expressions, and ways of speaking that would show their refinement and hide their emotions. Great emphasis was placed on elaborate dining rituals, the latest fashions, tournaments (games of combat between two men carrying lances on horseback), and humanist discussions—all as signs of their social superiority. Noblemen elevated themselves further by building grand castles in the mountains or expensive palaces in the countryside. In these magnificent dwellings they held banquets, staged hunts, and patronized the arts on a grand scale.

Monarchs occupy top rank

During the Renaissance and Reformation period, Europe was still fragmented into hundreds of indepen-

A French Renaissance manuscript illumination of a tournament. The second estate, or nobility, placed great emphasis on tournaments as a sign of their social superiority. ©Gianni Dagli Orti/Corbis. Reproduced by permission of the Corbis Corporation.

dent states. Heading these states were various types and ranks of rulers—popes, emperors, kings, cardinals, dukes, counts, and knights—who were called princes. At the highest level were popes, emperors, and kings, who ruled as monarchs. (A monarch is the sole head of a government.) The pope was the supreme head of the Roman Catholic Church as well as the ruler of the Papal States. The Holy Roman Emperor presided over his native land as well as other states within the Holy

Roman Empire. Kings were leaders of territories that included smaller states or provinces headed by noblemen such as dukes, counts, knights, and (in Germany) princes. Many dukes also had power nearly equal to that of monarchs, especially in the Italian city-states (see "The major city-states" in Chapter 2).

Monarchy was the most common form of government, and most monarchs were kings. Nevertheless, not all monarchies were created equal, as they varied greatly in size and type. Some were ruled by hereditary dynasties (rulers from the same family), such as Scotland under the Stuarts, England under the Tudors, and France under the Valois. Other monarchies, such as Poland, Hungary, Bohemia, and the Holy Roman Empire, were elective. Some kingdoms were relatively uniform in language or ethnic membership, but most contained varied regions where people spoke different languages and had come together over long periods of time. Some lands were united with others under the rule of one king, which was the case of Poland and Lithuania as well as Denmark, Sweden, and Norway.

Many monarchies made high-flown claims to power and independence. In the early sixteenth century Holy Roman Emperor Charles V (1500–1558; ruled 1519–56), who also ruled Spain as King Charles I (1516–56), headed the largest empire in history to that time. He saw himself occupying his thrones for the purpose of leading the Christian world against the enemies of God: Islam (a religion founded by the prophet Muhammad), the Lutherans (followers of Martin Luther, who initiated the movement to reform the church), and other heretics (those who violate the laws of God and the church). Admirers of French monarchs came close to defying their rulers, calling the king a "vicar [earthly representative] of Christ in his kingdom" or a "second sun on Earth," and even likening him to a "corporeal god" (God in human form).

Renaissance kings spent vast sums on upholding the highest image of the monarchy. They commissioned painters, sculptors, and engravers; patronized poets and playwrights; and mandated architects, heralds, and iconographers (artists who created symbols or images to celebrate the king and kingdom) to inflate the reputation of the monarch and his dynasty. Kings displayed themselves in the most magnificent of finery wherever subjects needed to be reminded of the ruler's authority and majesty (see "Life at court" section later in this chapter). However, no European monarchy of the time ever achieved absolute rule. Kings had to deal day to day with the complex and confusing machinery of government and political obligations. There seems to have been no master plan on the part of Renaissance monarchs to solve these challenges.

Kings versus popes

Kings first had to come to grips with their relationship with the church and particularly the papacy. Henry VIII (1491–1547; ruled 1509–47) took the

Church of England entirely out of the jurisdiction of the pope and made himself supreme head (see "England" in Chapter 3). The Spanish monarchs Ferdinand II of Aragon (1452–1516; ruled 1479–1516) and Isabella I of Castile (1451–1504; ruled 1474–1504) won the right to name church officials. During the Spanish Inquisition, they had control of the highest church court in the realm, virtually independent of the pope (see "Spain" in Chapter 3). In 1516 the French monarchy negotiated a concordat (agreement) with Pope Leo X (1475–1521; reigned 1513–21) by which it could control the choicest church offices in the realm (see "France" in Chapter 3). French kings had the right to censor papal bulls (official declarations). Thus the leading western European monarchies had won significant victories over the church before the Reformation. A degree of control over the church guaranteed monarchs not only certain economic benefits but also the influential loyalty of the clergy. Loyal noblemen could also look to the crown as the source of church careers for their family and clients.

Financing the monarchy

An unceasing problem for Renaissance monarchs was finding enough money to support their administrative responsibilities and ambitions. The cost of warfare had escalated: mercenaries (hired soldiers), warships, artillery trains, musketeers (soldiers who carried muskets, a type of rifle), and fortresses did not come cheaply. Massive building programs, such as those undertaken by Henry VIII and

A man paying taxes. In order to finance their extravagant lifestyles, Renaissance monarchs often had to impose taxes on their subjects. ©Archivo Iconografico, S.A./Corbis. Reproduced by permission of the Corbis Corporation.

King Francis I of France (1494–1547; ruled 1515–47), were also drains on royal treasuries. Kings met this challenge by selling royal lands and state offices. In fact, many kings invented new offices strictly for the purpose of sale. These measures opened careers for the middle class and reinforced the view of royalty as the center of authority. Loans could be obtained from banking houses or forcibly imposed on prosperous subjects. In the end, however, monarchs had to consider raising taxes.

In most countries it was recognized that a king seeking new taxation required the consent of his subjects, through the approval of a representative institution such as a parliament or a regional assembly. Parliaments and assemblies were seldom eager to see taxes raised, but at the same time they did not want to impede the legitimate demands of government. As kings developed a growing administrative framework for enforcing their wills, they also increasingly had to contend with the opinions of their subjects. Noblemen had always claimed the right to be appointed as councilors to their monarch and to take part in the rule of the kingdom. Even in the sixteenth century, when most kings had won the right to staff their councils as they saw fit, they knew they had to appoint members of old noble families who had remained loyal to them. Increasingly, however, monarchs looked outside the great families for their professional administrators and came to favor the sons of the lesser nobility and the prosperous middle class. There often was tension between the older nobility and the bureaucrats.

During the Renaissance and Reformation period, kings, royal councils, princely courts, some parliaments, and regional assemblies all gained power. No realm could function without cooperation among these various groups. Nobles continued to dominate the military and politics, middle-class professionals contributed legal and administrative expertise, and the king served as patron, negotiator, and moving force behind the growing state.

Third Estate

The Third Estate originally began with rural laborers, but it eventually grew to include commoners from both town and country. This class had a very broad range of members. At the upper level were lawyers, professors, physicians, merchants, and magistrates (judges), among others. In the lower levels were bailiffs (sheriffs' employees), soldiers, artisans, and peasants.

Urban society

Prior to the sixteenth century many urban members of the Third Estate gained status through international trade, manufacturing, and land ownership in town and country. From the sixteenth century on, many businessmen and industrialists turned to investing in lands and loans and pursuing careers in law. By the sixteenth century, particularly in France and Spain, members of the Third Estate were able to rise to the Second Estate by acquiring wealth. Businessmen converted their fortunes and capital in-

Two women displaying Elizabethan clothing. The woman on the left is wearing clothing typical of the nobility while the woman on the right wears the clothing of a commoner. *Reproduced by permission of The Granger Collection.*

vestments into land holdings, which were more prestigious than money. They bought titles and adopted noble behavior. People also raised their status through outstanding public service to a ruler or the state, or by marriage into the nobility.

The middle class, which became the core of the Third Estate, began developing as a result of urbanization after the year 1000. Level of education, profession or occupation, and wealth were the primary criteria for membership in the middle class. Lawyers, government officials, physicians, and intellectuals were at the top. They were followed by merchants, masters, journeymen (workers who have learned a trade and work for other persons) apprentices (those who learn a craft from a master), urban laborers, and domestic servants. Wealthy professionals, merchants, and manufacturers formed powerful and prestigious corporations and confraternities. These professional organizations exerted political influence, performed charitable deeds, and staged elaborate pageants, all symbols of their status. Guild members followed the professionals in rank, and in some cities they exercised considerable social and political influence. In Florence, for example, the fourteen major and seven minor guilds were divided both politically and socially, but they shared business activities, economic values, and moral values.

Guild membership separated masters, journeymen, and apprentices from those in the laboring class, who were lower in status than artisans. Status was associated with active participation in the guilds and confraternities. It required both wealth and social prominence. In contrast, laborers were unorganized, had no legal rights, and at times lived on the edge of poverty. Unlike guild masters, they were prohibited by law from meeting and organizing. Yet even within the laboring

class social status was attached to certain jobs. Tasks that required more physical strength than skill earned little or no respect.

Rural society

Rural society was also divided into social ranks. The first included high prelates who owned land and prominent lay families who spent part of their time in the city. The second, landlords and farmers, leased their properties from the first group. In western Europe the third group included independent peasants and peasants who rented land from landlords and relied on their own efforts for support. They were followed by the highly mobile, landless agricultural laborers, who depended on landlords for animals, seeds, and fertilizers. The position of these last two groups was always precarious because of high rents, taxes, usury (high-interest loans), crop failure, war, and epidemics. While serfdom still prevailed in some parts of western Europe, for the most part peasants achieved free status with the possibility of some mobility and the right to lease or own land. In contrast, peasants in eastern Europe were reduced to servile workers. They were deprived of any rights to land in east Germany, Silesia, Bohemia, Poland, Russia, Hungary, and Romania. Their movement was severely restricted, while their labor dues and services multiplied. Throughout Europe, the status of most country dwellers, particularly agricultural laborers, was regarded as inferior to that of townsmen. Urban dwellers often

Guilds

The corporations known as guilds played a significant part in urban life in Europe throughout the Renaissance. Guild members included artisans, merchants, peddlers, and shopkeepers. Originating in the thirteenth century, guilds controlled market conditions for foodstuffs, clothing, and construction. They also set standards for manufacturing. Another function of guilds was to provide training for apprentices. The training of an apprentice, which usually lasted for several years, provided the trainee not only with skills but also with shelter, meals, and lodging. Young, unmarried apprentices in particular were kept off the streets and to some extent out of trouble. Municipal authorities thus approved of guilds as protection against social unrest.

In many instances, guilds were also the basis of political life. In Florence and London, guild membership was essential to make a man eligible for office. Guilds also had a spiritual function. Members were Roman Catholic, and they met to celebrate their patron saint's festival. Each member was guaranteed a funeral, which everyone was required to attend. A guild maintained a local church through an agreement with the parish priest. Many guilds became patrons of the arts as they commissioned artists to decorate the church. The guilds tried to outdo one another with works by such masters as sculptors Donatello (c. 1386–1466) and Lorenzo Ghiberti (c. 1378–1455). The trade guilds and confraternities of Venice commissioned cycles of paintings from Tintoretto (also known as Jacopo Robusti; c. 1518–1594) and other famous artists. Beginning in 1535 the guilds of London organized the pageant for the Lord Mayor's Show.

mistrusted peasants, and law codes in various cities described them as natural-born inferiors who were malicious, insolent, and stupid.

Life at court

A ruler's court, the concept of which had developed during the Middle Ages, was the center of social and political life for the Renaissance nobility. It was based in the castle or palace of a pope, king, emperor, or duke, who was generally referred to as a prince. Most rulers were men. Salic Laws stated that only the male heirs of a ruler could take his place as the leader of a kingdom or state. Nevertheless, many women, such as Queen Isabella I of Castile and Queen Elizabeth I of England, came to power when there were no men in direct line to the throne. The court brought together numerous levels of the nobility as well as people from other social classes. A Renaissance court was typically composed of two concentric circles (one circle inside another). Within the inside circle were the councilors (members of a council) and officials whose work was directly supervised by the ruler. In the outer circle were the household officers who served the ruler's personal needs. The ruler's husband or wife had a separate household, but it too was part of the court. The function of the court was to regulate access to the ruler and to maintain the splendid surroundings and elaborate ceremonies that promoted the ruler's prestige.

Another important function was to involve rich and powerful people in the government. Because the court was the center of patronage (financial support), the atmosphere was always tense. Ministers, aristocratic and middle-class councilors, ladies of the court, secretaries, artisans, and even jesters and dwarfs jostled for favor and patronage. The ruler's household was usually presided over by a chamberlain (attendant), who organized it to give the ruler protection from the unending demands for patronage. The outer circle of the court was supervised by a steward (manager or supervisor), who kept the ruler in contact with the government and his or her subjects.

Court is status symbol

Courts became more elaborate during the Renaissance. New dynasties (rulers from the same family), such as the Sforza dukes in Italy and the Tudor monarchs in England, made their palaces and castles especially splendid to cover up the fact that they had only recently come to power. The people and the nobility were dazzled by court festivals, which were often used to make a weak ruler appear stronger. The rise of diplomacy, or political negotiation, likewise favored the growth of the court. Visiting princes or their emissaries (representatives) were treated to grand spectacles designed to impress them with the wealth and power of their host. Solemn entry processions, such as those greeting the arrival of a visiting sovereign or a bride for the prince, became occasions of spectacular display. Artists, architects, artisans, actors, musicians, courtiers (members of court), and eventually the entire populace (as spectators) cooperated in these celebrations. As rulers continued to cultivate an image of power and prestige, access to them was made more difficult. Elaborate ceremonies created distance between the ruler and visitors, further enhancing his aura. Courtiers gave great importance to dress and protocol, which revealed differences in rank and made the favors of the sovereign even more significant. The preening and display of majesty reached its peak in 1520 when Francis I and Henry VIII met at the Field of Cloth of Gold. The splendor of the French king's tent was said to outdo the Egyptian pyramids and the Roman amphitheaters, and the dress of the participants was so costly that it was said they "carried their mills, forests, and meadows on their backs." In other words, they bought clothes with the income they received from their estates.

The ceremonies of the papacy (office of the pope) were imitated by

A manuscript illumination depicting members of a king's court surrounding the monarch on his throne. ©*Historical Picture Archive/Corbis. Reproduced by permission of the Corbis Corporation.*

rulers' courts. The papacy had perfected its protocol (system of proper procedures) while the pope was in exile (absence from Rome, Italy, the official seat of the Roman Catholic Church) in Avignon, France, during the Great Schism (1309–1377; see "Crisis in the papacy" in Chapter 1). The papal master of ceremonies was in charge of the pope's court. One important ritual was the kissing of the pope's foot, a practice that was derived from the court of Byzantium (center of the Orthodox Eastern Church). At solemn banquets the pope was served in a ceremony that resembled the Roman Catholic mass (a worship service in which communion is celebrated). Butlers tasted his food and wine, which was then offered to him by servers on bended knee, while cardinals and other church officials either stood around or ate at lower tables. When the pope washed his hands or drank, laymen genuflected (touched a knee to the floor) and clergy stood, mimicking the ritual of the mass. The development of court etiquette was also spurred by permanent embassies (official offices of representatives of foreign countries) at the papal court. Ambassadors jealously watched the reception of rival

Field of Cloth of Gold

In June 1520, King Francis I of France and King Henry VIII of England met outside Guînes, France, at the Val Doré (Gold Valley). From June 7 until June 24, the kings and their courts engaged in "feats of arms" that were considered extravagant even by the standards of the Renaissance. Observers came up with the name "Field of Cloth of Gold" to describe the sight of so many luxuriously dressed nobles and servants.

The occasion was the celebration of a treaty signed by France and England in March 1520. The agreement promised a new era of harmony among the major European powers: France, England, Spain, and the Holy Roman Empire. Henry and his entire court set sail for France, while thousands of French laborers completed work on magnificent tents, pavilions, and stands for the spectators. The French nobility erected elaborate tents of velvet and cloth made of gold. Francis's grand tent, also made of gold cloth, was supported by two masts from a ship (poles that support sails) tied together and surmounted by a life-size statue of Saint Michael (angel of the sword). Henry outdid Francis by building a temporary palace outside Guînes with a brick foundation, walls of timber and canvas fashioned to look like brick, and large windows.

ambassadors, and they were frequently offended at perceived slights or evidence of favoritism. For instance, at a public audience (meeting with the pope) in 1570, the pope called for a stool to seat the grand duke of Tuscany. This privilege was normally reserved for the Holy Roman Emperor, so the ambassadors of other powers stormed out in protest.

Princes seek privacy

Kings were expected to have the most magnificent court and elaborate protocol, but territorial lords such as dukes often competed with them. Great nobles expanded their households into small courts. In his treatise on cardinals, the Italian humanist Paolo Cortesi (1465–1510) described one cardinal's palace and court that could easily employ sixty gentlemen attendants and eighty servants. Cristoforo di Messisbugo, the steward to Duke Ercole II of Ferrara (ruled 1534–1559), listed the personnel of the Ferrara court: the duke's family; court nobles, gentlemen, councilors, ambassadors, secretaries, chancellors; doctors, chaplains, and musicians; chamberlain and staff, including the master of the wardrobe and staff, valets (male personal servants), pages (youths who served knights), and doorkeepers; master of the house, steward and staff, including butlers, purveyors (food suppliers), cooks, carvers, servers, porters

On June 7 the kings and their courts of equal number, mounted on horseback, proceeded to the Val Doré and halted at opposite ends, as if arrayed for battle. Then, at the sound of a trumpet, Henry and Francis left their attendants behind. They galloped their horses toward each other, as if to engage in combat. Halting at a spot marked by a spear, the two kings embraced. After withdrawing to a nearby tent, they emerged two hours later and ordered their nobles to embrace one another. The "feats of arms" were meant to strengthen the embrace of reconciliation. The celebration commenced on June 9 and consisted of jousting (combat with spears on horseback), open-field tournaments, and combat on foot. The only contest between the two kings appears to have been an impromptu wrestling match, in which Francis bested Henry. The celebration was solemnized in a mass on June 23. The next day, at the conclusion of the tournaments, the kings bade farewell and vowed to build at Val Doré a chapel dedicated to Our Lady of Friendship and a palace where they could meet each year. In 1521 England repudiated the treaty with France. In the aftermath the Field of Cloth of Gold appeared as an act of frivolous diplomacy.

(baggage carriers), sweepers; master of the stables with grooms and muleteers; master of falcons and falconers, master of the hunt and huntsmen; and castellan (governor of the castle), with architects and warders (watchmen). Many clerics and noblemen endured secret misery as they lived beyond their means while trying to compete with kings. Princes themselves were constantly trying to cut down on ever-increasing court expenditures and to reduce the numbers of courtiers entitled to meals.

In the Middle Ages center of the court was the bedroom of the prince. An ambassador would initially be greeted with a formal reception in an outer chamber or a great hall and then escorted to a less public setting. A private interview in the prince's bedroom was the highest honor. During the Renaissance the prince's private study, not the bedroom, became the center of the palace. Princes found the endless ceremony tedious, and many created hideaways for themselves. As rulers sought more privacy, their households became isolated. At Rome, for example, the "palatine family," or private household of the pope, was a separate division of the curia (the papal court). Pope Innocent VIII (1432–1492 ; reigned 1484–92) built Villa Belvedere, a private residence on the hill above the Vatican Palace. Seeking greater freedom from the pleadings of courtiers, the first Tudor king, Henry VII (1547–1509; ruled 1485–1509), instituted the privy chamber (private room). It was served by mere gentlemen, not nobles, and presided over by an officer unique to the English court, the groom of the stool. Kings and princes throughout Europe built hunting lodges and country villas to escape the pressures of the court. Life at court was wearying for courtiers as well. They endured long waits in cold, drafty rooms, sleepless nights in uncomfortable—and generally shared—beds, bad food, tedium, snubs, and numerous other discomforts. These problems were made even worse when a ruler's court traveled around the kingdom. There were rewards, however, such as festivities, feasts, and above all the chance for advancement, which was the whole purpose of being a courtier.

Major courts

In the mid-fifteenth century, Burgundy, now a region in eastern France, was the preeminent court headed by a nobleman. Olivier de la Marche, master of the household and captain of the guard for the duke of Burgundy, Charles the Bold (ruled 1467–1477), wrote that elaborate ceremony ruled every aspect of court life. Court ideology centered on knighthood, and foreign visitors were particularly awed by the magnificent gatherings of the Order of the Golden Fleece. The order was created to integrate the great nobles into the Burgundian court, but even kings were flattered to be enrolled. By 1474 more than a thousand office-holders, most of whom had their own servants, lived at the Burgundy court at Charles's expense.

Italy had an abundance of princely courts that, as part of the Renaissance cult of magnificence, were centers of patronage and instrumental in the evolution of arts and literature. After the papacy, the leading Italian courts were those of Naples and Milan. The sixteenth-century humanist Paolo Giovio (1483–1552) thought the Renaissance had begun at the court of Galeazzo II Visconti of Milan (1321–1378; ruled 1354–78). The opulence of Visconti's court spurred the princes of Italy, including Pope Nicholas V (1397–1455; reigned 1447–55), to create equally magnificent courts. The humanist scholar Petrarch (1304–1374) was Visconti's guest for several years. Although Petrarch's fellow humanists complained of lack of leisure for their studies, they generally preferred appointments at court to university teaching. Humanists were able to promote their new educational program as schoolmasters and tutors to young princes and their noble companions. The schoolmasters could then count on being appointed secretaries to their students when the young men reached adulthood. Renaissance artists also benefited from being part of a court because they were freed from their status as mere artisans who worked under urban guilds.

While the courts of Naples and Milan were among the most significant, Asolo, the tiny court of Caterina Cornaro (1454–1510), the former queen of Cyprus, was also well known.

It produced one of the most influential works of the Renaissance, *Gli asolani* (Asolan dialogues; 1505), by the Italian cardinal and scholar Pietro Bembo (1470–1547). Similarly, the small court of Urbino holds a lasting place in history. The court was established by Duke Federigo da Montefeltro (1422–1482; ruled 1444–82) in an exquisite palace designed by the architect Francesco da Laurana (c. 1430–1502). Urbino was featured in the immensely popular *Libro de cortegiano,* or *Book of the Courtier* (1528) by Baldassare Castiglione (1478–1529), a book of advice for members of court. Equally brilliant was the Gonzaga court at Mantua, especially in the time of the famous marchioness (duchess), Isabella d'Este (1474–1539). Florence became the capital of a grand duchy (territory ruled by a grand duke) under Cosimo I de' Medici (1519–1574; ruled 1537–74). He used an extensive patronage system as a means of enhancing the power and prestige of the Medici dynasty.

Under King Francis I, France had a glorious court. Francis was know for his extensive patronage (inspired by his Italian visits) and his magnificent palaces, particularly Fontainebleau. In England the elaborate court of King Edward IV (1442–1483; ruled 1461–70, 1471–83) included the departments of the chapel, privy wardrobe, jewels, and signet. It assembled heralds, physicians, knights, esquires, carvers, servers, cupbearers, ushers, pages, minstrels, and servants. Under Henry VIII, the king's privy chamber became more public, welcoming royal favorites, many of whom served as diplomats. Under Queen Elizabeth I (1533–1603; ruled 1558–1603) the privy chamber once again became private quarters. The privy chamber was staffed by women who were allowed by the queen to participate in patronage but not in politics.

In Spain the independence of the traditional nobility limited the role of the court, though King Charles I (later Charles V, Holy Roman Emperor) attempted to introduce some of the practices he had seen at the court of Burgundy. He later did so in Germany, but the Holy Roman Emperor's court always had to compete with the rich and powerful courts of kings and princes in that country. Since Emperor Maximilian I (ruled 1493–1519) spent most of his time in the relatively insignificant city of Innsbruck, his court, despite its splendor, never fulfilled the function of integrating the German nobility.

Court determines proper manners

Courts throughout Europe decided the rules of etiquette, or proper behavior, for the regions they ruled. The nobility had long sent their sons to court as pages to learn manners, which gave the court its identity and made courtiers superior to other ranks of society. The emphasis on correct manners created a highly civilized society. In *Book of the Courtier,* Castiglione noted that courtiers were expected to be graceful in speech and behavior, have strong morals and intellect, and cultivate a humane outlook. In spite of the emphasis on proper manners, however, members of court were extremely competitive and they went to great lengths to win the favor of the sovereign. They learned to read every nuance of a ruler's glances, and they carefully controlled their own words and gestures in order to gain advantage over other members of court. They were constantly plotting against their rivals, and they were on guard against slander and intrigue.

The court was also a place where morals were corrupted. The mistresses of Renaissance princes were often prominent at court. Madame d'Étampes (1508–c. 1580), the second official mistress of King Francis I of France, acquired so much influence that she was able to bring about the fall of the constable (public officer responsible for keeping the peace and for performing minor judicial duties) of France, Anne duc de Montmorency (1493–1567). Duke Federigo II Gonzaga (1500–1540; ruled 1519–40) of Mantua, who lived at Francis's court as a youth, made his mother, Isabella d'Este, miserable by advancing his mistress over her. Vigilant queens and duchesses did their best to protect young court ladies. The walled garden, a famous feature of the Renaissance, was originally created as a refuge for the women of the palace to enjoy the outdoors in private, free from the intrusion of men.

Life in the city

Approximately one out of four western Europeans lived in or near urban centers. The proportion was even higher in the densely populated regions of northern and central Italy, southern Germany, and the Low Countries (Belgium, Luxembourg, and the Netherlands). The size of towns and cities differed considerably. For instance, towns were settlements of fewer than 500 inhabitants, whereas thousands of people lived in major urban centers. In the sixteenth century Venice had a population of 190,000, and Paris had 220,000 inhabitants. A small minority of cities concentrated on specialized activities such as large-scale industrial production, military training and provisioning, and maritime services for ports. Nevertheless, even the larger towns had a distinct agriculture character. During the mid-1550s in Aix-en-Provence, France, for instance, agricultural workers represented the largest occupational group. Pigs and geese were a common sight in the streets. Even within walled areas of the town, large spaces were commonly devoted to crops and orchards. The continuous stream of agricultural workers moving into larger towns and cities brought rural behavior patterns that shaped urban society, particularly among the poor.

People of different occupations, social classes, and customs were constantly brought together in large towns and cities. Each day people and goods flowed into and out of town gates. This constant activity caused serious traffic problems—we call them traffic jams today. Narrow winding streets, lined with shops and homes only inches from the curb, were not

The Renaissance town of Augsburg. People of varying professions and economic groups were often brought together in large towns and cities such as this. ©*Historical Picture Archive/Corbis. Reproduced by permission of the Corbis Corporation.*

built to accommodate large numbers of pedestrians and vehicles. Adding to the congestion were colorful, noisy processions that clogged the already crowded streets at carnival time—celebrations to honor a holy day and entertain residents and guests. A frequent source of conflict was deciding who had the right of way. Wheeled vehicles carrying goods or passengers had to compete with artisans whose work spilled onto the street outside their houses, or with pedestrians swarming into streets and squares. Traffic snarls became particularly severe during the later sixteenth century, when coaches and carriages came into fashion for persons of importance. In 1610, while caught in one of the many Parisian traffic jams, King Henry IV (1553–1610; ruled 1589–1610) of France was assassinated in his coach. Laws intended to reduce congestion were passed in many cities. A one-way traffic system was introduced in Amsterdam in 1615, and attempts were made in London to license hackney (hired) carriages in order to keep down their numbers. But in both cases the rising demand for wheeled transport only compounded the problem. Eventually, wealthy residents called for the construction of new residential districts with wide streets and squares in order to get relief from the noise, congestion, and unpleasant odors of everyday life.

Center of religion, education, government

Organized religion was a major part of urban life. Church buildings dominated the skyline, and parish churches functioned as social and cultural centers. Guilds also offered spiritual and social benefits. Towns were centers of education of all kinds. Dame schools (schools run by women in their own homes) provided basic instruction in reading writing for purposes of doing business and understanding church teaching. Latin grammar schools and universities offered vocational training. There were also schools for legal professionals, craftsmen, and even paupers.

Cities were also the center of government. Urban governments legislated the conditions in which markets were held, the level of taxes to be raised, and the management of clutter in the streets. They were also faced with unprecedented levels of immigration, severe economic fluctuations, and conflicts with state authorities. Committees were set up to deal with matters such as public health, fire prevention, defense, the maintenance of order, and poverty relief. With the exception of a shrinking number of city-states, however, most urban centers lost political independence to territorial rulers. Soon princely courts replaced the traditional oligarchies (groups of leaders who ran municipal governments) and fueled a wave of construction. Throughout Europe the new symbols of authority were palaces, which expressed the dominance of princes over the cities.

Life in the country

In the sixteenth century, during the height of the Renaissance and Reformation period, Europe was overwhelmingly rural. The majority of people were peasants who lived in villages and small towns, which formed the foundation of European society. Rural communities all over Europe included many kinds of peasants who practiced trades and crafts in addition to their activities as agricultural workers. They included shopkeepers, artisans (craftsmen), traders, carters (those who transported goods), and others who catered to local and outside customers. Furthermore, the boundaries between rural and urban society were often quite hazy. All towns and cities had residents who went out to work in the surrounding fields and pastures. They could therefore be called peasants, though they were citizens of large urban communities. There was also a considerable difference between villages and cities, making it more difficult to distinguish between rural and urban society.

Peasants' status changing

Prior to the Renaissance period, peasants had lived as serfs under a

Carnival Adds Color to City Life

Foreign visitors, especially in Italian cities, frequently wrote about the spectacle of urban life in their journals. One popular topic was carnival time, when religious and civic processions poured into the streets. Often accompanied by music and dancers, these parades were colorful, noisy events that attracted townspeople and peasants alike. Carnival had a serious purpose, such as celebrating a holy day, but it also provided entertainment for both participants and spectators. Visitors commented on the relative freedom with which women circulated in public, or the way townspeople mingled with peasants. People took time to stop and stare—and to shop. Salesmen made quick profits from the medicines, perfumes, and novelty items they sold to spectators lining squares and other public places along the parade route. Townspeople considered carnival an invitation to engage in extreme behavior, and peasants welcomed the chance to take a break from work. Yet in some ways it was just part of daily life in towns, where people moved around in order to see and to be seen.

The entertainment of the street was increasingly replaced by indoor activities. This trend occurred primarily because the urban elite classes wanted to separate themselves from the poor and the socially inferior. They held dances and gambling parties, which were often as elaborate as the street spectacles. Dances were held in town halls. In Nuremberg, Germany, the list of those permitted to take part in the dances became the legal basis for membership in the elite. Gambling could take place in comfortable and attractive surroundings that excluded the poor and the disreputable, who played cards in taverns. New forms of entertainment also developed, particularly at the end of the Renaissance: opera, theater, private poetry readings, and discussion groups.

social and economic system called feudalism that had dominated life in Europe throughout the Middle Ages (see "Feudalism" in Chapter 1). The serfs lived on vast estates owned by wealthy lords, where they worked the land. They were bound for life to the lord, to whom they owed obligations such as a portion of their crops in exchange for protection. During the fifteenth and sixteenth centuries, peasants in western Europe broke free of serfdom and started producing crops for sale on the open market. A minority of these peasants became wealthy, often buying up the lands of their neighbors. Others were merchants and businessmen, leading to an increasing number of different occupations held by members of the rural community. When rich peasants or other powerful parties gained control of the local government, they often took over the village commons (public open areas), undermining the old village communities. Royal governments further weakened the villages by finding pretexts to seize and sell communal lands.

Although peasants valued stability and self-sufficiency, they had regular contact with the outside world. They were highly mobile, often moving to other villages and rural regions, or to towns and cities. Usually they moved to take advantage of economic opportunities or to seek marriage partners. Those most likely to migrate were the landless and the young. Throughout Europe, a substantial proportion of peasant boys and girls went through a period of domestic service as a phase in their lives before settling down as adults. These adolescent servants usually found jobs with families in neighboring villages, but sometimes they ended up in regions far from their birthplace. Adult peasants frequently took seasonal jobs, harvesting crops in distant parts of their own country or even in foreign countries. During slack periods of the agricultural calendar, many peasants became muleteers (mule drivers) or carters. These occupations often took them to distant locations and sometimes enabled them to find better work situations.

Villages have own government

Villages were governed by local assemblies (representative bodies) who elected their own officials and drew up their own local laws. Village self-rule was tolerated by outside political authorities such as church officials, noblemen, and town leaders.

They realized that local people needed to make certain decisions pertaining to their own lives. Typically, the village assembly met in the local church, under a large tree, or in some other public place. Elected officials often displayed political skill, both within the village and in dealing with external authorities. In theory, participation in the government was open to all local citizens on equal terms. With the passage of time, however, village councils throughout Europe tended to fall under the domination of wealthy local landowners or merchants.

Through local assemblies and governing councils, peasant villagers regulated the use of resources such as forests, pastures, and farming lands. The aim was to protect and guarantee equal access to these lands. The local community also took charge of building and maintaining roads, wells, ovens, and other projects that benefited the village. Almost everywhere, peasant communities shared land, work, and products. These communities coexisted with private estates owned by noblemen. The community structure of the village gave it a leadership role in the defense of peasant rights. Village governments were active in hundreds of peasant rebellions. Many of these uprisings, such as the Germans Peasants' War (1524–26), became quite violent (see "German Peasants' War" in Chapter 5). However, the uprisings nearly always began as protests against violations of peasants' rights. Typically, peasant revolts were provoked by the growing power of the nation-state, which demanded higher taxes. In the end, the state's superior military forces usually crushed peasant armies. But the victorious state often introduced reforms that satisfied some of the major peasant grievances.

Social outsiders

During the Renaissance and Reformation period, Muslims, Jews, and slaves lived outside the mainstream of society in western Europe. They experienced legal restrictions, economic hardship, and segregation. Women, too, stood in a group apart. A woman's status mirrored first that of her birth family and later, if she married, that of her husband (see "Women in the family" in Chapter 13).

Muslims

During the Middle Ages, European Muslims (followers of Islam, a religion founded by the prophet Muhammad) lived primarily in Spain. They were descendants of Muslim Arabs and Berbers (wandering tribes) called Moors, who invaded the Iberian Peninsula (Spain and Portugal) in 712. At the time of the Moorish invasion, Christianity was the dominant religion. The Moors established a new culture on the Iberian Peninsula, but the Christians recaptured Spain in 1085. In 1233 Pope Gregory IX (before 1170– 1241; reigned 1227–41) established the Inquisition (now known as the medieval Inquisition; see "Inquisition" in Chapter 1). This official church court was charged with finding and punishing heretics (those who did not adhere to the laws

A scene depicting various Renaissance professions. © *Gianni Dagli Orti/Corbis. Reproduced by permission of the Corbis Corporation.*

of the church), namely Jews and Muslims. During the Inquisition thousands of non-Christians were killed by mobs, while thousands more tried to save their own lives by converting to Christianity. "Converted" Muslims who still secretly practiced Islam were called Moriscos.

More than two hundred years later, in 1474, Pope Sixtus IV (1414–

1484; reigned 1471–84) gave Spanish monarchs Ferdinand II of Aragon and Isabella I of Castile permission to conduct the Spanish Inquisition, separate from the medieval Inquisition. In 1502 Moriscos in Castile were given one last opportunity to make a sincere conversion or leaving Spain. This policy continued for more than twenty years. Then on December 9, 1525, King Charles I gave a similar choice to Moriscos living in Aragon. The following year he established an Inquisition court at Granada, a heavily Muslim province, as a final effort to force Moriscos to accept Christianity or leave the country. The church then sent Franciscans and Jesuits (members of Catholic religious orders) into Granada and Valencia to apply pressure on the Moriscos. Many Moriscos paid considerable sums of money to Catholic Church officials so they could stay in the country. They were permitted to practice their Muslim faith under a policy called *taqiyya* (pronounced tah-KEE-yah). By the mid-1500s, between 350,000 and 400,000 Moriscos were living in the Spanish provinces. The majority of Moriscos were farm laborers, though many worked in various trades such as the silk and leather industries. Others had even entered the ranks of nobility.

In the mid-1500s tensions increased between Spain and the Ottoman Empire, a vast Muslim kingdom in parts of Asia and North Africa. Throughout the Middle Ages, Christians had feared that the Ottomans would take over Europe. In Spain, Christians were becoming impatient because only a few Moriscos had actually converted. Moriscos were also fiercely opposing the efforts of the Inquisition. On December 24, 1568, Moriscos in Granada staged a rebellion and continued to fight Spanish armies for nearly two years. During the standoff, in 1569, King Philip II (1527–1598; ruled 1556–98) ordered all Moriscos—including those who were not involved in the conflict—out of Castile, Estremadura, and central Andalusia. More than eighty thousand people were deported. Government and church officials then debated what to do about Moriscos in the rest of Spain. Some contended that conversion was the best policy. Others proposed measures such as genocide (mass killings of members of a specific group) as well as the less extreme solution of deportation to the New World (the European term for North and South America). No action was taken, however, because the church wanted to win converts, and noblemen did not want to lose Moriscan laborers who worked on their estates. By the early seventeenth century, however, Spanish people had become convinced that Moriscos were plotting with Muslim and Protestant enemies to overthrow the Catholic state. On April 9, 1609, King Philip III (1578–1621; ruled 1598–1621) signed a decree of expulsion. From 1609 until 1614, between 300,000 and 350,000 Moriscos were forced to leave Spain. Most settled in North Africa, while others went to Turkey, France, and Italy. Children, slaves, and "good Christians" numbering in the tens of thousands were allowed to remain in Spain.

Jews

Jews had lived in western Europe since ancient times, but throughout the centuries Christians had become increasingly hostile toward them. This attitude was heavily influenced by the mistaken belief that Jews were the murderers of Christians (and the killers of Jesus Christ, the founder of Christianity). This notion was called the blood libel. According to the blood libel, Jews killed Christian boys to use their blood for "magical" rituals such as circumcision (removal of the foreskin of the penis) and the baking of unleavened bread, or matzos, used for the Passover holiday (matzos, a form of unleavened bread—bread without yeast—are eaten during the celebration of the ancient Hebrews' liberation from slavery in Egypt). Circumcision and the baking of unleavened bread were ancient practices of the Jewish religion, but Christians associated them with sorcery (use of magic to activate evil spirits). Although there was no basis for the blood libel, Christians throughout Europe intensely feared Jews. Between 1290 and about 1655, Jews were not legally allowed to live in England. After riots against Jews in Spain in 1391, Jews were massacred and all survivors were forced to convert to Christianity. These New Christians, the *conversos* (converted), were known as Marranos, the Spanish word for pigs. In 1475 in Trent, Italy, the Jewish community was destroyed after someone accused Jews of murdering a Christian boy. All the males were executed on a charge of ritual murder, and women and children were forced to convert.

Christians were also suspicious of Jewish money lenders who became prominent in Italy during the Renaissance. A significant number of money lenders were Jews because anti-Semitism, or prejudice against Jews, restricted Jews' job opportunities and forced many to go into fields like money-lending, which mainstream society considered an undesirable profession. Some Catholic preachers linked blood libel with money lending. The Italian priest Bernardino da Feltre (1439–1494) said that money loaned to Christians by Jews was like blood flowing in the veins, and that Jews were like gangrene poisoning, which had to be cut out. In Germany, Jews were viewed as an evil force that undermined the unity of the state. Since the state was considered the Corpus Christi (body of Jesus Christ), Christian reactions against Jews were frequently violent and resulted in riots.

After the Protestant Reformation in the mid-sixteenth century, Catholic suspicions of Jews were matched by Lutheran ones. Martin Luther (1483–1546), leader of the Reformation and founder of Lutheranism, initially wanted to convert the Jews. His goal was not so much to win new converts as it was to challenge the teachings of the Catholic Church by demonstrating the superiority of Lutheran doctrines. When his quest failed, he lashed out against Jews with an anti-Jewish tract titled *Von den Jügen und jren Lügen* (The Jews and their lies; 1543). This work was not about the failure of his conversion efforts but was instead an expression of his suspicions of

Jews. In a later tract he stated his concerns about negative Jewish influences on new Protestant groups such as the Sabbatarians. The Sabbatarians were a Protestant group who, like the Jews, observed the Sabbath on Saturday, in strict obedience to the fourth commandment in the Old Testament of the Bible (often called the Hebrew Bible).

Renaissance attitudes toward Jews were often shaped by humanists who based their ideas on ancient texts, which they were reading for the first time. Ancient Roman law, which had been adopted by the Holy Roman Empire as the set of laws for all of western Europe, contained statutes against Jews. Humanists were also influenced by legal scholars at the University of Padua in Italy. These scholars advocated separating Jews from Christians in order to prevent what was called the pollution of Christians and Christianity through any form of contact with Jews. By contrast, some of the greatest Renaissance legal experts, associated with the University of Perugia in Italy, supported a more moderate approach that balanced Jewish privileges with certain restrictions. Jewish privileges were quite limited, however. For instance, the general view was that Jewish children should be "saved" at any price, including forcibly baptizing them as Christians, even if their parents did not give approval.

Jewish communities In the fifteenth century Jews were living in Spain, Portugal, Italy, the Low Countries, and Germany. There were no Jewish communities in England and France. By the late sixteenth century, however, Jews were being forcibly converted to Christianity or driven out of Europe. In 1492, during the Spanish Inquisition (a Catholic Church court established to seek out and punish non-Christians), all unconverted Jews were expelled from Spain (see "Roman and Spanish Inquisitions" in Chapter 7). In 1497 the Jews of Portugal were converted, then forced out of the country by the Portuguese Inquisition in the 1530s. The Jews of Sicily, which was under Spanish rule, were forced to flee, and those of the Kingdom of Naples were ousted by 1541. Jews living in Germany were either driven out or subjected to constant attack. Jews of the Low Countries lived under cover as Christians until the seventeenth century.

Any Jews remaining in Europe lived exclusively in northern and central Italy. They formed communities based on a *condotta*, a limited contract allowing small groups of Jews to settle in a city and establish banks for providing loans to the poor. These contracts obligated the bankers to remain in the town for periods of five to ten years and were regularly renewed. Jewish communities were restricted mainly to larger cities. They were kept out of most towns for centuries, and some towns never accepted them. Jews settled in Venice proper in 1516, but only within the quarter long known as the Ghetto Nuovo (the origin of the term "ghetto."). In the 1530s the pope issued charters of privilege allowing Portuguese Jews to settle in Venice and Ferrara in order to promote commerce and international trade. Jewish

Court Jews

During the Renaissance many Jewish merchants and traders served on the courts of Italian rulers. Through their connections with Jewish traders in the Ottoman Empire, European Jews were ideally suited to supply armies with grain, timber, horses, and cattle. They also supplied rulers with diamonds, precious stones, and other luxury items. Jews were valued for what were perceived as good organizational skills. Rulers turned to individual Jews who were able to offer reliable, speedy, and extensive supplies of foodstuffs, cloth, and weapons for the army, the central instrument of the prince's power. Court Jews were often employed as tax administrators and court minters (those who made coins), and they engaged in secret and delicate diplomatic efforts on the ruler's behalf. Forming strong personal bonds with the ruler, court Jews were entrusted with arranging transfers of credit and providing assistance to the ruler.

Court Jews were especially prominent in the states of the Holy Roman Empire following the Thirty Years' War (1618-48), a conflict that involved all of the major powers of Europe. The war had left the Holy Roman Empire seriously weakened, and rulers within the empire needed people who were loyal to them. Jews with extensive trading and political connections were attractive figures. Some rose to positions of unique influence and affluence and were regarded as indispensable by their ruler. A typical example was Samuel Oppenheimer (c. 1630–1703), who served in the court of Holy Roman Emperor Leopold I (1640–1705; ruled 1658–1705), a member of the Habsburg dynasty based in Austria. In the early 1670s, only a few years after Leopold had expelled more than three thousand Jews from Vienna, Oppenheimer helped supply the Habsburg army. Awarded the title of imperial military factor, Oppenheimer developed an extensive operation that included many agents, contractors, and subcontractors throughout the empire and beyond. These connections enabled him to provide substantial supplies and foodstuffs to the Austrian armies and huge sums of money to the emperor. He also engaged in diplomatic activity on the emperor's behalf. Oppenheimer's activity, like that of some other court Jews, was performed in the face of adversity, as various forces within the Habsburg court plotted against him and tried to curtail his power.

refugees from Spain settled in 1541 in the Ghetto Vecchio. Eventually they were joined by Portuguese refugees.

Between 1591 and 1593, the grand duke of Tuscany brought a similar group into Livorno. Jews in this city handled a large percentage of Tuscan commerce with North Africa through the eighteenth century. By the end of the sixteenth century, about 60 percent of Italy's 20,000 Jews lived within the Papal States (territory ruled by the pope), primarily in Rome, Ancona, and Ferrara. The Jewish community of Rome, which dated back to the ancient period, were given papal privileges as early as 1402. Roman Jews were allowed to collect funds from Jews throughout northern Italy. Most important, they were considered *cives Romani,* or Roman citizens. During the Renaissance, many Jews held positions in rulers' courts, becoming highly influential and successful.

Jewish autonomy ended The Italian Jewish communities were essentially collections of individuals who were given authority by outside rulers to administer Jewish internal affairs—and to collect taxes. They were allowed to base their communities on Jewish law, but their autonomy (right to self-rule) was limited. For instance, the pope was constantly interfering in the work of Jewish tribunals (courts), even to the point of instructing these tribunals how to interpret Jewish law. In 1631 Venetian authorities discovered that Jewish statutes threatened to excommunicate (expel from the community) Jews who turned to non-Jewish courts. The Venetians then accused the Jews of trying to operate their own republic within the Republic of Venice.

Jewish community life was affected by the Roman Inquisition (see "Roman and Spanish Inquisitions" in Chapter 7). In 1555 Pope Paul IV (1476–1559; reigned 1555–59) established a ghetto in the Papal States. The following year he attacked Jews of Portuguese Christian origin, burning twenty-five of them at the stake. As a result, people fled to larger communities and many others converted, which was the pope's goal. A second and even greater dislocation took place in 1569, when Pope Pius V (1504–1572; reigned 1566–72) forced the Jews of the Papal States to live solely in Rome and Ancona, and in the French papal possessions around Avignon. The flourishing Jewish community of Bologna came to an abrupt end. Jews were also expelled by secular leaders of various small settlements in the Italian northeast, such as Vicenza, Treviso, and Cividale. For the remainder of the Renaissance and Reformation period, Jews in western Europe were confined to the ghettos of Italy.

Slaves

In western Europe during the fifteenth and sixteenth centuries, slavery was practiced mainly on the Italian and Iberian peninsulas. Even there, however, slavery was never crucial for social and economic development, and it did not exist on any great scale. Nevertheless, varieties of slavery were present. There were two distinct types of slavery: agricultural (rural) and domestic (urban). Some rural slaves worked in manufacturing on country estates. Much of the employment of domestic slaves was unproductive labor, for slaves were usually assigned as servants, guards, and sexual partners for masters. Most of the ordinary manufacturing of goods for everyday consumption took place in workshops within the homes of artisans. In these workshops a few domestic slaves could aid

Slavery Shapes Europe

During the thousand years from the end of the Roman Empire to the beginning of European expansion in the Atlantic Ocean, slavery was practiced in the Christian world. It was encouraged by European contact with the highly developed slavery system run by Muslim traders in Africa. The growing influence of Roman law, which contained regulations on slavery, provided a ready-made set of rules to be put into force when slavery became economically beneficial to Europe. The resurgence of slavery in the sixteenth century was due to the creation of the sugar plantation system in the New World. Sugar growing and re-fining required intensive labor, but there were not enough Native American or European workers to meet the needs of Spanish and Portuguese plantation owners. Portuguese traders therefore turned to slave-trading networks that were already operating along the West African coast. They captured thousands of Africans and transported these human cargoes across the Atlantic. The persistence of slavery throughout the Middle Ages thus helped shape the colonial societies in North and South America, and, in very real ways, influenced the evolution of modern society throughout the Western Hemisphere.

their artisan owners. Small-scale slavery, in which a few slaves were added to the urban or rural households as domestics and additional workers, was characteristic of both Renaissance Europe and the Islamic world. Gang slavery, which we associate with the slave system in the New World, was not present at all in Europe.

Slaves in Renaissance Europe came from two sources: birth to slave mothers or capture in warfare or raids. They were of many nationalities, and not exclusively African. When slaves entered western European households, they lived under the control of their masters, who legally had the power of life and death over them. Masters could sell, transfer, and move their slaves at will and could use them as sexual partners. Captives were often ransomed or exchanged. Despite their lack of legal standing, many slaves took advantage of laws that permitted them to attain freedom in several ways. For example, slaves could become free through self-purchase or by their master's gift during his lifetime or following his death. Freemen and freewomen suffered legal limitations, but children born to them were fully free.

Italy needs workers Slavery increased during the fifteenth century as a result of numerous plague epidemics that swept Europe in the fourteenth and fifteenth centuries and killed one-quarter to one-third of the European population (see "Black Death" in Chapter 1). As a consequence of the high death rate, European workers who might otherwise have become household servants found good jobs in the countryside or the cities. Death struck poor and rich alike, but many of the elite who survived increased their fortunes by receiving inheritance money from relatives who had died due to the disease. Slavery grew largely because additional workers and domestics were needed. The unrestricted importation of slaves from outside Italy was permitted by the government of Florence beginning in 1363, with the sole requirement that the slaves be of non-Christian origin. Perhaps as a result of the large influx of slaves over the preceding two decades, Venice prohibited slave auctions in 1366. Venetians were still permitted to import slaves, though all sales had to be by private contract.

Genoa continued to receive enslaved Tatars (a tribe from east central Asia), Russians, and Circassians (a group of people from the Caucasus, a region in southeast Europe) during this period, but their numbers declined in the second half of the fifteenth century when access to the Black Sea was cut off. The Genoese rectified the situation by going to the western Mediterranean. From North Africa, Spain, and Portugal, Muslim slaves were purchased in increasing numbers. In order to distinguish among Islam's varying ethnic groups, the Genoese categorized their slaves by skin color—white, black, *indaco* (indigo), *lauro* (mulatto), and *olivegno*

(olive). Relatively few black slaves reached Genoa or other northern Italian cities, though they were fairly common in southern Italy and Sicily.

Eventually non-Christian slaves were forbidden in Italy, so the Venetians turned to indentured servants to meet the demand for domestic servants. Known as "souls" (*anime*) by the Venetians, these indentured servants were predominantly young, purchased from their parents in Dalmatia, Albania, Istria, and Corfu by Venetian ship masters. Distinguished legally from ordinary slaves and bound only for a defined period of service, servants could buy back their freedom if they had the money. Although Venetian law prohibited their exchange or sale to another master, the Venetian government had to ensure that they were not taken elsewhere in Italy, where they were in danger of being sold into perpetual slavery.

African slave trade The situation was similar in Spain and Portugal. The Iberian states were part of the European world, where slavery gradually declined as serfdom and free labor grew more available at the end of the Middle Ages, in the fourteenth century. Yet, unlike the rest of western Europe, many Iberian kingdoms remained frontier states well into the sixteenth century sharing borders with non-Christian states whose inhabitants could be raided or enslaved with complete legality. This condition meant that slavery persisted there longer and more vigorously than elsewhere in Christian Europe.

The Portuguese and Spanish developed a large-scale trade in African slaves. Many of the African slaves went to the Atlantic islands, and many more went to the Americas as the pace of development increased there in the sixteenth century. Other black slaves ended up in Europe, causing changes in the ethnic composition of the servant population of several European regions. Blacks had been present in Europe in small numbers since the Roman period. From the ninth century, if not before, Muslims brought African slaves across the Saharan Desert for sale in the ports of the Mediterranean. Aside from Italy and the Iberian countries, however, blacks remained rarities in Europe until much later.

The Portuguese were the main slave traders of Europe in the late fifteenth and early sixteenth centuries. By the 1480s the Portuguese monarchy had established a Casa dos Escravos (slave house) in Lisbon to administer the trade. By the mid-sixteenth century, black slaves and freemen made up some 2.5 to 3 percent of the total Portuguese population. Only a minority of the Africans in the Portuguese slave trade actually arrived or remained in Portugal. Portuguese traders supplied slaves to the new Portuguese plantations in São Tomé (an island off western Africa), the Cape Verde, and Madeira (an island in the east Atlantic Ocean). They also sold slaves to African rulers and merchants at São Jorge da Mina. The Portuguese sold other slaves to Castilians in the Canary Islands off the coast of northwest Africa. Of those who were taken to Portugal significant numbers were later delivered elsewhere in Europe, particularly to Spain but also to Italy.

Greatest number in Seville The greatest number of slaves were held in Seville, Spain. Slavery had been a feature of the life of Seville since Roman times. By the thirteenth century, while still under Muslim control, the city had large numbers of slaves. Between the time of the Christian reconquest of the city in 1248 and the mid-fifteenth century, most of the slaves in Seville were Muslims, captured in the constant warfare between Christians and Muslims.

African slaves became more common in the fourteenth century as Spanish and Italian merchants purchased them in North African ports. By the middle of the fifteenth century, black slaves arrived in Seville by sea or overland from Portugal. Once in Seville, most of the newly arrived slaves were sold to private buyers. Seville had no regular slave market, unlike Lisbon, where slaves were sold at the Casa dos Escravos. Slave dealers in Seville took their human merchandise through the streets and arranged sales on the spot, making private arrangements with prospective purchasers. The buyers, at least in the period from 1484 to 1489, were predominantly from the artisan class. Age, sex, and physical condition determined the prices slaves would bring. Children brought the lowest prices because, before they could be put to work profitably, they needed lengthy care and training, and they were subject to disease and death.

Most slaves in Seville were used as domestic servants. Well-off families usually had at least two slaves. Wealthier families owned greater numbers, much as their contemporaries in Italy did. Slaves were also used in smaller numbers for income-producing ventures, such as the soap factory of Seville and the municipal granary (a place where grain is stored). Slaves were employed as porters and longshoremen, as retail sellers in the streets and plazas, and as assistants for shopkeepers and merchants. Some of the slaves acted as agents for their merchant-owners, and in some cases slaves ventured on business trips to the Spanish settlements in the Americas. Slaves were excluded from membership in the crafts guilds, though some did work as helpers for guild masters.

Mediterranean Europe had other cities in which slavery flourished in the period, even if they were not so racially mixed as Seville. One of those cities was Valencia, a major center for slavery in the fifteenth and sixteenth centuries. Slaves were not so numerous in Valencia as they were in Seville, but they were more varied in their ethnic origins. Most Valencian slaves were Muslim in origin, either from Spain itself or from North Africa. Non-Muslim slaves came from many other places, brought to Valencia by the slave traders. Within the western Mediterranean, the Balearic Islands also served as a hub of the Christian slave trade and as a place where slaves were used.

Social problems

Like societies in the past, people living during the Renaissance and Reformation period experienced social problems. Two of the most prevalent were poverty and crime.

Poverty

In the great cities of Europe, between 50 and 70 percent of the population could be classified as destitute. They suffered from financial hardship, lack of political power, and lack of social esteem. About 4 to 8 percent of the people were dependent on relief. They included the very young, the aged, invalids, and those who were mentally afflicted or physically impaired. Some were beggars, some were infants in the care of wet nurses, and some received relief in their own homes. In famine years their numbers swelled due to an influx of refugees from the devastated countryside, who struggled toward city gates in a desperate quest for food from granaries and alms from citizens.

Beyond the helpless and destitute lay a much larger circle of ill-paid laboring poor, comprising journeymen and their families, porters, and other casual workers. Among them were women who took on spinning and other tasks in the textile trades, widows burdened with young children, agricultural workers living within town walls, and unemployed servants. Dependent on irregular, seasonal work, they had no extra money or savings. Poor people could scrape out a living for much of the time, but sudden rises in the price of bread would immediately plunge them into reliance on charity. They were known to tax collectors as *miserahili,* people who have nothing, and they comprised at least another 20 percent of the urban population.

There was also an outer circle of craftsmen, shopkeepers, and minor officials, who had no real financial security in the face of illness or disaster, such as a plague epidemic. They were probably the people described by Carlo Borromeo (1538–1584), archbishop of Milan, when he visited Varese, Italy, in 1567. Borromeo mentioned seeing people who had some possessions but needed assistance because they had many children who they could not support. Those in the outer circle of poverty would never have begged openly, but few would have refused charitable contributions toward their daughters' marriage portions, or dowry (the amount of money or goods that a woman had to bring to a marriage).

Levels of poverty Most societies recognized levels of poverty, which were created by the superior classes. A privileged group of "shamefaced poor" generally claimed the largest allowances and enjoyed the most discreet and considerate treatment from charitable associations. They included nobles or burghers who were threatened not with starvation but with loss of honor because they could not afford to maintain the lifestyle appropriate to their social position. In fifteenth-century Florence the "shamefaced"

also included respectable artisans and shopkeepers. They resembled the "house poor" of sixteenth-century Germany or the "decayed households" in sixteenth-century England.

The "poor of Christ" were identified by the Catholic Church as those who represented the suffering Christ. It was thought that these people could transform earthly donations into heavenly treasure. They included widows and orphans as well as those who patiently accepted their misfortune and disability. In Catholic countries members of certain religious communities deliberately renounced all worldly goods. They were also considered the "poor of Christ," especially if, like the strict Franciscans (members of the order of Saint Francis of Assisi), they owned no property and lived by begging. Special hospitality was given to pilgrims who took long, grueling journeys to the great religious centers of Rome and Loretto in Italy and Compostela in Spain. There was little room, however, for such claims by the religious poor in Protestant societies. Their practices were perceived as mistaken attempts to pursue salvation through socially useless "works." Those who were poor through no choice of their own, however, received assistance from the Protestants. Huldrych Zwingli (1484–1531), the Swiss religious reformer wrote that voluntary poverty is simply a human act, whereas involuntary poverty follows the will of God. No doubt the largest body of poor people at any one time consisted of ordinary laborers who had no wealth or property and had to rely on their own physical strength for survival.

Below the laboring poor were the outcast poor, such as vagrants (wanderers), beggars who were not actually poor (they found it easier to beg than work), and brothel prostitutes (women who lived in houses that specialize in selling sexual favors). Widely accepted, at least from the thirteenth century, was the notion that not all the poor were the poor of Christ. In literature of the fifteenth century these people were depicted as being part of an organized anti-society, devoted to tricking the pious and stealing the alms of the truly poor. Prostitution, while to some extent licensed in Spanish and Italian towns, and in France and Germany before the coming of Protestantism, was at the same time stigmatized. In Dijon, France, in 1554 it was considered a form of female vagrancy. During the sixteenth century the outcast poor were increasingly portrayed as brute beasts. According to this view, they could be made human only by the Christian teachings of which they were woefully ignorant. As habitual sinners mired in sloth and vice, they were lost souls in need of redemption. This redemption could be achieved by confining them to an institution where they were forced to live like monks and nuns.

Formal and informal charity

Poverty was alleviated in numerous informal ways. People gave small gifts to beggars, and neighbors and families helped one another. Landlords and farmers sold grain to the local poor at less than the current market prices. Alehouse keepers and bakers gave generous credit. In addition to these forms of relief, most towns and some townships and villages maintained confraternities (religious brotherhoods), hospitals, and credit institutions. Management of these institutions gave well-to-do, leisured citizens the opportunity to improve their social standing by becoming patrons of the poor. Many wealthy people provided beds or pensions for their own favored dependents, and some were commemorated for their good works. Hospitals employed a large staff in relation to the number of inmates, and there was often no great difference in wealth between the poor admitted to the hospitals and the ward attendants who looked after them.

Confraternities help poor Catholic cities generally contained large numbers of confraternities and a much smaller number of sororities for women. Most of these confraternities and sororities were societies of laypersons who followed a rule similar to that practiced by official religious orders. Laypersons were taught how to gain salvation (forgiveness of sins) by practicing good works and correcting their faults. Among these good works were acts of mercy prescribed in the twenty-fifth chapter of the Gospel of Saint Matthew (a book in the New Testament of the Bible): almsgiving, caring for the sick, visiting prisoners, and taking in strangers. Catholic Church tradition had added another act of mercy, burial of the dead. This pious duty usually involved financing masses (Catholic religious services) for the souls of the departed. Those suffering the pains of Purgatory (the region between heaven and hell) were considered worthy recipients of charity from living people. In addition, presiding at masses provided welcome employment for impoverished priests. After the Black Death (a prolonged plague epidemic in Europe; see "Black Death" in Chapter 1), at least in Italy, it also became increasingly common to give relatively large sums as dowries for the marriage of poor girls of good reputation.

Confraternities functioned partly for the benefit of their own members and partly for the benefit of outsiders. From the late fifteenth century, there were increasing numbers of devout confraternities that directed much of their energy outward, toward people too poor or disreputable to belong to a religious brotherhood. Among these groups was the Compagnia del Divino Amore (Company of Divine Love) in Genoa, Italy, and elsewhere. Confraternities could be socially exclusive clubs, or they might embrace everyone in a community or parish, making only modest demands on people's time and purses. In the Spanish town of Zamora in the late sixteenth century, there were 150 confraternities serving at most 8,600 residents, or one organization for every fourteen households. There were five for clerics, ten for nobles, and more than a hundred for commoners.

Although confraternities were mostly confined to artisans and people above them socially, it was possible—as in the Italian cities of Rome, Florence, Milan, and Venice—to organize confraternities of approved beggars, especially blind and lame ones. Elected officers were in charge of fair distribution of alms collected on the street by the more skillful and appealing beggars. In sixteenth-century Bologna, Italy, street porters and others formed a Company of the Poor for the purpose of attracting rather than dispensing charity. The wealthier confraternities did not confine themselves to outdoor relief. They were quite capable, for example, of running hospitals or almshouses (poorhouses), and could be dedicated to almost any charitable or pious purpose.

Hospitals aid the sick In the fifteenth and sixteenth centuries, hospitals provided shelter but not necessarily medical care. To provide hospitality was not their only task, for they might also serve as general almshouses to their communities. Infants in their care were placed in foster homes, often in the nearby countryside. Three major functions of hospitals were the reception of pilgrims, the care of orphans and abandoned children, and the care of old people and widows. Attention to the sick went hand in hand with caring for the poor and helpless: people were poor because they were sick, and sick because they were poor. Certain hospitals, among them Santa Maria Nuova in Florence, enjoyed a high reputation for the quality of their

Pawnshops for the Poor

In addition to assisting the poor through confraternities and hospitals, many towns ran credit institutions. During the fifteenth century, Italian towns especially attempted to provide small loans at controlled rates of interest for the "poor of money," people who had goods to pawn. These people were distinct from the "poorer poor," who had no goods. Town officials might license a Jewish pawn broker, or establish a cut-rate Christian pawnshop known as a *monte di pietà* (mount of mercy), or they might resort to both methods. Similar pawnshops arose in Spain and the southern Low Countries. In the seventeenth century so-called *prêts charitables* were opened in France. They served not only as pawnshops but also as disaster banks, from which the commune (town government) was entitled to borrow in emergencies. In country districts the equivalents of the urban *monte di pietà* were grain banks, which lent seed corn to peasant farmers. These loans were backed by guarantees from the farmers' more prosperous neighbors.

medical care. Some kept wards specifically for the "shamefaced poor." Hospitals were unlikely to attract well-to-do people, even those who needed sophisticated medical treatment not available in their homes.

In the late Middle Ages, innumerable small hospitals were founded by private individuals, lay and clerical groups, and associations such as confraternities. In the fifteenth and sixteenth centuries, many large cities in Spain, France, and northern Italy attempted to draw most of their local hospitals together in a single organization run on the community's behalf. They did this to promote efficiency and avoid corruption. In Italy at least, responsibility was taken from unsupervised wardens and given to boards of governors recruited from the principal social orders in the city.

However, these metropolitan superhospitals seldom succeeded in drawing all hospitals under their wings, and before long new institutions were added. Among them were plague hospitals, which were in part quarantine centers for people and goods suspected of being contaminated by the plague. Hospitals for "incurables" originated about 1500 during a virulent outbreak of sexually transmitted disease. These institutions soon began to deal with other conditions that required prolonged treatment. From about 1560, hospitals designed to admit all beggars in the city began to be erected, amid much controversy over the desirability of keeping destitute people away from the public gaze. Certain cities staged "Triumphs of Charity" processions, which involved assembling local beggars and marching or carting them off to their new quarters, accompanied by a selection of their benefactors. Some triumphs were short-lived. In Rome, for instance, few such hospitals possessed the resources to carry out effective housing of the poorest of the poor.

Poor relief reforms From the early sixteenth century many town councils and some state governments endeavored to establish a more rational and coordinated system of poor relief. Their schemes had several common characteristics. They aimed to suppress or restrict public begging, encouraging each town to look after its own poor people and turn others away. Many governments organized censuses (official counts) of the poor and set up work programs for the unemployed. Another goal was to provide trade training for beggar children and orphans. Several Protestant towns in Germany dissolved Roman Catholic religious institutions. They then put the property and money into Common Chests controlled by boards of laymen, which were used for the education and relief of the deserving poor. Some Catholic cities also attempted to pool resources and establish centers for poor relief. In the sixteenth and seventeenth centuries public authorities became increasingly involved as poor relief agents. Many towns ran public granaries as a defense against famine. Efforts were made to control disease by controlling the outcast poor. Catholics and Protestants alike condemned idleness and undisciplined begging, but each religious group had its own type of institution. Catholic confraternities disappeared from Protestant towns, which ran public agencies, while the great beggars' hospitals continued their work in Catholic cities.

Crime

There was no uniform system of justice during the Renaissance and Reformation period. Europe was fragmented into hundreds of states, and each state determined its own laws. In general, however, laws were created by the common will of the people, by church courts, and by the government. Criminal behavior was divided into two categories: crimes against persons and crimes against property.

Crimes against persons Crimes against persons were frequent, and the seriousness of such crimes varied with the level of importance of the victim. Monarchs, for example, were considered far more important than the general population. The reason was that substantial power was given to a monarch by Roman law (the Codes of the ancient Roman Emperor Justinian). Roman law was introduced in the late Middle Ages in an attempt to apply a single system of laws throughout western Europe. With the growing acceptance of Roman Law, assassination, attempted assassination, and conspiracy against a monarch's government were considered especially serious crimes.

Other forms of crimes against persons ranged from verbal insult (a speech act that was legally recognized as violence) to assault and murder. In Italy, some types of verbal insult were accompanied by various acts, such as placing animal horns over a person's doorway, smearing excrement over a door, or posting signs in public places. A chance encounter between enemies on a public plaza could lead to an exchange of insults. At such a point, each man was determined to defend his own honor, and violence usually erupted.

Feuds and Outlaws

One of the most highly organized forms of violence was feuding, or acts of violence between prominent families. Governments tried to stamp out feuding because it threatened the stability of the state. Venice eliminated feuding among its ruling families by the end of the thirteenth century, and England stamped out feuds in the sixteenth century. Feuding persisted elsewhere during the Renaissance, especially in mountainous areas, remote regions, and along borders between states.

The main participants in feuds were adult male members of a family or clan. Boys and women were typically not attacked. Feuding murders were usually committed in public, rather than in ambushes at night, so the murderer could make himself known. The code of feuding was based on hunting customs, so that victims were sometimes treated as if they were hunted prey. They were butchered like animals and fed to dogs. Feuds among aristocratic families could sometimes trigger widespread social violence. An example was a devastating peasant revolt in Friuli, Italy, in 1511. Feuding families employed armed guards called bravos, who engaged in organized violence not only against their employer's enemies but also against helpless peasants and citizens.

Goverments combated feuding by sending the guilty parties into exile. But this punishment simply encouraged men to become outlaws—exiles who survived by turning to robbery, murder for hire, or smuggling. In Italy networks of exiles constantly agitated to return home, creating a kind of rebel force that lurked along the borders of virtually every state. Some of these outlaw-exiles were hired as soldiers in the armies of warring princes. During the last half of the sixteenth century the increased use of the rapier sword and the pistol made combat much more deadly. Whereas warring families previously had had street fights and brawls, they now were staging duels, which were conducted according to highly complex rituals. The dueling fad spread from Italy to the rest of Europe as warring families and clans abandoned group violence in favor of this more controlled method of settling feuds.

Not even the poorest Europeans engaged in violence without the use of some kind of weapon. Every man who was not a cleric (member of the clergy)—and an unarmed man was always assumed to be a cleric—carried at least a cudgel (club) wherever he went. If a confrontation occurred in a large city such as sixteenth-century Florence, where all weapons were banned within the city gates, then both men and women fought with anything at hand. They used rocks, pots and pans, and other items that could inflict injury, but they never simply fought with their fists. The Italian countryside of the sixteenth century had a true "arms race," as warring groups made or obtained firearms.

The rape of women was also considered a violent crime. Then, as now, rape was a display of male power over women. The major difference was that during the Renaissance era, when family feuds were involved, rape could be part of the violence used to carry out a vendetta (planned revenge).

Penalties The criminal justice system dealt with crimes of violence by imposing various penalties, often in combination. Flexibility was the rule. Fines were imposed on those convicted of minor violations, but the level of punishment could escalate sharply if the crime was linked to a serious flare-up of a vendetta. Even a verbal insult, if it led to injury or death during a vendetta, could be punished with fines that matched the severity of injury. The most severe penalty was death.

Complicating matters everywhere in Europe was the fact that an accused person could easily evade punishment by fleeing the court jurisdiction where the crime was committed. There was a risk involved, however, for those who fled. They were automatically banned from the area, deprived of the protection of law, and subject to being killed or captured by anyone without recourse (the right to defend themselves). But this was a risk worth taking, because a fugitive from justice could avoid spending a long time in jail before trial. In effect, the justice system was forced to bargain with the accused so he would return. At times a suspected criminal could even negotiate a lesser punishment as a condition of return. Such a deal might include a limited period of exile (forced absence from his home region), payment of a fine in money or kind (for example, personal property), or some combination of these penalties.

In northern Europe there was a growing reliance on a system called afflictive penalties, which was supposed to make punishments equal for rich and poor alike. Thus the rich were prevented from getting off with lighter punishment because they could more easily pay fines. After the 1530s the city of Florence increasingly imposed exile, known as *confino,* for a fixed period somewhere within the state, such as in the town of Livorno. Execution was reserved for the rare career criminal, for the worst murderers, and for bandits involved in brigandage (plundering of property). When caught, brigands were immediately hung in groups.

Crimes against property Crimes against property were less frequently committed than crimes against persons. Such offenses were many and varied, but they were clearly on the increase throughout the sixteenth century, when more laws dealing with these crimes went on the books. Theft covered a broad range of violations, from stealing a fish or a loaf of bread at market to the occasional fraudulent bankruptcy. The latter was considered a form of theft, comparable to a failure

Hanged men outside of a town. Death was often used by the Renaissance justice system to punish criminals. *Reproduced by permission of The Art Archive/Santa Anastasia Verona/Dagli Orti.*

to pay off a legitimate debt, and was a jailable offense. In the countryside, highway robbery was a special problem since, unlike theft in the city, it was invariably done with the aid of a deadly weapon. Highway robbery dif-

fered from brigandage in severity and frequency. Brigandage was widespread in the sixteenth century. It had to be treated as a military problem, because of the number and size of the bands of brigands. The usual solution was to organize an expensive temporary search party to hunt down the thieves.

Beginning in the sixteenth century in Florence, royal decrees established new types of property crimes. After 1537 fishing and hunting were declared off-limits to those without permits in large areas of Tuscan forests and rivers. These lands had formerly been open to everyone for gaming and fishing but were now reserved only for aristocrats. The motivation for creating these reserves was twofold: to establish hunting as an activity associated with the aristocracy, and to create monopolies on fish and game, which would be sold to supporters of the powerful Medici family. This practice was adopted by the nobility of other northern European countries. French nobles, for example, annexed land for their own private use.

Other categories of crime against property were created when property owners tried to protect new uses of their land. One example was converting land to pasture for raising sheep or for planting mulberry trees to cultivate silkworms. Violators—for instance, poor people who used the land for farming—were punished by criminal courts instead of civil courts. Wealthy people preferred criminal courts because civil procedures were too long and too expensive, and the outcome was less certain than in criminal courts.

Criminal justice system European systems of criminal justice dealt differently with commoners and aristocrats.

Distinctions were made between people according to their social status, and criminal courts recognized these distinctions. Another important factor was the severity of the crime.

The courts dealt with all classes and persons except for church officials and members of the royal family. A member of a royal family seldom committed a crime. When he did, it was usually one of violence and was swept under the rug. Aristocrats, such as those linked to the Medici regime in Florence, committed crimes, but the Medici rulers dealt with them outside of the regular system or by manipulating the system. Sometimes aristocratic criminals were ignored. Women did not appear in court nearly so frequently as did men. They were accused of a very limited range of crimes, most often fights with other women, small thefts, and other nonviolent offenses. They were given the same kinds of punishment as men, usually fines or *confino*. The most serious crime of which women were accused was infanticide (killing their children). However, prosecutions were rare because it was a difficult crime to prove in either civil or church courts.

Crimes against the regime, such as conspiracy (plot against a government), assassination, or attempted assassination, were the most serious crimes. Viewed as crimes against the royal person—who *is* the state—such offenses were punished by execution, imprisonment, or long periods of exile. Crimes of the poor against the wealthy, usually property crimes, were punished with fines, or exile within the state, or both. Crimes among persons of the same social status, notably the poor, were given these same penalties. The authorities found crimes of violence between feuding families particularly disturbing but punished them with fines or exile. They often suspected foreigners of thievery, since most professional thieves came from countries outside the one in question, and the punishment was execution or banishment. The occasional thrill-seeking noble might also become a thief.

Inquisitorial procedure adopted By the sixteenth century, the legal codes of northern Europe and Spain followed the Italian codes by adopting Roman law. They investigated alleged crime through inquisitorial (from the Latin *inquirere, inquisitum,* to inquire into or to search for evidence) procedure. This system was adopted first by the Roman Catholic Church to deal with heretics (those who violate the laws of the church). Inquisitorial procedure was used by Italian communes (town governments) in the twelfth century, and by the sixteenth century it was common throughout western Europe. Under this system government officials conducted the entire investigation in order to establish the facts and find the objective truth. They were usually successful. Exceptions occurred when the ruler had a personal stake in the outcome. Occasionally a case might prove embarrassing or inconvenient to the prince. Then the accused might be murdered

in his prison cell, or taken into exile without benefit of a trial.

Difficulty in financing the justice system played a crucial role in determining its character and operation. Those accused of crimes were usually held for long periods of time in uncomfortable public jails because they could not afford bail. The law required them to pay their own jail expenses, but most could not do so. Hence, the government had to support the prisoners, but very little state funding was granted for this purpose. Thus, those in jail, whether guilty or innocent, suffered hunger and other discomforts. The Florentines dealt with the problem by clearing the jails every six or nine months by releasing those unable to pay their fines.

The use of torture to obtain confession was common when no other reliable evidence could be found, usually in cases of professional theft. Torture was intended to shorten the time that people spent in jail, which reduced costs. The courtroom was often simply a place where lawyers exchanged documents, and hardly any examination of witnesses and oral arguments took place. The justice system therefore did not offer adequate protections for the accused. The overall quality of judges was uneven. Men without legal training served as judges in England, Germany, and Florence. Trained legal professionals presided in the French criminal justice system, which had adopted the inquisitorial procedure.

Education and Training

12

In the early fourteenth century, Italian humanist scholars began introducing new ideas about human knowledge and experience. They based their concepts on works written by ancient Greek and Roman philosophers, who placed value on the individual. The humanists' innovations led to the Renaissance, a cultural and social revolution that had an impact on every aspect of life throughout Europe. A major goal of the humanist movement was to change traditional methods of education developed in the latter half of the Middle Ages (c. 800–1200). At that time elementary schools, called Latin grammar schools, and universities were run by the Roman Catholic Church (a Christian religion based in Rome, Italy, and headed by a pope). Christian doctrine (religious beliefs) was the basis of all knowledge and learning. The purpose of education was to train the sons of noblemen—girls were not allowed to attend school—to become church officials. Similarly, the sons of kings and princes were educated to become Christian rulers. Classes in both grammar schools and universities were conducted in Latin, the official language of the Catholic Church and the Holy Roman Empire (the central government for most of Europe). Rules were quite rigid and did not permit students to learn about their world or to express their own ideas.

A new approach to education began emerging in 1350, when the Italian humanist Petrarch (1304–1374) discovered parts of the *Instituto oratoria*, a work written around A.D. 94 by the Roman orator and teacher Quintilian (A.D. c. 35–c. 100). The complete text was discovered in 1416 by the Italian humanist Poggio Bracciolini (1380–1459). In the *Instituto oratoria* Quintilian described the education of a perfect orator who would also have the qualities of a good man. According to Quintilian, education should begin in the home during infancy and continue into adulthood. He advocated a teaching method that was adapted to a child's abilities and character traits, progressing from simple to more complex lessons. Quintilian advised that recreation be combined with children's studies. Since he believed that the young are naturally inclined to learn, he did not approve of rigidly applied rules and physical punishment. The *Instituto oratoria* had a strong impact on education during the Renaissance. It was one of the first printed books in Italy—after the development of the printing press in the mid-1400s made it possible to widely distribute printed materials—and one hundred editions were published by 1496. Scholars later discovered works by the Roman orator Marcus Tullius Cicero (106–43 B.C.) and others, which led to an emphasis on the teaching of rhetoric (effective writing and speaking).

Humanist education developed

In the early fifteenth century several Italian humanists began developing their own theories of education. The most prominent theorist was Pier Paolo Vergerio (1370–1444), who wrote *De ingenuis moribus* (On noble customs) in 1404. Although Vergerio developed his teaching methods for the son of a nobleman, his ideas had an impact on the education of other social classes in both Italy and Europe. Vergerio stressed the importance of liberal studies (history, moral philosophy, and poetry) and the seven liberal arts (grammar; dialectic, which deals with discussion and reasoning; rhetoric: music; arithmetic; geometry; and astronomy). He advised that students be taught according to their own personalities and mental abilities, and he rejected harsh punishments. Vergerio recommended the use of discussion as a learning tool, and he even suggested that students teach other students. Finally, he required that pupils receive physical training (then called the art of war). His theory was that educating both the mind and the body would produce virtuous and wise men.

Other humanists emphasized the role of education in creating good citizens. For instance, Francesco Barbaro (1390–1454), one of the first Italian noblemen to become a humanist, insisted that liberal education was beneficial to society. He believed it enriched cultural life and improved the character of political leaders. Barbaro recommended that students per-

The interior of a medieval schoolroom from the signboard of a schoolmaster by Ambrosius Holbein. *Reproduced by permission of Hulton Archive.*

form writing exercises—paraphrasing poetry into prose, translating Greek into Latin and vice versa, and imitating passages from the classics. Passages from Cicero's works were to be read aloud, and large portions committed to memory. Latin was to be spoken among students both in and out of class. Educators also stressed the importance of a graceful writing and speaking style. These ideas were quickly adopted in the princely courts of northern Italy and among merchants and professionals there as well. Soon a humanist education, called *studia humanitatis,* became a requirement for secretarial, diplomatic, and political posts.

Italian schools start movement

In the fifteenth century, humanist education moved quickly from Italian households into Latin grammar schools. It then spread rapidly into the rest of Europe throughout the sixteenth century. Vittorino da Feltre (1378–1446), known as the greatest schoolmaster in the Renaissance, started one of the first humanist schools in Italy. In 1423 he established a boarding school, Casa Giocosa, at the court in Mantua. His patrons (financial supporters) were the dukes of Mantua, who belonged to the Gonzaga family. Vittorino taught the Gonzaga children as well as the children of other noble families. He also admitted poor children to the school free of charge if they showed promise and were recommended by friends and family. Pupils began their education as early as the age of four or five with reading and spelling. Later, his students were expected to memorize numerous texts by Latin poets and historians. Teachers dictated passages from Latin texts, and students wrote them down. Students were also required to recite passages in Latin, with stress on correct pronunciation. The goal of this training was to enable students to become skilled at both writing and speaking Latin.

Vittorino introduced classical Greek to a select number of older pupils who studied the works of such ancient philosophers as Cicero, Aristotle (384–322 B.C.), and Plato (c. 428–c. 348 B.C.). Teachers were available to give instruction in mathematics, astronomy, and geometry. Vittorino also made sure that his pupils devoted time to games and strenuous physical activity. He stressed the development of mind, body, and character, especially for those who wanted to enter the professions or public service. Vittorino had a strong sense of Christian duty, so he insisted that students attend church often.

Another noted fifteenth-century humanist school was opened by Guarino Guarini (pronounced gwah-REE-nee; c. 1374–1460) in Ferarra, Italy. Guarini required memorization, repetition, catechism (religious instruction), composition, and imitation (imitating passages from the classics). He also concentrated on both Latin and Greek texts

in order to provide better understanding of the classics. Guarini's lessons involved defining terms, explaining the text, and analyzing problems of interpretation. His students took detailed lecture notes and were encouraged to make extensive reading notes.

The main humanist curriculum, or plan of study, was generally limited to liberal studies and the liberal arts, as specified by Vittorino and Guarini. Instrumental music and drawing were added by the end of the fifteenth century. Military training was a also a major part of humanist education. For those boys who did not plan to become soldiers, the physical side of their education consisted of ball games, dancing, archery, fencing, gymnastics, riding, and swimming. Most humanist educators insisted that students attend worship services, go to confession regularly, and say their prayers. Humanists understood that they were teaching future advisers to princes, and they were molding the lives of boys who, as men, would have an influence on public life. By the middle of the fifteenth century Venetian noblemen, for example, were committed to humanistic education, either in the public schools or in study with private teachers. By the 1470s southern Italian schools also began to hire humanist teachers. Historians estimate that by the end of the fifteenth century nearly all Latin grammar schools in Italy provided a humanist curriculum.

Latin grammar books

The humanists' emphasis on classical Latin texts created a demand for new Latin grammar books. At the beginning of the fifteenth century, grammar teachers in Italy were using the same basic books that a thirteenth-century grammar teacher would have used. In 1473 the Italian educator Niccolò Perotti (1429–1480), a student of Vittorino, wrote *Rudimenta grammatices* (Basic grammar). This manual incorporated many classical Latin examples used by humanist teachers. The trend in new grammars then moved to the rest of Europe during the latter part of the fifteenth century. In 1487 the Spanish humanist Antonio de Nebrija (pronounced neh-BREE-ha; 1441–1522) published *Introductiones latinae* (Latin introductions). To help Spanish readers learn Latin, Nebrija placed a translation in Castilian (a dialect of the Spanish language) alongside a column of Latin text. The *Introductiones* was reprinted often and exported all over Europe. In 1598 the Royal Council of Castile ordered that no other Latin grammar be used in Spain or Portugal. Nebrija also compiled the first Spanish-Latin dictionary in 1492.

The most popular grammar text was the *Grammatica,* which was published by Johannes Despauterius around 1520. In France, Scotland, and the Low Countries (Belgium, the Netherlands, and Luxembourg), it was the basis for Latin grammars until the twentieth century. In 1572 the Portuguese Jesuit educator Manoel Alvers published a book that became the official grammar text in schools run by the Society of Jesus (the Jesuits; a Roman Catholic religious order). Humanist schools throughout Saxony (a

Lily's Latin Grammar

At the beginning of the sixteenth century in England, teachers at Magdalen College at Oxford and the grammar school at Saint Paul's Cathedral in London produced many new Latin grammars. The only text with a real humanist emphasis was *Rudimenta grammatices* (Basic grammar) by William Lily, who served as headmaster at the Saint Paul's school from 1512 until 1522. In 1540 and 1542 *Rudimenta grammatices* was the basis for two Latin grammars that were authorized by the king. One was written in Latin, the other in English. These books were used by teachers well beyond the Renaissance, during the reigns of Protestant and Catholic rulers alike.

district of Germany) used an elementary Latin grammar by the religious reformer Philip Melanchthon (1497–1560). It consisted of short sentences, prayers, psalms (poem songs), and fables (tales that feature animals as characters and provide a lesson about life). These brief exercises allowed students to learn grammar and vocabulary from reading and memorization. Melanchthon's grammar book was used in Germany until the eighteenth century.

Commonplace books

Humanist grammar schools also used commonplace books, which

were collections of phrases widely used in speech and writing at the time. Pupils were assigned commonplace books in their early schooling, as soon as they had a grasp of basic Latin. To compile a commonplace book, students were instructed to assemble a large notebook with blank pages. On each page they would write headings and subheadings on topics suggested by their teacher. A typical heading was *pietàs* (loving respect), which might include such subheadings as respect for God, for country, and for teachers. Under these subheadings, pupils inserted quotations from the Latin prose and poetry they were studying. At first teachers assigned the quotations, and later students selected their own passages. Usually commonplace books contained short, witty phrases or proverbs, which pupils were required to memorize and recite orally in class.

Soon humanists were recommending a new form of education. This method required students to learn Latin by imitating classical authors in their own Latin compositions instead of memorizing grammar rules. In 1512 the Dutch humanist Desiderius Erasmus (c. 1466–1536) published *De copia verborum* (Foundations of the abundant style), an anthology, or collection, of excerpts from classical works. Erasmus's book encouraged the new form of learning. During the sixteenth century it was printed in more than one hundred editions and was the preferred textbook in grammar schools throughout northern Europe.

In addition to commonplace books, humanist grammar schools relied on books called colloquies. These texts consisted of fictional dialogues written in classical style that served as models for speaking Latin outside the classroom. The most popular was Erasmus's *Colloquia* (Colloquy), which was published in 1518 and went through twelve editions by 1533. Other colloquies were *Exercitatio linguae latinae* (Schoolboy dialogues; 1538) by the Spanish humanist Juan Luis Vives (pronounced BEE-bahs; 1492–1540) and *Colloquiorum scholasticorum* (School colloquies; 1556) by Mathurin Cordier (1479–1564). Cordier's colloquy was still in use in English schools in the nineteenth century.

France starts humanist *collèges*

Italian humanist education became extremely popular in France in the 1520s and 1530s. Leading the way was the French king, Francis I (1494–1547; ruled 1515–47), who inspired leaders in cities and towns throughout the country to start schools called *collèges* (colleges). Local leaders believed that humanist education contributed to the common good, honored the king, and preserved the republican form of government. Officials in one French town even believed that education was more beneficial than all of the hospitals in the world. The movement barely touched village schools, however. By 1520 universities in Paris had established classical Latin and Greek studies as the foun-

Teaching Greek

Classical Greek was introduced in Italy by the Greek-born scholar Manuel Chrysoloras (pronounced kris-eh-LOHR-ehs; c. 1350–1414) in the 1390s, who taught classes in the language in several cities. While teaching the classes Chrysoloras produced *Erotemata sive quaestiones,* which was published many years after his death, in 1476, and provided some Greek grammar rules. Greek grammars were written by other scholars later in the fifteenth century. All of these texts were adapted for a Latin-speaking environment with simple rules, explanatory notes, and Latin translations. Students of Greek could expect to begin with some easy Greek prose plus the Gospels (books in the New Testament) in Latin, placed alongside a version in Greek. They went on to read works by major ancient Greek writers.

The introduction of Greek into the humanist curriculum was first attempted by Guarino Guarini at Venice and by Vittorino da Feltre at Mantua. Vittorino taught Greek in a broad style, giving explanations of such subjects as mythology, geography, and important people as well as teaching the actual language. Latin translations were used side by side with the Greek. For Guarini, the goal of Greek learning was to aid the study of Latin, though some students learned to translate from Greek to Latin. Students were not expected to write or speak Greek. In the latter part of the fifteenth century, with the introduction of printed Greek texts, Greek grammar became common in humanist schools in Italy. Even then it was normally taught only to older students.

dation of arts and theology (study of religion).

Masters of *collèges* in Paris developed a plan of study that moved from grammar to oratory (public speaking), logic (thinking based on reason), and natural philosophy (natural science; the study of such fields as physics, chemistry, and biology). Students progressed through the curriculum according to their abilities. The Paris *collèges* served as models for schools throughout France. Under this system students were divided into classes by age and ability. They studied classical Latin works and learned to translate from French into Latin. They also had lessons in Greek grammar and read a few classical Greek works. By the mid-sixteenth century nearly every town of sufficient size contained such a public school. Staffed by a principal and four to six teachers, each school normally taught several hundred students from a variety of social backgrounds. One of the most famous schools was the Collège de Guyenne in Bordeaux, where the essayist Michel de Montaigne (1533–1592) was educated. The humanist educator Mathurin Cordier served as the grammar master at Guyenne from 1534 to 1536. He then moved to Geneva, Switzerland, where he introduced Guyenne methods to the humanist curriculum of the Collège de la Rive.

The *collèges* began to decline in the 1570s because of a lack of funds and a shortage of qualified teachers. Town schools had also become a battleground for differing religious views. Large numbers of schoolteachers were attracted to Protestantism, while city and state leaders tried to enforce Catholicism. By 1610 Catholic priests and religious orders were teaching a modified humanist curriculum as a part of religious training. In addition, after 1600 both the church and the king expressed concern that society had too many educated laymen (people who are not members of the clergy), which may threaten the church's and king's power. The humanist curriculum was gradually overshadowed by an emphasis on French culture. Humanism had not been accepted by most members of the French aristocracy, who preferred military training and more practical forms of education. For them humanist learning was associated with Roman and Italian culture and had little importance to France.

Spain and Portugal influenced by Italy

Humanist education in Spain and Portugal began in the courts of kings and noblemen during the fifteenth century. Spanish and Portuguese humanism was heavily influenced by methods used in Italy. For instance, Spanish courts had direct contacts with the court of Alfonso V (1396–1458; ruled 1416–58), king of Naples and Sicily. The Spanish also had contacts with Rome and Florence. Large numbers of Spanish students attended Italian humanist schools, especially the Spanish College of San Clemente at Italy's University of Bologna. Portuguese students were supported by the royal court to study in Paris. Humanism took root in Spain in the last quarter of the fifteenth century. It was encouraged by Queen Isabella I of Castile (1451–1504; ruled 1474–1504) and spread by the production of classical texts by Spanish printing presses. Beginning in the 1490s, Isabella invited humanists such as Pietro Martire d' Anghiera (c. 1447–1526) and Lucio Marineo Siculo (died 1533) to make the palace school into a Latin academy. The royal court established two schools of classical Latin, and aristocratic families hired humanist tutors, a practice that continued into the eighteenth century. By the beginning of the sixteenth century, the Portuguese court had hired a humanist tutor from Spain.

The humanist curriculum was probably adopted in numerous Latin grammar schools in Spain and Portugal by the early sixteenth century. These Latin schools were competitive with church schools, and by 1600 they existed in hundreds of communities. Historians estimate that virtually every town with a population of more than 500 had a humanist Latin school. In the second half of the sixteenth century the Jesuits rapidly

Jesuit Schools

The Jesuits were among the first to establish humanist schools. As required by their religious order, they began to educate external (non-Jesuit) students at a school in Gandía, Spain, in 1547. Another school was founded at Messina in Sicily the following year. A Jesuit education began with Latin grammar on three grade levels. Beginning Greek was originally taught at the fourth level, along with Latin humanities. The humanities were then followed by rhetoric at the fifth level. In some schools these five levels were followed by the study of philosophy and theology. Students also continued reading texts in Greek and Latin and occasionally Hebrew. The schools were divided into distinct classes designed to meet the educational needs of each scholar. Jesuit teachers made demanding assignments in writing and public speaking. Pupils also studied mathematics, geography, history, and astronomy. All of these subjects were based on the original Latin texts.

Jesuit schools promoted public performances—theatrical presentations, public debates and orations—that advertised their institutions. The Jesuits were dedicated to both the intellectual and spiritual progress of their students. The education was free and brought in boys from all social classes, though the colleges tended to attract elites. Demand for Jesuit schools put strains on the expanding order. In 1551 Ignatius Loyola, the founder of the Society of Jesus, established the Collegio Romano, a high school in Rome for boys and young men. He intended Collegio Romano to be a center for the education of future teachers. By the time Ignatius died in 1556, Jesuits were running 33 colleges in seven European countries. By 1586 there were another 150 colleges, and, by 1600, a total of 236, ranging from Japan to Peru and Mexico. Jesuit schools became models for Italian seminaries and the schools of other religious orders.

dominated secondary schools in Spain and Portugal. By 1600 there were 118 Jesuit schools in Spain's major towns and cities, educating perhaps 10,000 to 15,000 boys each year.

New schools in England and Scotland

The best-known English humanist school was founded by John Colet (1466–1519) at Saint Paul's Cathedral in London in 1509. Colet reorganized the school to teach 153 students free of charge. He appointed William Lily (c. 1468–1522), a scholar who had traveled widely and had studied classical Latin and Greek in Italy, as schoolmaster. Lily taught Greek at Saint Paul's and also produced several short guides to Latin grammar. Colet's instructions for his school required the use of texts by Erasmus and empha-

John Colet, founder of Saint Paul's School, the best known English humanist school.

sized Christian piety, or devotion. Colet viewed school as a sacred space, giving special attention to the prayers of schoolboys and the depiction of Christ as a schoolchild.

The driving force behind humanist education in England was Erasmus. He agreed with Colet that education and Christian piety should be combined. Erasmus visited England for the first time in 1499, becoming a friend of Colet and humanist Thomas More (1478–1535). Erasmus visited England again in 1505 and returned in 1509 for his longest stay. During this time he wrote *De ratione studii*

(On the method of study; 1511). In this work he asserted that children should begin life speaking Latin, a task more easily accomplished in a wealthy household. It was less easily accomplished by students learning in a grammar school environment. Students should read extensively, he noted, and not simply memorize grammatical rules. Erasmus's last essay on education, published in 1529, was *De pueris instituendis* (On the education of boys). It included an attack on current educational practices, especially in monastery schools, where rules were strict and the emphasis was on religion. Erasmus recommended that parents either choose a public school or keep their child at home. Children should be molded from birth, he said, and the proper education of children requires sensitive and supportive teachers. More set up his own household to function as a school based mainly on Erasmus's ideas.

The most famous humanist school in England was at the royal court. There the children of kings Henry VII (1457–1509; ruled 1485–1509) and Henry VIII (1491–1547; ruled 1509–47) were educated along with children of noble families. One of the schoolmasters was Roger Ascham (1515–1568), who taught the future Queen Elizabeth I, daughter of Henry VIII. Ascham and other humanist educators saw education as a means toward reform of the nation and the community. The north of England was slower to embrace humanism in the grammar curriculum. In the 1540s and 1550s most schools in the north were large public institutions in which the curriculum may have been humanist but there was a strong emphasis on discipline. Humanism reached Scotland in the 1560s and 1570s, but there was no consistent curriculum. Many schoolmasters used humanist ideas to compile their own Latin grammar books.

Organized education in Germany and Low Countries

Humanism reached Germany and the Low Countries in the late fifteenth and early sixteenth centuries as the result of contact with humanists from Italy and France. A humanist education was first available at abbeys (monasteries attached to Catholic churches) throughout northern Europe. By the end of the fifteenth century, city schools in the Low Countries offered a humanist curriculum. These schools sometimes competed and even collaborated with schools associated with the Brethren of the Common Life (a Protestant religious group). In one case the Brethren's school at Liège, Belgium, was picked by the town council to be the main Latin school. Humanism was successfully blended into the Brethren curriculum. In other cases Brethren schools were pushed aside. The new Latin schools could be quite large, with a faculty that was divided into forms (academic years) and that specialized in particular subjects.

One of the most notable educators in the Low Countries was Juan Luis Vives, the Spanish scholar, who had adopted Bruges, Belgium, as his home. Vives was known for his ideas on human psychology. His major plan of study, *De disciplinis libri xx* (Twenty books on education), was published in 1531. In this work Vives advocated public schools in every township, and he stressed the equality of all languages. That is, he believed that the language spoken in a country (called the vernacular) should be studied alongside Latin and Greek. He also felt that students should learn from their own experience and observation. According to Vives, schoolmasters were engaged in the holy service of teaching children to better their God-given minds.

Throughout Germany and the Low Countries, education took on an organized form, with specialized subjects and classes divided into grades. In Zwickau, Germany, for example, a 1523 *Schulordnung* (school order) described six classes, going from sixth to first. The lowest class, the sixth grade, learned Latin grammar and German. Students in the fifth class started reading humanist texts and learned beginning Greek. In classes four to one, students learned more Latin and Greek texts and studied the New Testament in Greek. The second and first classes continued the study of Latin and Greek texts. They also read the Old Testament in Hebrew as well as in Latin and Greek translations.

Strasbourg has famous school

A complete humanist education was offered at Strasbourg, Germany, in a gymnasium (secondary school that prepared students for a university) led by Johann Sturm (1507–1589). The Strasbourg Latin school was established in 1538, with Sturm as rector (head), in an effort to consolidate two earlier humanist schools. Sturm's students studied Latin grammar, rhetoric, and dialectic based mainly on Cicero and Aristotle, along with Greek, mathematics, science, and biblical texts. Classical plays, orations, and defenses were presented on stage. Some Hebrew was introduced in the final year. The school was divided into eight highly structured classes, and strict exams were required for promotion. Sturm's gymnasium influenced schools throughout Europe. Although the Strasbourg gymnasium was open to sons of the poor, it actually educated about five hundred sons of wealthier citizens.

The numerous printing presses in the Low Countries and Germany strengthened educational opportunities with the printing of grammars and of Greek and Latin texts. The number of schools increased along with the explosion of printed schoolbooks. Efforts also were made to regulate and standardize education. By the mid-sixteenth century, humanist grammar education, combined with religious instruction, was required by both Protestant and Catholic states in Germany and the Low Countries.

Education for women promoted

During the Renaissance the humanist curriculum was nearly always written with the education of boys and the careers of men in mind. Nonetheless, a few educators promoted classical education for women. They may have been influenced by Quintilian, who gave examples of learned Roman women in his works. He also urged that both parents of a child be as learned as possible. Other influences were powerful women who were active in northern Italian courts in the fifteenth century and female rulers in Europe throughout the sixteenth century. Since humanists believed that children should begin to learn at an early age, they emphasized the need for home education. Usually this education involved a child's nurse or mother. For example, the Italian educator Enea Silvio Piccolomini (1405–1464; later Pope Pius II) referred to perfectly cultured mothers who served as models for sons.

Different educators had different reasons for supporting the education of girls. The Dutch humanist Erasmus argued that girls should learn how to study so they would be less idle and more virtuous. On the other hand, Erasmus's friend, the English humanist Thomas More, provided a classical education for his own daughters because it gave them greater access to a spiritual life. It also increased their chances of forming a marriage based on true companionship. In fact, the general attitude during the Renaissance was that women should be educated in order to prepare them for their roles as wives and mothers. A few writers suggested a link between classical education for women and civic life. For example, the English humanist Thomas Elyot (c.

1490–1546), in his *Defense of Good Women* (1545), described a sophisticated, learned, and successful female ruler. In 1638 Anne Marie van Schurmann published an essay titled *On the Capacity of the Female Mind for Learning,* in which she argued that learning was an end in itself—not necessarily a means to a career or a husband—and therefore suitable for both women and men.

Achievements of Renaissance women

The list of learned Renaissance women is long. Especially prominent were women who participated in court life in northern Italy. Many were educated from an early age. Among the students of Vittorino da Feltre at the Gonzaga court was Cecilia Gonzaga (1425–1451). She was introduced to Greek texts at age seven and was writing Greek at age ten. Laura Cereta (1469–1499) of Brescia, who was educated by her father in classical Greek language and literature, left behind a collection of letters. Isotta Nogarola (1418–1466) of Verona wrote Latin prose and poetry, corresponded with humanists, and participated in learned conferences and debates. Cassandra Fedele (1465–1558) was tutored by a humanist in Latin and Greek. She delivered orations before members of the University of Padua, the people of Venice, and the Venetian doge (duke). At the age of ninety-one she delivered an oration welcoming the queen of Poland to Venice. Costanza Varano (1426–1447) was educated partly by her grandmother, Battista da Montefeltro. Varano made

several public addresses and left behind letters, orations, and poems. Olympia Morata (1526–1555), tutored by a German humanist at the court of Ferrara, mastered both Latin and Greek. She left behind a volume of poems, letters, and dialogues, some of which are in Greek.

Other European women were also involved in learning and intellectual pursuits. In Spain Queen Isabella supported her Latin tutor and companion, Beatriz Galindo, called La Latina. A more classically trained female humanist was Francisca de Nebrija, daughter of Antonio de Nebrija, who substituted for her father as a lecturer in humanities at Alcala in the early sixteenth century. Luisa Sigea, a Latin tutor at the court of Portugal, wrote Latin poems as well as letters in more than one classical language. Another early sixteenth-century humanistically trained lady at the Spanish court was Ana Cervato. She memorized all of Cicero's orations, displaying an extensive knowledge of the classics.

Learned humanist women were quite active in northern Europe, especially in the convents. For instance, Caritas Pirkheimer (1467–1532), who had extensive knowledge of Latin, was head of the scholarly convent of Saint Clare in Bavaria (a district of Germany). Pirkheimer and a number of nuns in other convents regularly exchanged letters with humanist scholars. When nunneries were disbanded in parts of Germany that converted to Protestantism, the convents were turned into schools for girls. The education offered in these schools, however, appears to have been based on the study of Scripture and the German language, and humanism was not part of the curriculum.

Future English queens are educated In England there were voices raised in favor of educating women, who had not traditionally attended grammar schools. The daughters of King Henry VIII—both future queens of England— Mary Tudor (1516–1558; ruled as Mary I 1553–58) and Elizabeth Tudor (1533– 1603; ruled as Elizabeth I 1558– 1603), were taught by humanists. For Mary, Juan Luis Vives designed a rigorous "plan of study" that included the Latin and Greek as well as works by humanists. Elizabeth was tutored by Roger Ascham and became fluent in Latin. She also studied Greek and humanist culture. During Elizabeth's reign the aristocracy did not follow the royal lead in providing a humanist education for their daughters. In addition, Catholic convent schools were destroyed when the Church of England was established, and no alternative schools for girls took their place. The education of women was therefore restricted to households and to elementary schools, with few opportunities for classical training.

The first female humanist of note in France was Margaret of Navarre (1492–1549), author of *The Heptameron* (1531), an important Renaissance work. Although she was trained in Latin, Greek, and Hebrew, she wrote in French and Italian. Another Margaret, the daughter of King Francis I, was likewise humanistically trained and actively supported humanists. Mary Stuart, queen of Scotland (1542–1587), received a humanist education at the French royal court in the 1550s. She read classical Latin texts and works by Erasmus. Her notebook of Latin exercises included several humanistic arguments in favor of the education of women. She addressed the subject of learned women in an address she gave to the court at age fourteen. The humanist education made available to Scottish royalty at the French court did not reach convent schools for girls in Scotland until well into the seventeenth century, however. Public schools in the cities were open to girls at the elementary level but not at the secondary level. Therefore, most girls were not able to take advantage of a humanist education, though they could learn to read and write.

Humanistically educated women became increasingly rare in the seventeenth century, as English educator Bathsua Makin (c. 1600–c. 1674) noted in *An Essay to Revive the Ancient Education of Gentlewomen in Religion, Manners, Arts, and Tongues* (1673). She argued that women should receive an extensive classical education, especially in ancient languages. Makin herself taught these languages to women at the English court, but her efforts had no real impact on the general education of women in England.

Universities flourish in Renaissance

Only a tiny fraction of the male population taught or studied in universities, yet institutions of higher learning made an immense contribution to Renaissance culture and trained the leaders of society. In 1400, at the beginning of the Renaissance, there were twenty-nine universities in Europe. By 1601 sixty-three new universities had been founded in Italy, Spain, France, Germany, Denmark, Sweden, Belgium, Switzerland, Poland, England, and Scotland.

The main reason for starting new universities was a demand for higher education; increasing numbers of men wanted to learn (women were not permitted to enroll in a university). Society also needed more trained professionals because monarchs, princes, and cities required civil servants, preferably with law degrees. The adoption of Roman law in central Europe created a demand for lawyers and judges trained in this field. Numerous Germans enrolled in Italian universities, which were centers for the study of Roman law. A medical degree enabled the recipient to become a private physician, a court physician, or one employed by a town. Numerous clergymen earned theology degrees and then taught novice clergymen, especially in the schools of the large Catholic orders.

Sometimes princes and city councils founded universities for economic reasons. If a local university existed, young men who lived in the state could study at a considerably lower cost than if they had to go elsewhere. And parents could keep a closer eye on their sons. A university also brought prestige to a city or a ruler. Just

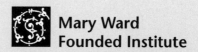

Mary Ward Founded Institute

Mary Ward (1585–1645), an English Catholic, established a network of humanist schools for girls. These schools were patterned after the Jesuit schools for boys. Ward had received a Latin education, and she was inspired by the English Jesuit college at Saint-Omer, a region in northern France. In 1609 she organized the Institute of the Blessed Virgin Mary, and her followers were popularly called Jesuitesses. By 1631 the Institute had three hundred female lay teachers and ten houses supervising numerous schools, one of which, in Vienna, enrolled as many as five hundred pupils. The curriculum included Latin and Greek (as well as vernacular education), mathematics, and the performance of Latin plays. The order was suppressed in 1631 by the English government because England was officially a Protestant country. Ward was imprisoned, though she subsequently established another Institute. Her followers have continued her work to the present.

as artists created works of art to grace a court, and writers praised a city, the presence of eminent professors at a local university proclaimed that the prince or the city encouraged learning. Most governments at one time or another tried to guarantee a large student body for the local university by forbidding young men from studying elsewhere. But these laws were seldom enforced. At the same time, civic leaders often dreamed that the local institution would attract students from other countries in Europe, as did universities in Paris, France, and Bologna, Italy. Considerable income was brought into a town by wealthy foreign students who purchased lodging, food, servants, and sometimes tutors. Princes and cities exercised control over universities by appointing and paying professors and heads of colleges. They made decisions about adding or eliminating subjects. After Europe divided into Catholic and Protestant lands, state and city leaders imposed religious requirements on faculty and students. University graduates, in turn, often played major roles in ruling the state.

Share common structure

All universities shared a common structure. Students attended lectures on required texts for several years before presenting themselves for degree examinations. Professors presented lectures on Aristotle's works on logic, natural philosophy, and metaphysics (the study of the nature of reality and existence). The works of Greek physicians Hippocrates (c. 460–c. 377 B.C.) and Galen (A.D. 129–c. 199), and the Muslim scientist Ibn Sinā (also known as Avicenna; 980–1037) were the basis of lectures on medicine. Law professors lectured on *Corpus juris civilis* (Body of civil law) and *Corpus juris canonici* (Body of canon law); civil law is state law, while canon law is that of the church. The theology faculty based their lectures on the Bible and *Sententiarum libri 4* (Sentences) by the Italian theologian

Peter Lombard (c. 1095–1160). All texts were written in Latin, and lectures, disputations, and examinations were conducted in Latin. Students were required to attend lectures for one to three years for a bachelor's degree in arts, five to seven years for doctorates in law and medicine, and twelve or more years beyond the master of arts degree for the doctorate of theology. These requirements were sometimes shortened. Professors and students participated in academic exercises, such as disputations, which were formal debates conducted according to the rules of logic.

When he felt prepared, the student submitted himself to a degree examination. A so-called college of doctors, a committee composed of professors and graduates of the university in the degree subject, examined the candidate. If the examiners were satisfied with the student's performance, he received one or more degrees recognizing him to be an expert in a subject and authorizing him to teach it anywhere in Europe. Approval of degrees came from charters issued by the pope and the Holy Roman Emperor authorizing universities to grant degrees.

The size of universities varied greatly. The University of Paris enrolled several thousand students, and several hundred teachers lectured at various levels. This was because Paris had numerous younger students, and older clergymen came to the university as both teachers and scholars. The clergymen taught liberal arts subjects to the teenage students while studying for advanced degrees themselves.

Bologna, the largest Italian university, had seventy-five to one hundred professors and fifteen hundred to two thousand students in the fifteenth and sixteenth centuries. Other universities were smaller. A typical university had thirty to forty professors who taught three hundred to five hundred students. Some universities had only ten to twenty professors teaching two hundred to three hundred students. But even the smallest provincial university was immensely important to the intellectual life of a region. The number of university students and degrees awarded increased in Europe as a whole between 1400 and 1600, in spite of many obstacles. Numerous wars forced universities to close temporarily, and the Protestant Reformation produced a sharp enrollment drop in German universities. The increased number of degrees suggests that society valued learning, or perhaps only the degree, more than it had in earlier centuries.

Students could easily attend more than one university because the texts were the same and all instruction was in Latin. Students sometimes traveled from university to university, following a famous professor. As a result, universities competed for a few renowned professors, especially in civil law. Attracted by higher salaries, these fortunate professors moved from one university to another. The majority of professors, however, spent their entire careers at a single university.

During the Middle Ages university students had organized themselves into "nations" corresponding to

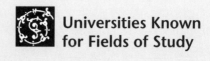

Universities Known for Fields of Study

Although European universities shared common characteristics, the subjects emphasized and the level of instruction varied greatly from institution to institution. The University of Paris in France and Oxford University in England emphasized instruction in arts and theology. Medicine and law were much less important. Indeed, Paris did not teach civil law. Paris and Oxford had many teenage students and awarded numerous bachelor's degrees. Universities in central Europe tended to pattern their curriculum on the University of Paris. Spanish universities, and French universities outside of Paris, tended to concentrate on law.

Italian universities were centers for instruction in civil (state) law, canon (church) law, and medicine at the doctoral level. They taught liberal arts subjects, such as logic and natural philosophy, as preparation for medicine, but they offered few theology courses before the second half of the sixteenth century. Doctoral degrees normally included the master's degree, which gave students the right to teach. The bachelor's degree had disappeared from Italian universities by the early fifteenth century.

their homelands. They elected student leaders to represent them in the city where they were attending a university. These organizations asserted student rights against local governments and helped choose professors. During the Renaissance student organizations retained their prestige but lost much of their power. City and town governments appointed professors and increasingly dominated other aspects of university life.

Impact of humanist education

The most important change in universities during the Renaissance was the introduction of humanistic studies into the curriculum. Professors who taught ancient Latin and Greek texts began to appear at Italian universities in the first half of the fifteenth century. They took university posts in northern European universities in the early sixteenth century. Sometimes they faced strong opposition from theologians who were already on the faculty. Humanists stressed better understanding of ancient Latin and Greek. Most important, they read texts critically within a historical context: By the late fifteenth century, and especially in the sixteenth century, humanist professors of philosophy were reading the works of Aristotle in Greek, rather than in medieval Latin translations. They also read the ancient Greek commentaries on Aristotle, which had been neglected because, prior to that time, few scholars knew Greek. The results were strong criticism of medieval commentators and new interpretations of Aristotle's works.

Professors of medicine used their newly acquired humanistic skills to examine the medical texts of Galen, the Greek philosopher (see "Medicine" in Chapter 10). The scholars found the medieval Latin translations inadequate, so they produced new Latin translations based on a better understanding of the original Greek. This process is sometimes called medical humanism. Other changes in university medical research included greater emphasis on anatomy as a result of more frequent and more detailed dissection of human bodies. In 1545 the Universities of Padua and Pisa simultaneously established the first university botanical gardens in order to improve the study of the medicinal properties of plants. Clinical medicine (medical instruction based examination and discussion of patients) began in 1545 when a professor at Padua took students to hospitals in order to lecture on a disease at the bedside of an ill patient. These innovations, in combination with medical humanism, produced a revolution in teaching and research of medicine at Padua by 1550. Other universities quickly followed Padua's lead.

Humanism also influenced the study of law. The new scholarly procedures produced the field called humanistic jurisprudence, which meant the attempt to reconstruct the social context of ancient Roman law. Scholars wrote commentaries on law, based on their discoveries. Sixteenth-century French universities welcomed humanistic jurisprudence, but Italian universities did not incorporate the new field into their curriculum.

Professional Training

Law, medicine, the civil service (government administration), the church, and teaching were the major professions in Europe during the Renaissance and Reformation period. Membership in these professions gave a man a higher status than other citizens, with the exception of rulers and aristocrats (noblemen) who enjoyed privileges based on birth. Becoming a professional required specialized training, often a university degree, and acceptance by a regulatory body.

Training to enter a profession began at an early age because nearly all professions required the ability to read, write, and sometimes speak Latin. Lawyers, physicians, university professors, clergymen, notaries (officials who certified legal documents), and governmental secretaries and administrators used Latin daily. A boy had to begin studying Latin as early as the age of six or seven in order to acquire this skill. Boys who attended Latin schools could enter the professions. Those who did not attend Latin schools usually took jobs as workers or artisans (see "Artisan training" section later in this chapter).

Law and medicine

Most lawyers and some physicians had to have university degrees. In Italy and southern Europe a boy began university studies at the age of seventeen or eighteen and emerged five to eight years later with a doctorate in law or medicine. In northern Europe boys aged thirteen or fourteen began to attend a residence college in a university town, where they were taught by masters and advanced students. After four or more years of study they obtained bachelor's degrees in arts, then they might continue to

study for doctorates in law, medicine, or theology. In England residence at one of the Inns of Court in London often completed the training of an aspiring lawyer or civil servant.

After receiving a degree, the new lawyer or physician had to be accepted by the professional association in the town in which he wished to practice. Called a guild (for example, the guild of physicians and apothecaries) or a college (for example, the college of lawyers and notaries), this body regulated the profession and determined who might practice. Local sons, especially of prominent families or those with male relatives in the guild, found easy acceptance. Anyone not locally born had more difficulty and was sometimes rejected. Once accepted, the young lawyer might establish a private practice or work for the town or state. Physicians practiced privately or were hired by the community to treat poor people who were ill.

Probably only a minority of men who practiced medicine were university trained. The rest included surgeons and empirics (practical doctors) who dealt with wounds, fractures, and rashes. Also in this group were barbers, who did cupping (drawing blood to the surface with a heated glass) and bleeding (draining blood from the body). These men learned as apprentices (those who learn by experience from a skilled member of a profession) or taught themselves by reading texts of practical medical advice. Medical guilds accepted surgeons and empirics if they passed a practical examination but rejected barbers. These

An anatomy lesson being conducting in the barber-surgeon hall. Few men who practiced medicine during the Renaissance had been university trained. ©Bettmann/Corbis. Reproduced by permission of the Corbis Corporation.

members of the medical profession did not enjoy the prestige or income of university-trained physicians.

At the time of the Renaissance and Reformation, states were rapidly expanding. They therefore employed an increasing number of administrators, secretaries, judges, and prosecutors—all professionals with specialized training. Sometimes the state established special schools to train boys for careers in government. Notaries were also essential for both government and business, because they recorded business partnerships, contracts, prop-

erty sales, marriage agreements, and wills. Licensed by the state and members of a guild, notaries wrote Latin in a handwriting so difficult to read and full of special formulas and abbreviations that it protected their professional status. Prospective notaries learned from experienced notaries and sometimes had university training.

The clergy

Many men became religious professionals during the Renaissance and Reformation era. The Roman Catholic Church had a great variety of clergy such as parish priests, priests who served bishops in many capacities, bishops, cardinals, diplomats, Vatican officials, and the pope. The church had its own courts, which required clergymen with legal training, and large staffs of secretaries, who served popes and bishops. Another group treated as clergymen were unordained monks, friars, and lay brothers who were members of religious orders.

While most clergymen were ordained priests, training varied according to a man's professional aspirations. Indeed, education helped determine how high a clergyman could rise within the church. Parish priests often received only a few years' education in a local Latin school and informal guidance from an established priest. A priest who hoped to rise into the highest ranks of the church needed a university degree, and he often obtained a law degree. The overwhelming majority of Italian popes, cardinals, and bishops in the fifteenth and sixteenth centuries held degrees in canon law, or in both civil and canon law. Clergymen expecting to become teachers and scholars of theology obtained theology degrees. This situation changed somewhat by the late sixteenth century. The development of Catholic seminaries and schools founded by new religious orders, such as the Jesuits, gave future clergymen training in liberal arts, philosophy, and theology. These subjects were more appropriate to the religious profession. Protestant churches also established schools for their clergy, which emphasized Bible study, theology, and preaching.

Social position linked to education

A person's social position was determined by his education and profession. An example is teachers, whose training and social position varied. University professors had degrees and shared the world of lawyers and physicians. Teachers at the secondary level, especially those who taught at Latin schools, came close to the training and social position of professors. But elementary-school teachers, a few of whom were women, lacked social distinction and received low salaries. Anyone could become a teacher, because the profession lacked regulatory organizations. The vast majority of professionals outside the church came from professional families. Hence, dynasties of lawyers and physicians were formed during the Renaissance, as father, son, grandson, and nephew all became lawyers, or all became physicians. For example, numerous members of the Sozini family in Siena, Italy, became lawyers, judges, and professors of law in the fifteenth and sixteenth centuries.

Artisan training

Artisans (also called craftsmen) were skilled workers who made items to be sold in the extensive trading networks that had been developing since the eleventh and twelfth centuries. A craft guild was an organization of all the producers of one particular item in a town, such as shoemakers or blacksmiths (those who make objects out of iron). Each guild set standards of quality for its products and regulated the conduct of its members. The guild also set procedures for the training of its members. To become a shoemaker, for instance, it was necessary to spend about seven years as an apprentice (one who learns a trade under the supervision of a master). Apprentices or their parents normally paid the master for their training, and apprentices remained with one master for the entire period of their training.

The apprentice then spent another seven years as a journeyman (one who travels from job to job) working in the shop of a master shoemaker. Journeymen received room and board and sometimes a small wage. They often traveled from master to master gaining skill and experience until they were ready to make their own masterpiece—a fine example of their craft that demonstrated their expertise. The masterpiece had to be approved by the other master shoemakers, who decided if the market for shoes was large enough in their town to support another shoemaker. Once the masters approved the journeyman's masterpiece and gave him permission to work in the town, he became a master and opened his own shop. Although the time required to be an apprentice and journeyman varied slightly from craft to craft, all guilds followed the same training procedures.

Artists

In book thirty-five of *Natural History,* the ancient Roman scholar

Pliny the Elder (A.D. 23–79) tells of the ancient Greek artist Pamphilus (after 390–350 B.C.), who was "the first painter highly educated in all branches of learning, especially arithmetic and geometry, without the aid of which he maintained art could not attain perfection." Pamphilus trained the most famous painter of Greek antiquity, Apelles (fourth century B.C.). Pamphilus put his pupils through what was effectively a twelve-year course of study, and through his influence the art of painting was elevated to the level of a liberal art. Pliny's account of Pamphilus's training methods provided a model for Renaissance artists—painters and sculptors. Between 1400 and 1600, artists sought to elevate the status of their profession and to expand artistic training by introducing liberal studies. At the beginning of this period painters and sculptors, like most artisans of the time, underwent an apprenticeship with a master. By the end of the Renaissance, in the late sixteenth century, both private and state-sponsored artistic academies had been founded to give students practical instruction along with exposure to art theory, mathematics, and anatomy.

Apprenticeship Throughout the Renaissance period, a young artist learned his craft by apprenticing with a master. Historians have determined the nature of these apprenticeships by investigating documents from the period. These documents include guild or municipal regulations, contracts between individual masters and pupils,

Musical Training

Little is known about music education during the Renaissance. Some formal instruction was given in cathedral choir schools in France and Flanders (located in parts of present-day France, Belgium, and the Netherlands). Similar training was given to choirboys at the major Italian cathedrals. In general, however, most musicians received individual instruction at home, a practice that was especially true for girls. The printing of musical primers began in the late sixteenth century, but knowledge of music was usually passed down from a master to a student rather than through textbooks. Many singers and composers were clerics (church officials), particularly in Catholic countries. A few, like the French composer Guillaume Dufay (c. 1400–1474), performed throughout Europe, while others, like the Flemish composer Heinrich Isaac (c. 1450–1517), were given honored positions at the court of the Holy Roman Emperor. But the employment situation for musicians and composers was unstable. They were often fired from their positions when a new duke gained power at court or when a major church made financial cutbacks. If a composer wanted to publish his music he had to find a patron who would subsidize (help pay for) the printing costs. The composer would then dedicate the work to the patron. Although some musicians, such as the famous Italian composer Giovanni Pierluigi da Palestrina (c. 1525–1594), became wealthy, many depended on their jobs as chapel masters or directors of music in churches for an income.

As a rule, most musicians and patrons were men. Nevertheless, a few women made contributions to music of the period. Historians know that noblewomen in Italy, France, and Flanders acted as patrons. Among the most prominent was Isabella d'Este, duchess of the Italian city-state of Ferarra, who played a role in the development of songs called frottole. A famous woman musician was Laura Pevenara, who performed at the court of Ferrara. Women were also active in music outside the court. Presses in Antwerp, Belgium, printed music performed by amateur female musicians. During the late sixteenth century Italian nuns in Bologna, Milan, and Verona became increasingly involved in the music world.

handbooks or treatises (largely Italian) written by practicing artists, and surviving drawings and prints.

Local artists' guilds regulated apprenticeships to varying degrees. The goal was to equalize practices among the various artists' workshops and to ensure a consistent level of quality in their products. Hence, guild statutes might specify how many apprentices a master could take into his shop at a time and how long an apprenticeship should last. Statutes also stated that a pupil should not leave one master for another during his apprenticeship, or that a pupil could not sell works independently. Specific terms were also set out in contracts drawn up between the master and the father or guardian of the potential pupil, who was typically a male between twelve and fourteen years old. Some contracts specified that in addition to receiving food, lodging, and clothing, the apprentice would be paid a salary. Others required that the master be paid a yearly fee, which could be reduced as the training progressed—and as the youth presumably became more useful to the shop. A contract that required payment of the master was apparently the norm in northern Europe. Italian apprenticeship agreements might be of either type, suggesting that, at least in Italy, the profession did not draw exclusively from one economic class.

The lengths of time mentioned in these contracts varied widely, from one to eight years, and sometimes ignored guild statutes. If the apprentice did follow the full course of training and could afford to pay dues to the guild, he could open his own workshop and take on apprentices himself. In some cases, mostly in northern Europe, guild certification involved submitting a piece of work to demonstrate mastery (that is, a masterpiece). If the fully trained artist did not have the funds to pay guild dues and start up a workshop, he often hired himself out as a journeyman or assistant until his financial position improved.

The actual training program for an apprentice artist is not addressed in guild statutes and is usually only hinted at in contracts. A fuller picture of Italian training is found in *Il libro dell'arte* (Craftsman's handbook), which was written by the painter Cennino Cennini (c. 1370–c. 1440) around 1400. Cennini apprenticed in the late fourteenth century under the Florentine painter Agnolo Gaddi (c. 1350–1396). Although his book was apparently composed while he was at the court in Padua, his was probably the typical apprenticeship of a painter in Tuscany. Cennini claimed to have spent twelve years of study under Gaddi. He described essentially a thirteen-year training period. He spent the first year copying artistic models with a stylus (pen used for drawing) on a small wooden panel. For the next six years he learned basic tasks such as mixing pigments and preparing panels to be painted. During the final six years he mastered the techniques of painting on a panel and a wall.

At the end of the fifteenth century the Tuscan artist Leonardo da Vinci (1452–1519) began preparing notes for a treatise about painting. One of his goals was to develop an ideal training course for an apprentice. Leonardo's notes reflect the new emphasis on studying perspective and proportion that was taking place in the Renaissance art world. Yet he indicated that the central feature of artistic training was drawing, which began with copying two-dimensional examples from the works of other artists and then moving on to three-dimensional examples, like sculptures. The final stage was drawing objects in living nature. The imitative practices described by Cennini and Leonardo are reflected in numerous drawings made by Renaissance artists.

Informal and formal academies

In the 1570s and 1580s academies for the training of artists were being formed in Italy and northern Europe. The concept of an academy originated in Italy in the early sixteenth century, when artists gathered for group drawing sessions after the work day was over. Both Cennini and Leonardo discussed the practice of apprentices drawing in groups. Although Leonardo was concerned that pupils might be distracted by the presence of others, he noted that these sessions could stimulate healthy competition among young artists. In 1531 the Italian artist Agostino Venenziano put the word "Academia" (Academy) on an engraving. It depicted artists drawing statuettes by candlelight in the studio of the Italian sculptor Baccio Bandinelli. A later engraving by the Italian artist Enea Vico, made around 1550, shows a group of artists drawing by lamplight. The items in the studio include skeletons, perhaps suggesting that by the mid-sixteenth century apprentices were doing anatomical studies.

Informal academies were also appearing in northern Europe. The Dutch artist Karel Van Mander (1548–1606) is said to have formed an academy for drawing with several other artists in Haarlem during the 1580s. Van Mander had visited Florence and Rome in the mid-1570s, and it is likely that he imported the practice of group drawing sessions from Italy. In fact, by the time Van Mander passed through Florence, a formal artistic academy, the Compagnia e Accademia del Disegno (Company and Academy of Design), had been founded in that city by artist Giorgio Vasari (1511–1574). The academy had developed out of the Company of Saint Luke, an artists' social organization called a confraternity. It provided an educational program for artists, eventually replacing the functions of painters' and sculptors' guilds. After 1571 painters and sculptors were no longer required to belong to a guild. Vasari received support from Cosimo I de' Medici (1519–1574), the duke of Florence. The Compagnia e Accademia del Disegno became a sort of sister organization to the Accademia Fiorentino, the state-sponsored literary academy that promoted the Tuscan language. The Accademia del Disegno became a model for institutions in other Italian cities, such as Rome, Bologna, and Milan. In 1648 in Paris, the last chapter in the early history of modern artistic education was begun with the founding of the state-sponsored Académie Royale de Peinture et Sculpture (Royal Academy of Painting and Sculpture). Various national academies followed in Vienna, Austria; Madrid, Spain; St. Petersburg, Russia; and other European capitals.

13

Women in the Renaissance and Reformation

Several questions arise when describing the condition of European women in the Renaissance: Did their social or economic condition improve? Did they gain greater access to power? Were they able to express themselves in different ways than in the Middle Ages? Finally, was there a Renaissance for women? These questions can be addressed by looking at women's lives in three settings: the family, religion, and elite culture (the lives of female rulers, artists, and thinkers).

Women in the family

Women played several roles in their families, depending on their age and marital status. First a woman was a daughter and then a wife, mother, or widow. In contrast, male roles were generally defined by social position or occupation—merchant, knight, priest, peasant, barrel maker, weaver, and so on. Female roles were more sharply defined in upper-class society than in peasant society. The main reason was economic. Upper-class daughters, wives, and widows had a share in the family estate, so they were regarded mainly as a way to hold onto or expand. Therefore their lives were strictly regulated and controlled. In contrast, peasant women generally had more freedom. Wives, daughters, and even widows were actively involved in helping to support the family by maintaining the household and working along with men on the farm or in the shop. Therefore it was not practical to regulate and control their lives.

Daughters

A daughter was called a "virgin," that is, one who has not engaged in sexual intercourse. Daughters were expected to remain virgins until they were married, or for their entire lives if they were not married. The ideal of virginity had roots in the Christian New Testament (the second part of the Bible), in Greek philosophy, and in writings of early Christian leaders. These works were based on the concept of the patriarchal family (a family headed by the father) as the foundation of society. A person's identity depended on his or her descent through the male line. During the eleventh century this ideal was strengthened by reform movements within the church. Around the twelfth century in western Europe the requirement of virginity for daughters received new emphasis, first in the households of the high nobility and then in the property-owning classes. Property was passed along almost entirely to male heirs. Therefore, the main purpose of daughters was to serve as brides who linked two family lines together. To assure the legitimacy of any male heirs resulting from a marriage, it was necessary that the bride's father be able to assure her future husband that she was a virgin.

Increasingly in the Renaissance era, the concept of honor also depended on virginity. The violation of a daughter's virginity brought dishonor not only on the girl, but also on all of her male kin. Therefore, a young woman was usually held responsible for being raped (forced to have sexual relations) because this assault meant she was no longer a virgin and she had thus dishonored her family. Even though the young women was the victim of the rape, she was the one who was punished. Punishment often varied with the social standing of the woman's male relatives. For example, the daughter of a nobleman was punished more severely than the daughter of a laborer because the nobleman had a more honored place in society. When some young girls lost their virginity through rape or seduction, they were then abandoned by their male kin and often turned to prostitution (having sexual intercourse in exchange for money), which was the only way they could support themselves.

Wives and managers

In addition to preserving their virginity, daughters were required to master skills that they would later use in marriage. Most important were textile crafts such as spinning, weaving, and embroidering, which were generally taught by the older women of the household. Young girls also learned to manage finances, to supervise servants, and to nurse ailing household members. Finally, girls were instructed in chastity (refraining from sexual intercourse), obedience, and silence, all qualities that were thought to prepare a daughter for her role as a wife.

Wives had many responsibilities as workers and as managers of a household. Peasant women performed numerous duties, from tending fowl and sheep and a vegetable garden to brewing beer and assisting with the harvest. Artisan wives did skilled craft work alongside their husbands, or did the work themselves during their husbands' absence. Sometimes women became members of craft guilds in this way. (A guild was an organization that trained apprentices for a craft or trade and set standards for quality.) Wives of merchants tended shops, helped keep accounts, or managed other business records. Among wealthier patrician and aristocratic families, women performed the textile work that women everywhere were expected to do, but they generally made luxury items such as gold-thread embroidery. Their primary role was the running of the household: seeing to the purchase, storage, and replenishment of supplies; entertaining their husbands' visitors; supervising the servants; and nursing the ill, whether servants or family members.

The dowry

In most regions of Europe, when a woman of the propertied classes got married, she was expected to bring to her new husband's house-hold a portion of her father's wealth. Called a dowry, that portion usually represented the woman's claim on her inheritance. The function of the dowry was to remove a woman from her father's line so that she had no further claim on his property. Her share of her inheritance was to be as small as possible, to minimize the burden on the father's estate. At the same time, the dowry had to be large enough to attract—in effect, "purchase"—a husband with the highest social status. A marriage could reflect glory on the bride's kin, win them political allies and access to power, or increase the family's wealth. If a woman's family could not afford a high-status husband, she had to be satisfied with a lesser one who could be acquired with a smaller dowry. Even among the poorest ranks of the peasantry, a bride was expected to bring some goods to a marriage, if only a few pots or stools to furnish her new home.

The dowry technically remained the woman's property for life, but in fact it was managed by her husband. When the woman died the property was passed on to her heirs, female as well as male, if local laws permitted her to make a testament, or will, and name special gifts. In some regions of Europe, a wife might possess property in her own name in addition to the dowry. Sometimes that property was bestowed upon her by her father, who determined the value of the dowry. Again, depending on local custom, the woman might be able to pass the property along to her heirs when she died. Women were often entitled to use real estate (land), jewelry, and clothing that belonged to a male relative, who had the right to reclaim it as needed.

Rights for Jewish women Unlike Christian women, Jewish women had some legal independence. Prior to the creation of ghettos that placed all Jews under the system of Roman law in Italy (see "Roman and Spanish Inquisitions" in Chapter 7), Jewish communities had their own laws. Women had the right to sign contracts, represent themselves in court, and initiate legal actions. A number of women were bankers and full members of partnerships. In Turin, Italy, a Jewish father's wealth was funneled directly into his daughter's dowry. The reasons for this practice were many, but mainly it was intended to protect family property. As a result, the woman holding the dowry occupied an enviable position. The middle-class status of most Italian Jews played a role in balancing power between men and women. Even the richest Jewish men could not acquire great wealth or elite social status because they were barred by society's restrictions on Jews. As a result of these restrictions, women had an opportunity to gain equal status with them.

Marriage

A woman had virtually no role in choosing her husband. In the propertied classes most marriages were arranged by a woman's male kin, perhaps in consultation with her mother.

Renaissance women working at an outside loom. Women had many responsibilities as workers and managers of the households. *©Archivo Iconografico, S.A./Corbis. Reproduced by permission of the Corbis Corporation.*

Many women married men they barely knew or had never met. In most parts of Europe peasants of both sexes married fairly late (in their twenties). Among the upper classes, however, a teenage girl often married an older man (perhaps in his late twenties or thirties) who was already established in commerce, government, or aristocratic society. Sometimes a young woman married a man who was even more advanced in age and who had already been married. In these circumstances, it is difficult to know whether love played a role in the marriage. Many upper-class wives and husbands led separate lives because of the disparity in their ages, their lack of acquaintance prior to marriage, and their very different daily occupations. For instance, the husband might be involved in his business or in political activities while the wife's life was focused on the home. Companionship seemed to be more possible in marriages among the lower classes. Often spouses were engaged in the same kind of occupation—for example, they were both skilled craftspeople, or they operated a tavern or a shop together.

Marital problems Preachers, humanists, and other moral instructors promoted the ideal of a close relationship between wife and husband. They thundered against adultery (having sexual relations outside marriage), bigamy (having more than one spouse), desertion, and abuse. Adultery was consistently viewed as a wife's crime—not a husband's—and a very serious one. In many locations, a husband was excused for killing his wife if she was caught committing adultery. In some places, such a murder was not even designated a crime. Among the wives of European royalty, adultery was considered treason (a crime against the state) and generally punishable by execution. Meanwhile, men regularly engaged in adultery, sometimes with concubines or mistresses who lived in the family home. Wives were expected to raise children from these illicit relationships. Such arrangements were more typical of high-status families. Among the poorer classes, marital problems were more often expressed through bigamy or desertion. A man who found marriage unsatisfactory might leave his parish and marry again

in a more remote location. A man left his wife if he felt burdened by her, in which case the woman had no legal rights and she was reduced to dire economic conditions.

Abuse could be found everywhere, and among all classes. Wife-beating was permissible, as was the physical punishment of children and servants. Some moralists urged moderation and others deplored the use of beatings altogether. Men might, furthermore, imprison, starve, and degrade their wives and other family members. Prior to the Protestant Reformation, divorce was not available as a solution for a broken marriage. Among the upper classes, annulment (declaring a marriage invalid) was a possibility on grounds that the marriage had not been consummated (the couple had not had sexual intercourse), the couple were closely related kin, or there had been some flaw in the marriage ritual. Some Protestant reformers argued for divorce in cases of adultery or hopeless incompatibility. Their arguments were fundamental to later legislation permitting civil divorce.

Acts of cruelty by Jewish men in domestic relations are mentioned in documents of the period. Among these acts were broken engagements, abandonment, nonsupport, physical and verbal abuse, and the refusal to acknowledge or support a child born out of wedlock. A woman might threaten to bring the child to the synagogue (Jewish house of worship) or to pressure lay leaders to come to her aid. The rabbis of Catholic Europe were much less willing than the rabbis of Islamic countries to force a man to divorce his wife. This reluctance was a reflection of the Catholic belief that a marriage could never be dissolved. It was also further evidence that during the Renaissance women had no opportunity to extricate themselves from bad marriages.

Motherhood

The primary responsibility of all wives was the conception, bearing, and rearing of children. Women of child-bearing age spent most of their lives being pregnant, giving birth, and caring for children. Birth control was strongly discouraged. For women who wanted to terminate a pregnancy, abortions were sometimes performed. The method involved herbal remedies, recommended by midwife-healers, that posed great risk to the mother. Lactation (production of milk in a woman's breasts for nursing babies) frequently resulted in a period of infertility and relief from pregnancy, but when it did not, women often conceived anew within weeks of giving birth. Such a pattern is seen in the high birthrates in certain social groups—twenty or twenty-five children from one mother were not uncommon—and indicate that a woman had an average of one child per year. Although wealthy people viewed frequent childbirth as desirable, the birth of a single child could be seen as excessive to a poor or unmarried woman who was unable to care for the baby. That situation often led to child abandonment or even infanticide (killing of babies).

During the fifteenth and sixteenth centuries the infant mortality (death) rate was high throughout Europe. From 20 to 50 percent of all infants died. A high mortality rate up to age twenty was also frequent. It was not unusual for a woman who had given birth to eight or ten children to see only one or two of them reach adulthood. Women also risked dying in childbirth. The chance of death in any single childbirth event was about 10 percent—much higher over a lifetime in which a woman experienced childbirth several times. Mortality in childbirth was a leading cause of death among women, a great number of whom predeceased their husbands, who might proceed to marry one or two other wives. Moralists therefore used the possibility of death in childbirth as one argument for a woman to remain virginal and not marry.

Child rearing A woman's responsibility for her healthy newborn infant varied according to social class. Poor women generally nursed (breast-fed) their own infants for about two years, but women in the upper classes usually did not. In elite circles arrangements were made, often by fathers, to send a child to live with a wet nurse. A wet nurse was frequently a lower-class woman whose own baby had died or who had recently weaned her own infant from the breast (ended breast feeding). Sometimes wet nurses weaned their own babies early so they could be paid to breast-feed the baby of an upper-class couple. Infants spent about one or two years with their wet nurses (female infants were perhaps weaned sooner than males) before returning to their mothers. In the meantime, the mothers might have gotten pregnant once again.

A mother was responsible for a child from the time of birth until the child reached the age of six or seven. At that point it was believed a child was capable of rational thought. Young children were taught skills and moral values by their mothers, except in some wealthy families where servants were given these responsibilities. Girls were kept closely confined and supervised, trained in household skills, and taught chastity, silence, and obedience. Boys were prepared for further instruction under their fathers, either by a school or tutor, or in apprenticeship (training for a craft or trade). Peasants trained male and female children in agricultural skills. In the case of the very poor, both male and female children were often sent out of the home at age eight or nine to work as servants in upper-class households. Virtually the only education they received was the early childhood instruction offered by their mothers.

When a mother of young children died, her children were reared by their father and his female kin, his servants, or his new wife. When a father died, his male kin took responsibility for rearing children. In his will he may have invited his widow to remain in the household to tend her children, or she might be welcomed in that role by her late husband's brothers or cousins. But children were not understood to belong to their mother. If she did not, as a widow, remain in her deceased husband's household, she would relinquish the care of her children to her husband's family. Generally she would not be able to claim her offspring as her own.

Widowhood

Widowhood presented difficulties not only for the widows (women whose husbands have died) but also for society. These difficulties involved issues of kinship and morality: To whose household did a widow belong? How could the behavior of a sexually experienced woman be controlled? A widow was faced with several possible fates. Depending on where she lived, she might remain in her husband's household, especially if young children survived. She might return to her father's household or to that of other male kin. She might also marry again, enter a convent (a house for religious women) or other religious community, or live alone. Competing interests surrounded the woman as this decision was made, and usually she had little say in the matter. Her birth family might wish her to remarry or to return, with her dowry, to their household. Her husband's family might want her to stay with them so that her dowry could continue to support their household. Church officials and social leaders would urge chastity upon a widow and express anxiety about her moral supervision. In Catholic regions, she might be urged to join a convent or religious community. Elsewhere she might be advised to remarry. Living alone was risky for a woman because it might signify that she was impoverished and or had been abandoned by her kin. If she had property she might become the object of suspicion. The Dutch humanist Desiderius Erasmus (c. 1466–1536) argued that a self-sufficient widow could remain chaste and lead a productive life alone, but few people agreed with him at the time.

Women and religion

During the Middle Ages and the early part of the Renaissance, most European women were Catholics. Those who wished to devote their lives to the church entered convents. This situation changed after the Protestant Reformation in the sixteenth century. Women who converted to Protestantism expressed their religious commitment as wives and mothers or as activists in the new faith.

Catholic holy women

Catholic women entered convents for a variety of reasons. Some were adults drawn to the religious life; some were widows or refugees who sought a safe haven or were placed in safety by male kin; some were young girls placed by their kin permanently or temporarily in convents also for safekeeping, or as an alternative to marriage. Some of these women subsequently made permanent vows. Although some women lived in convents because of a sincere religious vocation, others were there to bide

 Benvenida Abravanel

Under Jewish law, women had many more rights than Christian women. Yet even Jewish women who had converted to Christianity (converted Jews were sometimes called New Christians) enjoyed more independence. An example is Benvenida Abravanel (born 1473), a Portuguese New Christian who settled in Italy and was a teacher to the daughter of the Spanish viceroy (royal governor). As a widow, Abravanel ran a loan-banking business, served the Medicis (the family of the dukes of Florence and Tuscany), contributed to charity, and was active in Christian causes. The Jewish playwright and poet Judah Sommo called Abravanel a "Princess."

their time, or despite their own personal choice or interest. Most women who resided in convents for any of these motives came from propertied and even aristocratic families. Convents required an entrance fee termed a "dowry," just as in a marriage. During the Renaissance, in some areas (such as the wealthier Italian cities) the number of women entering convents because of their family's economic interests skyrocketed.

In addition to those who sought to pursue a religious vocation in the convent there were others whose quest for holiness led them elsewhere. They joined communities of religious women that were not

Two nuns praying in a convent. During the Renaissance women entered convents for a variety of reasons. ©*Leonard de Selva/Corbis. Reproduced by permission of the Corbis Corporation.*

strictly cloistered, or separated from society. These women sought the less strict life because they preferred it or because their families did not provide the dowries necessary for admission to a convent. Nevertheless, they were supervised in some manner by members of the male clergy. A few others pursued saintly careers as single individuals. They followed strict routines of religious observance while living in the household of a male. Many were wives or widows who did charitable work with hospitals or religious orders. The Catholic Reformation greatly curtailed this kind of religious expression.

Women seeking to follow religious vocations were largely limited to the single option of the convent. At the same time, they were placed under even stricter regulation by male clergy. Holy women were closely scrutinized for evidence of heresy, witchcraft, or for pretending to be sacred.

Protestant reformers

The hold of the patriarchal family on women increased under Protestantism. Both men and women followers of this faith were faced with a new set of beliefs and standards of

Teresa of Ávila

Teresa of Ávila (1515–1582) was one of the great holy women of the Catholic Church. The founder of the Reformed Discalced (Barefoot) Carmelite Convent of San Jose, Spain, she is famous today for her mystical writings. She was born Teresa de Ahumada on a farm near Ávila, Spain. After a life-threatening illness she entered the Carmelite Convent of the Encarnacion (Incarnation), where she became a nun in 1537 and took the name of Teresa de Jesus. In 1554 Teresa experienced the first of several visions during which she saw a statue of the wounded Christ. She continued having visions and began writing her autobiography, later titled *Life*. When Teresa finished her book, she was called before the Spanish Inquisition, a church court set up to apprehend and punish heretics. The inquisitors told her to expand the book because they wanted to know more about her visions. She completed the longer version of *Life* in 1559.

By 1560 Teresa had made a decision to reform the Carmelites. She had long been troubled by the lax standards at her convent, and she wanted to return the Carmelites to strict observance of the original rules of the order. After much opposition and struggle, in 1562 Pope Pius IV granted her permission to start the Discalced Carmelites. Before her death she produced numerous books, which are now considered classics in mystical literature. Teresa was instrumental in reforming not only Carmelite convents for women but also Carmelite monasteries for men. She is credited with reviving Catholicism at a time when Protestantism threatened to bring down the church.

moral behavior. For women, it meant the disappearance of convents, which had been disbanded in Protestant countries. Convents still provided alternative living situations for unmarried or widowed Catholic women. A Protestant woman, however, was expected to live with her own family or her husband's family, under the supervision of men for her whole life.

Grumbach and Zell promote reform A few opportunities for female leadership emerged in the earliest days of Protestantism. Some female advocates of reform circulated their views in writing. Among them was Argula von Grumbach, who was born into an aristocratic and well-educated family near Beratzhausen, Germany. She was orphaned in 1509 while being educated at court in Munich. In 1516 she married Friedrich von Grumbach, an administrator for the Bavarian dukes of the Franconian town of Diefurt. She was then drawn to Protestantism, probably by Paul Speratus, a scholar and cathedral preacher who was a champion of church reform. Inspired by the pamphlets of Protestant Reformation leader Martin Luther and other reformers, Grumbach immersed herself in reading Scripture (the text of the Bible). In 1523, after witnessing the mock trial of a student who was a follower of Lutheranism, she challenged Catholic theologians to a debate about their coercive conduct. When they refused to participate, she published a pamphlet that eventually went into fourteen editions. In six open letters to German princes and to officials in the cities of Ingolstadt and Regensburg, she outlined a reform program for society as well as the church. She also published a poem to defend herself against unfounded accusations that she had a sexual attraction to a man named Arsacius Seehofer. After 1524 Grumbach produced no more pamphlets, but she did exchange letters with Luther and the Lutheran theologian Andreas Osiander. She also promoted the Reformation locally. In 1533, three years after the death of her Roman Catholic husband, she married again, but she was widowed again in 1535. Grumbach's unpublished family papers give insights into such matters as early Protestant educational ideals and the legal and financial difficulties of widows.

A few Protestant women became lay (unordained) preachers. The best known was the German reformer Katharine Schütz Zell (c. 1497–1564), who worked toward religious tolerance as a writer, speaker, and adviser. In 1523 she created a controversy by marrying Matthäus Zell (1477–1548), a Catholic cathedral preacher and re-

former. Katharine soon became known for her hospitality to reform leaders. She also took in refugees, attended to victims of the plague (an epidemic disease; see "Black Death" in Chapter 1), and visited sick people in jails. Zell kept in touch, by letter or in person, with many of the leading Protestant reformers such as Huldrych Zwingli (1484–1531) and Oecolampadius (also known as Johannes Huszgen; 1482–1531), who headed independent reform efforts. By the mid-1500s there were deep splits among Protestants because they could not reach agreement on a statement of faith. The Zells sided with radical groups (those who hold extreme views) that were pushing for the elimination of Catholic elements in Protestant doctrine (beliefs).

Between 1524 and 1558 Katharine published five works, including a defense of her husband. In 1557 she wrote an open letter to Ludwig Rabus, the Lutheran preacher in Ulm, who had criticized her radical views. In the letter she appealed to the common sense of the people of Strasbourg. She supported the efforts of radicals such as Zwingli and Kaspar Schwenckfeld von Ossig, both of whom had been guests in her home. Zell also expressed admiration for the Anabaptists (a Protestant group that advocated baptism of adults, not infants), whom she preferred to call Baptists. The Anabaptists were being persecuted as heretics by mainstream Protestants, however, and Zell was accused of heresy for supporting them.

Grumbach and Zell were members of the first generation of

Anabaptist Anneken Hendriks being burned at the stake in Amsterdam, Holland. Anabaptists were often persecuted as heretics by mainstream Protestants. *©Bettmann/Corbis. Reproduced by permission of the Corbis Corporation.*

Protestant reformers. By the late sixteenth century women no longer participated as either critics or advocates of reform efforts and the movement was dominated by men. Many women among the persecuted sects, notably the Anabaptists, openly professed their faith and were executed by Protestant leaders. These women gained fame as martyrs.

Women in high culture

The role of women in "high" culture—the elite world of power, ideas, and artistic creation—was significantly expanded in the Renaissance era. A few women served as monarchs who were instrumental in shaping not only political events but also cultural developments. Cultivated women of the high middle class or aristocracy headed salons that spread new scientific and philosophical ideas and set standards of literary taste. During the sixteenth and seventeenth centuries women became increasingly active in the humanist movement, which was given impetus by salons. The participation of women in intellectual life represented a major advance: for two thousand years they had been excluded from such pursuits because they were denied access to formal education. The new humanist emphasis on the worth of the individual began breaking down traditional barriers. As a result, an unparalleled number of women became writers during the Renaissance era. There were hundreds and perhaps thousands of women authors, mainly in Italy, France, and England. After 1500 they were encouraged by the growth of the printing industry, which permitted women authors to deal directly with publishers and bypass male-dominated institutions such as universities.

Women writers contributed to the beginning stages of modern feminism (support of the equality of women with men), which gained momentum in the eighteenth century. Women also wrote poetry, romances, stories, novels, and plays, which they translated into other languages. A few women who were learned in Latin or Greek translated works of classical or humanist authors. In addition, they wrote diaries, family histories, and advice books. Women painters and illustrators also gained fame in the flourishing art world. Although women were prevented from entering the professions because of their lack of access to formal education, they did make contributions to the emerging field of medicine.

Women rulers, intellectuals, writers, and artists did not influence Renaissance culture so greatly as did their male colleagues. Nevertheless, women and their supporters were included in major social and political issues from the outset. Their participation contributed to changes in ideas about women's moral and intellectual capabilities, laying the foundation for the modern feminist movement. In this sense, there surely was a Renaissance for women.

Queens and queenship

During the Renaissance the question of whether women could or should be monarchs was a much-debated issue. Only a few women were actually reigning queens (those who occupy the throne), and those women became powerful rulers in spite of concerns about women monarchs. Even where laws limited women's right to inherit the throne, as in France and Aragon (a region of Spain), queens consort (wives of kings) still had considerable influence. Numerous regents, queen mothers, and kings' mistresses also performed a variety of official and unofficial duties. A regent was a queen consort who ruled in the absence of the king while he was on a mission to another country or in the place of a son who was too young to take the throne. A queen mother is the mother of a reigning king. A mistress was a woman who had an ongoing intimate, sexual relationship with a king who was married to another woman.

Reigning queens Reigning queens had greater difficulties than male rulers. Every queen was expected to marry and produce male heirs to continue the dynasty (rulers in the same family line). The queen's selection of a spouse was especially controversial. It was difficult for members of a patriarchal society, in which husbands were heads of households, to distinguish between a woman's status as a private wife and as a public ruler. Some court officials feared civil war if she married one of her subjects, and others feared political problems if she wed a foreigner. Men dominated the royal bureaucracy as well as local offices. The general feeling was that a woman could not lead a government composed of men. For instance, in 1558 the Scottish Protestant reformer John Knox (1513–1572) asserted that a kingdom with a female ruler was like a monster with its feet where its head ought to be. Warfare created even more problems, for a woman did not fit into the traditional role of a military leader.

Isabella I, queen of Castile. As a queen married to a powerful king, Isabella had an easier time ruling a male-dominated system than the unmarried Queen Elizabeth I of England. *Reproduced by permission of Archive Photos/Popperfoto.*

Two reigning queens, Isabella I of Castile (1451–1504; ruled 1474–1504) and Elizabeth I of England (1533–1603; ruled 1558–1603), responded to these difficulties in different ways. Isabella's marriage to King Ferdinand II of Aragon (1452–1516; ruled 1479–1516) in 1469 won acceptance because it led to the unification of their realms as the kingdom of Spain (see "Spain" in Chapter 3). Elizabeth lacked such a convenient choice. She succeeded her half-sister,

Queen Mary I (1516–1558; ruled 1553–58), who had wed Philip II of Spain (1527–1598; ruled 1556–98) in 1554 (see "England" in Chapter 3). Elizabeth was aware of the discord that could result from a foreign marriage, so she was reluctant to choose a husband from another country. Political divisions among her advisers over the selection of a husband finally prevented her from marrying. The issue of a male heir to the throne therefore remained unresolved during her reign.

Elizabeth's status as a single woman did offer some advantages. Until the last years of her life she used the possibility of getting married as a bargaining tool in negotiations with other countries. As a queen married to a powerful king, though, Isabella had an easier time ruling a male-dominated system. In contrast, Elizabeth presented herself as both a male and a female monarch in public announcements and ceremonies. As she grew older, her subjects honored her with the image of the "Virgin Queen," which associated her with the Virgin Mary (mother of Jesus Christ). In warfare both queens assumed the role of warrior. Isabella accompanied the Spanish army on its campaigns to expel the Moors from Spain. In 1588, after Spain declared war on England, Elizabeth dressed in armor and gave a speech to her troops at Tilbury to inspire them to defeat the invading Spanish Armada (see "English defeat Spanish Armada" in Chapter 3).

Lower-ranking queens Like other wives, queens consort had the responsibility of giving birth to a male heir. If they failed in this duty, their husbands might divorce them or even have them executed. An example was Anne Boleyn (c. 1507–1536), the wife of King Henry VIII of England (1491–1547; ruled 1509–47) and the mother of Elizabeth I. Henry ordered that Boleyn be beheaded when he discovered that she was having an affair. As consorts, they also had symbolic power, which was especially strong if they had been honored and blessed in a coronation ceremony. Without ruling authority, their influence depended on several factors. Foremost was the survival of their male children, for whom they might serve as regents. Queens consort also exerted control if they possessed strong personalities or came from royal lineage. The latter was especially true for a woman coming from a foreign dynasty who could advance the interests of her family at her husband's court.

Regents had some authority to govern, since they acted on behalf of rulers who were relatives. One example was Mary of Hungary (1505–1558; ruled 1531–55), who controlled the Netherlands for her brother, Holy Roman Emperor Charles V (1500–1558; ruled 1519–56). Another was Catherine de Médicis (1519–1589), who ruled France for her minor sons (see "France" in Chapter 3). Regents with the least power were queens consort, who served for short durations during their husbands' absences. For instance, Katherine Parr (1512–48), the last wife of Henry VIII, was regent for three months in 1544 when the king was on a military campaign in France.

Queen mothers could provide much-needed stability during times of emergency. Louise of Savoy (1476–1531) ruled France for her son, King Francis I (1494–1547; ruled 1515–47), on two occasions. In 1515 she served as regent while Francis opened the second phase of the Italian Wars (1494–1559), a conflict between France and Spain over control of Italy (see "Italian Wars dominate Renaissance" in Chapter 2). She was regent again in 1525 after Francis was defeated at the Battle of Pavia in Italy and was held prisoner in Spain. Sometimes women who were not officially members of a royal family wielded power by manipulating the actions of their monarch lovers. An example was Diane de Poitiers (1499–1566), the mistress of King Henry II (1519–1559; ruled 1547–59) of France. (A mistress is a woman who has a continuing sexual relationship with a married man who is not her husband.) She influenced the decisions of the king, virtually replacing his wife, Catherine de Médicis, as queen.

Reigning queens, regents, and even kings' mistresses were in the position to patronize artists, musicians, humanists, and poets. One of the greatest patrons was Margaret of Austria (1480–1530), who served as regent of the Netherlands (1507–15; 1519–30) for her nephew, the future Emperor Charles V. She collected a fine library and supported outstanding artists and musicians. Women who married rulers of foreign realms also could introduce political and economic connections and new trends into their adopted lands. The activities of these women established their importance as political and cultural leaders. They remained influential in France, where they had helped to forge absolutism (absolute power invested in one or more leaders). Reigning queens made the greatest gains in England, but the increased power of Parliament (main ruling body of Great Britain) led to a weakening of royal control by the seventeenth century.

Salons

Women began making important contributions to Renaissance culture through their participation in salons. A salon was an intellectual and literary discussion that became popular in the 1600s. It was held at a royal or noble court and headed by an aristocratic or high-born woman called a *salonnière*. The terms "salon" and *salonnière* were introduced in the nineteenth century. During the Renaissance salons were known as *ruelles* (companies). Many women who headed and attended these gatherings exchanged ideas, then published their views in books and pamphlets.

Early forms of the salon could be found in northern Italy in the 1400s. Examples were literary gatherings in Brescia, where the humanist scholar Laura Cereta (1469–1499) presented her essays, and discussions headed by Marchioness Isabella d'Este (1474–1539) at her famous court in Mantua. Similar events were held in convents, where women could more easily express their views without the

Diane de Poitiers

Diane de Poitiers (pronounced deh pwah-tyay; 1499–1566) was a French noblewoman and mistress of King Henry II of France. She wielded considerable power during the king's reign, virtually replacing his wife, Catherine de Médicis, as queen. In 1514 Diane married Louis de Brézé, the grand sénéchal of Normandy, and had two daughters with him. Her exceptional beauty, which she maintained until late in life, gained her entry to the court of King Francis I. In 1530 she met Henry when he and his brother returned from serving as hostages in Spain for their father's ransom. After her husband's death in 1531, she became the love of Henry's life. Although she was twenty years older than Henry, he remained devoted to her until his death. She also maintained friendly relations with Catherine de Médicis.

When Henry became king in 1547, Diane received the title of the duchess of Valentinois; she also received the château (large country house) of Chenonceau. At court she was instrumental in manipulating the principal rivals for the king's favor, Anne de Montmorency (1493–1567; in this case Anne is a male name) and the family of Guise. She took the side of whichever party seemed to be most powerful at the moment. Diane also supported Henry's anti-Protestant policies. She extended patronage to the group of poets known as the Pléiade, who honored her with many laudatory poems. Her beauty and position also made her the subject of numerous artworks, including the famed *Diana the Huntress* attributed to the painter Jean Goujon (c. 1510–1568). The painting was placed in her second château, Anet, which had been reconstructed and was one of the highlights of mid-sixteenth-century French Renaissance culture. After Henry was killed in a jousting tournament (a game of combat with lances), Catherine de Médicis took Chenonceau away from Diane, who retired to Anet.

fear of ruining their reputations. Other pioneers of the Renaissance salon were French noblewomen Madeleine des Roches (c. 1520–1587) and Catherine des Roches (1542–1587) in the city of Poitiers. One of the first salons was the *chambre bleue* (blue room) established by the French hostess Madame de Rambouillet (also known as Catherine d'Angennes; 1588–1665) at her townhouse in Paris in the 1630s. Devoted to literature and cultured conversation, Madame de Rambouillet's salon had a strong influence on the development of French literature. The salon became especially popular in Paris, but such gatherings were also found in Berlin, Germany; Vienna, Austria; and London, England.

The salon was only one form of intellectual discussion attended by women. They were also welcomed at coffeehouses, academies, clubs, and masonic lodges (meeting places for the Free and Accepted Masons, a fraternal organization). The salon was different from these other social gatherings, however, in that it attracted a diverse range of participants and featured a varied program. It was also held in a more intimate setting, at the home of the *salonnière*. She presided over the conversation and set standards of etiquette (proper manners) to prevent disruptions and rivalries during the discussion. For the *salonnière,* the salon might serve as a means of education or a way to gain influence in society. The image of a *salonnière* was borrowed from such works as *Il cortegiano,* or *The Book of the Courtier* (1528), by Baldassare Castiglione (1478–1529), which defined proper manners for male and female members of the court (see "Life at court" in Chapter 11). Castiglione portrayed women as delicate, sensitive, beauteous, and selfless, and the *salonnière* was expected to possess these qualities. Nevertheless, the prominence of women afforded by salons was one of the most criticized aspects of these gatherings. The French writers Michel de Montaigne (1533–1592) and Molière (also known as Jean-Baptiste Poqueline; 1622–1673) were the best-known critics. They lamented that placing salons in the hands of women threatened not only manly virtues but also the seriousness of intellectual work and the stability of society.

New ideas promoted The salon was a place where writers might gain patronage for advancing their careers, either from the social elite with whom they mixed there or from the *salonnière* herself. Events held at a salon provided a forum for introducing new knowledge to a nonlearned audience. Authors read their writings aloud and commented on one another's work. Salons featured debates and dramatic performances and emphasized the art of conversation. Intellectual innovations and technical advances were worded in clear terms that were understandable to the nonlearned audience. This technique facilitated the transformation of new ideas into accepted ways of thinking.

The subject matter of salon discussions varied over time and from place to place. In seventeenth-century Paris, for instance, salon gatherings were devoted to refining the language and promoting style and clarity of expression. Typical topics of discussion were the nature of love, marriage, and patriarchal authority. Several literary genres originated or were developed in these social settings. Among them were the portrait, novel (a long prose story about human experiences), maxim (a wise saying), occasional verse (a poem composed for a specific occasion), and newsletter. A number of women who participated in seventeenth-century salons published their own writings, many of which incorporated themes and conversations common to salons. These authors included the poet and novelist Madeleine de Scudéry (often known as Sappho; 1607–1701) and the novelist Marie-Madeleine de La Fayette (1634–1693).

Scudéry is best known for *Artamène ou le Grand Cyrus* (1649–53) and *Clélie* (1654–60). La Fayette's works included *La Princesse de Montpensier* (1662), *Zayde* (1670), and *La Princesse de Clèves* (1678). By the eighteenth century, however, topics pertaining to women became less popular and women engaged in intellectual discussions less frequently.

Feminists

The activities of Italian women humanists led to the beginning of the modern feminist movement. In the mid-sixteenth century feminists appeared in France. Among them was Louise Labé (c. 1524–1566), a poet who urged women to take up scholarly pursuits. Other notable feminists were Madeleine des Roches and Catherine des Roches, whose salon was known as the school of learning or academy of honor. The salon was attended by humanists who encouraged the Rocheses to pursue their studies and publish their work. Among the first feminists in England were Jane Anger, Ester Sowernam, Rachel Speght (born c. 1597), and Constantia Munda. Although these writers identified traditional spiritual virtues with women, they saw men as also being capable of such qualities. Such traditional virtues included modesty, gentleness, selflessness, and piety (holiness). Their work helped promote the concept of androgyny (having characteristics of both sexes). A number of women in London from the 1570s until the 1620s acted out their androgyny through cross-dressing (wearing men's clothes) and were often referred to as hermaphrodites (people who have both male and female reproductive organs). In January 1620 King James I (1566–1625; ruled 1603–25) ordered ministers to preach against cross-dressing in their sermons. The following month a treatise titled *Hic mulier,* or, *The Man-Woman* was published, reaffirming the idea that women have a fixed nature.

Similar radical stirrings were in the air in seventeenth-century France. Louise-Marguerite of Lorraine, princess of Conti established a salon-in-exile at her château at Eu. There she wrote her memoirs of the court of King Henry IV (1533–1610; ruled 1589–1610) and read them at her salon. She then handed the manuscript over to writers in her circle, asking them to rewrite it for publication as a novel. This practice became a pattern crucial to the early history of the French novel. The novels created at Eu used a historical setting to develop plots composed equally of political and amorous adventures. They were written by men and women alike, but a woman's name was attached to each.

In the 1620s, 1630s, and 1640s—a wartime period in France called the Fronde—the *femme forte* (strong woman) emerged in French literature. The *femme forte* was portrayed as a Christian Amazon (mythical woman warrior) fighting, hunting, shooting, and riding. She dressed like a man while engaging in these pursuits. During these years Madeleine de Scudéry published *Artamène, ou le grand Cyrus,* which was initially a political novel. As the Fronde ended, novels focused on intellectual matters through dialogue. The years 1653 through 1660 were important in establishing a change from the *femme forte* to the *précieuse* (woman lay intellectual). The novels of Scudéry and others chronicled the salon life of intellectual conversation.

Three Italian women also expressed strong feminist views. Lucrezia Marinella was the first female writer to confront male authorities directly. In *La nobilità et l'eccellenza delle donne, co' diffetti e mancamenti de gli huomini* (The nobility and excellence of women, with the defects and vices of men; 1600) she responded to *I donneschi difetti* (The defects of women; 1599) by Giuseppe Passi. Refuting Passi's charges that women are weak and depraved, or evil, by nature, Marinella gave examples to show that women are more virtuous than men. In a second edition of her work the following year, Marinella criticized the negative views of women portrayed by the Italian male writers Boccaccio, Sperone Speroni, Torquato Tasso, and Ercole Tasso. All of these men, she said, made assumptions about all women on the basis of the behavior of one woman. Another Italian woman writer, Moderata Fonte, published *Il merito delle donne* (The worth of women; 1600), in which she used the voices of seven noblewomen to document female inequality in Venice. Inequalities included no opportunities for education, mistreatment by men, and lack of access to dowries. A third Italian feminist writer

was Arcangela Tarabotti (1604–1652), whose *La tirannia paterna* (Paternal tyranny) was published after her death as *La semplicità ingannata* (Innocence deceived; 1654).

In many of these texts women began to see themselves as actors who must shape their own destiny. Before the end of the seventeenth century European feminists had developed a consciousness of themselves as a group. In 1792 the English author Mary Wollstonecraft (later Mary Godwin; mother of author Mary Wollstonecraft Shelley; 1759–1797) wrote *Vindication of the Rights of Woman,* in which she called for equal rights and education for women. Historians note that Wollstonecraft's work would not have been possible without the efforts of her feminist forebears in the Renaissance.

Querelle des femmes An important part of Renaissance feminism was the *querelle des femmes.* The phrase means "the woman question" and refers to the literary debate over the nature and status of women that began around 1500 and continued beyond the end of the Renaissance.

The German physician and philosopher Heinrich Agrippa of Nettesheim (1486–1535) brought the woman question to center stage with *Declamatio de nobilitate et praecellentia foeminei sexus* (Declamation on the nobility and preeminence of the female sex; 1529). He dedicated the work to Margaret of Austria, governor of the Netherlands. Since the declamation was soon translated into English,

French, German, and Italian, Agrippa's ideas were repeated endlessly by a broad spectrum of writers. Arguing that women were better off in the ancient world, he reinterpreted biblical, Greek, and Roman texts to "prove" women superior to men. Agrippa reread the Bible to show, among other things, that men and women were created equal in soul and that the New Testament makes it clear that women not only prophesied (spoke as if divinely inspired) in public but also served as church leaders.

Perhaps even more controversial was Agrippa's contention that the oppression of women was based not on their biological nature but instead on social tradition. Although he did not see women as being inferior by nature, he did not advocate an expanded social role for them. Castiglione also took up the woman question, in Book Three of *Book of the Courtier*. While acknowledging that male sovereignty places a limit on women's freedom, he never challenged the male right to this sovereignty. Much more pro-woman was the Italian poet Ludovico Ariosto (1474–1533), who wrote *Orlando Furioso* (Mad Roland; 1532), which is considered the greatest epic (long) poem of the Italian Renaissance. In this work of forty-six cantos (major divisions) he raised questions about whether women can be chaste (he answered "yes" in cantos 4 and 5), whether women are morally inferior to men ("no," cantos 27 to 29), and whether men have a greater potential for depravity than women ("yes," can-

tos 42 and 43). Ariosto urged women to write their own history instead of depending on men to do it for them, an idea picked up in Italy by Luigi Dardano and in France by François de Billon and Guillaume Postel.

Should women be rulers? Discussion of the woman question in England was initially based on whether women should be rulers. In 1523 the Spanish humanist Juan Luis Vives (1492–1540) wrote *De institutione foeminae christianae* (Instruction of a Christian woman). At the request of the queen consort Catherine of Aragon (1485–1536), Vives's work was translated from Latin by Richard Hyrde in 1540 for the guidance of her daughter Mary Tudor (future Queen Mary I). On the basis of Vives's views it was concluded that Mary should not govern because women are weak, though Hyrde tried to put Vives's work in a more positive light. In *Defence of Good Women* (1540) the English humanist Thomas Elyot (c. 1490–1546) argued against Vives, saying that women can rule as well as men, though they should do so only under special circumstances.

In 1558 the Protestant reformer John Knox lashed out against women rulers in *First Blast of the Trumpet against the Monstrous Regiment of Women*. At the time Catholic women occupied the throne in three countries—Catherine de Médicis was queen consort in France, Mary of Guise (1515–1560; regent 1554–59) was regent in Scotland, and Mary I led England. Knox's work appeared, at the time, as a Protestant, Elizabeth I, became queen of England, but he made the issue a critical one thereafter. In 1559 John Aylmer (1521–1594) responded to Knox with *Harborowe for Faithfull and Trewe Subjectes*. Aylmer contended that Elizabeth ruled by divine intervention—that is, God had decreed that she become queen because she was an unusually gifted woman, who possessed more intelligence and skill than other women. However, since God had specially chosen Elizabeth to rule, her reign should not be used as evidence that women should be monarchs in the future. The poet Edmund Spenser (c. 1552–1599) introduced a version of the same argument in *The Faerie Queene* (1590, 1596), where Elizabeth is presented as being a unique person who was chosen by God (see "Literature" in Chapter 8).

By the end of the sixteenth century, writers had concluded that virtue was the same for both men and women. The question now became how to make this equality real, and during the seventeenth century the emphasis shifted to education. The Dutch humanist Anna Maria van Schurman (1607–1678) published a tract in the form of a logical discourse titled *Dissertatio de ingenii muliebris ad doctrinam et meliores litteras aptitudine* (Whether a Christian woman should be educated; 1638). As the first woman to study at a Dutch university, Schurman wrote that women who had leisure time could become scholars. Nevertheless, she did not see any role for women outside the home. At the end of her life she abandoned intellec-

tual pursuits and became involved in the Protestant reform movement.

The French writer Marie de Gournay (1565-1645), who corresponded with Schurman, took a firmer stand. In *Égalité des hommes et des femmes* (The equality of men and women; 1622), Gournay argued for equality of mind between men and women and asserted that if women were educated as men are, they would excel to the same degree. In a later essay, *Grief des dames* (The ladies' grievance; 1626), she satirized the failure of men to take women seriously and to consider them as equals in conversation. Gournay won this last argument, for in the second half of the seventeenth century social conversation between men and women was generally accepted as morally appropriate and enjoyable. One of the best-known published dialogues of the *querelle* was *De l'egalité des deux sexes* (The equality of the two sexes; 1673) by François Poulain de la Barre. It consists of a conversation in which both women and men contribute much to the discussion.

Throughout the seventeenth century, however, insistence on the subordination of women in marriage remained firm. Indeed, a major argument for Queen Elizabeth's single status was that as a ruler she governed all men but if she were to marry she would be subordinate (as wife) to her husband. Neither men nor women who participated in the *querelle* were able to bridge the gulf between arguments for the equality of the sexes and the subordination of women to men in the political and social arena. The conclusions and problems of the *querelle* established the terms and arguments of the issue for the coming centuries.

Other women writers

Italian women writers continued to make contributions in the century after Christine de Pisan's death in about 1430. Among the most acclaimed was Vittoria Colonna (1492–1547), the "literary queen" of the Italian Renaissance, who was at the center of intellectual and political developments of her day. Widowed from an unhappy and childless marriage at the age of thirty-three, Colonna spent the remaining twenty-two years of her life traveling, writing, and attracting a wide and important circle of acquaintances. The most famous was the great Italian painter Michelangolo (1475–1564; see "Renaissance Art" in Chapter 8), with whom she shared a long and fruitful correspondence. Colonna's published works consisted of books of verse that explore love in its various forms. Laura Terracina (1519–c. 1577), a contemporary of Colonna, lived a solitary life in her native Naples. From 1548 through 1561 she published moral lamentations, poems of praise for her relatives and friends, and reminiscences of her early years as a member of the Neapolitan Academy of Incogniti (The Unknowns). Most importantly, she wrote a forty-two-canto poem titled *Discorso sopra it principio di tutti i canti d' Orlando furioso* (Interpretation of the first cantos of Orlando furioso; 1549). Another significant writer at the time was Moderata Fonte

(1555–1592). Born into the Venetian nobility, she published religious poems and musical dramas in verse. She also wrote an important four-hundred-page prose work on women before her death at the age of thirty-seven.

Marriage for Fonte and other Italian Renaissance women proved somewhat stifling to their literary achievement. This problem did not apply to courtesans, who were freer to develop their intellectual and literary capabilities. (A courtesan was a prostitute, a woman who is paid to engage in sexual intercourse, whose clients were courtiers and other wealthy or upper-class men.) Veronica Franco (1546–1591) and Gaspara Stampa (c. 1523–1554) made major contributions to Renaissance love poetry. Tullia d'Aragona (c. 1510–1556), another upper-class courtesan, also established herself as a literary figure in her own right by publishing works of lyric poetry, epistolary sonnets, and the *Dialogo della infinità di amore* (Dialogue on the infinity of love; 1547).

In sixteenth-century France, love was also the theme of a few women who established themselves as writers. Margaret of Navarre (1492–1549), sister to the king of France, was an important Renaissance patron. She also wrote the great collection of stories known as the *Heptaméron* (1558). Women writers became especially prominent in England during the seventeenth century. Among them was Margaret Cavendish (1623–1673), who displayed great versatility and skill in her writings. The most famous writer of the late Renaissance period in Eng-

"Mad Madge"

The English writer and intellectual Margaret Cavendish (1623–1673) wrote in the greatest variety of genres of any women, or even men, of the late Renaissance period. She sought fame through her works, but during her own lifetime she was a social outsider. Nicknamed "Mad Madge," she was ridiculed for her self-promotion, her willingness to debate famous male thinkers, and her strong feminist views.

Cavendish was born into a wealthy family from the Colchester area. In 1643, at age twenty, she joined Queen Henrietta Maria's court in Oxford. The following year, during the English Civil War (a conflict in which rebel forces overthrew the monarchy), she accompanied the queen into exile in Paris. By 1645 she had met and married William Cavendish. The couple remained in Paris until 1660, when the monarchy was restored in England. Margaret published *Poems and Fancies,* the first of many works, in 1653. She went on to write about natural philosophy (natural science; the study of such fields

as physics, chemistry, and biology), two volumes of plays, fantasies, essays, letters, an autobiography, and a biography of her husband. She was criticized for her lack of training—she knew no foreign languages and did not have a classical or scholarly education—and her failure to produce polished works.

Cavendish was a complex figure. While she was a strong royalist (supporter of the monarchy), she published essays and letters critical of England's social hierarchy (class structure) and royal rule. She produced radical critiques of women's low social, political, intellectual, and legal standing, yet she often described women as weak, emotional creatures dependent on the goodness and competence of men. While others saw her as privileged, she often portrayed herself as an intellectual and social outcast. In the late twentieth century her works gained serious attention from literary scholars, historians of science, women's historians, and those studying women philosophers.

land was Aphra Behn (1640– 1689). She earned an independent living by her plays, songs, translations, and an epistolary novel, many of which were dedicated to female patrons.

Jewish scholars and writers Jewish women had to persevere against great odds to receive an education and be

admitted into literary and spiritual circles. Rabbis (Jewish spiritual leaders) expressed significant ambivalence, or mixed feelings, toward Jewish women receiving education beyond the skills necessary for managing a household. They feared that additional learning would inflame the passions of women and therefore endanger their honor. During the sixteenth century, Jewish literature about the nature of women showed many similarities to the Christian *querelles des femmes* discussion of the status of women. Some Italian rabbis reacted strongly against giving women greater freedom and even advocated physical punishment of disobedient wives. Rabbi Azriel Dien (died 1536) expressed the view that "over his women, every man shall be ruler to his house and rebuke his wife" (*Sheelot u-teshuvot,* no. 6), making it clear that men did not always have their way.

Nevertheless, a few scholarly Jewish women emerged in sixteenth-century Italy. Among them were Diana Rieti and her sister Fioretta (Bat Sheva) Rieti Modena, who both knew the Torah (books of Jewish wisdom and law), the Talmud (Jewish traditions), the midrash (explanations of early Scripture), the works of the Jewish philosopher Maimonides (also known as Moses ben Maimon), and Kabbalah (also cabala; Jewish mysticism). Late in life they set out to live in Safed, a community of mystics in Palestine (present-day Israel), the Jewish equivalent of entering a convent. Other Jewish women served as teachers of Italian and even Hebrew to young girls, at least in the fundamentals of reading. Some Jewish women were called *Rabbanit,* a title of distinction for a woman who had attained a significant level of learning. They joined in rabbinic discussions and participated in healing and birthing. Educated Jewish women in Italy found opportunities to work as scribes and printers, and their contributions are preserved in the colophons (statements of publication information) of many books.

Some educated Jewish women became writers. Debora Ascarelli of Rome and Venice gained recognition for her rhymed translations of liturgical poetry from Hebrew to Italian. These works were completed in about 1537 and published in Venice in 1601 and again in 1609. It was the first publication by a Jewish woman. Another writer was Sarra Copia Sullam. She was born to a prominent Italian Jewish family in Venice and received an education that included instruction in Italian and Spanish. She gathered around her a salon of men of letters in exchange for financial backing, intellectual conversation, and brilliant letters. After being accused of denying the immortality of the soul, she sat down and in two days wrote a strong defense of her views. It was published as *The Manifesto of Sarra Copia Sulam, a Jewish woman, in which she refutes and disavows the opinion denying the immortality of the soul, falsely attributed to her by Signor Baldassare Bonifaccio.*

Artists

During the fifteenth and sixteenth centuries, European women worked in virtually every artistic field. The most numerous women artists were nuns, though they were rarely identified because they created objects and images primarily to honor God's glory. Historical records show that an extensive art industry was conducted by nuns and that convents were often artists' workshops. Nuns were cloistered (lived inside walled convents), so they learned their craft with limited outside instruction. For instance, Marguerite (or Grietkin) Scheppers, a professional limner who was not a nun, taught her art to Sister Cornelie van Wulfskerke, a Carmelite nun of Notre Dame de Sion in present-day Switzerland. (A limner was an artist who made illuminated manuscripts, that is, painted the pages of books with brilliant colors). Sister Cornelie, in turn, taught and collaborated with Sister Marguerite van Rye in illuminating missals (prayer books) and small books of music.

Another group of women artists were the daughters of artists. They learned their craft and perfected their skills under the guidance of their fathers. Among them were Deanna Mantuana, the daughter of Giovanni Batista Mantuana, and Lavinia Fontana (1552–1614), the daughter of Prospero Fontana. Mantuana learned engraving by copying her father's drawings, then used her skills to promote the architectural career of her husband, Francesco da Volterra. In 1575 she was authorized by the pope to make and market prints. Fontana came the closest to achieving professional status equal to that of male artists. Despite pressure to limit herself to painting portraits, she painted biblical stories and mythological figures.

A third category of women artists belonged to the lesser nobility (lower rank of the aristocracy). Members of the nobility—men and women alike—were discouraged, and some

Sofonisba Anguissola was one of the few members of the Renaissance nobility to pursue a career as an artist. *Reproduced by permission of Hulton Archive.*

cases legally barred, from becoming artists because such a career was considered a form labor for the lower classes. A striking exception was Sofonisba Anguissola (c. 1535–1625). The eldest of six children, Anguissola studied painting with the Italian artists Bernardino Campi (1522–c. 1591) and Bernardino Gatti. Her father promoted her career, and in 1561 she became a lady-in-waiting (court attendant) to Queen Isabella I of Castile. In addition to producing portraits of the royal family and members of the court, she instructed the queen in the art of painting.

Women and science

During the Renaissance women participated in the background of the academic world of science. By the fourteenth century the university had become an important center for scientific learning, most notably the study of writings by the ancient Greek philosopher Aristotle (384– 322 B.C.) and the pursuit of learned medicine. Scholasticism (a scholarly movement devoted to combining ancient philosophy with Christian theology) had made Latin the language in which all discussions of knowledge took place (see "Scholasticism" in Chapter 1). Women were prevented from receiving formal education in Latin, so they were excluded from traditional intellectual pursuits. In addition, while there was no specific rule barring women from universities, the assumption was that the purpose of higher education was to prepare men for careers in the church or for professions such as law and medicine. The development of humanistic education outside of universities created opportunities for a few women to participate in conversations about knowledge. In northern Italy especially, learned fathers occasionally educated their daughters in Latin and Greek. Some women courtiers had access to a kind of learning equivalent to that of the university. They also enjoyed the company of physicians, philosophers, mathematicians, and engineers who increasingly came to the Renaissance courts in search of patronage for their projects.

Access to knowledge is not the same as full participation, however. While there were successful women writers and artists by the sixteenth century, it is difficult to identify any women who were known independently for their science. More typically, wives, sisters, and daughters of prominent natural scientists (astronomers, physicists, and chemists) participated fully in a scientific household. For example, the Danish nobleman and astronomer (scientist who studies planets, stars, and other heavenly bodies) Tycho Brahe (1546–1601) was assisted by his sister Sophie in observing the nova (new star) of 1572 (see "Astronomy" in Chapter 10). She also shared the secret of his elixir (medicinal remedy) to ward off the plague (an epidemic disease) and generally involved herself in scientific conversations at the Danish court. The Italian naturalist (biologist) Ulisse Aldrovandi (1522–1605) married his second wife, Francesca Fontana, for her learning as well as her dowry. She participated actively in the maintenance of his expanding natural history collection and in the preparation of his encyclopedia of nature. The English mathematician and magus (magician) John Dee (1527–1608) at times made his wife, Jane Fromond, the object of his experimental imagination, recording her menstrual cycle and reproductive activities. In all of these instances, women facilitated the work of men as part of their household responsibilities.

Midwives compete with physicians

Medicine was the one field in which Renaissance women enjoyed a greater degree of independence. Although women were not allowed to practice as physicians and surgeons, many communities relied on women healers for medicinal and herbal knowledge. In some instances, prominent practitioners (unlicensed physicians) such as the French midwife (one who assists in childbirth) Louise Bourgeois (1563–1636) circulated pamphlets about their treatment methods. They demonstrated that their experience rivaled academic knowledge of the human body.

Throughout the Renaissance many women became successful and sought-after midwives. Midwifery was more often practiced as a skill than as a trade or profession, but it was also a form of community service, particularly in more rural areas. The primary attendant at a birth might be an experienced and skilled midwife who had served an apprenticeship under a senior midwife. She could also be a friend, neighbor, or family member with some experience in these matters. Records indicate that on the European continent from the fourteenth century onward, midwives were employed by some municipalities to ensure care for their female residents. Midwives often testified as expert witnesses in matters of rape, abortion, infanticide (killing of infants), and illegitimacy, and verified the pregnancy claims of female prisoners standing trial.

Midwifery was first licensed and regulated in the towns of south-

Although not legally allowed to practice medicine, women like French midwife Louise Bourgeois demonstrated that their experience rivaled that of academic knowledge. *Reproduced by permission of The Granger Collection.*

ern Germany during the fifteenth century. Examinations were administered by a committee of physicians or women of high social standing as part of the licensing process. The growing web of regulations reflected a greater concern with the moral, rather than technical, qualifications of the midwife. These regulations often defined the midwife's place in the medical profession. For example, midwives were banned from prescribing drugs or performing surgery, and they were required to call for a learned physician in difficult cases. The movement to limit the activities of midwives came at approximately the same time that prosecutions for witchcraft (the use of magic to control evil forces) were occurring in Europe (see *"Malleus Maleficarum* triggers witch hunts" in Chapter 7). Some historians believe that midwives came under suspicion because they possessed what some considered to be dangerous knowledge associated with witches, specifically the use of herbal remedies that inhibited conception (becoming pregnant) and induced abortion (expelling a fetus from the womb). Nevertheless, examinations of trial records have shown that midwives appeared more often as expert witnesses than victims in witchcraft trials.

The practice of midwifery began to decline in the sixteenth century, primarily because male physicians were trying to establish medicine as a legitimate profession for themselves. They wrote numerous books in which they attacked midwives as being ignorant and making "popular errors"—that is, practicing outside the academic community. By the seventeenth century physicians were replacing midwives as experts in the delivery of babies.

Daily Life

14

How does one define daily life in any period of the past? Doing so involves looking at a wide variety of factors. How did people dress, and what did they eat? What did they do for fun? Did the rich and the poor do the same things? To understand daily life, we must look at these issues along with politics, warfare, art, economics, religion, and the effects of illness and disease on families and social groups. In this chapter we will look at the different areas of Renaissance Europe, examine the customs of various peoples during the early and late Renaissance, and examine the social and economic factors that affected people's everyday lives.

A diverse society

Renaissance Europe was not a single, unified society with the same traditions throughout the land. Each region had distinct languages, ethnic makeups, and geographic factors that shaped everyday life. Broadly, Mediterranean societies experienced hot, dry summers and cool, rainy winters, while the North experienced mild, temperate summers and long, cold winters. The Mediterranean region had arid (dry) or semiarid mountain ranges, while the North was characterized by broad expanses of fertile plains and forest. The Mediterranean Sea connected the South with more ancient cultures and peoples of northern Africa and Asia. Consequently, cities, long-distance shipping, and trade were features of life in the South much more so than in the North. The exceptions were the Hanseatic cities (cities belonging to a trade network called the Hanseatic League; see "Hanseatic League" box in Chapter 4) of northern Germany and the cosmopolitan industrial cities of the Low Countries (Belgium, the Netherlands, and Luxembourg).

Everywhere else, Europe's population was thinly spread throughout rural areas. In these regions peasants and nobles sometimes rubbed shoulders with sheepherders on the plains when the sheepherders brought their flocks down from the high pastures in the fall and looked for work in the winter. Europeans were often on the move, going to market, traveling to political centers to pay taxes, or embarking on religious pilgrimages. Southerners traveled from one port city to another on ships; they crossed over land by foot or uncomfortably on the back of a donkey. Northerners traveled by foot or, increasingly, by boat on canals and rivers. Hosting travelers were numerous inns, taverns, and religious establishments.

Gender and class also shaped daily life. Upper-class women were confined to the home or the court.

Someone accompanied them (or they went in groups) when they went to the market, church, or special civic or religious events. Middle-class and poor women spent much time working. Middle-class women were artisans or shopkeepers, and poor women worked in the fields if they were peasants or in households if they were servants. Women of the elite classes supervised a domestic staff and oversaw the education of their children. Noblemen spent their time at court, at war, or managing their country estates. In urban areas, especially in Italy, some men engaged in business activity. Political life was open to some, but opportunities for nobles to have a meaningful impact on politics declined as princes and kings gained more and more power. In smaller urban areas nobles of middle rank directed local politics under the authority of capitals of territorial states. Sometimes they ruled on their own if they had not yet been made part of the political structure of a regional state. Whatever the setting, political life was almost entirely the domain of upper-class men. Rural males participated in village affairs through parish or village councils, which were directed by priests or local lords.

Economy divides classes

In Renaissance Europe the economic cycle that lasted from 1450 until 1550 began and ended in crisis. In the earlier stages, around 1450, Europe was recovering from population losses and the consequent economic depression that followed the "Black

Death," a widespread disease epidemic (see "Black Death" section later in this chapter). As population levels began to recover, people became more prosperous, and workers' wages bought more and better food. From this time until 1550, the wages of an average worker were enough to provide good food and a warm, clean home for the family. Then prices began to rise rapidly, and by 1600 increases had reached 200 to 300 percent above what they had been fifty years earlier.

To some extent, this rise in prices, called inflation, was due to large amounts of gold coming in from European colonies in the Americas. The severity of inflation varied from region to region, as did the ability of workers to live on their wages. In rural areas the expansion of a money economy (an economy that runs on cash, not credit or goods) initially produced a problem for both lords and peasants: how to convert wealth in land and goods into increasingly necessary cash. The seignorial (lord) class solved this problem by forcing peasants to pay cash instead of working off their obligations (peasants were required to give lords a percentage of crops and other products). Peasants then had to find some means of getting cash to pay the lord. Some would find extra jobs and work for wages, while others would produce surplus goods (such as growing extra food or making pottery) that they could sell at the local market. Some were forced to become criminals and began smuggling goods to raise the extra money. In the meantime, the gap between rich and poor was widening. The upper and merchant classes took advantage of the money economy to establish thriving banks and businesses that formed the basis of modern capitalism (private or corporate ownership of goods).

Family and kinship

Kinship loomed large in the life of the Renaissance. It was referred to by a variety of terms, among them lineage, house, race, blood, and family.

Structures

Kinship was defined by the incest prohibitions (laws against having sexual relations with family members) of the Roman Catholic Church. Kinship comprised everyone with a common ancestry going back four generations (that is, extending out to third cousins). Also included were the spouses of these relatives and some connected by god parentage (a godparent is one who sponsors a child's baptism). Some secular (nonreligious) laws gave inheritance rights to descendants of even more remote common ancestors. In reality, however, kinship was seen more narrowly, being limited to individuals whose names were known and who saw one another from time to time. The idea of kinship also varied according to social position and wealth.

The standard way of reckoning descent was through fathers. Mothers were invisible in most genealogies (documents tracing generations of families). As a member of a family

Powerful Families

Kinship was different for the nobility than for the majority of people. Ordinary people did not have the resources to know as many different relatives, whereas the elite could claim knowledge of even remote ancestors. The largest, most extended families were those in the upper levels of society. The Renaissance was an era of dynasties (families who hold power for many generations)—not only royal dynasties, but noble, patrician (aristocratic), and mercantile (merchant) ones as well. Names of dynasties were as least as important as names of individuals. In fact, the chief political players were not individuals, but families. Among the most powerful families of Renaissance Europe were the Colonnas and Orsinis of Rome, Italy; the Medicis and Strozzis of Florence, Italy; the extended Contarini family of Venice, Italy; the Fuggers of Augsburg, Bavaria (in southern Germany); the House (family of rulers) of Habsburg in Austria and Spain; the House of Tudor in England; and the House of Valois of France.

First among the symbols of powerful families was the surname (last name or family name). The use of a surname was fairly new in the early fifteenth century. It was at first associated with important families, who took the names of important ancestors or the names of territories they controlled. More visible symbols were coats of arms (emblems with family symbols), which decorated houses, furniture, the clothing of servants, and a variety of other items. The public works of a pope (supreme head of the Roman Catholic Church) were even marked with the arms of his family. Houses were family symbols, too, and the size and appearance of a house proclaimed power and wealth. Inheritance was the key to family power in modest families and well-to-do families alike. Property was passed down through a succession of individuals who were expected to preserve and enhance what they received.

line, an individual belonged to a group of agnates, or people related by blood through male parents. However, maternal blood relatives were also important. Tracing ancestry through both parents was very much in practice at the time, in spite of the greater emphasis on paternal lines (family lines descending from the father). Relatives with no connection by blood could also be important. The church included both affinity (relationship by marriage) and consanguinity (of the same blood or origin) in its definition of kin, and advantageous in-law relationships were the prime objective of many marriages.

Ancestry is important

There was hardly any aspect of an individual's life that was not affected by kinship, especially for someone in an important family. Nobles and patricians were acutely aware of their ancestors. They constructed genealogies that were sometimes partly fictional, such as naming a hero from antiquity as the originator of the family line. Preserving the memory of ancestors became important to Christian families. Elaborate funeral ceremonies, monuments, and family chapels have preserved the names of some great families into the present day.

Every member of a great family shared in the family's reputation. However, it is difficult to know if the same was true of lower-class individuals. Great families overshadowed other ones, especially in matters of state, and sometimes seemed to be the only families in a particular region. The loss of family honor was a collective burden. An individual convicted of a serious crime not only shamed his kin but also might cause them to lose for generations the legal privileges they enjoyed as members of the nobility. Women had a special responsibility for maintaining the honor of their husbands' families by being above reproach sexually. That is, women were expected to be virgins (one who has not had sexual relations) upon marriage and to remain true to their husbands. All kinsmen got involved in rivalries with other families. Feuds and long-held grudges were a feature of Renaissance culture (see "Feuds and Outlaws" box in Chapter 11).

It was assumed that individual desires were never so important as the needs of the family. Marriage choices were based on what was good for the family, as were career choices. Family members in positions of power had an obligation to help their kin. Wealthier kinsmen were expected to come to the rescue of family members. Even in the lowest classes the first source of help for paupers (poor people) was kin. While the laws in England obligated only fairly close relatives—like grandparents and aunts or uncles—to support kin, members of great families assumed they had a right to approach distant relatives for help.

The system of family obligations and family power can be summed up in the word "nepotism," the practice of favoring one's family members over others. Far from being thought of as corrupt, favor of one's family was admired. The most famous examples are found in the Renaissance papacy, the office of the pope. In the course of what was usually a short reign, a pope would act quickly to advance the careers and status of his relatives, most often in the immediate family of a sister. The pope would award honorary titles, give away property, arrange powerful marriages, and name nephews as cardinals (church officials ranking directly below the pope). Popes did on a grand scale what other members of the nobility did if they had the opportunity. Royal ladies-in-waiting (court attendants to queens), for example, took care of husbands, brothers, and children. Whenever possible, the goal was to put a relative in a position where the family would benefit from future favors and, most notably, acquire some-

Private Life

An important development during the Renaissance was the concept of private life. This notion involved a general change in mental outlook that came from the humanists' emphasis on individualism. During the Middle Ages the public and private spheres were intertwined. The needs of the individual were never so important as the needs for the community or group. The situation changed in the fifteenth century (and much earlier in Italy) with the development of commerce, cities, and wealth. Some people then had the means and the desire to distinguish themselves from others. In addition, monarchs and princes who busied themselves by accumulating wealth and political power created a state in which individuals defined themselves by what they owned. Changes in religious life also affected society, and individuals began to look inward and focus on communion with God. Also important were the changes in the role of the family. From as early as the seventeenth century in some regions, the home became a place where one could hide from the gossip and judgment of the public.

thing valuable that could be passed on to future generations.

Households

During the Renaissance, the word most often used to refer to a household was "family." Although

"family" also had other meanings, it was primarily a synonym for household.

Types of households

By far the most common household structure was, as it is today, the nuclear-family or conjugal household, based on one married couple and their children. Another common type, found among peasants using a system of inheritance in which property passed to a single heir, has been termed the "stem-family" household. The heir to family property remained in the household with the parents after he or she married, forming a second family that might produce a third household generation. Less common was a structure referred to nowadays as the "extended-family" household, but more accurately termed the "joint-family" household. It was based on a married couple and their sons, all of whom remained in the household after they married, along with their children.

The conjugal household was generally the smallest in size. Joint-family households sometimes were quite large. For example, a family in early fifteenth-century Tuscany included forty-seven members, all related by blood or marriage. This was unusual, however. The chief determination of family size was wealth. There was a differences between the majority of less-privileged households, whatever their structure, and the households of the economically and socially privileged. Most households averaged five or six members. Some had one or two members, but households of moderate means might reach nine or ten. Elite households were large even if they were conjugal in structure, because parents and children were not the only inhabitants. Renaissance households almost always included people who had no kinship ties with each other, usually categorized as servants. A peasant household might at most have two or three servants, but the household of a lord might have forty or more. Elite households expanded in the fifteenth and sixteenth centuries and slowly shrank after that, though still remaining huge in comparison to most.

Some members of households were hard to categorize, even for contemporaries. Orphans who lived with aunts and uncles were sometimes considered servants. Elderly relatives might be in a similar position. Stepmothers, half siblings, and children born out of wedlock further complicated household structure, as did lodgers (people who paid a fee to live in another family's house), who were neither servants nor kin.

Household activities

Households were centers of production, and most were engaged in agricultural activities—at all social levels. Noble households were organized for the use of land, usually managed by the lords' officers, who were servants of relatively high status. Peasants called sharecroppers produced for both the lord and themselves, selling excess goods at the local market when they could. Whether tenants, share-croppers, or direct owners, peasants used the labor of their whole household—their children, servants if they had any, and wives. Great households were also the centers of political power, from the households of kings and princes down to the households of lords of small manors. Various levels of justice were administered by household officers of manorial and territorial lords, including church lords like abbots. The main political function of lesser households was that they constituted units that were ruled. Heads of households were taxed rather than individuals.

The consumption of goods was different from today. Consumption in poorer households could hardly be separated from production, since the production was meant to sustain a livelihood. By contrast, consumption in great households was plentiful. The very size of houses was a way of indicating wealth. Exterior appearance was meant to convey power and importance. Interior decoration was meant to impress, often with reminders of an owner's distinguished ancestry. Large numbers of servants also proclaimed an owner's status. All this was usually displayed when households would receive guests, a frequent occurrence in most wealthy homes.

Sharp contrasts in housing

The quality of housing, both urban and rural, followed a slow but steady course of improvement during the Renaissance. Europeans were the best housed and fed among civiliza-

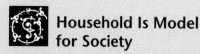

Household Is Model for Society

Most Renaissance writings on household management endorsed a power structure in which the master, or household head, was the supreme authority whom all other members were expected to obey. Very large households were supposed to be organized into various levels of authority. Notions about the household affected the way many other institutions were run. A monarchy was supposed to be little different from a well-run household. A major complaint against King Richard II of England (1367–1400; ruled 1377–99) was that he did not manage finances like a good housekeeper. Monastic institutions were organized like households, as were schools and colleges, partly because some of them were schoolmasters' homes and partly because the model seems to have been inescapable.

tions and cultures on the major continents. Those of the seignorial class who had not fallen on hard times lived relatively comfortably in wooden or stone castles or manor houses. The movement toward building with stone increased from 1400 on, with an emphasis, especially in France, on remodeling medieval (a term for the Middle Ages) structures in stone according to architectural standards established in Renaissance Italy (see "Architecture" in Chapter 8). The peasantry lived in houses made of wood or earth, with thatched roofs and

earthen floors. The major improvements in these dwellings came with the practice of installing tile flooring, which was plentiful and inexpensive. There was little besides a screen to divide one room from another and separate the human occupants from their farm animals. Fleas and other insects were probably a constant problem, especially in the summer. Bathrooms and chimneys were unknown until the seventeenth century.

Furnishings differed according to status. In the homes of lords, beds, tables, and chairs were comfortable and elaborate. Metal plates were fashionable in Italy during the fifteenth century, and ceramic (pottery baked at a high temperature in a kiln) dinnerware was a specialty of the Romagna region. Among the poor, straw mattresses, chairs or a table fashioned from barrel halves were common. Cooking and eating might have centered on a metal stove, with a cooking pot and a copper drinking cup.

Only the elite classes in cities enjoyed style, comfort, and beauty in housing, furnishings, and food. Italy was in the forefront of quality of life among the well-to-do. For example, towns in northern Europe did not change their building materials from wood to stone until the sixteenth century. The Italians began building with stone in the Middle Ages, however, and brought the process to a high standard with the construction of Renaissance palaces in the fifteenth century. Around that time elaborate and beautiful ceramic dinnerware, which was less expensive and improved the taste of food, replaced metal plates of the earlier period. Table manners first emerged among the Italians, along with relatively refined cookery, which then made its way to France from about 1550 onward. The urban poor lived less well, showing evidence of the growing gap between the rich and the poor in cities.

The urban poor lived in terrible conditions, as can be seen in inventory records made of their possessions after death. A typical poor person had a few low-quality eating utensils, a blackened metal cooking pot, frying pans, dripping pans, and a board for kneading bread. Other personal belongings included a few old clothes, a stool, a table, and a bench that also doubled as a bed, perhaps with a few sacks of straw serving for a mattress. Items such as these furnished life in crowded rented rooms, which were generally dark and dirty and located on the upper floors of buildings—floors reserved for the poor. The homeless poor lived in shantytowns (assemblies of small, temporary homes)—in 1560 in Pescara, Italy, for example, four hundred people out of a population of two thousand lived in such conditions. In Genoa, Italy, the poor sold themselves as galley slaves (people who manned oars on large ships called galleys) every winter. In Venice, destitute people lived in small boats near quays (platforms along banks) or under bridges of canals. In each city the poor lived with fleas, lice, and other pests. Poverty and destitution were visible everywhere.

Marriage

In Renaissance society, marriage was the foundation of the household and kinship, which in turn were the foundations of society and the state. In most parts of Europe, starting a household and beginning married life were essentially the same thing. Kin were very aware of their connections by blood and by marriage, which was an instrument for extending and strengthening kinship. Marriage alliances between ruling families sealed peace treaties and sometimes created empires.

All religions agreed on the value of marriage to prevent sinful sexual behavior. Marriage was a spiritual and respected institution. In 1439 it was officially declared a sacrament, or religious obligation, of the Roman Catholic Church. Protestants believed marriage to be a relationship singularly blessed by God. Unlike Catholic priests, who could not marry and took vows of chastity, Protestant ministers were encouraged to get married. Until the Reformation, the church, not the state, legally defined and oversaw marriage.

Finding a partner

Although a fairly large number of people remained single, marriage was considered the normal lot of ordinary people. In addition to religious celibates (those who choose not to have sexual relations in order to please God), the unmarried included those who could not afford marriage and those who were social outcasts (perhaps due to a physical or mental handicap or deformity). Marriages tended to be among people of similar social and financial backgrounds, and were usually limited to the local area. In rural villages and urban neighborhoods courtships developed from the contacts of daily life. Marriage was different for the very wealthy. Young people of higher status were more closely supervised, and the marriage pool for them had to be wider if they were to be wisely matched. Members of the highest nobility married people from other regions or even other countries. For them courtship took place only after a mate had already been selected by parents or other kin. Such arrangements could be protested and called off, but this rarely happened. In lower classes the choice of a mate was sometimes made by young people, but the selection was subject to parental approval. These selections were rarely rejected by the parents, but the church often had a say in the approval of a prospective marriage. For those in the nobility, political alliance through marriage was important, and there was often the danger of marrying someone close in the bloodline. The Protestant church reduced the number of forbidden marriages (by both blood relation and marriage ties), while the Catholic Church kept all of its limitations but often gave permission to couples who were distantly related.

Although sexual intimacy before marriage was not condoned, a number of lower-class women were pregnant at the time of their weddings. Village youth groups, which had some control over marriage choices, discouraged what they considered to be inappropriate matches. Marriages that might be objected to were those in which there was a wide age difference or in which one of the parties was an outsider. Typically, even these marriages would be agreed upon if both parties were serious about marrying. In upper classes the bride was rarely pregnant at the time of marriage, and the rituals of courtship were highly formal. Traditional gifts were exchanged and the man was expected to assume the role of "servant" to the woman, who was his "mistress." These terms were simply part of the formality of courtship and the wedding itself, however; after marriage, the man became the master of the household and the woman generally possessed very little power.

Betrothal is binding

Courtship led to betrothal, an important stage in the process of getting married that began to lose its central place only toward the end of the seventeenth century. It was often a formal ceremony that might be performed in front of a priest at the church door. Betrothal bound the couple in a relationship that could be broken only by mutual consent, which was supposed to be as public as the betrothal itself. The legal difference between a betrothal and a wedding was not easy to understand, and church lawyers wrestled with it for a long time.

In most cases, betrothal led directly to marriage after an interval of a

Marriage: A Business Agreement

The idea of marrying for love is relatively new, and rarely was it the reason for marriage during the Renaissance. While there were probably romantic couples like Romeo and Juliet, the young lovers in Shakespeare's play, marriage was first and foremost a business arrangement. For centuries, throughout world cultures, marriage was the decision of the family (usually the father, although the mother would typically have some say) and not of the individuals getting married. Marriage negotiations between families might extend over weeks or months and were more complicated among the higher social classes. The most common concerns discussed during these negotiations were the dowry contributed on the bride's side and how the possessions of the couple would be distributed after death. The dowry was a financial offering made by the parents of either the bride or the groom, a tradition that is almost as old as history itself. The family of the bride would be particularly concerned about her financial support in the event of the husband's death. Most widows (women whose husbands have died) would receive a contribution (known as a dower in England) from the husband's side of the family. The details were spelled out in a contract. If the bride and her family did not make specific agreements about such issues, the bride could possibly have to return home and be supported by her birth family. For her parents this could be an undesirable and economically difficult situation.

month or two. There were some exceptions. For instance, betrothals sometimes lasted for years, or one of the parties in an informal betrothal might go back on his or her word. One party in a formal betrothal could refuse to break it at the request of the other. A pregnant woman might insist that she was actually married since she was betrothed to the man with whom she had conceived her unborn child. Perhaps the hardest case was one in which a woman sued a man who, she claimed, promised to marry her. The courts had to decide if a betrothal had occurred. Such cases were known as "clandestine marriages" and took up much of the time in church courts. In the sixteenth century, after the split between the Catholic and Protestant churches, both churches focused more on the vows exchanged during marriage, but betrothal remained important.

Church wedding required

Wedding ceremonies varied widely. Some took place in church or, more often, at the church door. Some were held in private homes. In much of Italy, the "wedding" consisted of so many steps that it is hard to know which one actually resulted in a legal marriage. It may have been the appearance before a notary (a public officer who certifies legal documents), who recorded what he witnessed. Each region had its own version of the words that were traditionally spoken. In general, the couple agreed to be husband and wife and, in many versions, the bride's father gave his daughter into the keeping of the bridegroom. There were symbols like the ring and gestures like the kiss. One common gesture was the clasping of hands, which was a synonym for a wedding (or a betrothal) in many places.

Until the middle and late sixteenth century, the legal requirements for marriage were a confusing combination of canon (church) law, decrees from the church, and local civil laws. Then the church became a legal part of the marriage ceremony. Most Protestant towns and governments adopted ordinances requiring a wedding to take place in a recognized church in the presence of a minister. Similarly, the Catholic Church defined a valid marriage as one in which consent was exchanged in front of a priest and other witnesses. It may be that of all the religious changes of the Reformation period, those that most affected ordinary people were in marriage practices.

Many wedding customs and celebrations remained unchanged. The signing of the marriage contract, when there was one, preceded or closely followed the exchange of vows. There were processions to or from the church, there were communal meals with traditional foods, and there were dances, music, and songs.

All of these activities often took place out of doors with many participants. On higher social levels there was a trend toward more private and more restrained weddings. Church authorities were generally in favor of eliminating all elements of paganism (religions native to areas before the spread of Christianity) and superstition in wedding celebrations. Protestant authorities in particular attempted to ban noise, music, and dancing. Yet the Roman Catholic Church had long disapproved of weddings that were too private, and discouraged such aristocratic practices as midnight ceremonies in private chapels. Class differences continued, but the popular practices that were most offensive to church officials gradually disappeared.

A small number of couples eloped (married without their parents' knowledge), usually because of parental disapproval. Since the Roman Catholic Church never required parental consent, an elopement was acceptable in the religious and legal sense. Nevertheless, it was often looked down upon in society. Many Protestant ordinances required parental consent, especially for people under a certain age. No matter how strict regulations became, however, there were always couples who managed to avoid them.

Married life

According to the common view of married life, the husband was superior to the wife. After the period of courtship, in which the male suitor was a servant to the female, the man became the master of the household. Women had few legal rights. Scholars generally agree, however, that women were usually treated well and enjoyed a degree of equality with their husbands. A man may have had authority over his wife, but he was expected to provide for her, protect her, treat her kindly, and make sure she was taken care of in the event of his death. In addition, individual relationships created different types of marriages. If a man was much older than his wife, there tended to be more inequality, as was the case in many upper-class marriages. In the lower classes there was likely to be less of an age gap, and the husband and wife had usually both worked as servants before they married. Therefore they had a basis for a relationship. In practice, many marriages were economic partnerships. Rural wives in particular did work in the household and on the land that complemented the work of their husbands. Men frequently depended on their wives' judgment and ability more than they might admit. Some literate upper-class men expressed admiration for their wives and confessed to being at a loss in household affairs after their wives' deaths. Husbands' wills sometimes gave considerable power to their widows.

Infidelity: a double standard While love was not commonly considered a proper basis for marriage, the feelings that developed between a woman and a man once they were married—as they lived together and shared responsibilities—often came to include love and af-

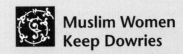

Muslim Women Keep Dowries

During the Renaissance and Reformation period, the man was considered the master of the household. A wife was therefore subservient to her husband, and laws and religious customs supported this inequality. No matter how large a dowry a wife had brought into a marriage, the husband assumed control of it. Generally speaking, wives could not act for themselves either in law or in commerce. It is important to note, however, that this was true of Christian marriages but not of Muslim marriages. In Islamic law, found in the Koran (the holy book for Muslims, followers of Islam), women kept their dowries and had a greater level of economic control than their Christian sisters. Islam was not tolerated in most of Europe, especially after the Crusades (Christian religious wars against Muslims) of the Middle Ages and the expulsions of Muslims and Jews from Spain in 1492.

fection. Many couples worked together, were active parents, and were also bedfellows. Sexual pleasure was an important aspect of marriage, but it had to be kept within bounds. Husbands and wives were expected to satisfy one another sexually, something called the "conjugal debt." Sometimes cases were brought to ecclesiastical (church) courts by spouses who complained that the debt was not being paid.

Religious writers warned that too much sex in a marriage was just as dangerous as adultery. Adultery is defined as a married person having a sexual relationship with a person other than his or her spouse, and it was considered a serious sin. Both husbands and wives were capable of cheating on their spouses, but the infidelity of a woman was considered the greater of the two evils. Secular and civil laws alike reflected this attitude. The double standard became a strong part of Christian culture at this time. Wives of husbands who cheated were expected to endure the infidelity as long as it was conducted in private. Husbands who allowed themselves to be betrayed by their wives, however, were publicly mocked and scorned. One of the worst social insults was to be called a "cuckold" (a man whose wife is unfaithful). From every indication, wives were rarely unfaithful, and the few who were found guilty were severely punished. The unlikelihood of a woman committing adultery did not prevent male jealousy from being one of the most common themes in Renaissance literature.

Divorce not condoned Most marriages did not end until one of the partners died. Yet marriages rarely lasted long because the death rate was so high. It was not uncommon for men who married in their late twenties to die in their forties. Furthermore, many women died in childbirth after only a few years of marriage. Some couples separated before death. Divorce was not available as a real option, though some Protestant jurisdictions allowed it. The Catholic Church allowed legal separation ("divortium"), and most Protestant authorities preferred separation to outright divorce, in which remarriage was permitted. The usual ground for separation was adultery, and few believed that a person who had committed adultery should remarry. Other grounds included abuse, but it was not easy for ordinary people to be granted permanent separations.

People in power had more options. Especially when policy seemed to require a new marriage alliance, a ruler might ask for an annulment, which stated that a legal marriage never existed. An annulment was often granted on a variety of grounds. Among them were lack of consent on the part of one party or another, and the lack of freedom to marry in the first place because of blood relations between the parties. But an annulment for a marriage that had existed for several years and produced children was always a problem. The most famous annulment of this period was the "divorce" of Henry VIII and Catherine of Aragon, the king and queen of England (see "England" in Chapter 3). When the pope would not grant Henry's request for an annulment, Henry broke away from the Catholic Church and founded the Church of England. Some marriages of lesser folk were annulled fairly easily, usually because they had never been consummated (the couple had not had sexual relations).

People tended to stay in unhappy marriages, but some took the most direct route to divorce: desertion. It was usually men who deserted. A wife was left in the position of being one who had lost a husband but was still married and unable to remarry. The lack of communication among different regions made it possible for the husband to go elsewhere and remarry without his wife ever finding out. If it was discovered that one of the parties was married to two people, the later marriage was annulled and the offending party was severely punished.

Remarriage is frequent The normal way of looking at marriage was that it was a union of young people who had never been married before. Yet many people, perhaps 20 percent of the population, were married for the second or third time because of death in previous marriages. A widower (a man whose wife has died) was likely to marry again after a fairly short interval. A widow (a woman whose husband has died) was somewhat less likely to remarry, but much depended on age and circumstances. Families were often eager to use young widows to form desirable new alliances, but some more mature widows clung to autonomy they had never enjoyed before in their lives. Second marriages generally had much less festivity surrounding them, and the ceremonies even eliminated certain solemn sayings. Second marriages were often the source of social mocking as well, especially in France.

Childbirth and infancy

Even though birth and infancy were common to all in the Renais-sance, very little firsthand information is available because women did not write about the subject and men were seldom witnesses. Previously untapped sources, like church records and burials, have recently given some valuable information about the experiences of ordinary people. What is clear is that birth and infancy were filled with danger, especially for the child.

Midwives assist childbirth

The most important attendant at a birth was the midwife (one who assists in the delivery of a baby). She was typically of a social rank not far removed from that of the mother and was generally an older woman who had already given birth to several children of her own. Her skills were greatly respected, even by physicians. She was trained by a practicing midwife, who passed along her knowledge much as masters trained apprentices (young men who learned a trade from a craftsman). Midwives were often the target of men's suspicions about secret activities involving women. They were sometimes feared as witches who might give the soul of the child to the devil before the child could be baptized (initiated into the Christian religion by being anointed with water by a priest).

The basic techniques of midwives seem to have worked well in most births. The woman in labor was encouraged to sit up and bear down to ease the passage of the baby through the birth canal, often using a birthing chair. Some problem births were handled effectively. Midwives knew how

Men, Childbirth, and Medical Knowledge

Women gave birth in the company of many women. It was an occasion for the gathering of relatives and neighbors, not only to give help and comfort but also to make social contact. This custom went across geography and class. Even medical men were completely excluded, and thus their knowledge of childbirth was mainly drawn from books rather than observation. While men were generally forbidden from taking part in birthing, male painters frequently depicted birth scenes, usually as part of cycles on the lives of saints. (A cycle, or series, of paintings would cover the birth, life, miracles, and death of a holy figure.) These paintings cannot be considered accurate but do show the presence of many women. While men did not attend the actual birthing, many physicians attempted to improve the safety of the process. The first medical work on childbirth written since antiquity was a manual for pregnant women and midwives by the German physician Eucharius Rosslin. First published in 1513, it was printed in England three decades later as *The Burth of Mankynde.* The work was translated into other languages and republished many times until the end of the seventeenth century. Rosslin's aim was to combine medical knowledge taken from classical antiquity with what he could find out about midwives' methods. His goal was to improve the childbirth process, not replace midwives. The emergence of male midwives, or obstetricians, came much later.

to turn infants who were incorrectly positioned. Complications that could be dealt with only by using instruments required the intervention of a surgeon—however, this usually meant the child would not survive. If the birth canal was blocked, a surgeon used hooks and knives to remove the infant in pieces. Cesarean sections (the removal of a child from the womb by making an incision in the mother's abdomen) were performed only if the mother died and there was a chance of saving the infant.

Although the danger of death in childbirth was great, most women survived and gave birth many times. Nevertheless, many writers, mostly male, expressed a fear of childbirth. They spoke of illness, pangs, torment, even "pains of hell" and "snares of Death." The main cause of childbed death was probably infection, usually a consequence of a hand or an instrument being inserted into the birth canal. For example, a midwife might attempt to remove a placenta (organ that connects the fetus to the mother's uterus) that had not been expelled. This kind of contact probably caused most cases of postpartum (after birth) illness and death. In such cases a woman who had a seemingly normal delivery could develop a prolonged fever, and death would come within a month.

Feeding infants

The normal food for newborns was human milk. Most mothers breast-fed their babies, particularly in the lower classes. A few lower-class babies could not be nursed by their mothers, who had either died or were ill. Some infants were fed animals' milk or wheat gruel (a liquid substance made of wheat grain and water or milk). Breast-feeding by the mother had the enthusiastic approval of respected authorities. The medical profession recommended it, and the clergy was strongly in favor of it. The Italian theologian Saint Bernadino of Siena (1380–1444), among others, preached against women who neglected their breast-feeding duty in order to indulge in sinful behavior, such as vanity and sensuality. These were common themes in many sermons of the time. The image of the nursing Madonna (the Virgin Mary; mother of Jesus of Nazareth) became a central theme of Renaissance art.

Wet-nursing a thriving business In spite of the overwhelming approval of maternal nursing, many mothers of the upper classes hired wet nurses to breast-feed their babies. A thriving business, wet-nursing may be the best-documented part of infancy in the Renaissance. The typical wet nurse was a married peasant woman whose own infant had died. If her child was not

dead she might decide to suckle it along with an additional infant, but that was a highly unlikely and undesirable situation. Wet nurses usually stayed in their own homes, so situations frequently arose where an infant was sent to live in a strange house more modest than that of his or her parents. A few exceptionally wealthy families kept at least some of their infants, most often their sons, at home, with a wet nurse living with the family. This assured that the infant would get the nurse's undivided attention and would be well rested and well nourished.

Renaissance society expressed mixed feelings toward wet-nursing. Writers who recommended that mothers nurse their own babies also offered advice on how to select wet nurses. The reasons for using wet nurses were fairly complex. Christian moralists thought wet nurses could prevent marital infidelity (having sexual relations with a person who is not one's spouse) on the part of the husband, which was a risk because nursing mothers were not supposed to be sexually active. The prospect of uninterrupted sexual relations was appealing to couples, but this meant that wives would become pregnant more often. There seems to have been a feeling, rarely expressed directly, that a nursing woman was reduced to subhuman status. While breast-feeding may have been acceptable for common women (who could not afford wet nurses anyway), it was not appropriate for women of higher status. Whether these ideas were consciously held by all people in the privileged classes is not known, but it is clear that they routinely avoided having to deal with such issues.

Many upper-class women had mixed feelings about hiring a wet nurse. The practice of avoiding nursing stood in stark contrast to the artistic images showing the Virgin Mary breast-feeding the baby Jesus. There were other sources of ambivalence as well. Milk was thought to carry with it character and personality traits, so that a baby was formed as much by breast milk as by the environment of the womb. The Italian artist Michelangelo (1475–1564) joked that he became a sculptor because his nurse was a stonecutter's wife. It was assumed by some that a baby could take on the undesirable peasant characteristics from its nurse.

The business of wet-nursing operated in much the same way throughout western Europe. The father chose the nurse and made a contract with her husband, who received regular payments. Some cities had nurses' registries (places where nurses would register their services), which were privately run or under government control. The best-known registry was founded in Paris before 1350. Like a careful father, a registry was supposed to check that nurses were of good moral character and had pleasant dispositions. Their milk was tested and judged as to thickness, color, and taste. One function of registries was to provide nurses for foundlings (abandoned babies) and orphans in the care of religious institutions or municipalities.

Mortality rate is high

Life was precarious for newborns. The infant death rate remained more or less constant throughout the Renaissance. Between 20 and 40 percent of all babies died before their first birthday. At that age they still had only a 50 percent chance of surviving past the age of ten. These figures applied to all classes. The main reason for this widespread phenomenon was that infants had difficulty fighting off illness. In addition, infants' digestive and respiratory systems are less able to withstand environmental hazards like extremes of weather and impure water. Poverty added more dangers, such as malnourished nursing mothers. Poor orphans were exposed to the worst hazards in the crowded houses of overworked, inattentive wet nurses. Even the better conditions of the rich could not prevent the overwhelming dangers of infant diseases.

How infants were treated is difficult to determine. Some experts believe that the high mortality rate was due to parents investing little or no emotion into their children. Others claim that it is difficult to know how specific parents felt as the historical record gives little indication of the personal feelings of grieving parents. Many children were certainly showered with love and attention, and the parents were overcome with grief in the event of death. What is left out of history is how the mother felt, because first-hand accounts of women's lives are lacking. People seem to have accepted to a large degree the inevitability of frequent death. Some families even reused the name of a dead infant for another child. The tenderness shown in artists' images of the infant Jesus could have reflected an attitude toward babies in general. There was much concern that a baby be baptized as soon as possible to avoid the risk of its soul remaining in limbo (place where the unbaptized remain after death) for eternity should it die prematurely.

Care of infants

Soon after birth a baby was wrapped in swaddling clothes, an intricate arrangement of cloth that kept the arms and legs straight and the body warm and easy to handle. For most children the clothes were changed from time to time, but there was frequent changing of clothes for babies under the care of live-in nurses in well-to-do homes. Breast-feeding lasted at least a year, sometimes more than two years. The preferred food for weaning, before the child switched to a regular adult diet, was a mixture of fine white wheat and water, which the child was fed with a spoon.

Supervision of infants was not so concentrated as it is today. Most children lived in small houses and were placed in cradles by the fire until they reached an age where they could get around by themselves. The mother, a servant, or an older child would keep an eye on the baby while going about other tasks. Swaddled infants were often victims of fatal accidents. They were burned after being placed too near unwatched fires or smothered when sleeping in large beds with

adults. Poor people often slept in the same bed with their infants out of convenience and warmth, and "overlaying" (that is, people turning over onto babies) was often listed as a cause of infant death. In larger houses there were usually servants to mind the children. No historical records suggest that the home, rich or poor, was child-centered. Wealthier children were better fed and safer, but they were no more visible, since they spent most of their time in the world of women that men had little to do with. Once out of swaddling clothes, babies were not encouraged to crawl freely or walk without walkers or leading strings (similar to leashes). Poorer children were probably subject to less control. Untended children who could walk might knock over (and be burned by) scalding liquids, fall into ditches, or be attacked by animals. The lives of Renaissance children, mainly boys, did not enter into historical record until they were older, which makes it nearly impossible to know much about the earliest stages of life.

Childhood

Children were important primarily because there were so many of them. During the Renaissance more than half the population was under twenty-five, an age distribution not unlike many of the developing countries in the twentieth and twenty-first centuries. They were also the instrument of one of the fundamental organizing principles of Renaissance society: inheritance. Young people were often treated in contradictory ways. They were expected to be obedient and respectful, yet once they had survived infancy, the difficulty of taming their rebelliousness and transforming them into moral beings proved a constant challenge.

Meaning of childhood

Childhood was commonly thought to begin at age seven and end at fourteen. Children under seven, the stage known as "infancy," belonged to the world of women. After seven, children were regarded as capable of being instructed. In some places the laws considered children under fourteen to be capable of committing adult crimes. Confirmation (conferring the gift of the Holy Spirit) and first communion (service in which bread and wine are symbolic of the body and blood of Christ) took place between the ages of seven and fourteen. Many children started to work before the age of fourteen. Some boys were legally declared "emancipated" (released from parental control) as young as nine, and some were required to bear arms in times of war at an even younger age.

Historians have disagreed about the experience of childhood in this period. At the time it was thought that children had to be tightly controlled to prevent them from acting on their impulses. Moralists claimed that great effort was needed to tame children's wildness, which resulted from original sin (the human condition of being sinful at birth). Dealing with children was assumed to be a bat-

tle of wills, in which the only good outcome was their surrendering to authority. Children also needed protection against the forces of evil. The devil's work (evil) was closely associated with sexuality. Some scholars note that children were not protected from exposure to coarse and blasphemous language, or to gambling and excessive drinking. Such behavior was impossible to avoid in ordinary village and town life and in the confines of most houses. In spite of this environment, sexual activity outside of marriage was considered the most sinful behavior. Apart from the household, most institutions intended for children were segregated by gender.

Upbringing depends on class

While many variations existed depending on the social class of a child's family, play was a part of childhood at all social levels. The few toys that have survived look much like the balls, sticks, hoops, dolls, and marbles of later times. There were occasional references in writing to games, and it is unlikely that children played by themselves. Children of the poor who lived in very small houses probably did most of their playing out of doors. Some experts have claimed that children were raised in households where they received little love and attention, yet many writers in the Renaissance period frequently told parents to stop spoiling their children. It was thought that children needed to be raised in a disciplined and controlled manner. While it was commonly believed that the lower classes were most likely to

Children's Games by Pieter Bruegel the Elder. This painting depicts the typical games that Renaissance children played. ©*Francis G. Mayer/Corbis. Reproduced by permission of the Corbis Corporation.*

spoil children with love and attention, Thomas More (c. 1478–1535), the prominent English humanist, was one example of a cultured person admitting to loving his children dearly.

Many children were motherless, fatherless, or completely orphaned. Relatives took orphans into their homes, sometimes in spite of not wanting to do so. It remains uncertain whether life for orphans was more difficult than life for other children. The most deprived children were those who were abandoned and left to be raised in foundling homes like the Os-

pedale delgi Innocenti (Hospital of the Holy Innocents) in Florence. Some of these homes were run by religious orders, while others were under the control of local government.

Training and education Serious training started around the age of seven and usually took place within a household. Peasant children of both sexes started helping around the house even before they were seven. One form of early work was looking after younger children. In wealthy households children were likely to pass from wet nurs-

Religion and Childhood

Children started learning about religion at a very early age, often from women. The heads of larger households led regular morning and evening prayers. In wealthy households a chaplain led prayers. The pressure to make religion a part of the household routine became even greater after the Reformation. Many believed that stories from the Bible should replace the traditional fairy tales and stories that were usually told to children. Humanist advisers of women held that the reading of stories distracted from religion and morality. After the Reformation, disapproval of stories based on superstition intensified under both Catholics and Protestants, but their criticism did little to change tradition. Parents would remember how the stories had moved or even frightened them as children and would pass them along to their own children.

es into the hands of governesses (women hired to care for children) and tutors (male teachers). As in peasant households, training was determined by gender differences. Girls learned needlework and basic household management skills, while boys were taught horsemanship and hunting. At the age of five, six, or seven, some boys and girls began formal schooling, whether inside or outside the home. The form (whether in Latin or a native language) and extent of education depended on the economic and social status of the family, the sex of the pupil, the expectations of parents, and the availability of schooling.

In northwestern Europe both urban and rural children commonly left home. Peasant children of both sexes often went to live in other peasant households and sometimes to great country houses or to better-off urban ones. Some children became apprentices with craftsmen or, if they were of the appropriate social rank, with merchants of professionals like physicians and lawyers. At the highest social levels children entered the houses of great nobles or princes. There was no set age at which children left home, and the length of time spent away from home depended on various factors. Peasant children might return after a year or two, spend some time working at home, and then leave again. Apprenticeships usually lasted for several years and generally meant a permanent separation from home. People who took in children also took on the educational and disciplinary roles of the children's parents. Arrangements with craft masters were usually made by the children's parents. In one form or another, this experience was common up and down the social scale. In Italy, upper-class families were less likely to send their children away from home. Even craft apprentices in Italy tended to work with their own fathers or with masters in the same town and continued to live at home.

Books on courtesy and etiquette (proper manners) give an idea of the elaborate code of behavior expected of nobles who frequented the courts of the powerful people. These books were directed at young boys and stressed the importance of good manners and the skills of serving a noble lord at the table. The sons and daughters of gentlemen learned a great deal at court. They also formed links between their families and the families they served and made valuable contacts for their own later careers. Fathers who chose not to give their sons this experience were thought to have done them a great disservice.

Youth

The transition from childhood to youth during the Renaissance is difficult to define. Almost everything that has been said about childhood also relates to youth. Youths were still expected to be respectful to elders and obedient to authority. In spite of this, the signs of physical maturity made a difference. These signs seem to have appeared fairly late, past the conventional age marker of fourteen. Research suggests that this was true not only of menstruation in girls but also of the development of voice change and facial hair in boys.

Strength, health, and beauty were youthful characteristics that were praised and envied. Adults tended to be nostalgic about their own youth. Many remembered it as a carefree time rather than one of obedience and hard work. In reality, most master craftsmen made their apprentices do full-scale, difficult projects without paying them. Another characteristic of youth was irresponsibility. Sports and games became more rambunctious, especially when combined with drinking and gambling, activities specifically forbidden in apprenticeship contracts. Youth groups organized seasonal celebrations, often following tradition, and supervised courtship behavior. Courtship was similar to modern-day dating, but with more elaborate rules and customs. Membership in such groups was generally limited to unmarried males, which was the definition of "youth."

For most people of both sexes, being a servant was equated with youth. The conventional view was that servants were both young and single. If they had not left home before the age of fourteen, they were likely to do so shortly afterward. Especially in the countryside the period of service could go on for many years and usually consisted of a series of relatively short stays with different masters. Servants were able to move freely from village to village, town to town, and, for females especially, from rural areas to urban ones. These servants were not independent but were always forced to rely on their employers. Young people's apprenticeships sometimes continued well into their twenties and was the form of service with the most well-defined rules. Stereotypes of apprentices—that they were abused by masters or that they were difficult to control—repeated the stereotypes of youth in general. For some young people the stereotypes were true, but for most they were not.

The end of youth came only with a change in legal status. Not surprisingly, youth was the time for courtship. The primary entry into adulthood was marriage, which brought with it a certain degree of autonomy, or independence. It usually coincided with the end of apprenticeship and other kinds of service, for men and women alike. Women, however, did not achieve the same legal autonomy. They passed from childhood to the dependency of wifehood. Some men chose not to marry and passed from childhood to an adulthood of partial dependency in monasteries (religious houses for men). Some men became technically autonomous without getting married if their fathers chose to emancipate them. Age did not define adulthood, but marriage certainly terminated childhood and youth.

Food and drink

Although the basic outlines of the Renaissance diet would be familiar to anyone living today, the way Europeans thought about food and drink was quite different. Patterns of fasting (abstaining from food) and feasting were set by the Christian calendar. A system of medicine, concentrating on "humors" (body fluids, such as blood) taken from the Greeks, informed their ideas about what food was healthful to eat (see "Medicine" in Chapter 10). Banqueting was the courtly ideal of dining, whereas the masses ate simple meals and plain food.

Bread is basis of diet

Bread was the single most important item in the European diet for all social classes. It was not only central to the Christian religion in the form of the Eucharist (communion), but it was also the principle agricultural product and a staple of all meals. Wealthier Europeans preferred fine bread made of carefully bolted (or sifted) wheat flour. Less refined brown bread containing more bran and sometimes including barley or rye—and in times of need, beans or chestnuts—was eaten by the lower classes. Typically, before the use of individual plates, bread served as a platter for holding other food. Cooked grains were also central to the diet and were easier and cheaper to prepare because they did not require a bread oven. In the south various forms of porridge were made of cooked barley or millet (grass made into a grain). In the north, spelt (a form of wheat) or oatmeal was used more commonly. People living in extreme poverty used vetches (vegetable-bearing plants) and lupines (a type of flower-bearing herb) instead of grains. Rice had been introduced into the European diet relatively recently.

The most common drink in southern Europe was wine, and entire regions were devoted to the production and trade of wine. Monasteries, whose monks made wine for use in the Catholic mass, maintained many of the oldest vineyards. Although the majority of wines were locally manufactured and consumed, there was a large export trade from regions such as Bordeaux (in the south of France). Expensive sweet wines were also imported from Crete (an island off the coast of Greece) and Madeira (islands in the

North Atlantic belonging to Portugal). Stronger spirits, such as aqua vitae (an alcoholic liquid for medicinal purposes), brandy, and whiskey were also available. In northern Europe beer or ale was the most common beverage, and many households brewed their own. In some regions, such as Normandy (in France) and the southwest of England, cider pressed from apples was the usual drink. In eastern Europe, mead, one of the earliest types of an alcoholic drink, was made from fermented honey. Water was rarely consumed by itself, probably for fear of contamination, though it was typically mixed with wine. Whether the water was meant to dilute the wine or the wine to improve the water was a matter of debate in the Renaissance.

The preferred form of fat is another major distinction between southern and northern European diets in the Renaissance. Olive oil dominated in the south and butter in the north. Because it is an animal product, however, butter was not supposed to be used during Lent (a forty-day period—it used to be forty weekdays—separating Ash Wednesday and Easter Sunday, during which Christians are supposed to fast and pray). There was a conscious effort to enforce the use of olive oil in the north during Lent. Animal fats such as pork or goose might also be a central part of the diet in certain regions.

Animal products

The most commonly raised domestic animals included cows, sheep,

Diet for Rich and Poor

Renaissance Europeans were unique in comparison with the rest of the world's peoples because of the amount of meat and fish they ate. The relatively small human population left ample space for raising herds of cattle, pigs, goats, and sheep. Flesh was eaten by all classes, though in more variety and in larger quantities by the wealthy. Workers in sixteenth-century Flanders (now a region in Belgium) ate rye bread, peas, beans, and cured herring (a type of fish). When the poor ate meat, it was salted (preserved). Tuna fish was also available. The very poor might survive on a diet of two or three pounds of bread a day and nothing else. The rich ate every variety of flesh available—roasted, grilled, or baked meats and fish prepared several ways. Meats would be heaped together on metal plates, called *mets* in France, and the diners would help themselves. Dinner might consist of as many as eight courses, beginning with meats in broth and ending with fruit. The presentation of food was important only among the higher social classes and usually only on special occasions. Otherwise, quantity was more important than presentation.

and goats. Their milk was used to make a wide variety of fresh and aged cheeses. When used as meat, these animals were typically eaten while young as veal, lamb, and kid. They could also be consumed at more mature ages.

Pigs were important in all parts of Europe, and their meat was preserved throughout the year. Domestic fowl included chickens, duck, geese, and pigeons. Hunting wild game was common, though the privilege to shoot venison (deer) or boar (wild pig) might be reserved for the nobility. Small wild birds such as turtle doves, as well as rabbits, hares, and even hedgehogs were frequently served.

Depending on the location, fish were also extremely important in the European diet. In the Mediterranean, along the Atlantic coasts, and in the Baltic region, fish were either consumed locally or preserved for export. In the north, herring and cod were among the preserved fish, while in the south, anchovies, sardines, and bortago (salted belly of tuna) were prepared. These products were important during Lent, when they could be transported inland. The major river systems provided salmon and trout, and ponds offered a steady supply of fish to an inland community. Whale meat and porpoise were also among the more expensive and elegant foods.

Vegetable products

Fruits and vegetables were an integral part of the European diet, though physicians typically warned against excessive eating of these items. Generally the poorer a family, the greater amount of vegetables they consumed. The sixteenth century was a period of growth. Inflation and a drop in real wages increasingly tightened the average worker's budget, re-

sulting in the family spending more money on cheaper foods. Grains and vegetables became a central, and sometimes only, part of the diet. This change meant less meat was consumed, and it may have been a reason the European diet became increasingly deficient. Some vegetables were specifically associated with lower classes: beans, cabbage, garlic, and onions in particular. Fruits like peaches and melons, on the other hand, were very popular in European courts.

When adding spices, Renaissance cooks depended on native herbs such as parsley, basil, oregano, marjoram (a type of mint), thyme, sage, tarragon, fennel, dill, bay, coriander, sorrel, saffron, and mustard. There was also an active trade in spices from Asia and Africa. Late medieval and Renaissance cooking made liberal use of spices. Spices were expensive because they had to be shipped across Europe, with numerous middlemen handling them, so they became a significant marker of social status. The more heavily one could season a dish, the more wealthy and impressive one would seem. The idea that spices were used to mask the odor of rancid meat makes little sense—anyone who could afford spices could also afford fresh meat. Apart from the spices still used in the twenty-first century, there were a number of others commonly imported. "Grains of Paradise," or melegueta pepper, was brought from the west coast of Africa until the Portugese feared it would cut into their pepper profits and banned its import in the sixteenth century. The importance of spices cannot be overstated, and it should be remembered that the Italian explorer Christopher Columbus (1451–1506) was primarily looking for spices, not a new world, when he reached the Americas in 1492. Sugar, used liberally as a spice in this period, later formed the backbone of several New World (the European term for the Americas) slave economies, especially in the Caribbean and Brazil. The attempt to find a sea route directly to Asia for spices also inspired the Portugese to travel around the southern tip of Africa. They eventually started colonies in India, Indonesia, and China for the spice trade.

Ideas about food

Attitudes toward food in Renaissance culture were informed by several different traditions. Some diets were basic and simple, while others were extravagant and rich. For the average European, the patterns of feast and fast were set by the seasons and the requirements of the Christian calendar.

Christian calendar There were many Christian holidays throughout the year, and individual communities might also have celebrated their own patron saints with festivals and feasts. But no celebration better demonstrates the attitude of excess more than carnival, or *carne-val,* from the Latin word "meat." Generally this festival was designed as a way to consume all remaining meat before Lent, when the eating of meat (except fish) was forbidden. Carnivals were a way

The Columbian Exchange

Although many New World food products did not gain wide acceptance until long after the Renaissance, some crops from the Americas made their first appearance in Europe after being introduced by Christopher Columbus and later explorers. Tomatoes, potatoes, corn (maize), peppers, certain types of squash and beans, turkeys, allspice, tobacco, and chocolate are all from the Americas. In many cases they were used in combination with other foods. Corn, for example, was made into polenta, a type of cornmeal mush; potatoes were turned into dumplings. In much of Europe, though, these foods were consciously avoided. Tomatoes did not catch on in Europe for centuries. (Many believed watery vegetables were not meant for human consumption.) Tobacco was also thought to be dangerous by some medical doctors.

to indulge in food, violence, and sex. The festival climaxed in Mardi Gras (fat Tuesday, or Shrove Tuesday) the day before Ash Wednesday, which is the first day of Lent. It often included a staged battle between a fat personification of Carnival bearing sausages and an old thin woman armed with herring, which represented Lent.

In stark contrast to these scenes were the official fasts. Lent, extending forty days from Ash Wednesday to Easter (commemoration of Christ's resurrection, or rising from the dead), was the most important though not the only time meat, milk, butter, and eggs were forbidden. One could get permission to break the rules, and this was apparently done somewhat regularly. For instance, beaver's tail and puffin (a seabird) were defined as fish products and therefore suitable for Lent. Otherwise most Europeans did survive on fish and vegetables, but for some this did not involve any hardship. Rare and exotic fish, as well as elaborate varieties of fruit, were common among the wealthy, overshadowing the purpose of Lent as a period of prayer and atonement. Protestants did not observe Catholic rituals for Lent. Nevertheless, some rulers declared periods of "political" Lent, as did Queen Elizabeth I of England (1533–1603; ruled 1558–1603), to prevent the supply of meat from dwindling and its price from soaring.

Nutritional theory The second major influence on European foods in the Renaissance was nutritional theory. Renaissance physicians used a system they had inherited from the Greeks and Arabs, based on the four humors, or vital fluids, of the body (see "Medicine" in Chapter 10). According to this theory, human health depends on the balance of the humors: blood, phlegm (mucus), black bile, and yellow biles. It was thought that one particular humor was dominant in every individual and determined his or her complexion, or temperament—sanguine (cheerful; relating to blood), phlegmatic (slow; relating to mucus),

melancholic (sad; relating to black bile), and choleric (angry; relating to yellow bile). Therefore, Renaissance nutritional experts believed they could classify every food according to the humors and how they might affect the individual.

Animals and plants also have their own complexion. Although there was wide disagreement among nutritionists about how to classify certain foods, flavor was the dominant factor. Spicy, aromatic, and salty foods were all classified as hot and dry and were thought to increase hot and dry (choleric) humors in the body. This diet was thought to be an advantage for people who had an excess of phlegmatic humors, for the food acted as a counterbalance. Sour foods and condiments were considered cold and dry. They were used to treat those with an excess of bile. It is possible that many popular food combinations were originally designed with this in mind. For example, cold and moist pork could be balanced with hot and dry mustard. Sweet dishes (hot and moist) might be balanced with sour (cold and dry) condiments.

Beyond their dominant humors, individual foods were also assigned specific properties: power to open or close the body's passages, aid digestion, cause sweating, and promote sleep. Thus, the order of a meal was considered important. Certain foods should precede other foods; foods that can rot easily, like melons and cucumbers, should never be allowed to rest at the top of the stomach where they might go bad before being digested. The list of rules and the resulting arguments waged in professional circles was endless. Numerous dietary guidelines were published during the Renaissance.

Cookbooks are popular From the evidence provided by the first cookbooks, food in the early Renaissance was not very different from that of preceding centuries. The only major change was the appearance of distinctly regional styles of cooking, as opposed to the more international character of medieval cuisine. The first printed cookbook was *De honesta voluptate* (Of honorable pleasure; 1475) by the Italian humanist Bartolomeo Sacchi (1421–1481), who was called Platina. It contains recipes borrowed from a compilation made in the Middle Ages. Platina's recipes reflect medieval influences, such as heavy use of spices and sugar, as well as unique ingredients such as almond milk, rosewater, defrutum (reduced grapes), and verjus (juice of unripe grapes). Platina's work, which also contains much nutritional and historical information, was the best-selling book about food during the Renaissance period. It was translated from Latin into Italian, German, and Dutch. A French translation ran through dozens of editions throughout the sixteenth century.

The most detailed cookbook of the Renaissance was the *Opera* of Bartolomeo Scappi, chef to Pope Pius V (1504–1572; reigned 1566–72). Scappi had access to the latest kitchen equipment, and there are detailed illustra-tions in his book. Among the most recent inventions was the fork. His recipes, which numbered in the hundreds, show Italian food of the Renaissance period breaking away from medieval cuisine. The recipes for pasta and stews are similar to those of today. Apart from cookbooks designed for actual use, several other food-related books became popular. Books about the eating habits of ancient Greeks and Romans, as well as guides for kitchen management and carving also became best-sellers in Renaissance courts.

Clothing

Clothing and fashion were important in the Renaissance. The economic, social, and political changes of the time were reflected in popular styles—the raising of hemlines for men (and the lengthening of them for women), the shift toward military uniforms, the impact of the Protestant Reformation on clerical dress, and the evolution of class distinctions through clothes. Clothing was central in the shaping of identity, as color, cut, fold, and draping took on great importance. As a result, changes in clothing revealed as much about class distinctions and national character as they did about masculinity and femininity and ideals of beauty.

Clothing trade flourishes

Economic conditions toward the end of the fourteenth century became favorable for the clothing trade. Political stability, greater wealth, and

Examples of sixteenth-century dress and the classes that wore them. From left to right: a nobleman's attire, a military habit, middle class style, noble ladies' attire, and a London merchant's clothing. *Reproduced by permission of Hulton Archive.*

an expanding market made it possible for industries to emerge in Italy and elsewhere based on the production, importation, and exportation of luxury goods and cloths. In Lucca, Italy, silk weaving—which had been introduced by the Jews in the tenth century—expanded considerably after the mid-fourteenth century. Venice benefited from its commercial network and large fleet to import precious silks and textiles (cloth and materials for making cloth) from the East. Silk in general underwent an expansion in Spain and later in France, but Italy remained central for the production not only of silks but of such luxury materials as satins, velvets, taffeta, and eventually lace. Wool and linen would remain the most used fabrics of the age, but the wearing of luxury cloth became such a large part of society that laws were passed to limit the manufacturing and consumption of these fabrics. The main purpose of the laws, called sumptuary laws, was to limit the consumption of luxury items. The laws also determined who could wear what, while regulating the shape and style of garments.

With the increased import of precious metals after Columbus's journey to America, Italy was challenged by new manufacturing and trade centers in the north. These developments resulted in Italy increasing its production and trading in luxury cloths and silks. For northern countries, new manufacturing equipment that had previously been prohibited by old guild regulations began to appear. (Guilds were medieval craft and trade groups that trained apprentices and set standards for production of goods.) First on the scene was the fulling mill (a mill where woolen cloth was processed) and later the knitting machine (invented by William Lee in 1589). At the same time, technological innovations improved processes of weaving and dying. In England, landowners increased their own wool production by turning part of their land into pasture, so wool-bearing animals would have more space to graze.

Elite fashion

Fashion was extremely important to the Renaissance man, especially when he was at court. Every day the fashionable man undertook his dressing with the aid of a servant, who was required to tie up the points (pieces of lace that held a garment together), lace the doublet (a close-fitting jacket), arrange the stomacher (a piece of cloth heavily jeweled or embroidered, worn at the center of the bodice), and fasten the frilled shirt. Costume varied across nations. In general, however, men's long garments—which still prevailed at churches and universities—became much shorter. The surcoat, an outer coat or cloak, went out of fashion in favor of the exposed hose-enclosed leg. Attached to the hose was the pourpont, a chest-and-waist-fitted doublet made of lined and quilted rich fabric that took many forms and cuts over the years and across regions. Regions, in turn, influenced one another. For instance, when the French king Charles VIII (1470–1498; ruled 1493–98) invaded Italy in 1494, the French and Italians exchanged clothing styles.

Toward the end of the sixteenth century, Spain began to set standards of fashion that would eventually dominate throughout Europe. The Spanish preferred a simple and somber line of clothing. Softness was replaced by a straight and stiff silhouette, the doublet was designed to emphasize the slimness of the waist, and black became the preferred color for Spaniards. In France, King Henry II (1519–1559; ruled 1547–59) and his court were especially fond of dark hues over-traced with gold, with none of the Italian ornamentation that was usually found in clothing. During the reign of King Henry III (1551–1589; ruled 1574–89), the French briefly returned to the Italian style. Noblemen at the court of King Henry IV (1553–1610; ruled 1589–1610) had to have as many as thirty suits and were expected to change them frequently in order to maintain respectability. It was during this time, especially in Elizabethan England, that the ruff (a large round collar of pleated muslin or linen) around the neck grew increasingly pronounced in size. By 1579, ac-

Fashion: Elaborate and Uncomfortable

During the Renaissance women's fashion became increasingly elaborate. Sumptuary laws attempted to limit the measurements, the amount of jewel trimming, and the cut of women's clothing. By the end of the fifteenth century, throughout Europe the gown replaced other garments for women except for the elegant surcoat. Both the gown and the surcoat fitted tightly to the upper part of the body while the skirt flowed and trailed on the ground, lengthening the line and accentuating the waist and hips. Necklines could vary—the square neckline came from Italian styles, while Burgundians favored pointed neck openings—and sleeves tended to trail. In the sixteenth century, women, like men, adopted Spanish fashions, most notably the farthingale, hoops worn under a skirt to expand it at the hip. The farthingale was a favorite garment of Marguerite de Valois (1553–1615), queen consort of Henry IV. It could take on many variations and required the building of special high chairs to accommodate the hoops when the woman sat down.

cording to one writer, the wearers could barely move their heads.

Women also used a variety of cosmetics, jewels, headgear, and accessories. Queen Elizabeth I, who made clothing a central part of her political strategies, wished to preserve the complexion of a "virgin queen" (nickname given her because she was unmarried). She did so by applying a thick layer of white powder makeup to her already pale face. Accessories became more important than ever, for men as well as women. Earrings, which had disappeared in the Middle Ages, became widely popular, as did handkerchiefs. Gloves were central to fashion and could be made of gold cloth encrusted with hundreds of pearls. Fans, hand mirrors, and elaborately embroidered objects, especially during Elizabeth's reign, completed the costumes that were in essence women's weapons in their social encounters. Prostitutes (women who have sexual relations for money) were given more leeway in dress and ornamentation than their more constricted, domesticated sisters, especially in cities such as Venice. Their dress influenced that of respectable women. Prostitutes often started fads such as wearing high wooden platform shoes—shoes so tall that one commentator described the spectacle as watching a creature of half wood and half woman totter down the street.

Fashion and the body

Clothing covered the body but it also changed, shaped, squeezed, and exaggerated the human form. For Renaissance men, puffy doublets gave the broad-shouldered appearance of a soldier in armor, while coats were padded with hay and straw at the shoulders. With hose, male legs received new emphasis, as did the waist, which was usually set off by a form-fitting doublet or tightened with a belt. In addition, the increasingly prominent codpiece (a flap or bag concealing an opening in the front of breeches, or pants), which had originated in Germany, exaggerated the male groin area. The shell shape was particularly popular. Women also wore clothing that enhanced or exaggerated their bodies. In sixteenth-century Italy, women "full of flesh" were favored and compared to wine barrels. To emphasize this full-figured ideal, women's clothes were layered with jewelry made of gold, emeralds, and pearls. Following Spanish influences, however, women's waists were gradually squeezed in, leading to increasingly rigid and torturous whalebone bodices that also tightly compressed the breasts.

Clothes of the lower classes

Clothing was simple and tended not to vary much among the lower orders. For peasants, underwear came into use in the thirteenth century. Legs might be bare and feet were uncovered except for a flat sole held by a leather strap wound around the leg. Some peasants in Flanders wore wooden shoes, as did the urban cloth workers in Florence. Women wore skirts and aprons tucked up for work and topped with tight bodices and enveloping cloaks, while men dressed in buttoned jackets, short breeches, and wide-brimmed hats. Material consisted primarily of coarse wool or unbleached linen, while colors were restricted primarily to black (in women's clothing) or dull browns and grays. Those who worked in a luxury industry attempted to imitate the higher classes by wearing velvet on special occasions. In general, however, embellishments to these drab clothes consisted of silver buttons, taffeta (a plain-woven, elegant fabric) scarves, or the occasional muff (a tubular item, normally made of fur, used to warm the hands). Only at the end of the seventeenth century would developments in industrial production offer the lower classes a wide variety of fabric and color. The very poor continued to wear hand-me-down rags or coarse wool garments donated by trade guilds or religious fraternities.

The military look

Fashion in the Renaissance took many elements from the military, from breeches to the wearing of swords, which noblemen wore for ceremonial decoration at court. Beginning in Germany, an obsession for slashes and puffed sleeves moved across Europe and peaked in the sixteenth century. The style was said to have been derived from the tattered clothing of Swiss mercenaries (hired soldiers) returning from a victory against Charles the Bold (1433–1477), duke of Burgundy, in 1476. The Swiss had seized the garments off defeated dead soldiers. The returning warriors found the clothes too tight, so they slashed them or allowed the seams to rip, causing the garments to puff out. Germans, who first noted this look, were responsible in turn for the military-like "lattice" breeches made of wide strips of material and worn by the papal Swiss Guards today. The Thirty Years' War (1618–48) seems to

Evolution of Military Uniforms

After the sixteenth century the rise of infantry warfare involving masses of men generated a need for uniforms. Early versions of the uniform could be found in the fifteenth century, when Swiss soldiers wore short, brightly colored slashed doublets and tight breeches. Another example could be found in the sixteenth century, when troops in the imperial army in Nuremberg, Germany, wore red coats. Around the same time English soldiers under the duke of Norfolk wore suits of blue trimmed with red. German *Landsknechten* mercenaries, recruited from the lower orders, pioneered the use of long breeches and cloaks in battle, as well as widened slashes and puffed sleeves. In general, however, uniforms of a more simple and useful variety would not develop until the means of mass production were available at the end of the seventeenth century.

have been especially influential in spreading amongst the larger population the soldier's soft, broad-brimmed hat (which later became the three-cornered tricorn), the broad collar, and the rows of buttons that decorated the seams of trousers.

During the fifteenth and sixteenth centuries, armor (a protective metal suit worn in combat) became increasingly unnecessary in the face of changes in warfare, such as the use of massed troops and artillery (guns and cannons). Nevertheless, armor reached new levels of decoration that served more ceremonial than practical functions. In the sixteenth century the master armor maker was Filippo Negroli of Milan, Italy, whose detailed helmets and shields were made for such leaders as Holy Roman Emperor Charles V (1500–1558; ruled 1519–56) and King Francis I of France (1494–1547; ruled 1515–47). Negroli drew upon themes in traditional Greek and Roman art. A fourth-generation member of an armor-making dynasty, he specialized in *all'antica,* a contemporary type of armor fashioned in the style of antiquity that featured images of lions, dragons, and Medusa heads. (Medusa was a monster in Greek mythology who had snakes for hair.) Among the more elaborate of his designs was a helmet that was a kind of monster mask. It consisted of flying batwing cheek pieces, fangs thrusting from the jaw, and a pair of ramlike horns positioned on the top of the head.

Religious clothing

Popes, cardinals, and other clergy were not immune from embracing the clothing trends of the time. As a result, in 1464 Pope Paul II (1417–1471; reigned 1464–71) issued vestimentary laws (laws relating to the clothes, or vestments, of the clergy) that were intended to regulate occasionally outrageous costumes. Although not typical, Cardinal Francesco Gonzaga (1444–1483) went into debt with his purchase of Turkish floor-length robes of crimson and green damask, various velvets and woven silks, and other garments. In another reaction to these displays, the Italian monk and preacher Girolamo Savonarola (1452–1498) inspired many "bonfires of vanities" in Florence in the 1490s. These bonfires were ceremonies in which luxury items were burned in protest against the extravagance of the clergy and laity alike. Precious veils and cosmetics, ornaments, and masses of false hair—blonde was the fashionable color—were thrown onto the fires. The Dutch humanist Desiderius Erasmus (c. 1466–1536) also commented upon the increasingly elaborate clothing of the clerical orders. He noted their obsession with girdles, cowls (hoods on cloaks), gowns, and tonsures (a shaved portion of the head, usually the crown). The Protestant Reformation also had an impact on clothing, as white gowns, plain white surplices (long outer garments with open sleeves), and black scarves distinguished men of the new faith.

Theatrical and festive costumes

Festivals, processions, and special events became more frequent in the Renaissance. These events were generated by the increased spending power, princely and civic displays, and a general desire for showmanship. As a result, clothing became more elaborate, especially in the seventeenth century when the masque (a form of drama in which actors used masks) became a fully developed theatrical court genre (see "Court masque" in Chapter 9). The masque was so important in England that the scientific scholar Sir Francis Bacon (1561–1626)

wrote a treatise (study) on the subject. Since performances were always at night and usually illuminated by candlelight, the most flattering colors were thought to be white, carnation (red), or a kind of "sea-water green." Costumes could also be made of "tynsell" (tinsel; sparkling metal thread), beads, and sequins (small disks of shiny metal), and further adorned with gold tassels, gilt bells, fringing, and silver and gold lace. Masks were usually made of velvet and built up to produce a dramatic effect. Foreign visitors often thought the costumes to be outrageous and bizarre.

The French were most noted for the dress displayed at glittering court events, gaining a reputation for spectacles of unparalleled magnificence. In seventeenth-century France, ballets became ways for performers to dress as Indians, Moors, Africans, and Asians. French court members indulged in their own kind of theater by dressing, at special events, as Persian shahs, Turks, rajas (Indian princes), and Native Americans.

Festivals

Renaissance festivals may be usefully classified in several different ways. Both religious and civic festivals aimed at representing the established order in a favorable light and at creating an impression of harmony and security in the empire. Some festivals took place annually or were organized for unique occasions. Others were popular and folkloric, celebrating a tradi-

Religious Feasts and Processions

The calendar of religious feasts and processions was meant to give a sense of harmony between human history and the universe. When civic officials took part in religious processions, they were showing that spiritual and everyday (called secular, or nonreligious) life were one. An example was the Palm Sunday (the Sunday before Easter) processions in Venice. For Italian city-states, feast days were the equivalent of modern-day celebrations such as Bastille Day in France or Independence Day in the United States. In Florence, symbolic tribute was offered on the Feast of Saint John the Baptist (last Jewish prophet and forerunner of Jesus Christ; June 24), and there were often parades with patriotic floats. In Siena, the Assumption of the Virgin (August 15; the day when the Virgin Mary was believed to have been raised to heaven) was the national holiday. Venice celebrated not only the Feast of Saint Mark (one of Jesus Christ's twelve disciples; April 25), but also several other holidays recalling the saint's connection with the republic.

tion based on a popular myth or folk tale. Many involved elite and learned participants. Some festivals were meant to defy normal religious and social customs, if only for a day. For example, an old tradition in some cities allowed the common people to destroy the canopy under which a religious official had just ridden. At Fer-

rara, Italy, in 1598, even Pope Clement VIII's horse was taken as a prize by the over-excited crowd.

State occasions

Civic pageantry was also aimed at presenting a unified image of the state and society. Military processions and local ceremonies would often put the head of state and other government officials on display to the people. Foreign ambassadors, delegations of foreign merchants, and representatives of local guilds were often featured as well. These public displays implied a harmony among the various social classes and even among the nations of the Christian world.

The routes taken by civic processions similarly suggested an integration of church and state, as well as the link between the ruler and the ruled. Visiting monarchs stopped at city gates to receive greetings from town fathers. Then they proceeded to the local cathedral to be received by the bishop and to make a show of personal devotions. Only after this ceremony were they free to go to the palace where they would be staying. In some cities, such as Naples, Italy, which had five *seggi* (seats; district governments), monarchs stopped at designated points along the entry route to receive the homage of local authorities. New popes, in their procession to take possession of Saint John Lateran (an ancient basilica, or church), paused to accept the civil allegiance of the Jewish colony in Rome and to confirm its civil rights. New sovereigns in England and France noted messages from various groups in their first grand progress through London and Paris. Official accounts of these processions tended to be positive, and it seems that public enthusiasm was enormous. Awareness of injustices were suspended temporarily as people were caught up in a feeling of civic pride.

Royal and dynastic weddings

Civic unity was also promoted by celebrations of royal and noble weddings. If the bride came from another state or country, joyous entries into the city were part of the ceremony. A series of courtly entertainments usually took place as well. An example was the wedding of the duke of Florence, Cosimo I (1503–1572) and the daughter of the Spanish viceroy (official who represented the king) of Naples in 1539. The union represented a significant political alliance between Spain and Florence. The themes of the entry decorations celebrated this alliance. Courtly entertainments included banquets, indoor pageants, tournaments or other contests of chivalry, fireworks, and (especially in Italy) the performance of comedies. Wedding festivities were, after carnivals, the principal occasion for the staging of comedies. In Ferrara, Italy, for the 1502 wedding of Lucretia Borgia (1480–1519) and Alfonso I d'Este (1486–1534), the comedies of the Roman playwright Plautus (c. 254–184 B.C.) were performed in Italian. Later in the century, original neoclassical comedies in the vernacular (local language), called *commedie erudite* (learned come-

The marriage of Princess Elizabeth of England to Frederick V of Bohemia. Royal weddings such as this often promoted civic unity.
Photograph by Renold Elstrack. Reproduced by permission of Cambridge University.

dies), were put on in Florence, Mantua, and Ferrara. The first performance of neoclassical comedy in France took place when Queen Catherine de Médicis (1519–1589) visited Lyon.

Elaborate nuptial (wedding) festivities also became common in northern Europe. The wedding of the Danish king Frederick II (1534–1588;

ruled 1559–88) in 1572 was celebrated with banquets, a tournament, and a grand passage of the bride through the streets of Copenhagen. The celebrations for the wedding of the Scottish king James VI (also known as James I of England; 1566–1625; ruled Scotland 1567–1625) to Anne of Denmark apparently included the playing of comedies both in Latin and in Danish, first at Oslo, Norway, and then at the Danish court. Northern European courtly entertainments eventually became more elaborate than the Italian, moving toward a lavish style called baroque. In 1634 in Copenhagen celebrations for the wedding of prince-elect Christian included a ballet, two musical comedies, and an extremely elaborate display of fireworks. The art of court festivals became an international affair. Italians were often employed in the north, and the English architect Inigo Jones (1573–1652), who had Italian experience, almost certainly designed festival material for Hamburg, Germany, in 1603. English actors performed in Germany and Denmark.

Celebration of Palilia

Humanist professors and students in various cities amused themselves at times by reviving classical festivals or by celebrating events in Roman history. This practice was carried furthest in the *Studium* (university) at Rome, where in the late fifteenth century Julius Pomponius Laetus and some colleagues renewed observance of the Palilia. The celebration had originally been an agriculture festival but in classical times it also commemorated the anniversary of the building of Rome. In the early years of the revival there was more drinking than eating, with a Latin oration in praise of the city being the central ceremonial element. In 1501 the festivities were moved to the Campidoglio, the ancient Capitolium, and officials from the Vatican and the city government began to participate.

In 1513 the Palilia was the occasion for the most remarkable and learned festival of the Renaissance. The new pope, Leo X (1475–1521; reigned 1513–21), asked the city government to grant honorary Roman citizenship to his brother Giuliano Medici (1479–1516) and his nephew Lorenzo de' Medici (1492–1519). The flattered officials resolved to conduct the proceedings with as much style as possible. Making the citizenship ceremony coincide with the Palilia, they commissioned the construction of an enormous neoclassical theater, with temporary statues and paintings that depicted events in ancient history. Paintings and inscriptions concentrated on the supposedly friendly relations between the early Romans and Etruscans. The Etruscans were ancient peoples who settled the region in central Italy now known as Tuscany, where Florence is located. The Romans and Etruscans were continually at war with one another in ancient times. In the ceremony the Romans were named the symbolic ancestors of the Medicis, while the Etruscans were named the symbolic ancestors of the Florentines. Proceedings included a mass (the only religious element in the ceremony), a Latin oration in praise of Rome and the Medicis, and the presentation of a diploma of citizenship. An elaborate banquet of more than twenty courses was served, a complex pageant was performed in Latin, and Plautus's *Poenulus* was performed in Latin. Both female and male roles were filled by male students. Afterward the Romans took fierce pride in what they had accomplished. This event was one of the last times Latin was used as the main language in a public Roman celebration. Pope Leo X authorized annual celebrations of the Palilia, but there was never again such splendor.

Festivals of misrule

Festivals that served as protection from popular resentment or as subversions of public order have attracted the attention of historians in recent years. An undoubted ancestor of many Renaissance festivals of this kind can be seen in the Roman Saturnalia, which was celebrated around the time of the winter solstice (beginning of winter; about December 22). During one stage of the ancient feast, the social order was turned upside down. Masters and slaves exchanged clothing, and the masters served the slaves at table.

Feast of Fools The Feast of Fools (Latin *Festum Stultorum,* French *Fête des Fous,* German *Narrenfest*) was long celebrated in religious communities over most of western Europe. It was held shortly after Christmas, near the time of the old Saturnalia. Hierarchy (social order) was reversed as a young cleric or monastic novice was elected bishop, and things normally held sacred were made fun of, notably in mock masses. Some places observed, more or less in association with the Feast of Fools, a *Festum Asinorum* (Feast of Asses), in which a donkey was brought into church and both priest and congregation brayed (harsh cry of a donkey) at certain points of the liturgy. High church officials took steps to stop this custom, and by the sixteenth century such celebrations were in decline. Secular festivals of misrule, however, continued to be practiced.

Abbeys of misrule In the fifteenth and sixteenth centuries, France and other European countries had organizations (especially of young men) that were sometimes called abbeys (kingdoms) of misrule (*abbayes de maugouvert* in French). These associations elected abbots or kings who led them in a variety of activities for regular festivals like Christmas and carnival. They also led *charivaris* (shivarees), rowdy events that humiliated men (known as "henpecked husbands") who were dominated by their wives. Often the wives themselves took part in the festivities. In sixteenth-century England, among the higher social classes, a court of misrule was sometimes convened for Yuletide (period of time before and after Christmas) celebrations. On January 3, 1552, George Ferrars, who was appointed abbot by King Edward VI (1537–1553; ruled 1547–53), staged a mock triumphal entry into London.

Abbots could also have official functions, such as meeting foreign delegations. At other times, as a great number of surviving songs and literary works reveal, abbeys were simply agents of good fun. They were not always involved with subversive activities.

Carnival

By far the most important annual feast of "transgression" was carnival. It was celebrated over most of central and western Europe, at least until the Reformation. Thereafter carnival was suppressed, along with Lent, in some (but not all) Protestant areas. Carnival was originally celebrated on Twelfth Night (the evening of Epiphany, the coming of the Magi after the birth of Jesus), close to the time of the old Saturnalia. During the Renaissance it was confined in most places to the last few days before Lent, whose date varied with that of Easter. Carnival was a period of licensed, authorized celebration of "the world turned upside down." The forms of celebrations varied with local tradition. Masking was perhaps the most common element, though it was periodically forbidden in reaction to various excesses. In really bad times, as at Rome in the years following the Sack of 1527 (invasion by the army of Emperor Charles V), the celebration of carnival was suspended. It was perhaps the most popular of all annual festivals, so people did not give it up easily.

Rome had one of the most elaborate series of carnival entertainments. Setting the annual program was the privilege and responsibility of the city government, the Campidoglio. The program had to be approved by the pope, who would help with expenses. Nearly all events took place in the week between the last two Sundays before Lent. There were several footraces: one for young men, one for Jews, one for old men, and, occasionally, one for prostitutes. There were also horse races, bullfights, and games involving other animals, some of them seeming very cruel to the modern mind. Several games took place on the second Sunday, at a hill called Testaccio outside the city walls. On certain other days contests of chivalry were held for young aristocrats. On Shrove Thursday the main pageant of carnival was held in Piazza Navona, then called the Agone, with a parade that included the single senator and the three *conservatori* (officials) of the city government, as well as a float depicting historical and mythological figures. Prominent writers and academics planned the floats, and first-rate artists sometimes decorated them.

The Roman celebrations thus included both learned and popular elements, both aristocratic and plebeian (common). While there was much blowing off of steam and relieving of tensions, truly subversive elements were not very visible. The pageant often flattered the reigning pope, as when that of 1536 recreated the triumph of Paulus Aemilius (Pope Paul III; 1468–1549; reigned 1534–49). The masking was no doubt politically risky, and popes forbade disguising for the purpose of mocking the clergy or religious ceremonies. Carnival harassment of the Jews was also strictly forbidden, indicating that such activity was likely to occur otherwise.

Carnivals are more elaborate Among other Italian carnivals, those in Florence and Venice were especially elaborate. In 1513, the Compagnia del Broncone and the Compagnia del Diamante, companies of young Florentines similar to the abbeys of misrule (see "Abbeys of misrule" section previously in this chapter), staged competing parades through town. The first had chariots portraying golden ages of the past and present (in reference to the recent return to power of the Medici family), and the second showed the three ages of man. Comedies were often performed for carnival in Florence, as in other Italian cities, and there arose a special lyric genre of *canti carnascialeschi* (carnival songs). These songs were a favorite of Lorenzo de' Medici (the Magnificent; 1449–1492), the city's ruler in the late fifteenth century.

Venice had a particularly long carnival celebration, beginning on Twelfth Night. The official climax came on Shrove Thursday, when the doge (duke) and other officials oversaw a bizarre celebration of a twelfth-century victory over the patriarch of Aquileia. In this ceremony, a bull and three hundred pigs were put on "trial" and executed, after being teased and chased around the piazzetta (plaza). In the Piazza San Marco, there were sometimes parades that mocked the official ones of the republic. These festivities were usually performed without any tensions between officials and the people. As in Florence, many carnival activities were carried out by groups of wellborn young men, here called Campagnie delle Claze. These groups sometimes staged pageants in the piazza on specially built platforms. They also held performances of comedies, usually in private houses. Many strangers came into town during the Venetian carnival, both for the spectacles and for the masking, which was performed for free.

The official activity of Italian carnivals was scarcely subversive, and often even supportive of government, but in Germany it was more daring. During the early years of the Reformation, carnival parades and floats in several cities mocked the pope and Roman Catholic clergy. At Nuremberg in 1539, on the other hand, the main float, a ship, made fun of the principal Protestant preachers who were an enemy of carnival pleasures. Nervous city authorities everywhere tried to prevent such embarrassments. Most plays, such as those performed in Nuremberg, usually spared official government institutions and officials from ridicule. The subject matter was usually human failings, such as envy and lust. France offers the exceptional example of a carnival celebration that turned to violence. In the Dauphiné town of Romans, social tensions had been high for some time when in 1580 a group of celebrators took advantage of the confusion of carnival and massacred a large number of reform-minded revelers (carnival participants). Scholars are still unsure whether or not the "upside down" atmosphere of carnivals laid the groundwork for the social, political, and religious revolution of the times.

Fairs

In the High Middle Ages (eleventh to thirteenth centuries), fairs became a significant feature of economic activity, and by the end of that period they existed in large numbers all over northwestern Europe. Less historical information is available about such events in eastern Europe and Italy. Most fairs were the expansion of a local weekly market into an annual event lasting a few days. Often fairs were held at the same time as the feast of a locally celebrated saint. A much smaller number were celebrated regionally or nationally, sometimes attracting merchants from a foreign country but without becoming a truly international celebration. The English fairs of Saint Ives, Boston, and Winchester, which were visited by Flemish merchants buying wool and selling cloth, are classic examples of this type. The annual cycle of six fairs in Flanders, comprising two at Ypres and one each at Bruges, Torhout, Lille, and Messines, were larger but did not rise much more above a regional status than did their English counterparts. The only true international fairs were the cycle of Champagne (in northeastern France), with two each at Troyes and Provins, and one each at Lagny and Bar-sur-Aube. By the end of the twelfth century these were the most energetic centers of trade in Europe, where Italians exchanged products for northern cloth brought by merchants from the Low Countries, France, and England. These fairs may be singled out also as the only occasions, before the fifteenth century, when money (whether in coin form or international bills of exchange) was a commodity. This feature helped maintain the importance of Champagne fairs until about the 1320s, even though as centers for trade in wares they had been declining for at least forty years before that.

A downturn in the economy in the fourteenth century caused a severe and widespread decline in fair activity. Recovery in the fifteenth and sixteenth centuries was patchy and accompanied by change. At first it appeared that Chalon-sur-Saône in Burgundy, France, might survive as an international successor to the Champagne fairs, but even before 1400 Geneva, Switzerland, had secured that position. For most of the fifteenth century its four fairs, spaced throughout the year, were massively attended by merchants from the Rhineland, the Low Countries, Italy, Spain, and France. Generally these merchants sold goods, bullion (coins), and financial instruments. In 1420 the French dauphin (eldest son of a king of France), later King Charles VII (1403–1461; ruled 1422–61), established fairs at Lyon, in Burgundy. Initially these events benefited from merchants coming from Geneva, Switzerland, but later the two cities became rivals. A turning point came in 1463, when Louis XI (1423–1483; ruled 1461–83) changed the dates of the Lyon fairs to be the same as the Geneva fairs. One early indication of the shift in importance was the transfer of a branch of the Medici bank from Geneva to Lyon in 1465. By the early sixteenth century the former was deeply overshadowed by the latter. The quarterly fairs of Lyon dominated Europe for the greater part of that century. They supported a prosperous trade in merchandise, especially silks and spices, but are best known for their role in the international money market. Loans were arranged there, bills cleared, and interest rates established. By the 1580s financial business was shifting to Besançon, another town conveniently positioned on the borders of France and the Roman Empire. Besançon flourished until well into the seventeenth century, purely as a money fair acting in close cooperation with similar fairs in Piacenza and Genoa in Italy and Medina del Campo in Spain.

Fairs in decline

The major Flemish fairs did not survive into the later Middle Ages and those of the northern Low Countries never became more than local events. In the fifteenth century a cycle of four important fairs was established in Antwerp, Belgium, and Bergen op Zoom in Brabant (now part of the Netherlands and Belgium). The growth of Antwerp as a major international center of trade and finance in the early sixteenth century caused these fairs to decline. Part of the reason fairs existed was that they allowed visitors and temporarily suspended local monopolies, but since Antwerp was an open city in this respect it did not need the fairs. In the early 1560s the English Merchant Adventurers Company, whose cloth trade provided a major stimulus to the fairs in the fifteenth century, tried with little success to restrict its members' business to the traditional fair structure of both towns.

In England many of the smallest fairs simply died out. Others changed their character and even increased their size by specializing in one or two products or types of livestock, often combining this with an annual labor hiring function. Some relics still survive under regional names, though very few retain any of their ancient characteristics. Among the few nationally significant fairs of this period, the most important were those at Bristol, England; at Beverly in Yorkshire, England; and above all at Stourbridge, near Cambridge, England. The last, unheard of in earlier times, flourished until the eighteenth century and was patronized by customers from all over England.

In northern Europe the great fair at Scania, in southern Sweden, survived until the mid-sixteenth century. Although basically considered a herring (a type of fish) fair, it was also a general distribution point for much of the west Baltic region. Apart from Scania, the Hanseatic (German) towns had little use for fairs and their civil ordinances prevented visiting English and Dutch merchants from attending the fairs in northern Germany and Poland. The most important German fair was that of Frankfurt am Main.

Scholars still wonder whether this was an international fair, or just an extremely large and successful regional one. Since textiles brought from Italy and southern Germany were sent from the fair to the Low Countries, with English and Dutch cloth distributed in the opposite direction, there seems no reason to doubt its international status. In the sixteenth century the fair became important for financial transfers between Germany and the Low Countries, but activity was not on the scale of Lyon and the other southern fairs. Leipzig may be included as the second German fair town and for its book fair, which still survives.

Sports

The medieval world was filled with sporting contests, from chivalric tournaments to church-sponsored ball games. The Renaissance world also celebrated such contests, but with the new sense of individuality, gender, education, and the body that accompanied Renaissance thought. For humanists such as the Italian scholar Leon Battista Alberti (1401–1472), the pursuit of sports was the perfect meeting of the body and mind. He claimed that the scholar who engaged in sporting activities would achieve the ideal combination of mental and physical development necessary to become a "universal man." Such a man was to choose carefully, and have a perfect balance among his sports: swimming, running, hunting, wrestling, and horseback riding. All of these sports, and certain ones that focused on "ball-play," were acceptable because they were played by the ancient Greeks. Not all Renaissance men agreed, however. Some, such as Erasmus, claimed that honesty and responsibility were important elements of sport, but the overall goal of the society should be to produce gentlemen and scholars, not athletes.

On the playing fields and among nobler classes, jousting tournaments continued in popularity despite the pleas of academics and scholars. The English king Henry VIII was an avid supporter and participant in such games. Contests of physical strength and skill could be important diplomatic events, such as Henry's wrestling match with the French king Francis I at the Field of Cloth of Gold pageant in 1520. Another enthusiast of chivalric games was King Henry II of France, who was killed in a jousting contest in 1559. His death left France open to religious wars that eventually tore the country apart (see "France" in Chapter 6). At court, sports served as important social events. According to the Italian writer Baldassare Castiglione (1478–1529), author of *Book of the Courtier*, it was the duty of the perfect courtier (member of court) to gain proficiency not only in the joust but also in other popular and military-influenced sports such as archery, swordplay, fencing, and horse racing. He also urged participation in running, hurdle jumping, swimming, and throwing. The court lady, according to Castiglione, was to stand by and cheer the athletic displays of her man. A courtier could also engage in contest with peasants. Castiglione warned,

King Henry VIII jousting in honor of Queen Catherine of Aragon and to celebrate the birth of their only son, Henry, Duke of Cornwell. *Reproduced by permission of Hulton Archive.*

however, that a courtier should be sure that he would win. For instance, it would be humiliating for a courtier if he were defeated by a peasant in a wrestling match.

Tennis becomes popular

One of the most popular sports of the Renaissance among the upper classes was tennis, which originated in medieval France and spread outward to other western European countries. Monarchs again set the fashion, with Henry VIII (the owner of seven rackets) joining Emperor Charles V in 1523 for a doubles match against the princes of Orange and Brandenburg. The game was played differently in various regions, which tended to complicate the rules. In 1555 a monk named Antonio Scaino de Salo wrote a treatise on tennis in which he attempted to universalize the rules of etiquette, scoring, and play. This work resulted in tennis becoming more popular among merchants, students, and artisans, all of whom would have had access to the book. Meanwhile, King James VI of Scotland (also known as James I of England) popularized the ancient sport of golf, which had originated in Scotland and was played not only by

Sports of the Lower Classes

While sports among the elite were played across national boundaries, sports among the lower classes differed from region to region. In popular culture, games such as *la soule,* born in the twelfth-century villages of France, involved teams of men divided according to parish or marital status (those who were married versus those who were unmarried, for example). These teams then battled against one another and attempted to drive a ball forward and past a goalpost with the foot, the hand, or sticks of various kinds. The church had long sponsored events such as *la soule,* though some clerics had called for its prohibition from the beginning. Some clerics even threatened excommunication (exile from the church) for those who engaged in a game that caused such competitive spirits to arise.

In England, football (known as soccer in modern-day United States), which may have derived from *la soule,* had a long legacy. A rumor had for years attributed the origin of soccer to a group of Englishman kicking a Dane's (person from Denmark) severed head amongst one another. Stool ball, a popular Renaissance game, is said to have begun among milkmaids who threw (or hit with bats) balls toward their milking

the king but also by his mother, Mary Stuart (also known as Mary, Queen of Scots). Golf's short-lived popularity among the English, however, was due more to their desire to please the king than to a love of the sport.

Sickness and disease

Wealthy people who lived during Renaissance times dealt with many of the same illnesses we have today: poxes (viruses causing pustules on the skin), scurvy (a disease caused by vitamin deficiency), cancers, fevers, rheumatism (any of a series of diseases in which the muscles and joints are severely swollen and inflamed), and gout (similar to rheumatism, with even more swelling of the joints and traces of uric acid in the blood). Some aristocratic families, such as the Medici family, struggled against tuberculosis (a highly communicable disease of the lungs), while others struggled to survive syphilis (a sexually transmitted disease; see "Epidemics widespread" section later in this chapter). Malaria (a bacterial disease often carried by mosquitoes) was an especially deadly disease that plagued Italy. Those who had to undergo surgery often suffered unpleasant chronic ulcers and infections, resulting in the need for continued surgery throughout their lives. For those who could afford such procedures, life expectancy could reach fifty or sixty years.

stools, trying to knock them over. By the Renaissance the game was associated with courtship and the Easter season and later evolved into the English ball-and-bat games of rounders and cricket. Finally, in piazzas across Italy the Easter season brought on games, including *calico,* in which uniformed (and only highborn) players kicked and hurled a leather ball filled with animal hair as a cheering crowd watched.

The possibility of disruption and violence in sports (and the problems that arose with gambling and dice games) had always been of concern to authorities. In the Renaissance even more people began speaking out against the "devilish pastimes," especially when they were played on the Sabbath (Sunday; a day for prayer and contemplation). Among the Protestant leaders, Martin Luther (1483–1546) was one of the few who publicly supported sporting events, especially bowling (*Kegels*). In general, however, such amusements as maypoles, bearbaiting, and cockfighting were denounced as sins of idleness. They were usually severely restricted, if not prohibited. Enforcement of these rules was uneven, as peasants often refused to stop participating in their favorite pastimes.

The majority of people living during the Renaissance also had to deal with persistent hunger, infection, overcrowding, and poverty. They were underfed and constantly in danger of being infected with a variety of diseases, and more often than not their cries for help fell upon the deaf ears of the wealthy. After the Black Death the poor lived a little better because prices stabilized, resulting in lower food costs, and wages increased. By the sixteenth and seventeenth centuries, however, the homeless and hungry became more numerous than before, due to prices once again rising faster than wage increases. For those who were wealthy, avoiding illness was easier. They were able to remain healthy because of proper diet and the ability to move to summer cottages in the countryside (disease was less common in rural areas and therefore spread more slowly than in urban areas). The rich often imported wines (which were believed to help stave off disease), took long steam baths, and had access to the newest medicines and treatments. The poor, however, did not have doctors to plan diets for them, nor could they afford the food if they did. The rich scorned the poor for eating trash, worms, insects, and grubs (wormlike larvae of insects). People who lived in poverty were regarded by the rich as vagrants and criminals, and they were thought to be less than human. On the other hand, very little of elite medicine (such as potions, powders, baths, and prescriptions) made sense to the poor. Anger and resentment was felt on both sides, widening the already massive gap between the rich and poor.

New diseases

During the Renaissance physicians and laymen began to see many "new diseases," sicknesses that had not been discussed in the medical texts of the ancients. For instance, injuries inflicted by guns, which were introduced in the fourteenth century, were at first treated with ineffective methods used in medieval times. By the sixteenth century, however, discovering new ways of treating illness could make a physician very successful and wealthy. Among the new or newly recognized sicknesses was the "great pox" (or syphilis, the "French Disease"). "Great" distinguished this illness from smallpox (a contagious disease caused by a virus, which produces severe skin sores) that was first discovered by the Arabs. Smallpox had become a serious epidemic in late sixteenth-century Europe. Miners' diseases (ailments suffered by those who worked in underground mines) were the first occupational afflictions described in detail in medical texts of the time. Epidemic typhus fever (a bacterial disease carried by body lice, which causes high fever) appeared suddenly in the early sixteenth-century wars. Scurvy and yellow fever were first described during the time of overseas conquest and colonization. Scurvy is a disease of the gums caused by a lack of vitamin C in the diet. During the Renaissance explorers regularly crossed the Atlantic to colonize the New World (the European term for the Americas). Many ships started carrying limes (citrus fruits are rich in vitamin C) in an effort to prevent sailors from contracting the illness. During trips to the New World, Europeans also contracted yellow fever, a disease caused by a virus-carrying mosquito, which results in high fever and jaundice (yellowing of the skin).

As new lands were "discovered," a wide variety of natural and organic plants were studied by doctors and laymen alike. Many new medicines and treatments, formed by using plants and minerals, became popular. The success of these medicines caused many to question the conventional ideas and treatments used by doctors. A philosophical debate exploded among scholars on how diseases where classified, and what made a disease "new."

Diseases and population

Lack of complete records from the Renaissance period make it difficult to know the numbers of people in the various social classes who were afflicted with disease. What is known is that 25 percent of all infants born never reached their second birthday, regardless of social class. In addition, fevers of various kinds and duration were the main cause of death at all stages of life. During epidemic years, even in the sixteenth century, mortality rates of more than 10 percent were common in urban areas. Deaths caused by plague alone in the great plague years (1520s, 1570s, 1590s, 1630) reached levels of 15 to 40 percent. These rates were as high as the levels witnessed during the Black Death in the mid-1300s. Wealthy people probably had a greater chance of survival because health practices during that time separated the rich from the poor in epidemic years.

Overall, the population of Europe began to grow after 1460 as more people moved from rural areas into urban centers. Yet among both urban and rural laborers, illness caused greater poverty and an increased dependence upon assistance from the government and private charities (see "Poverty" in Chapter 11). Any number of factors—plague, famine, illness, accident, an increase in the number of children, or the death of the mother in childbirth—could drastically change the economic conditions of a family. Hospitals and other traditional charitable organizations were rarely able to help families in any real way, and so the later Renaissance period was characterized by an even greater gap between rich and poor.

Death

From the fourteenth through the sixteenth centuries, Renaissance Europeans were fascinated with death. Perhaps the reason was the recurring epidemics of bubonic plague (a highly contagious disease that unexpectedly swept a region and killed large segments of the population). Greater awareness of death was expressed in new forms of funeral rites, mourning practices, and acts of remembrance. Accompanying these changes was a preoccupation with the *ars moriendi* (art of dying), a subject some authors began writing about extensively in the fifteenth century. The themes of physical decay and the triumph of death were central ideas in images, especially in the tomb art of northern Europe. Although every society must confront the inevitable loss of its members through death, the ways in which Renaissance Europeans faced the facts of death reveal much about their social values, religious beliefs, and overall health status.

Causes of death

The single greatest killer in Renaissance Europe was bubonic plague, which was known simply as the plague or as the "Black Death" (see "Black Death" in Chapter 1). The unsanitary conditions of the Middle Ages permitted bacillus-carrying fleas to infest and infect black rats, which then bit humans. The bite of the flea produces buboes, or lumps the size of chestnuts, usually in the groin and the armpit. This type of infection is known as the bubonic plague. It came to be called the "Black Death" because it produced open sores that turned black on people's bodies. Bubonic plague arrived first in Sicily in December 1347 and spread up the Italian peninsula by the summer of 1348. It reached pandemic levels throughout continental Europe, especially in urban areas, by the end of 1349. (Pandemic refers to the outbreak of disease over a huge geographic area,

A doctor treating a patient dying of the plague in 1491. The plague was the single greatest killer of people during the Renaissance.
Photograph courtesy of The Library of Congress.

affecting large numbers of people. In the twenty-first century, Africa has a pandemic level of citizens suffering from HIV/AIDS.) The first wave of the plague took an enormous toll on the population, with estimates ranging from one-third to one-half of local populations dying within those two years.

Beginning with the second appearance of the plague in 1362, the disease became a standard feature of life in Renaissance Europe. The plague returned every ten to twelve years until the last major outbreak in Lon-don in 1661, with some episodes being more contagious than others. Even though Europeans did not fully understand the causes of the plague, they knew that certain practical measures such as quarantine (confinement) and escape from infected areas were effective ways to reduce the spread of the disease. By the end of the fifteenth century, wealthy urban dwellers, especially those in the Mediterranean basin, fled every summer into the countryside where the plague was less easily spread. These practices gradually concentrated victims among the poor. After awhile local governments had formed harsh policies regarding those who suffered from the plague. By 1500 laborers and artisans were quarantined in plague hospitals. By the late sixteenth century the plague became a disease associated with poverty and poor hygiene.

Epidemics widespread Renaissance Europeans confronted other epidemic diseases as well. Most widespread among them was a strain of syphilis that acted like a virus. It first appeared in 1494 and was known as the "pox." The pox was a painful venereal (sexually transmitted) disease that killed its victims far more slowly than the plague. The onset of new, powerful, and incurable diseases like the "pox" resulted in a rise of charitable groups throughout Europe. The "pox" was blamed regularly on those outside of the immediate community. At some point the Italians, French, and Amerindians (Native Americans) all were blamed for having caused and spread the disease. Unlike the plague, which attacked all age groups and both sexes equally, syphilis was confined to sexually active adults. Treatises on morality blamed the spread of the disease on prostitution, which contributed to the closing of state-run brothels in the later sixteenth century.

Europeans also commonly suffered from deadly respiratory illnesses such as tuberculosis. Men routinely fell victim to accidents on their business travels or while doing agricultural work, while many women died during childbirth. Mortality was extremely high for children below the age of two, primarily due to illness. In times of economic hardship, infanticide (the killing of children) became a noticeable social problem, either because it actually increased as a way to limit family size or because it came to greater public attention as a criminal activity. Records from Italian courts show that infant girls were either killed or abandoned at roughly twice the rate of baby boys. Part of the reason for this was due to the fact that girls could not earn wages as high as those of boys. Girls also required more economic resources in order to fund the dowry required for marriage. Once children survived their critical early years, they had a reasonable chance of reaching adulthood.

Attitudes toward death

Renaissance Europeans had complicated views on death. Beliefs about the afterlife were a combination of Christian influences and classical Greek and Roman traditions. Perhaps the source that best reveals this cultural mix was *ars morendi*. Beginning in the early fifteenth century, writings in both Latin and vernacular languages started to teach a lay audience how a good Christian should approach impending death. These tracts stressed that death should be welcomed rather than feared, since it was death that gave meaning to life. In fact, life on Earth was seen as preparation for the afterlife. Since anyone might fall ill suddenly, the *ars morendi* writings emphasized the importance of making a "good death." The ill person was advised to confess to a priest, forgive friends and family gathered around the deathbed, and dispose of his or her personal belongings and wealth. One was also expected to make charitable donations or other financial compensation for past sins. These popular literary works stressed acceptance of death and planning for it as a way to control the unpredictable timing of one's demise. Making a good death helped the individual gain entry into purgatory (a region between heaven and hell) rather than be condemned to hell.

Visual imagery in northern Europe emphasized a darker sense of death than did the artistic representation of Italy and Spain. In France and Holland, the "dance of death," with its grim reapers and skeletons, became popular in the fifteenth century. Northern European artists also developed a form of tomb sculpture that portrayed an image of the living person placed over a decaying corpse.

Images, such as this one titled *Death and the Printers,* showing the "dance of death" became popular during the fifteenth century. *Reproduced by permission of The Granger Collection.*

This type of representation emphasized the belief that death triumphed over all persons regardless of wealth or status and reminded viewers that the physical organisms of the body did not last as long as the soul.

Attitudes and beliefs drawn from ancient philosophers were once again taken up by Renaissance Europeans. These attitudes were generally interpreted in ways that supported traditional Christian beliefs. Christian teachings were mixed with ancient Stoic philosophy. Stoic philosophy emphasized the importance of fulfilling one's duty to the living and also

stressed disciplined behavior. Renaissance thinkers claimed that mourners should control their sorrow through self-discipline. Comfort for their loss could be taken in work, duty, literary expression, and the Christian faith. Throughout the fifteenth century humanists in particular supported more restrained forms of mourning for both women and men.

Wills and bequests

The testament, or will, was a legal document witnessed by a notary that gave instructions about a person's wishes after his or her death. The will allowed a person to express wishes about the distribution of personal property, as well as instructions about burial. The *ars morendi* suggested that drawing up a last will was an important step in planning for a good death. Despite this advice, the vast majority of Europeans died without leaving a testament. Local customs therefore determined what would happen to their mortal remains and worldly goods. Normally wives were buried in the tombs of their husbands, and close relatives inherited property. Burial in one's local parish church or cemetery was the norm in the absence of other instructions.

Still, many thousands of testaments survive from the Renaissance period. These legal documents provide important sources for examining the social values of the time. Studies of French and Italian urban wills, for instance, reveal that more men than women left wills. In Italy during the 1300s and 1400s, wills made by women (mostly widows) were never more than 30 percent of the surviving documents. The transmission of property in these wills varied according to geographical location, class, gender, religious beliefs, and time period. Over the course of the Renaissance era, many people left great sums of money to buy a tomb or fund a memorial mass (Catholic religious service) to ensure that future generations would remember them. In some central Italian cities, men favored making large donations to one institution rather than several small contributions to charities. Most of these insti-

tutions helped poor young girls find husbands. In other cities, however, there was an opposite pattern of giving, with men splitting up their contributions into several donations. Women, especially widows, liked to give their money to nunneries (religious houses for women) at a rate much greater than that of men. They may have done so because they were related to nuns in particular convents or because they wanted to support the institutions. Scholars have yet to evaluate all the information available in these documents.

Rituals of death

Between 1300 and 1600 there were two main directions in the rituals surrounding death, mourning, and remembrance. The first trend was toward increased ceremony in funeral rites, especially in regions that remained Catholic after the religious reforms of the sixteenth century. This trend actually began in the early fourteenth century, predating the first outbreak of the plague in 1348. However, high death tolls from the plague gave greater significance to new forms of ceremony and ritual. Wealthy merchants, landowners, and aristocrats spent ever larger sums on funeral processions. They purchased such items as an expensive cloth to drape the bier (the stand on which a coffin is placed), a rich outfit in which to be buried, a great number of paid mourners and candles, and elaborate mourning clothes for relatives. Funeral pomp declared one's social status and may have helped some accept their own mortality. The funerals of ordinary people like artisans, small merchants, and shopkeepers also became more elaborate. This new flamboyance was also expressed in larger numbers of commemorative masses said for the deceased, which was believed to shorten the stay in purgatory. The beautiful family funeral chapels decorated in new Renaissance style were part of this new emphasis on ceremony.

Protestants stress simplicity The second major trend in death rites during the Renaissance period ran exactly counter to the first. After the rise of Protestantism in the sixteenth century, a more reserved ceremonial style was seen in those regions of Europe that had rejected Catholicism. Protestants had to develop new liturgical and ceremonial practices that better fit their beliefs. English Protestants tried to balance an appropriate, dignified display of social status without the pomp shown in Catholic ceremonies. Protestant preachers emphasized simple funeral ceremonies that focused attention on the afterlife. They also advised mourners to engage in only brief periods of grieving and rejected commemorative masses along with the concept of purgatory. By 1600 the ways in which Europeans buried and remembered their dead provided important clues about their deepest religious beliefs and helped distinguish Catholics from Protestants in everyday life.

Where to Learn More

The following list focuses on works written for readers of middle school and high school age. Books aimed at adult readers have been included when they are especially important in providing information or analysis that would otherwise be unavailable, or because they have become classics.

Books

Ackerman, James S. *Palladio's Villas*. Locust Valley, N.Y.: Institute of Fine Arts, New York University, 1967.

Ackroyd, Peter. *The Life of Thomas More*. New York: Nan A. Talese, 1998.

Anthony, Arthur. *The Tailor-King: The Rise and Fall of the Anabaptist Kingdom of Münster*. New York: St. Martin's Press, 1989.

Atil, Esin. *Suleymanname: The Illustrated History of Suleyman the Magnificent*. New York: H. N. Abrams, 1986.

Banville, John. *Kepler, A Novel*. New York: Vintage, 1993. (Fiction)

Barstow, Anne Llewellyn. *Witchcraze: A New History of the European Witch Hunts*. San Francisco: Harper, 1999.

Bellonci, Maria. *The Life and Times of Lucrezia Borgia*. Translated by Bernard and

Barbara Wall. London: Phoenix Press, 2000.

Brimacombe, Peter. *All the Queen's Men: The World of Elizabeth I.* New York: St. Martin's Press, 2000.

Brophy, James, and Henry Paolucci, eds. *The Achievement of Galileo.* New York: Twayne, 1962.

Burch, Joann Johansen. *Fine Print: A Story About Johann Gutenberg.* Minneapolis: Carolrhoda Books, 1991.

Canavaggio, Jean. *Cervantes.* Translated by J. R. Jones. New York: Norton, 1990.

Castiglione, Baldassare. *Book of the Courtier; An Authoritative Text, Criticism.* Edited by Daniel Javitch. New York: Norton, 2002.

Cavendish, Margaret. *The Blazing World and Other Writings.* Edited by Kate Lilley. New York: Penguin Classics, 1994.

Cervantes, Miguel de. *Don Quijote.* Edited Diana de Armas Wilson, and translated by Burton Raffel. New York: Norton, 1999.

Christianson, John Robert. *On Tycho's Island: Tycho Brahe and His Assistants, 1570–1601.* New York: Cambridge University Press, 1999.

Copernicus, Nicholas. *Nicholas Copernicus on the Revolutions.* Edited and translated by Edward Rosen. Baltimore, Md.: Johns Hopkins University Press, 1978.

Cox-Rearick, Janet. *The Collection of Francis I: Royal Treasures.* New York: Harry N. Abrams, Inc., 1996.

De La Bedoyere, Michael. *The Meddlesome Friar and the Wayward Pope; The Story of the Conflict between Savonarola and Alexander VI.* Garden City, N.Y.: Hanover House, 1958.

Dobson, Michael, and Stanley Wells, eds. *The Oxford Companion to Shakespeare.* Oxford: Oxford University Press, 2001.

Dommermuth-Costa, Carol. *William Shakespeare.* Minneapolis: Lerner, 2002.

Dwyer, Frank. *James I.* New York: Chelsea House, 1988.

Erlanger, Rachel. *The Unarmed Prophet: Savonarola in Florence.* New York: McGraw-Hill, 1988.

Evans, G. Blakemore, and others, eds. *The Riverside Shakespeare.* New York: Houghton Mifflin, 1997.

Farber, Joseph C. *Palladio's Architecture and its Influence: A Photographic Guide.* New York: Dover, 1980.

Fearon, Mike. *Martin Luther.* Minneapolis: Bethany House Publishers, 1986.

Ferino-Pagden, Sylvia, and Maria Kusche. *Sofonisba Anguissola: a Renaissance Woman.* Washington, D.C.: National Museum of Women in the Arts, 1995.

Finger, Stanley. *Minds Behind the Brain: The Pioneers and Their Discoveries.* New York: Oxford University Press, 2000.

Fisher, Leonard Everett. *Galileo.* New York: Macmillan, 1992.

Fisher, Leonard Everett. *Gutenberg.* New York: Macmillan, 1993.

Fletcher, Jennifer. *Peter Paul Rubens; With Fifty Plates in Full Colour.* New York, Phaidon, 1968.

Fontbrune, Jean-Charles de. *Nostradamus 2: Into the Twenty-*

first Century. Translated by Alexis Lykiard. New York: Holt, Rinehart, and Winston, 1985.

Friedman, Meyer. Medicine's 10 greatest Discoveries. New Haven, Conn.: Yale University Press, 1998.

Gäbler, Ulrich. Huldrych Zwingli: His Life and Work. Translated by Ruth C. L. Gritsch. Philadelphia: Fortress Press, 1986.

Garfield, Leon. Shakespeare Stories II. Boston: Houghton Mifflin Co., 1995.

Garrard, Mary D. Artemisia Gentileschi Around 1622 : The Shaping and Reshaping of an Artistic Identity. Berkeley: University of California Press, 2001.

Gelb, Michael. How to Think Like Leonardo Da Vinci: Seven Steps to Genius Every Day. New York: Delacorte Press, 1998.

Goldsmith, Mike. Galileo Galilei. Austin, Tex.: Raintree Steck-Vaughn, 2001.

Greef, Wulfert de. The Writings of John Calvin: An Introductory Guide. Translated by Lyle D. Bierma. Grand Rapids, Mich.: Baker Books, 1993.

Harp, Richard, and Stanley Stewart, eds. The Cambridge Companion to Ben Jonson. New York: Cambridge University Press, 2000.

Hillerbrand, Hans J., ed. The Protestant Reformation. New York: Harper Torchbooks, 1968.

Hutchison, Jane Campbell. Albrecht Dürer: A Biography. Princeton, N.J.: Princeton University Press, 1990.

Hyma, Albert. The Youth of Erasmus. New York: Russell & Russell, 1968.

Ibn Khaldûn, 'Adb al-Rahman. The Muqaddimah: An Introduction to History. Edited by N. J. Dawood, and translated by Franz Rosenthal. Princeton, N.J.: Princeton University Press, 1989.

Ignatius of Loyola. The Spiritual Exercises of St. Ignatius. Translated by Louis J. Puhl. New York: Vintage Books, 2000.

Kamen, Henry. Philip of Spain. New Haven Conn.: Yale University Press, 1997.

Kepler, Johannes. The Harmony of the World. Translated by E .J. Aiton, A. M. Duncan, and J.V. Field. Philadelphia, Pa.: American Philosophical Society, 1997.

King, Ethel M. Palestrina: The Prince of Music. Brooklyn, N.Y.: Theo. Gaus' Sons, 1965.

King, Margaret L., and Albert Rabil, eds., and trans. Her Immaculate Hand: Selected Works By and About the Women Humanists of Quattrocento Italy. Binghamton, N.Y.: Medieval and Renaissance Texts and Studies, 1983.

Knecht, R. J. Renaissance Warrior and Patron: The Reign of Francis I. New York: Cambridge University Press, 1994.

Krensky, Stephen. Breaking into Print: Before and After the Invention of the Printing Press. Boston: Little, Brown, 1996.

Lafferty, Peter. Leonardo da Vinci. New York: Bookwright, 1990.

Lapierre, Alexandra. Artemisia: A Novel. Translated by Liz Heron. New York: Grove Press, 2000. (Fiction)

Loewen, Harry, and Steven M. Nolt. Through Fire & Water: An Overview of Mennonite His-

tory. Scottdale, Pa.: Herald Press, 1996.

MacDonald, Alan. *Henry VIII and His Chopping Block*. New York: Scholastic, 1999.

Marguerite de Navarre. *Heptameron*. Translated by P.A. Chilton. New York: Penguin Books, 1984.

Maurier, Daphne du. *The Winding Stair: Francis Bacon, His Rise and Fall*. Garden City, N.Y.: Doubleday, 1977.

McGuigan, Dorothy Gies. *The Habsburgs*. Garden City, N.Y. Doubleday, 1966.

McLanathan, Richard. *Peter Paul Rubens*. New York: H.N. Abrams, 1995.

Medwick, Cathleen. *Teresa of Avila: the Progress of a Soul*. New York: Alfred A. Knopf, 1999.

Merriman, Roger Bigelow. *Suleiman the Magnificent*. New York: Cooper Square Publishers, 1966.

Michelangelo. *The Complete Poems of Michelangelo*. Translated by John Frederick Nims. Chicago, Ill.: University of Chicago Press, 1998.

Milton, Jacqueline. *Galileo: Scientist and Stargazer*. New York: Oxford University Press, 2000.

Montaigne, Michel de. *Selected Essays*. Translated by Donald M. Frame. New York: Van Nostrand, 1941.

More, Thomas. *Utopia*. Edited by Paul Turner. New York: Penguin Books, 1965.

Netanyahu, B. *Don Isaac Abrabanel: Statesman and Philosopher*. 5th ed. Ithaca, N.Y.: Cornell University Press, 1999.

Noll, Mark A. *Confessions and Catechisms of the Reformation*. Vancouver, B.C.: Regent College Publishing, 1997.

Nuland, Sheriwn B. *Leonardo da Vinci*. New York: Viking, 2000.

Olin, John C., ed. *The Autobiography of St. Ignatius Loyola*. Translated by Joseph F. O'Callaghan. New York: Fordham University Press, 1993.

Oliver, Isaac. *Art at the Courts of Elizabeth I and James I*. New York: Garland, 1981.

O'Malley, John W. *The First Jesuits*. Cambridge, Mass.: Harvard University Press, 1993.

Parker, T. H. L. *John Calvin, a Biography*. Philadelphia: Westminster Press, 1975.

Perlingieri, Ilya Sandra. *Sofonisba Anguissola: The First Great Woman Artist of the Renaissance*. New York: Rizzoli, 1992.

Petrarca, Francesco. *Selections from "Canzoniere" and Other Works*. Edited by Mark Musa. New York: Oxford University Press, 1999.

Pieter Bruegel the Elder: Drawings and Prints. New Haven, Conn.: Yale University Press, 2001.

Plowden, Alison. *The Young Elizabeth: The First Twenty-Five Years of Elizabeth I*. Stroud, Gloucestershire: Sutton, 1999.

Purcell, Mary. *The First Jesuit, St. Ignatius Loyola (1491–1556)*. Chicago: Loyola University Press, 1981.

Puzo, Mario. *The Family: A Novel*. Completed by Carol Gino. New York: Regan Books, 2001. (Fiction)

Rabelais, François. *Gargantua and Pantagruel*. Translated by J. M. Cohen. New York: Viking Penguin, 1976.

Raboff, Ernest. *Albrecht Dürer*. New York: Harper & Row, 1988.

Rady, Martyn. *The Emperor Charles V*. New York: Longman, 1988.

Richter, Irma A. *Selections from the Notebooks of Leonardo da Vinci*. New York: Oxford University Press, 1977.

Riley, Judith Merkle. *The Master of All Desires*. New York: Viking, 1999. (Fiction)

Ripley, Alexandra. *The Time Returns*. Garden City, N.Y.: Doubleday, 1985. (Fiction)

Roessner, Michaela. *The Stars Dispose*. New York: Tor, 1997. (Fiction)

Saint-Saëns, Alain, ed. *Young Charles V, 1500–1531*. New Orleans: University Press of the South, 2000.

Scheib, Asta. *Children of Disobedience: The Love Story of Martin Luther and Katharina von Bora: A Novel*. Translated by David Ward. New York: Crossroad, 2000. (Fiction)

Seward, Desmond. *Prince of the Renaissance; the Golden Life of François I*. New York: Macmillan, 1973.

Sharpe, James. *The Bewitching of Anne Gunter: A Horrible and True Story of Deception, Witchcraft, Murder, and the King of England*. New York: Routledge, 2000.

Shulman, Sandra. *The Florentine*. New York: Morrow, 1973. (Fiction)

Skinner, Quentin. *Great Political Thinkers*. New York: Oxford University Press, 1992.

Stanley, Diane. *Michelangelo*. New York: HarperCollins, 2000.

Starkey, David. *Elizabeth: The Struggle for the Throne*. New York: HarperCollins, 2001.

Stepanek, Sally. *Martin Luther*. New York: Chelsea House, 1986.

Summers, Montague, ed. *The Malleus Maleficarum* Malleus Maleficarum *of Heinrich Kramer and James Sprenger*. New York: Dover Publications, 1971.

Teresa de Ávila. *The Life of Saint Teresa*. Translated by J. M. Cohen. New York: Penguin Books, 1957.

Thomas. Jane Resh. *Behind the Mask: The Life of Queen Elizabeth I*. New York: Clarion Books, 1998.

Thrasher, Thomas. *William Shakespeare*. San Diego, Calif.: Lucent Books, 1999.

Veglahn, Nancy. *Dance of the Planets: The Universe of Nicolaus Copernicus*. New York: Coward, McCann & Geohegan, 1979. (Fiction)

Vergani, Luis. *"The Prince," Notes; Including Machiavelli's Life and Works*. Lincoln, Nebr.: Cliff's Notes, 1967.

Vernon, Louise A. *The Man Who Laid the Egg*. Scottdale, Pa.: Herald Press, 1977.

Viroli, Maurizio. *Niccolò's Smile: A Biography of Machiavelli*. Translated by Antony Shugaar. New York: Farrar, Straus and Giroux, 2000.

Voelkel, James R. *Johannes Kepler: And the New Astronomy*. New York: Oxford University Press Children's Books, 2001.

Vreeland, Susan. *The Passion of Artemesia*. New York: Viking, 2002. (Fiction)

Wedgwood, C. V. and the editors of Time-Life Books. *The World of Rubens, 1577-1640.* New York: Time, Inc., 1967.

Weir, Allison. *Henry VIII: The King and His Court.* New York: Ballantine Books, 2001.

Westman, Robert S., ed. *The Copernican Achievement.* Berkeley: University of California Press, 1975.

Zophy, Jonathan W. *A Short History of Renaissance and Reformation Europe.* 2nd ed. Upper Saddle River, N.J.: Prentice Hall, 1999.

Web Sites

"Alexander VI." *Catholic Encyclopedia.* [Online] Available http://www.newadvent.org/cathen/01289a.htm, May 20, 2002.

"Alexander VI." *Encyclopedia.com.* [Online] Available http://www.encyclopedia.com/html/a/alexand6.asp, May 20, 2002.

Ancient Medicine, from Homer to Vesalius. [Online] Available http://www.med.virginia.edu/hs-library/historical/antiqua/anthome.html, May 20, 2002.

"Anguissola, Sofonisba." *A Guide to the Collection of European Art to 1900.* [Online] Available http://www.mfa.org/handbook/portrait.asp?id=195.5&s=6, May 20, 2002.

"Anguissola, Sofonisba." *Art Cyclopedia.* [Online] Available http://www.artcyclopedia.com/artists/anguissola_sofonisba.html, May 20, 2002.

Artemisia's Letter. [Online] Available http://rubens.anu.edu.au/student.projects/artemisia/Artemisia%27s_Letter.html, May 20, 2002.

Artist Profiles: Lavinia Fontana. [Online] Available http://www.nmwa.org/legacy/bios/bfontana.htm, May 20, 2002.

Art of Renaissance Science: Galileo and Perspective. [Online] Available http://www.crs4.it/Ars/arshtml/arstoc.html, May 20, 2002.

"Bacon, Francis." *The Internet Encyclopedia of Philosophy.* [Online] Available http://www.utm.edu/research/iep/b/bacon.htm, May 20, 2002.

Baldassare Castiglione [portrait] by Raphael. [Online] Available http://www.theartgallery.com.au/ArtEducation/greatartists/Raphael/baldassare/, May 20, 2002.

"Bruegel, Pieter the Elder." *Britannica.com.* [Online] Available http://www.britannica.com/eb/article?eu=17000&tocid=869&query=bruegel%2C%20pieter%20the%20elder, May 20, 2002.

"Bruegel, Pieter the Elder." *Web Gallery of Art.* [Online] Available http://www.kfki.hu/~arthp/html/b/bruegel/pieter_e/index.html, May 20, 2002.

A Celebration of Women Writers: 1401–1500. [Online] Available http://digital.library.upenn.edu/women/_generate/1401-1500.html, May 20, 2002.

"Charles V, Holy Roman Emperor." *The Columbia Encyclopedia.* [Online] Available http://www.bartleby.com/65/ch/Charles5HRE.html, May 20, 2002.

Chu, Luthy. *Erasmus, Desiderius.* [Online] Available http://campus.northpark.edu/history/WebChron/WestEurope/Erasmus.html, May 20, 2002.

"Council of Trent." *Infoplease.com.* [Online] Available http://www.infoplease.com/ce6/society/A0849364.html, May 20, 2002.

Debus, Allen G. *Paracelsus, Theophrastus—Medical Revolution.* [Online] Available http://www.nlm.nih.gov/exhibition/paracelsus/paracelsus_2.html, May 20, 2002.

"Don Isaac Abrabanel." *Catholic Encyclopedia.* [Online] Available http://www.newadvent.org/cathen/01050b.htm, May 20 2002.

The Don Quixote Exhibit. [Online] Available http://milton.mse.jhu.edu:8006/, May 20, 2002.

"Dürer, Albrecht." *MSN Encarta.* [Online] Available http://encarta.msn.com/find/Concise.asp?ti=038AD000, May 20, 2002.

Early Modern Europe: The Witch Hunts. [Online] Available http://history.hanover.edu/early/wh.html, May 20, 2002.

"Elizabeth I." *Luminarium.* [Online] Available http://www.luminarium.org/renlit/eliza.htm, May 20, 2002.

"Erasmus, Desiderius." *MSN Encarta.* [Online] Available http://encarta.msn.com/index/conciseindex/5A/05A6E000.htm?z=1&pg=2&br=1, May 20, 2002.

Erasumus, Desiderius. *Praise of Folly.* [Online] Available http://www.stupidity.com/erasmus/eracont.htm, May 20, 2002.

The Essays of Francis Bacon. [Online] Available http://ourworld.compuserve.com/homepages/mike_donnelly/bacon.htm, May 20, 2002.

"Francis I." *Infoplease.com.* [Online] Available http://www.infoplease.com/ce6/people/A0819430.html, May 20, 2002.

Galilei, Galileo—Portrait. [Online] Available http://galileo.imss.firenze.it/museo/b/egalilg.html, May 20, 2002.

"Galileo." *MSN Encarta.* [Online] Available http://encarta.msn.com/find/Concise.asp?z=1&pg=2&ti=017E5000, May 20, 2002.

"Gentileschi, Artemisia." *Web Galleries.* [Online] Available http://www.webgalleries.com/pm/colors/gentile.html, May 20, 2002.

Gournay, Marie de (1565–1645). [Online] Available http://www.pinn.net/~sunshine/march99/gournay2.html, May 20, 2002.

"Gournay, Marie de." *Early French Women Writers.* [Online] Available http://erc.lib.umn.edu/dynaweb/french/@Generic__CollectionView, May 20, 2002.

"Gustav I Vasa." *Britannica.com.* [Online] Available http://www.britannica.com/eb/article?eu=39368&tocid=0&query=gustaf%20i%20vasa, May 20, 2002.

"Gustavus I." *Learning Network.* [Online] Available http://www.factmonster.com/ce6/people/A0822195.html, May 20, 2002.

The Gutenberg Bible. [Online] Available http://prodigi.bl.uk/gutenbg/, May 20, 2002.

"Gutenberg, Johannes." *Famous People in Printing History.* [Online] Available http://www.ssc.cc.il.us/acad/career/depts/technology/ppt/whatsup/trivia/gutenbrg.htm, May 20, 2002.

Gutenberg Museum. [Online] Available http://www.gutenberg.de/, May 20, 2002.

Hagen, J. G. "Copernicus, Nicholas." *Catholic Encyclopedia.* [Online] Available http://www.newadvent.org/cathen/04352b.htm, May 20, 2002.

Halsall, Paul. *Council of Trent—Rules on Prohibited Books.* [Online] Available http://www.fordham.edu/halsall/mod/trent-booksrules.html, May 20, 2002.

Halsall, Paul. "Elizabeth I." *Modern History Sourcebook.* [Online] Available http://www.fordham.edu/halsall/mod/elizabeth1.html, May 20, 2002.

Halsall, Paul. "Luther, Martin." *Letter to the Archbishop of Mainz.* [Online] Available http://www.fordham.edu/halsall/source/lutherltr-indulgences.html, May 20, 2002.

Halsall, Paul. "Petrarch, Francesco." *Letters—circa 1372.* [Online] Available http://www.fordham.edu/halsall/source/petrarch1.html, May 20, 2002.

"Henry VIII." *Britannica.com.* [Online] Available http://www.britannica.com/eb/article?eu=40871&tocid=0&query=henry%20viii, May 20, 2002.

"Henry VIII." *History Channel.* [Online] Available http://www.thehistorychannel.co.uk/classroom/alevel/henry1.htm, May 20, 2002.

"Henry VIII." *Image Gallery.* [Online] Available http://www.tudorhistory.org/henry8/gallery.html, May 20, 2002.

The Heptameron of Margaret, Queen of Navarre. [Online] Available http://digital.library.upenn.edu/women/navarre/heptameron/heptameron.html, May 20, 2002.

"How Nostradamus Works." *How Stuff Works.* [Online] Available http://www.howstuffworks.com/nostradamus.htm, May 20, 2002.

Hudleston, G. Roger. "More, Thomas." *Catholic Encyclopedia.* [Online] Available http://www.newadvent.org/cathen/14689c.htm, May 20, 2002.

Ibn Khaldûn—Iranian Muslim Philosopher. [Online] Available http://www.trincoll.edu/depts/phil/philo/phils/muslim/khaldun.html, May 20, 2002.

"Ignatius of Loyola, Saint." *Britannica.com.* [Online] Available http://www.britannica.com/eb/article?eu=50361&tocid=0&query=ignatius%20loyola, May 20, 2002.

Intelmann, Arthur. "Monteverdi, Claudio." *Unitel—"L'Orfeo."* [Online] Available http://www.unitel.classicalmusic.com/classica/112200.htm, May 20, 2002.

"James I." *Britannia.* [Online] Available http://www.britannia.com/history/monarchs/mon46.html, May 20, 2002.

"Jonson, Ben." *Luminarium Profile.* [Online] Available http://www.luminarium.org/sevenlit/jonson/, May 20, 2002.

"Jonson, Ben." *TheatreHistory.com.* [Online] Available http://www.theatrehistory.com/british/jonson001.html, May 20, 2002.

Kepler, Johannes—Kepler's Laws of Planetary Motion. [Online] Available http://zebu.uoregon.edu/textbook/planets.html, May 20, 2002.

"Kepler, Johannesi" *MSN Encarta*. [Online] Available http://encarta.msn.com/find/Concise.asp?ti=02F84000, May 20, 2002.

"Kepler, Johannes." *NASA Kepler Musem*. [Online] Available http://www.kepler.arc.nasa.gov/johannes.html, May 20, 2002.

Kirsch, J.P. "Savonarola, Girolamo." *Catholic Encyclopedia*. [Online] Available http://www.newadvent.org/cathen/13490a.htm, May 20, 2002.

Kurth, Godefroid. "Philip II (King of Spain)." *Catholic Encyclopedia*. [Online] Available http://www.newadvent.org/cathen/12002a.htm, May 20, 2002.

"Leonardo da Vinci." *Artcyclopedia*. [Online] Available http://artcyclopedia.com/artists/leonardo_da_vinci.html, May 20, 2002.

"Leonardo da Vinci." *MSN Encarta*. [Online] Available http://encarta.msn.com/find/Concise.asp?z=1&pg=2&ti=761561520, May 20, 2002.

"Leonardo da Vinci." *National Museum of Science and Technology*. [Online] Available http://www.museoscienza.org/english/leonardo/leonardo.html, May 20, 2002.

Letters of Philip II, King of Spain, 1592–1597. [Online] Available http://library.byu.edu/~rdh/phil2/, May 20, 2002.

Lipman, David E. "Abraham Senior." *Gates of Jewish Heritage*. [Online] Available http://www.jewishgates.org/personalities/2senior.stm, May 20, 2002.

Lipman, David E. "Isaac ben Judah Abrabanel." *Gates of Jewish Heritage*. [Online] Available http://www.jewishgates.org/personalities/2abrav.stm, May 20, 2002.

"Luther, Martin." *MSN Encarta*. [Online] Available http://encarta.msn.com/find/concise.asp?z=1&pg=2&ti=04875000, May 20, 2002.

"Machiavelli, Nicolo." *Internet Philosophy Encyclopedia*. [Online] Available http://www.utm.edu/research/iep/m/machiave.htm, May 20, 2002.

"Machiavelli, Nicolo." *MSN Encarta*. [Online] Available http://encarta.msn.com/find/Concise.asp?ti=05DD9000, May 20, 2002.

"Margaret of Navarre." *Infoplease.com*. [Online] Available http://www.infoplease.com/ce6/people/A0831778.html, May 20, 2002.

"Marlowe, Christopher." *Luminarium*. [Online] Available http://www.luminarium.org/renlit/marlowe.htm, May 20, 2002.

Martin Luther and the Reformation. [Online] Available http://mars.acnet.wnec.edu/~grempel/courses/wc2/lectures/luther.html, May 20, 2002.

The Medici Family. [Online] Available http://es.rice.edu/ES/humsoc/Galileo/People/medici.html, May 20, 2002.

"Medici, Lorenzo de', 1492–1519—Italian Merchant Prince." *Infoplease.com*. [Online] Available http://www.infoplease.com/ce6/people/A0832477.html, May 20, 2002.

"Michelangelo." *MSN Encarta*. [Online] Available http://encarta.msn.com/find/Concise.asp?z=1&pg=2&ti=761560125, May 20, 2002.

Michelangelo—Sistine Chapel Ceiling. [Online] Available http://www.science.wayne.edu/~mcogan/Humanities/Sistine/index.html, May 20, 2002.

"Michelangelo." *Web Gallery of Art.* [Online] Available http://www.kfki.hu/~arthp/html/m/michelan/, May 20, 2002.

Montaigne, Michel de. *Essays.* [Online] Available http://www.orst.edu/instruct/phl302/texts/montaigne/m-essays_contents.html, May 20, 2002.

Montaigne, Michel de. *On Cannibals.* [Online] Available http://www.wsu.edu:8080/~wldciv/world_civ_reader/world_civ_reader_2/montaigne.html, May 20, 2002.

"Monteverdi, Claudio." *Essentials of Music.* [Online] Available http://www.essentialsofmusic.com/composer/monteverdi.html, May 20, 2002.

Monteverdi, Claudio—Innovator and Madrigalist. [Online] Available http://web.azstarnet.com/public/packages/reelbook/153-4028.htm, May 20, 2002.

"Monteverdi, Claudio." *Milestones of the Millenium.* [Online] Available http://npr.org/programs/specials/milestones/990519.motm.monteverdi.html, May 20, 2002.

"More, Thomas." *The Lumminarium.* [Online] Available http://www.luminarium.org/renlit/tmore.htm, May 20, 2002.

"More, Thomas." *Redefining the Sacred.* [Online] Available http://www.folger.edu/institute/sacred/image8.html, May 20, 2002.

"Nogarola, Isotta." *Sunshine for Women.* [Online] Available http://www.pinn.net/~sunshine/march99/nogarla2.html, May 20, 2002.

Norton Topics Online: Van Schuppen, Engraving [portrait] of Margaret Cavendish. [Online] Available http://www.wwnorton.com/nael/NTO/18thC/worlds/imcavendish.htm, May 20, 2002.

"Nostradamus." *MSN Encarta.* [Online] Available http://encarta.msn.com/find/Concise.asp?z=1&pg=2&ti=761568156, May 20, 2002.

"Palladio, Andrea." *Palladian Buildings in Vicenza.* [Online] Available http://www.ashmm.com/cultura/palladio/copertuk.htm, May 20, 2002.

Palladio, Andrea—Palladio and Pattern Books. [Online] Available http://mondrian.princeton.edu/Campus/text_pattern.html, May 20, 2002.

"Paracelsus, Theophrastus." *Coelum Philosophorum.* [Online] Available http://www.levity.com/alchemy/coelum.html, May 20, 2002.

"Paracelsus, Theophrastus." *Infoplease.com.* [Online] Available http://www.infoplease.com/ce5/CE039437.html, May 20, 2002.

"Paul III." *Infoplease.com.* [Online] Available http://www.infoplease.com/ce6/people/A0837895.html, May 20, 2002.

Petrarch, Francesco—Petrarch's House. [Online] Available http://freia.dei.unipd.it/civici/civici/petra%24.html, May 20, 2002.

"Philip II." *Infoplease.com.* [Online] Available http://www.infoplease.com/ce5/CE040637.html, May 20, 2002.

Pioch, Nicolas. "Bruegel, Pieter the Elder." *WebMuseum.* [Online] Available http://sunsite.unc.edu/wm/paint/auth/bruegel/, May 20 2002.

Pioch, Nicolas. "Dürer, Albrecht." *Webmuseum.* [Online] Available http://metalab.unc.edu/wm/paint/auth/durer/, May 20, 2002.

Pioch, Nicolas. "Leonardo da Vinci." *WebMuseum.* [Online] Available http://mexplaza.udg.mx/wm/paint/auth/vinci/, May 20, 2002.

Pioch, Nicolas. "Michelangelo Merisi da Caravaggio." *Webmuseum.* [Online] Available http://sunsite.unc.edu/wm/paint/auth/caravaggio, May 20, 2002.

Plant, David. *Kepler, Johannes—Kepler and the Music of the Spheres.* [Online] Available http://www.astrologyworld.com/kepler.html, May 20, 2002.

Pollen, J. H. "Ignatius Loyola, St." *Catholic Encyclopedia.* [Online] Available http://www.newadvent.org/cathen/07639c.htm, May 20, 2002.

Portrait of Girolamo Savonarola by Bartolomeo, Fra. [Online] Available http://www.kfki.hu/~arthp/html/b/bartolom/fra/savonaro.html, May 20, 2002.

Protestant Reformation. [Online] Available http://www.mun.ca/rels/hrollmann/reform/reform.html, May 20, 2002.

"Rabelais, François." *Infoplease.com.* [Online] Available http://www.infoplease.com/ce6/people/A0840877.html, May 20, 2002.

"Savonarola, Girolamo." *MSN Encarta.* [Online] Available http://encarta.msn.com/index/concise index/4B/04BA3000.htm?z=1&pg=2&br=1, May 20, 2002.

The Schlietheim Confession. [Online] Available http://www.anabaptists.org/history/schleith.html, May 20, 2002.

Senfelder, Leopold. "Vesalius, Andreas." *Catholic Encyclopedia.* [Online] Available http://www.knight.org/advent/cathen/15378c.htm, May 20, 2002.

"Shakespeare, William." *Internet Editions.* [Online] Available http://web.uvic.ca/shakespeare/Annex, May 20, 2002.

"Shakespeare, William." *Shakespearean Homework Helper.* [Online] Available http://hometown.aol.com/liadona2/shakespeare.html, May 20, 2002.

"Shakespeare, William." *MSN Encarta.* [Online] Available http://encarta.msn.com/find/Concise.asp?z=1&pg=2&ti=761562101, May 20, 2002.

The Six Wives of Henry VIII. [Online] Available http://www.larmouth.demon.co.uk/sarah-jayne/wives/wives.html, May 20, 2002.

The Spiritual Exercises of St. Ignatius of Loyola. [Online] Available http://www.ccel.org/i/ignatius/exercises/exercises.html, May 20, 2002.

Suleyman the Magnificent. [Online] Available http://www.wsu.edu:8001/~dee/OTTOMAN/SULEYMAN.HTM, May 20, 2002.

Teresa de Ávila, *Way of Perfection.* [Online] Available http://www.ccel.org/t/teresa/way/main.html, May 20, 2002.

"Vesalius, Andreas." *Infoplease.com.* [Online] Available http://

www.infoplease.com/ce5/CE
054107.html, May 20, 2002.

Women and European Witch Hunts.
[Online] Available http://
www.kings.edu/womens_
history/witch.html, May 20,
2002.

Zimmerman, Benedict. "Teresa of
Jesus (Teresa de Ávila)."
Catholic Encyclopedia. [On-
line] Available http://www.
n e w a d v e n t . o r g / c a t h e n /
14515b.htm, May 20, 2002.

"Zwingli, Ulrich." *Zwingli and
Luther.* [Online] Available
http://www.bible.org/docs/
history/schaff/vol7/schaf176.
htm, May 20, 2002.

Sound Recordings

Don Quixote. St. Paul, Minn.: High-
Bridge,1997.

Man of La Mancha. New York:
Sony Classical, 1996.

Starry Messenger. Prince Frederick,
Md.: Recorded Books, 1997.

Video Recordings and DVDs

The Agony and the Ecstasy. Livonia,
Mich.: CBS/Fox Video, 1988.
(Videorecording)

Artemisia. Burbank, Calif.: Mira-
max Home Entertainment,
2001. (DVD)

Don Quixote. Los Angeles: TNT
Original: Hallmark Entertain-
ment Production, 2000.
(Video recording)

Galileo: On the Shoulders of Giants.
Toronto: Devine Entertain-
ment, 1997. (Video recording)

A Man for All Seasons. Burbank,
Calif.: RCA/Columbia Pic-
tures Home Video, 1985.
(Videorecording)

Man of La Mancha. Farmington
Hills, Mich.: CBS/FOX Video,
1984. (Video recording)

Martin Luther. Worcester, Pa.: Vision Video, 1990. (Video
recording)

*Masterpieces of Italian Art, Volume:
Da Vinci, Michelangelo, Ra-
phael and Titian.* New York:
VPI-AC Video Inc., 1990.
(Video recording)

The Private Life of Henry VIII. Los
Angeles: Embassy Home En-
tertainment, 1986. (Video
recording)

The Radicals [Anabaptists].
Worcester, Pa.: Gateway
Films-Vision Video, 1989.
(Video recording)

Suleyman the Magnificent. New
York: National Gallery of Art
and Metropolitan Museum of
Art; Home Vision, 1987.
(Video recording)

Index

A

Abacists *2:* 444
Abacus *2:* 464
'Abbās I *1:* 42
Abelard, Peter *1:* 32
Abrabanel, Isaac *1:* 121
Abravanel, Benvenida *2:* 547
Academia della Crusca *1:* 54
Académie Royale de Peinture et
    Sculpture *2:* 539
Accoppiatori *1:* 55
Acosta, José de *2:* 458
Act of Supremacy *1:* 252
Act of Treason *1:* 252–53
Acuña, Antonio de *1:* 126
Ad extirpanda 1: 24
Adoration of the Magi 2: 332
Adrian VI *1:* 209
Against the Jews and Their Lies, 1:
    225
*Against the Robbing and Murdering
    Horde of Peasants 1:* 213
Agricola, Rudolf *2:* 374
Agrippa, Heinrich *2:* 559–60
AIDS and Black Death *1:* 37

Albert II, Holy Roman Emperor *1:*
    149, 151, 183
Alberti, Leon Battista *1:* 77; *2:* 331
Albigensian Crusade *1:* 23
Albrecht, Dürer *2:* 446
Albuquerque, Alfonso de *1:* 136
Alchemists *2:* 467 (ill.)
Alchemy *2:* 466, 468–69
Alencon, Duke of Anjou *1:* 177,
    251
Alexander VI, Pope *1:* 49, 60, 66,
    82, 83 (ill.), 85, 96, 124,
    137–38, 270–71
Alexius I, Byzantine Emperor *1:*
    72
Alfonso V, King of Naples and
    Sicily *1:* 88–89; *2:* 522
Alfonso I, King of Naples *1:* 88,
    88 (ill.)
Alfonso I, King of Portugal *1:* 123
Alfonso II, King of Spain *1:* 89
Allen, Elias *2:* 461
Almagest 2: 429–30
Álvarez de Toledo, Fernando, *1:*
    130, 297
Alvers, Manoel *2:* 519

P

Pacioli, Luca *2:* 444
Padilla, Juan de *1:* 126
Painting, Italian *2:* 330, 331 (ill.), 332, 334–46, 348
Palestrina, Giovanni Pierluigi da *1:* 284; *2:* 364–66, 537
Palladio, Andrea *1:* 69, 82, 117; *2:* 358–59, 420
Papal States *1:* 21, 27, 192
Paracelsus *2:* 452–53
Paré, Ambroise *2:* 450
Parr, Katherine *1:* 109; *2:* 554
Pascal, Blaise *2:* 446
Passi, Giuseppe *2:* 559
Paul IV, Pope *1:* 274; *2:* 500
Paul II, Pope *1:* 58
Paul III and His Grandsons 2: 341
Paul III, Pope *1:* 128, 273, 273 (ill.), 294
Peace of Augsburg *1:* 147, 155, 226
Peace of Barcelona *1:* 86
Peace of Lodi *1:* 66, 74
Peace of Oliva *1:* 182
Peace of Saint Germain *1:* 245
Peace of the Pyrenees *1:* 103
Peace of Westphalia *1:* 20, 103, 144, 173, 177, 181, 251, 266–67
Peasant Dance 2: 411
Peasant Wedding 2: 411
Pepin the Short *1:* 81
Pépin III *1:* 13
Perotti, Niccolò *2:* 519
Pesaro Madonna 2: 341
Peter of Aragon *1:* 96
Peter III, King of Aragon *1:* 48, 87
Petrarch *1:* 8–9, 45, 80; *2:* 306–07, 324, 488, 516
Petri, Laurentius *1:* 238, 241–42
Petri, Olaus *1:* 238, 241–42
Pfefferkorn, Johannes *2:* 378
Phaedrus 2: 431
Philip Augustus, King of France *1:* 93
Philip of Hesse *1:* 209, 218, 221, 223–24
Philip I, King of Austria *1:* 124
Philip IV, King of France *1:* 25–26, 93, 191–92
Philip IV, King of Spain *1:* 134, 266

Philip II, King of Spain *1:* 111–13, 123, 129–32, 153, 174–77, 244, 249, 251, 254, 257–58, 297; *2:* 412
Philip VI, King of France *1:* 93
Philip III, Duke of Burgundy *1:* 104
Philip III, King of Spain *1:* 116, 133; *2:* 496
Piarists *1:* 281, 283
Pico della Mirandola, Giovanni *2:* 313–14, 380
Pietà (Michelangelo) *2:* 351, 353 (ill.)
Pirkheimer, Caritas *2:* 527
Pisan, Christine de *2:* 318, 320, 320 (ill.)
Pisanello, Antonio *1:* 77
Pisano, Nicola *2:* 351, 357
Pius V, Pope *1:* 294; *2:* 500
Pius IV, Pope *1:* 274
Pius II, Pope *1:* 43 (ill.), 44, 82
Pizzaro, Francisco *1:* 127
Plantagenets *1:* 43, 104
Plato *2:* 428
Pliny the Elder *2:* 536
Plutarch *1:* 9
Poggio Bracciolini *2:* 516
Pole, Reginald *1:* 111, 254
Poliziano, Angelo, Philologist *1:* 57
Polo, Marco *1:* 134
Porta, Giacomo della *1:* 82; *2:* 357
Portrait of a Nun 2: 346
Poverty *2:* 504–08
Pradanos, Juan de *1:* 290
Praise of Folly 2: 376
Prez, Josquin de *2:* 423
Primaticcio, Francesco *2:* 415, 417
Primavera 1: 7
The Prince 1: 8; *2:* 315
Printing press *1:* 6, 7 (ill.)
Procession to Calvary 2: 410
Prodigal Son 2: 406
Professional training *2:* 532, 534–35, 534 (ill.)
Professions *2:* 495 (ill.)
Protestant Reformation (See: Reformation, Protestant)
Ptolemy *2:* 429–30, 457
Punishment *2:* 512 (ill.)
Puritans *1:* 114, 117, 258

W

Waldo, Peter *1:* 102
Wallenstein, Albrecht von *1:* 262, 265
Walther, Bernard *2:* 461
Ward, Mary *1:* 287; *2:* 529
War of Kalmar *1:* 178
War of the Roses *1:* 43, 104–05
War of the Sicilian Vespers *1:* 48, 87, 96
Water test *1:* 302
Wat Tyler Revolt *1:* 37
Wedding Dance 2: 411, 413 (ill.)
West Roman Empire *1:* 1, 12
Wet Nurses *2:* 585–86
Whether a Christian woman should be educated 2: 561
Widowhood *2:* 546
Willaert, Adrian *2:* 423
William of Orange *1:* 130–31, 156, 174–75, 176 (ill.), 177, 249, 251
William I, King of England *1:* 14, 92
Wingate, Edmund *2:* 465
Wishart, George *1:* 256
Witchcraft trials *1:* 299, 302
Witches, execution of *1:* 303
Wollstonecraft, Mary *2:* 559
Wolsey, Thomas *2:* 382
Women during the Renaissance *2:* 543 (ill.)
World War I *1:* 151

Worship of Venus 2: 340
Wren, Christopher *1:* 117
Wright, Edward *2:* 447
Wulfskerke, Cornelie van *2:* 565
Wycliffe, John *1:* 36, 145, 195

X

Xavier, Francis *1:* 280

Y

Youth *2:* 591–92

Z

Zabarella, Jacopo *2:* 431
Zaccaria, Antonio Maria *1:* 277–78
Zell, Katharine Schütz *2:* 550
Zell, Matthäus *2:* 550
Žižka, Jan *1:* 167
Zodiac *2:* 471 (ill.)
Zubarán, Francisco de *1:* 133
Zwingli, Huldrych *1:* 145, 147, 169, 171 (ill.), 195, 218, 226–27, 228 (ill.), 229–30, 232–34